PERSISTENCE
OF
VISION

PERSISTENCE

OF

VISION

An Impractical Guide To Producing A
Feature Film For Under $30,000

John Gaspard & Dale Newton

Published by Michael Wiese Productions, 11288 Ventura Blvd., Suite 821, Studio City, CA 91604 (818) 379-8799 Fax (818) 986-3408.
Wiese@earthlink.net
http://www.earthlink.net/~mwp

Cover design by Art Hotel, Los Angeles
Final Copy Check by Bernice Balfour

Printed by Braun-Brumfield, Inc., Ann Arbor, Michigan
Manufactured in the United States of America

Copyright 1996 by John Gaspard & Dale Newton

Note: The information presented in this book is for entertainment and information purposes only. The authors are not giving business or financial advice. Readers should consult their lawyers, accountants and financial advisors. The publisher and its assignees are not responsible nor liable for how readers may choose to use this information.

Library of Congress Cataloging in Publication Data

Gaspard, John, 1958-

  Persistence of vision : an impractical guide to producing a feature film for under $30,000 / John Gaspard & Dale Newton,
        p. cm.
    ISBN 0-941188-23-X
    1. Motion pictures--Production and direction. 2. Low budget motion pictures. 3. Motion picture industry--United States--Finance. I. Newton, Dale, 1957- II. Title.
PN1995.9.P7G375   1996
791.43'0232--cc20   95-42044
                                                                 CIP

Books from
MICHAEL WIESE PRODUCTIONS

TABLE OF CONTENTS

ACKNOWLEDGMENTS

We always knew that filmmaking was a collaborative art, but we had no idea that a crowd was required to write a book as well.

There are many people to thank for their help and support in putting this book together. In no particular order, they are:

Richard Glatzer
Ruth Charny
Daniel Curran
Jennifer Howe
Janusz Kaminski
Eric Tretbar
Julie Chang
Robin Alper
Trent Harris
Walter Hart
James Babcock
Soodabeh Babcock
Eric Mueller
Julie Hartley
Andrew Peterson
Sean King
Michael Brillantes
Jeff Butcher
Nelle Stokes
William Bayer
Dave Reynolds
Randy Adamsick, Minnesota Film Board
Marc Kramer
Jane Minton, IFP North
Dawn Hudson, Matthew Waldman, IFP West
Deb Rose

Michael Paul Levin
Peter Moore
Bruce V. Assardo
Rachel Katz
Beth Gilleland
Tom Belanger
Cindy Widlund
Virginia Hoffmann
Tim Rice, Movie Maker Magazine
Thomas Vitale
Seth Kittay
Daniel Polsfuss
Jerry Nelson
Steve Lustgarten
Steve Molton
Mark Tusk
Marcus Hu
Strand Releasing
Walter Hart
Donna Smith
Al Cohn
Victoria Eide
Jeff Baustert
Wade Danielson
Roger Nygard
Daniel J. Berks
Jay Horan
Michael de Avila
Richard Seres
Amelia Oriani (for her excellent poof reading)

Special thanks to Kathy and Jenny for their infinite patience, and to Franny and Zooey for not throwing up on the manuscript.

INTRODUCTION

Buying this book was your first mistake.

Don't panic, though. In the overall scheme of ultra-low-budget film production, it isn't a large mistake. However, if you want to produce a movie for under $30,000, from now on you must remember these two key maxims:

- You never pay full price for anything having to do with your movie. Ever.
- And you never, ever buy what you can borrow or get for free. (Those of you who are going to read this entire book while standing in the stacks at Barnes & Noble can move up to the front of the class right now.)

Early on we considered titling this manuscript (with a nod to the late Abbie Hoffman's famous work), "Borrow This Book!" This phrase exemplifies one of the attitudes you're going to have to employ to succeed at this venture.

The following chapters outline, in gory detail, the steps to producing a professional feature film for under $30,000. Is it an easy process? By no means. In fact, people are going to tell you it's impossible. That's what they told us — often loudly and at great length. However, it can be done and it can be done well. All it takes is a strong vision, a little creativity, and a lot of persistence.

If you're looking for a definitive tome on filmmaking, we suggest you put this book back now (or peruse our bibliography for more likely titles). This book is not intended to be a short course on theories and themes and techniques of filmmaking. Its purpose is more specific: How to circumvent the traditional filmmaking routes in order to make a quality feature film for the remarkably low sum of $30,000 or less.

We recognize that the readers of this book may vary widely in their experience levels. We've tried to balance our approach, so as not to talk down to people who already have considerable film experience and not to confuse people who are just starting out. However, we recognize that we may not have been entirely successful. If you find yourself patronized or perplexed at any portions of this book, please accept our apologies now.

* * *

Before we get into the nuts and bolts of how you can make a feature for such a (relatively) paltry sum, please indulge us for a moment as we recount how we came to produce not one, but two feature films for a sticker price of less than what it costs for Arnold Schwarzenegger to say "Hasta la vista, baby" and "I'll be back."

Our first ultra-low-budget feature film, "Resident Alien," was the brainchild of Dale, resulting from three factors: a life-long interest in film, a premature brush with a mid-life crisis, and a visit to a Hollywood set where he realized the wizards of Hollywood hadn't built anything that he couldn't create in his own basement workshop.

With a two-day low-budget filmmaking seminar by Dov Simens for inspiration (a highly recommended program, by the way; see the "Other Resources" section in the appendix for details), Dale began working on the structure for his film, creating a script that fit all the requirements of the ultra-low-budget genre: A small cast, limited locations, and a story driven more by character than big-budget action scenes or costly special effects. In short, he successfully completed Step One of the process: He created a dream.

Step Two of the process is to involve others in the dream, which Dale tackled with equal aplomb. First on board was John, followed in short order by a host of people who generously gave of their time and talent to make "Resident Alien" into the little film that could. These people came from all walks of life, but they shared two important qualities: They believed in the movie, and they believed we could make it happen.

"Resident Alien" is the story of Cal, a former astrophysics graduate student — currently an apartment-building manager — who scans the night skies for a discovery that will help him regain his position in the scientific community. His only tenant, Leslie, is newly divorced, out of work, and at the end of her rope. One night they both witness, and are nearly incinerated by, what appears to be a crashing UFO. When a mysterious stranger, an unscrupulous UFO investigator, and a wily sheriff enter the picture, Cal and Leslie's lives are turned upside down.

"Resident Alien" Poster
Photo courtesy of Granite Productions, Ltd.

Using personal savings and investments from friends and family, we shot "Resident Alien" over four consecutive weekends in late 1989. Since most of the action takes place at the motel/apartment building Cal manages, a suitable motel in Lake City, Minnesota, was rented for our first weekend. We then dove into production, shooting nearly one quarter of the film in a frenzied, exhausting two-day marathon.

Arriving home late Sunday night, we were tired but satisfied: All things considered, the weekend had gone well. The location looked good. The actors were great. And the story seemed to be making that shaky leap from page to screen.

Monday morning the call came. The film was black. There was nothing on it. It was image-free.

Working with an unfamiliar camera, we had loaded the film wrong. For every shot. All weekend long. It was as if that weekend's work had never happened. All that effort, and we had absolutely nothing to show for it. Except for a sizable dent in the checkbook.

We were faced with a quandary: Should we abandon the project and cut our losses, or continue to throw money at this movie-making machine and hope for the best? Swallowing hard, Dale (the producer) decided to proceed. As it turned out, our trial by fire was to be a short trial, with an early acquittal, because once past that first bump, the rest of the production was smooth (albeit, slow) sailing.

The production was, by necessity, divided into two phases: Live-action shooting, which took about a month, and special-effects shooting, which took about a year. The effects included flying spaceships, explosions, miniature shots, and all sorts of things you're not supposed to be able to do on an ultra-tiny budget.

Many months later, in the fall of 1991, "Resident Alien" premiered to hearty audience response and favorable reviews. One reviewer even called the film "the best low-budget independent project ever to come out of the area," which is high praise, considering the number of independent features Minnesota has spawned.

Another critic mistakenly referred to our guerrilla filmmaking tactics as "Kamikaze Filmmaking," which may have been more true than we were willing to admit, because even before the premiere of "Resident Alien," we had already shot our second feature, "Beyond Bob."

"Beyond Bob" Poster
Photo courtesy of Granite Productions, Ltd.

"Beyond Bob," a romantic-comedy ghost story, was not originally conceived as an ultra-low-budget film. Written by John and his writing partner Michael Paul Levin (who also plays Bob in the film), the script was designed for a slightly larger budget. Although it required few locations, had no action sequences, and hardly any special effects, it did involve a larger cast than "Resident Alien" (seven major characters and two extended crowd scenes) and an ambitious soundtrack.

The ambitious soundtrack was a logical outgrowth of this story about college friends whose rock band disbanded after the untimely death of its leader, Bob. Years later the group gets together for a weekend, only to be visited by the ghost of Bob, who's intent on getting their lives back on the right track. It's "The Big Chill" meets "Ghost." (Or, for you lower-budget fans, "The Return of the Secaucus Seven" meets "Truly, Madly, Deeply.") One studio executive affectionately referred to the finished film as "The Little Chill." We think that was meant as a compliment.

We followed the same shooting schedule on "Beyond Bob" that we had with the first film, shooting over four consecutive weekends during the summer of 1991. However, the film had actually been in pre-production for much of the previous year, as the large cast had to be assembled, locations secured and much of the music written and recorded.

As with "Resident Alien," we suffered another short trial by fire a few weeks before shooting began on "Beyond Bob," when we lost three of our seven cast members to jobs that paid actual cash. The late additions who came to our rescue must have meshed well with the others, however, for one studio executive who looked at the film insisted that the cast had to have come out of New York or Los Angeles, and not from the large and talented acting pool in the Minneapolis/St. Paul area. That executive was wrong, but that's not surprising because he was also wrong about our budget, which he estimated to be about $900,000. Or 30 times higher than it actually was.

* * *

On both films, the road from original idea to finished film was a long one, but the end results were, at least in our eyes, well worth the effort. We learned a lot in the process, about filmmaking and about ourselves. But there's one important thing writing this book has taught us that making the films didn't: We are not alone. And neither are you.

There are a surprising number of people out in the world, struggling to do the same thing we did. While we researched this book, we heard stories about successes and failures, about profitable ventures and near bankruptcies. Despite the differences in experiences, in results, and in the films themselves, one similar trait shone through all the interviews and conversations we had with filmmakers from South Africa to Seattle, from Texas to New Brunswick: Each filmmaker had a fierce persistence of vision, best defined as a complete unwillingness to give up even when all signs and reason said they should.

Making any feature film is an enormous undertaking. Making a professional-quality feature film for under $30,000 is an accomplishment worthy of sainthood because it definitely qualifies as a miracle. The following pages explain how we — and other filmmakers like us — made our films. We'll also provide you with the tools you'll need to make your own ultra-low-budget feature. So if you're still standing in the stacks at Barnes & Noble, quit reading this introduction and get to the meat! You've got a miracle to make!

THE DREAM
Taking A Leap

Everything we're about to tell you is wrong.

Really? Well, no. Not really.

However, a healthy dose of skepticism will help sustain you on the long journey that lies before you. As you make your way down the twisted path toward a finished feature film, you're going to meet a steady stream of nay sayers, pessimists, and downright negative people who will tell you that you're insane, you can't do it, and you're a damn fool for trying.

Don't listen to them. Or, for that matter, even to us.

William Goldman, the author of such screenplays as "Butch Cassidy and The Sundance Kid," "All The President's Men," and "Marathon Man," will probably be remembered for one short statement just as much as he is remembered for all the books and screenplays he wrote. That statement is simply this: Nobody knows anything.

The investor who tells you that you'll never raise the money doesn't know anything.

The lab operator who tells you that you can't possibly make a feature film on your tiny budget doesn't know anything.

The cinematographer who says you can't shoot a decent feature film on an eight-day schedule doesn't know anything.

The distributor who says no audience will want to see your film doesn't know anything.

Even the two guys who wrote a book telling you the "right" way to make an ultra-low-budget feature don't know anything.

It's not that these people — and countless others that you'll meet — are ignorant. On the contrary, some know the movie business inside and out. It's just that the process of making an ultra-low-budget film requires breaking lots of rules. Sometimes all the rules. Even the rules we've laid out in this book.

However, if nothing else, the rules in this book can act as a good starting point and touchstone for you to return to as you make your way through the pre-production, production and post-production processes.

And how, you impatiently ask, do you start on this amazing, frustrating, and often exhilarating journey? With a dream.

Some have called filmmaking a "silver addiction" referring to the silver salts used in film stocks. As addictions go, it's a strong one. It has to be because often the dream of making your film is all that carries you over the long days/weeks/months/years that it takes to go from idea to entity.

With that in mind, your first task is to find your dream. To define it. To make it your own.

Since you're reading this book, odds are that you already have at least the beginnings of a dream.

- A story you're dying to tell.

- A character you'd love to see developed.

- An idea or issue you're burning to explore.

The next step is to look at that dream with a cold, realistic eye: Is it a reasonable dream? Can you produce it for $30,000? While there's certainly no absolute answer, there is a ballpark that you should at least try to play in if you're going to work at this budget level.

For example, is your story idea a historical costume drama, involving large crowd scenes and multiple, historically-accurate locations? If so, then keep dreaming.

Is your idea a small, contemporary dramatic (romance, comedy, suspense, horror, farce, mystery, melodrama, science fiction) story that can take place in just a few locations with a handful of characters? Great. Now you're in the ballpark.

We'll get into more specific constraints in the next chapter, but suffice it to say that if you're trying to re-do "Ben Hur" on this budget, you're setting yourself up for a painful fall.

* * *

Once you've defined your dream, you're ready to take the next important step. Start telling people that you're going to make a feature film. It doesn't matter where. At a cocktail party, after church, on a bus, or at the water cooler. It also doesn't really matter who. Your parents. Your significant other. Your co-workers. Your dentist.

It only matters that you say it. And that you say it out loud. "I'm going to make a feature film."

Why do you have to say it, say it out loud, and say it to someone else? Two reasons: The first is that, since this is a statement most people aren't used to hearing, you're bound to get some interesting responses. Responses along the lines of, "What's it about?" "Where are you getting the money?" and "Great. Can I help?"

While all these questions are valid and important, it's the last one that you're really listening for because once you've got the dream, the next step is to get other people excited about it. You need other people excited about your project because there's ABSOLUTELY NO WAY you can do it all alone.

The second reason you should begin telling people that you're going to make a feature — saying it often and out loud — is because it takes your dream and begins to make it real. Just saying it isn't going to make it happen, of course. But it does put your pride on the line. You're more likely to push forward if your friends start asking, "What ever happened to that film thing you were going to do?"

It also makes the idea more concrete and it raises other questions that you have to start thinking about. When will you start shooting? Where are you going to get the money? Who's going to be in it? When is it going to be done? How are you going to distribute it?

The following chapters will provide you with the means to answer those questions. But nobody's going to ask the questions until you make the statement. Out loud.

"I'm going to make a feature film." (Uh-oh. Now you've done it.)

* * *

Making a feature film, even for someone who's done it many times, is a daunting process. For someone who's never done it, it can be downright overwhelming. Take solace that it isn't one long process, but is instead a series of discrete and attainable steps. Each step leads logically to the next.

You also don't have to navigate these unfamiliar waters without charts. Others have done this before, or at least something similar. Us, for instance, and the other filmmakers you'll meet in this book.

Reading this book and others on writing, producing and selling movies can provide valuable background. Taking classes can be good preparation on specific parts of the process. Working on other people's films (regardless of the budget) can be an education in itself on what to do and what not to do.

One of the best sources of information we've found is people who have made a feature before. They're generally more than happy to talk to you. More likely than not, they'll tell you that you can't make a movie for $30,000, and then they'll proceed to give you three ideas on how to make it happen. In addition, they'll mention a few more pitfalls to watch out for, recommend some cast and crew people, suggest who else to turn to for free advice, and maybe even volunteer to help. At least, that's been our experience.

If there's one thing we learned, it's that dreams are contagious, and you should try to infect as many people as possible with yours.

You have a long, challenging journey ahead if you're going to start — not to mention finish — a feature film. Regardless of the length of your journey, however, there is a destination — the moment when the finished film begins to roll in front of an audience, and you can see the fruits of your labor — your dream — come to life. The audience laughs. They cry. They gasp. They applaud.

And your dream has become reality.

THE SCRIPT
(If It Ain't On The Page ...)

Analogy #1: Just as the basement is the foundation for your house, so too is the screenplay the foundation for your film. A strong foundation makes for a stronger house and a stronger film. However, unlike your basement, you can't fill up your screenplay with extra stuff you're not using. There's just no room in your film, in your shooting schedule, or in your budget.

Analogy #2: Your screenplay is your road map. It tells you, your cast, and your crew where you're headed and how you're going to get there. Without a good road map, you might make it to your destination but not before wasting a lot of time and money, two commodities that are in short supply.

A dramatic feature film is only as good as its screenplay and rarely any better. While this is certainly common knowledge, you'd be amazed at the number of filmmakers (and we're not just pointing fingers at Hollywood here; independents are just as guilty) who dive into production with a screenplay that simply isn't ready to be shot.

Therefore, be prepared to spend a lot of time on your script. It's a difficult process, but you'll be happier about it in the end, and the results will show in your finished film. Making a good film out of a bad script is not unlike the proverbial sow's ear and silk purse. It's simply not going to happen.

The Basics

While this chapter isn't intended to provide you with an exhaustive course in screenwriting, it will give you the basics you need to construct a script that's filmable on your ultra-low budget.

(For further reading on the finer points of screenwriting, along with sample formats, please refer to the bibliography in the appendix.

There are a number of excellent books out there on screenwriting; however, remember the words of our friend Mr. Goldman, "Nobody knows anything." For every absolute rule someone states about screenwriting, you can always find several examples of successful films that have broken that rule. The "Other Resources" section in the appendix also lists where you can buy screenplays of existing films, which can be an excellent educational resource.)

Story

As an independent filmmaker with no budget to speak of, story is your friend, your biggest asset, and your secret weapon. The reality of making movies on this scale is that you're not going to impress a distributor with your big-name stars (unless you're married to one), your exotic locations (unless you live in one), or your stunning crowd scenes (unless you have a stunningly large family). You simply don't have the bucks for them.

That leaves you with story, the one place where you can compete head-to-head with the Hollywood big kids. You can have a better story in your $30,000 feature than that $40 million box-office bomb starring the latest flavor-of-the-month star teetering on the rim of Mount Erebus.

Story is your best selling point. If the story is great, shortcomings in lighting, cinematography, sound, set design, and so on will be forgotten as the viewer is drawn into the story. Consider the early films of D. W. Griffith or Charlie Chaplin. No sound, only natural light, black and white, static camera shots. Yet they are still powerful, entertaining and remembered today because they presented engaging characters in interesting stories.

Three-Act Structure

Now, we're big fans of the three-act structure: Act 1 (otherwise known as The Beginning), in which you establish motivation and set the scene, which leads to a catharsis, crisis, or conflict that requires the main character to make a decision about what he or she wants to do.

Act 2 (also known as The Middle), in which the main character faces challenges and obstacles to carrying out that decision, leading to a scene of recognition in which the character reaffirms his or her commitment to the decision.

Act 3 (you guessed it, The End), in which the story reaches its climax, and the main character succeeds or fails to achieve what he or she wants.

This, of course, isn't the only way to structure a screenplay, but it's tried and true, and 90 percent of the successful and well-loved films follow this pattern.

There are, of course, exceptions to the rule. Quentin Tarantino took the classic three-act structure and turned it on its ear with "Pulp Fiction," which contained a three act structure, but ordered them as Act One, Act Three and then Act Two. Even a classic dramatist like Harold Pinter has put a spin on the three acts, structuring his film "Betrayal" (and the play of the same name) so that we see the story's conclusion at the beginning of the film and then work our way backwards so that the beginning of the story occurs at the end. If you have in mind a bold, innovative, stunning new screenplay structure, go for it. It just might be your ticket. If you haven't been struck by a bolt of inspired genius, stick to the proven, audience-tested structure.

Writing For A Tiny Budget

While the traditional three-act screenplay structure can apply to any film, there are special considerations that you must be aware of in crafting your ultra-low-budget feature script. And we do recommend writing the script specifically for a tiny budget. It's easier to make your limitations invisible if you aren't imposing them on a bigger-budget story.

With that in mind, here are some of the building blocks for your screenplay:

Creating Unique Characters

Any respectable film needs interesting characters that the audience cares about. This is doubly important to your project. Unique, unusual, remarkably-true-to-life, or endearing characters will help you attract an audience, which in turn will help attract the attention of distributors. But of more immediate concern, juicy roles will draw the high-quality actors you need. This is a case of one strong asset attracting another. Actors live by their resumes, so the better the role, the more good people who will be auditioning.

Along this same line of thought, give good lines to all the characters, even the waitress in the walk-on role. Speaking parts are the currency of an actor's resume. Since you can't pay them much — or any — money, give them something useful, a good scene for their reel.

Where would Bronson Pinchot be without his short, but memorable, appearance in "Beverly Hills Cop" as the art gallery assistant? Jeff Goldblum virtually launched his career with "I forgot my mantra" in Woody Allen's "Annie Hall." Even Richard Dreyfuss had a memorable line in his early, minuscule appearance in "The Graduate" ("You want me to call the cops? I'll call the cops.")

Bottom line: Give all your actors something interesting to play.

Mystery

A bit of uncertainty can really help propel your story forward. Don't tell the audience everything at once. Let the story be revealed. Make the audience want to see the next scene to learn the truth about a character, to see how a scheme unfolds, to find out what that crazy person was building. A little mystery can go a long way towards preventing your story from slowing down. But — and this is a big but — make sure the answers are worth the wait.

Twists

Keep your audience engaged in the story by turning the plot direction on its ear occasionally. (The heroine in peril was actually married to the villain! The bad guy is actually good! The dog can talk!) If they are concentrating on the story, they're less likely to notice that you couldn't afford a room at the Ritz for that romantic scene and are instead shooting in your parents' attractively paneled basement rec room.

Dramatic Tension

Don't forget to create conflict between your characters. Which are you most likely to watch, the couple on the corner quietly holding hands or the ones with the flailing arms who are shouting at each other? Make use of that most noble of human instincts, voyeurism. This is an easy point to forget, but the fact is that if your characters agree on everything, you don't have much dramatic tension. And without dramatic tension, you won't have much of a movie.

Testing Your Story

Test your stories on your friends — the ones who will tell you if it stinks. If you don't have any friends who are that honest, give it to people who don't like you. If you can win them over with your story, it's good. The point is, make sure you have a tale that people want to be told.

Screenwriter Paul Schrader ("Taxi Driver") has said that he makes a point of telling people the story of his screenplay as he's working on it, gauging their reactions to the story and adjusting his screenplay to match. At its heart, filmmaking is storytelling, and you've got to make sure you have something interesting to tell.

* * *

These are the things you need for a successful screenplay. Next we've got the list of things you can't have if you want to finish your ultra-low-budget feature film.

Cash constraints can be gratifying to overcome, and we think they bring out the true creativity of a production team. If you can just throw money at a problem, you tend to take the first solution that comes to mind, usually the one that's been done a dozen times before. If you have to come up with a novel solution to your problem, you've usually added a new creative element to your film. A tight budget can squeeze those creative juices out of you. So, here's a list of constraints to inspire your best ideas.

Number of Characters

Limit yourself to three main characters, or barring that, don't include more than three main characters all together in a scene or have them all interacting at the same time. For instance, if you have a party scene, break up the conversations into subgroups of three or less. Why? You don't have enough film stock.

We'll get into this in more detail later, but your budget will only allow for a three-to-one (3:1) or four-to-one (4:1) shooting ratio. What this means is that with a 3:1 ratio, you can shoot only 3 minutes of film for each finished minute of your movie.

For example, let's say you're shooting the climactic scene where Rhett walks out on Scarlet (apparently you've ignored everything we've said about historical costume dramas and crowd scenes). With a 3:1 shooting ratio, this gives you just enough film to shoot the scene in a master shot showing both of them and then to shoot two other takes of the scene, a close-up of Rhett and a close-up of Scarlet. That's 3:1, with no margin for error.

If Rhett said "Give a hoot" in the master shot, you can do a second take — which would move you up to a 4:1 ratio for this scene and force you to shoot some later scene in a 2:1 ratio to compensate — or you can make sure that you get him to say "Give a damn" in the close-up. Most of the time you'll try to work in a 3:1 or 2:1 ratio to save a little footage for that tricky shot that's going to take a 5:1 ratio.

So what's shooting ratio got to do with the number of main characters in your script? Let's add Ashley to the scene with Rhett and Scarlet, and you'll quickly realize that you're into a 4:1 shooting ratio — a master shot and three close-ups (Ashley, Rhett, Scarlet). And that assumes there are no mistakes that require a retake. The more group scenes like this in your script, the more your film stock expense has to go up to compensate, and the sad fact is that you don't have the money for more film.

So does this mean you can only afford to do a film with two characters? By no means. But on the other hand, you probably aren't going to do a story about a baseball team whose players are inseparable.

In "Beyond Bob," we had seven principal characters because the script was not originally written to be done on an ultra-low budget. When possible, the script was rewritten to break up dialogue among smaller groups of characters. We kept to a 4:1 shooting ratio only by making editing decisions in the camera and by breaking scenes into sub-groups of characters. Rarely do all the characters appear in the same sequence, and if they do, they don't all talk.

The perfect number of characters in a scene from "Beyond Bob."
Pictured, Kathryn O'Malley and Peter Moore.
Photo courtesy of Granite Productions, Ltd.

In summary, your life will be much easier, and your film much better, if you structure your screenplay to work within your limited shooting ratio.

Number of Locations

To stay on a $30,000 budget, you'll have to do all principal photography in four weekends or less. Trust us on this one. In order to accomplish this, you have to control yourself on the number of locations.

Now this doesn't mean you can't have a variety of locations; just that you need to have big chunks of sync-sound dialogue occurring at a limited number of locations.

The main reason is time. If you move your entire crew from one location to another during one day of the shoot, you'll lose a minimum of an hour for each move, in addition to the travel time itself. This is more than merely an hour because during that hour you're also paying equipment rental, you're losing daylight shooting time, and there's always the problem of having the crew and cast straggle off "to get a Coke." You also lose the momentum and pace your director has been trying to establish in order to shoot 12 pages of script a day. You don't want to do this. Enough said.

By keeping a couple of points in mind as you write your script, you can provide a nice variety of locations without wasting precious production time.

The first thing is not to introduce a new location without using it for a lot of pages of dialogue or action. However, this doesn't necessarily mean continuous use of the location within the story. Since you'll be shooting out of sequence, it doesn't matter when in the story you use this setting, just as long as it totals up to blocks of 12 pages — the amount you'll shoot in a day. This way, you can set up your crew and equipment at that location and shoot for the whole day. It's easy enough to switch locations overnight by just taking the equipment home and bringing it to the new location the next morning. No production time wasted.

If this seems like a stifling limitation, keep in mind that the same location can include many settings. For example, the house we used in "Beyond Bob" served up an easy dozen settings. A location also can be made to look completely different to create a different mood for a different scene. You can change lighting, add props and furniture, change characters, or completely change the interactions between the characters. All of these will reinvigorate the scene, and the audience will scarcely give a thought to whether they've seen this location before.

You can also pick a bland setting and redress it to serve as more than one location. If you could afford a sound stage and set pieces (which you can't, so forget it!), this is how you'd shoot all of your interiors for the same reason Hollywood productions do — to save the costs and time of moving cast, crew, and equipment. You can, however, find a location that can serve the same essential purpose for you.

For example, in "Resident Alien," we shot in Dale's living room and work room for one afternoon (we spent the morning shooting in his backyard, so the whole day really counted as one location). With the use of office partitions, desk, computer, file cabinet, chairs, and careful camera angles, we transformed the neutral-colored walls of the living room into a welfare office. Not three feet away, again using a few selected decorations and pieces of furniture, we created the interior of a North Dakota farm house.

Another 12 feet away in a workroom with unfinished sheetrock walls, we moved a few appliances, propped up a few more pieces of sheetrock for additional walls, and — voila! — we had a motel laundry room in central Minnesota. Four hundred miles of travel in less than two dozen feet of distance. And no one has ever suspected when seeing the finished film. So if you're planning to repaint the living room, pick something nondescript.

You may have noticed that we've mainly referred to interior locations. That's because your script should primarily take place indoors, unless you live somewhere where the weather is reliable (we don't).

On your fast-paced schedule, you need as much control as possible, so limit the outdoor dialogue scenes and try to locate them near an indoor location in case of typhoon, blizzard, tornado, or other acts of God.

If you own your own 16mm camera, such as a Bolex with a decent lens, then you can add a large number of establishing shots to your script as long as they don't require sync sound or extra lighting. (The sync-sound camera, the recorder for sync-sound, and the lights are going to be some of your most expensive rentals.) You can even have your actors in the shots as long as there isn't dialogue. This second-unit shooting is cheap and can be done as time permits.

We shot the first ten minutes of "Beyond Bob" — which was all essentially silent exteriors — as second-unit work over the course of three months after principal photography was completed. So, if you want other interesting locations, just write them as simple establishing shots in your script. We've even used miniatures of building signs and other exteriors to get the look of a bigger-budget film.

Remember, every time you introduce a new location, think of where else in your story you can use it.

Write What You Own

Another point you can never forget while writing the script is that you have no money! Nada! Zippo! All of your money is going for equipment, film stock, and food for the cast and crew. So don't write in any props or locations that you don't own, can't beg or borrow, or can't sneak into long enough to get your shot.

Forget about that old truism, "Write what you know." You need to write what you own. Robert Rodriguez, who made "El Mariachi," followed this rule, structuring his script around locations, vehicles and props he had easy access to: two bars, a jail, a ranch, a motorcycle, a school bus, and a pit bull.

Clearly, expensive set dressings are not going to be your strong suit. They're simply too time consuming and expensive. However, you can enliven your scenes by using unique props and costumes.

On "Resident Alien," we couldn't afford sets that you usually see in science-fiction films, but we knew the audience would be expecting a science-fiction look. To compensate, the main character was made into a science geek who is constantly using or working on homemade science gear. These props were easily transported to the locations, didn't cost much and gave us the requisite science-fiction look.

Also look around where you live. It may be old hat to you, but unless you live in Los Angeles or New York, it's a unique regional location for the rest of the world. What may be mundane to you may never have been seen by most audiences.

This is one of the biggest reasons we're fans of regional film-making. Ninety percent of the films released look like the terrain within 100 miles of Los Angeles. There are thousands of unique settings, urban and rural, that are rarities on the screen. So when you think of locations for your scenes, pick settings that are unique to your neck of the woods. What is an expensive location shoot for Paramount is a cheap back-yard set for you. Your neighborhood can add hundreds of thousands of dollars of visual impact to your film for next to nothing. This kind of thinking will have distributors guessing you spent a million bucks on your film.

It's also possible to use what you *don't* have to your advantage. When Kevin Smith made "Clerks," he had complete access to the convenience store that served as his primary location. The one drawback was that he only had use of the location at night, and his story took place during the day. His budget didn't give him enough money to set up huge lights outside the store to give the illusion of sunlight during his all-night shoots, so he took this disadvantage and made it his character's problem and not his own. Dante, the beleaguered store clerk, arrives at work to find that someone has jammed gum in the lock that secures the metal shutters over the front window of the store. As a result, he can't get the shutters opened. This is just one of the many problems that plague Dante throughout the day. Smith wisely found a way to take a problem and make it work to his advantage as part of his story.

This same thinking can be helpful at any budget level. When Richard Rush was making "The Stunt Man," he found that the California locations, and in particular the palm trees, were getting in the way of the World War I film-within-the-film that Peter O'Toole's character was directing. Then Rush, too, realized that it wasn't his problem; it was the character's problem. So in the finished film, O'Toole laments "Palm trees! Yet more palm trees! Who had the audacity to put palm trees there?! They will be in every shot! And what are palm trees doing waving around in a battlefield in Europe during the First World War? Answer me that." The answer is that the writer and director have cleverly taken a disadvantage and turned it around to their advantage.

Night vs. Day & Big vs. Small

Here's a simple mathematical equation: Lights = money. As you will have limited money for your production, it follows that you will have limited lighting. How does this affect the scripting process? Let us illuminate.

The first requirement is to not write scenes set in large locations that must be lit artificially. Now if you're reading carefully, you see that this doesn't prevent you from using large locations. You can use the Grand Canyon during the day; thanks to the sun, you don't have to rent lights to do it.

Night shots seem like a cheap idea, but they actually may require a lot of money — that is, light — to make them visible on film. Again, if you're reading carefully, you'll notice we said "may require." If you limit the size of the area you are trying to light, the simple lighting kit you can afford (four 1000 watt lamps) will be more than adequate. We even simulated a blinding UFO landing using this lighting kit by limiting the area we were lighting.

We were also able to shoot under-exposed shots during the magic hour just after sunset but before dark to simulate night. We could see headlights on vehicles and details in the dark trees and cars without using any artificial lights.

So, the lesson here is to write scenes requiring artificial lighting only for small locations or small parts of large locations. For large locations, keep in mind that they must be shot in daylight, during magic hour (this will have to be a short sequence that can be accomplished in less than an hour), or as miniatures that you can afford to light.

Surely, you are thinking, these are enough shackles to place on one project. Dream on.

Other Constraints

These are only the budgetary constraints you must suffer through. They'll seem easy once your project is facing the list of "artistic" requirements of most potential distributors. Most of these requirements are so lowbrow (more blood, more girls, more blood, more bikinis, more blood, more sex, more nudity, and did we mention more blood?) that we were glad we didn't pander to them.

Make a movie that's your vision, that you're proud of. When you face the inevitable rejections, you can sleep nights if you've followed your dream. It's hard to justify risking $30,000 if it's only to make a return on your investment. If you're only in this for the money, there are better investments that are a lot less work.

But just because most of this advice from distributors is fecal doesn't mean there aren't some valuable points.

The best piece of advice we've heard is to get your story moving in the first five minutes. "Resident Alien" doesn't kick into gear until about 15 minutes in. This is a long time without the aid of a well-known star or stunning visuals. We've been fortunate that most people are willing to wait for the good stuff that follows. However, attention spans are short in the world of distribution and increasingly so among audiences, so it's important that your story hits the ground running.

You need to make sure something intriguing, startling, or dramatic happens in the first five minutes to draw them into the story. And then you darn well better use the next 85 minutes to build on that opening. Ideally, the viewers will be so captivated by your story that they'll never get to think about it being an ultra-low-budget film again until it's all over. By that point, they won't care if you had a big-name star or a Riviera locale.

Finding The Write Stuff

So what do you do if you're not a screenwriter but you have everything else it takes to make a film? Obviously you need to find a screenwriter, which really won't be that difficult. The tough part will be finding the *right* screenwriter.

As with every other crew and cast position you'll need to fill, we recommend that you opt for excitement about the project and a positive attitude over experience. Not that we're knocking experience. Experience is great — when you can afford it. The main problem with experience is that by the time someone becomes really experienced in something — like writing, editing, photography, whatever — they often expect to receive a paycheck that is commensurate with their skills. And who can blame them? You can't, but you can't afford them, either.

The people you're looking for are the ones who are really excited about the project and who appear to have the basic skills necessary to get them through their tasks. In our case, it was often people who had experience in film production, but usually one or two steps down from the position they were taking on our film.

For example, a camera loader becomes a camera operator; a production assistant becomes a production manager; a boom operator becomes a sound recordist; or an assistant editor becomes an editor. These are people who want to move up but who haven't really had the opportunity. That is, until your film came along.

The same will probably be true of your screenwriter. Odds are you aren't going to get a working professional, card-carrying Writers Guild member to write your script for you. First, because you can't afford them, and second, because as union members, they can't work on your decidedly non-union film.

So how do you find this budding William Goldman? Well, if you followed our earlier advice (tell people that you're making a feature), you may have already heard from a couple writers. Word travels fast, and the word about feature films seems to travel at supersonic speeds. (We even had someone call us from New York to inquire about the possibility of being an extra in one of our films. In Minnesota. Trust us, word travels fast.)

However, if writers haven't started seeking you out, there are a number of ways to beat them out of the bushes. Here are a few:

• Many colleges and universities offer film-writing and play-writing courses. Call the professors at a school near you, and see if they can recommend any of their students. You may even get the professor interested.

• If you have a chapter of the Independent Feature Project nearby (see the appendix), check with them about putting an announcement in their newsletter or on their bulletin board (cork, voice mail, or computer). In the announcement, specify what you're looking for ("an ultra-low-budget script") as well as what you're not looking for (for example, "no slasher, horror, or exploitation" if that's your plan). This will save you and the respondents a lot of time.

• If your city or state has a film commission or office, talk to the people there for names of local people writing screenplays. Generally, film boards are in the business of bringing big-buck films into your area, but most of them also do their best to help out local folks interested in film work. At the very least, they'll have a directory of local production talent, which will come in very handy later on. Odds are, they'll even know who are the up-and-coming screenwriters in your area and will help put you in touch with them.

• If all else fails, you can place an ad in one of the Hollywood trade papers — Variety or The Hollywood Reporter. However, we'd recommend that this be your avenue of last resort, for a few key reasons.

First, it costs money to place an ad, and you don't have any money. Certainly not to be placing ads.

Second, you will be inundated with scripts. Your mailbox will be stuffed. Boxes of scripts will land on your doorstep. Your answering machine will explode from overuse. Your home will be swallowed by paper. Your body will never be found.

Perhaps we exaggerate. But not by much.

And, finally, 99.99% of these scripts will not be written for your budget level. And cramming a million dollar (or 20 million dollar) script into a $30,000 budget is not a pretty sight. Imagine Orson Welles in a Speedo.

If you feel you must take this approach, be sure to specify "ultra-low-budget" in your ad. This will tell the reader two things: Don't bother sending big budget scripts (they will anyway), and don't plan on getting paid. Also specify what you do or don't want, such as "no horror," "no period pieces," and so on. We've put the addresses for these trade papers in the "Other Resources" section of the appendix. Contact them for information on ad rates (and don't get mad when we say we told you so).

Once you've found your screenwriter, you need to settle on your story. He or she may have a story or script that can be adapted to your budget parameters. If so, great. Or you may need to outline the parameters and let the writer go off and stew on it for a while. Most writers like a challenge, and writing for a $30,000 feature certainly qualifies.

Of course, you may already have a story that you'd like the writer to adapt. This is a fine approach, with a couple caveats:

• If it's a story you made up, you're in great shape because that means you own the rights to it. You can do whatever you want with it.

• If it's a story that's in the public domain, you're also in good shape. Public domain means that the author is dead and has been for a good long time. As such, no one person owns the rights to the material, but it is now owned by the public. Shakespeare is a good example of a writer whose work is in the public domain. Danielle Steel is not.

However, with writers who are dead but not nearly as dead as Shakespeare, it's often tricky to figure out what's in the public domain and what isn't. If it's older than a hundred years, you might be okay, but you'll want to check with the Library of Congress to make sure.

If the story you're interested in adapting isn't in the public domain, you're going to have to get the rights from the author, and that's going to cost you money. Probably.

For example, if you've got your eye on a Sidney Sheldon or John Grisham story, forget it. These guys are out of your league. But if the story is by a less well-known author, you may be able to work something out. Regional writers are — not so surprisingly — great resources for regional stories and may be interested in seeing their work transferred to the big (or semi-big) screen.

As with everyone you bring on board, you'll need to establish a contract with your writer, so you have rights to use the finished script.

One final housekeeping note: Whether you write the script yourself or contract with someone else to write your script, be sure that you copyright the material and the writer registers it with the Writers Guild of America.

Technically, anything original that you write is copyrighted the moment you write it. However, it is a good idea to go through the simple copyright procedures when your script is finished.

To copyright your script, write to the Library of Congress and ask for their Form PA. You can find their address in the "Other Resources" section of the appendix. As of this writing, it costs $10 to copyright material.

You should also register your script with the Writers Guild of America. This registration doesn't take the place of copyrighting, but it does provide you with an additional level of security should there be any question as to the ownership of your script. Send them an unbound copy of your script, along with $20 (for non-members). Their address can be found in the "Other Resources" section of the appendix. An alternative is to mail a copy of the script to yourself by certified mail so it has a delivery date. Don't open this package, just put it away as proof of a date by which the script was completed.

* * *

Part of the creative challenge for the screenwriter of an ultra-low-budget movie is how to turn every penny into screen image. The right script for an ultra-low-budget film is literally worth hundreds of thousands of dollars in apparent value for the finished movie, so it's not a creative challenge to take lightly or to do quickly.

As you — or your new best friend, your screenwriter — shape your script, think of what it costs to do everything, and then think of how you can reuse that expense several more times to get maximum screen value for it.

Remember, your screenplay is the support structure for the rest of this project. Build this foundation with the strongest material you can find; it's got to carry a heavy load.

THE BUDGET
And How To Budge It

Putting together a $30,000 budget for a feature film is a lot like losing your job and finding out you can live on $100 a month.

All those things that were essentials suddenly become luxuries you have to do without. You sleep on your best friend's couch. You take more out of the church collection plate than you put in. You accept and even ask for handouts and favors. You distill your existence down to bare necessities. To succeed within this budget, you will have to discover how to make a film using only the barest of necessities.

Making an ultra-low-budget feature film may give you freedom and let you keep your integrity, but you've got to swallow a lot of pride and inhibitions along the way. And you have to discard many of your preconceived notions of how to put a film together. We found that working professionals in the film business were the people most skeptical of this kind of project. More than one director of photography told us it was impossible to shoot a feature film on this kind of budget, but we went on to do two.

It was impossible to them because they thought you had to have a lighting truck, a top-of-the-line Arriflex camera, a dolly, and a case full of lenses to do the job. Maybe they do, but you don't.

More than once as we planned and shot our films, we found ourselves following the model of the silent films of the 1910s and 1920s. There were few rules about how to make a film back then, and most films were done on shoestring budgets. They didn't have years of "standard practices" to constrain them.

To create your budget and your film, you have to throw off nearly 100 years of accumulated ideas about filmmaking. You don't need dressing rooms for the stars. You don't need most "standard" crew positions. You don't need a day to shoot one scene. You don't need that lighting truck or that new Arriflex or more than one lens. You don't need to follow the "rules." Once you've broken free of these mental shackles, you'll find developing your budget is a lot easier.

It's best to start your budget by including only items that would prevent you from starting and completing your film:

Essentials

- Script
- Camera, batteries, zoom lens, light meter, tripod, filters
- Film stock
- Film processing and work print
- Cast (unless your film is about inanimate objects)
- Very abbreviated crew
- Good food and drinks for cast and crew (to prevent mutiny)
- Film and sound edge numbering
- Editing facilities and supplies
- Music score
- Recording-studio time for sound effects, foley, dialogue looping, music recording
- Sound transfers to 16mm fullcoat magnetic stock for editing
- Recording-studio time for sound mix, 16mm magnetic stock for sound master
- Negative cutting and black leader for A/B roll
- Final print or video transfer

Once you start adding up the numbers, you'll be appalled to see that these items will chew up most of your budget, and any filmmaking experience you have will be screaming that you've left out a bunch of important stuff. We know. This is where you apply your creativity. You start looking at the list and figuring out what you can get for free, borrow, get for a discount rate, or can defer the payment for until your film grows up and starts earning its own money. Once you've done this (Don't panic. We'll give you some more help on this.), you will have an even-more-paltry sum of money available to spend on the almost essentials.

While the list of essentials included the items you need in order to make a salable feature film, the list of almost essentials will be governed more by the unique aspects of your project. You may be able to do without some of the items on this list or make limited use of them.

Almost Essentials

- Second unit camera and tripod (This is such a cost-saver that it should be on the essential list, but you can often borrow it for free.)
- Shipping cost for lab (unless you have one in town)
- Lighting equipment (If you can shoot in natural light, you can get away with just light control devices such as bounce cards, scrims, and reflectors.)
- Tape recorder (Many of the classic spaghetti westerns had their entire sound track and dialogue looped in post-production. No sound was recorded on the set.)
- Shotgun mike, wind screen, and boom pole
- Audio tape stock
- Token payments to cast and crew
- Titles (do-it-yourself ones)
- Rental of film vault space for negatives and audio masters
- Publicity photos, publicity packets
- Photocopying for scripts, maps to locations, cast and crew phone lists, etc.
- Preview video tapes for distributors and film festivals
- Postage for publicity and preview tape mailings

If you still have a few pennies left after including all the essentials and almost essentials, then you can move onto the luxuries:

Luxuries

- Release print with optical sound track
- Camcorder (for taping auditions, playback of a few critical scenes on the set, and making quick video dubs)
- Video dubs of the workprint (for the composer and for use in looping dialogue, foley, sound effects, and for special effects production)
- Wardrobe rentals or purchases
- Makeup
- Models and miniatures
- Vehicle rental
- Location rental
- Camera dolly
- A small-name actor or personality for a cameo role
- Festival entry fees
- Film market entry fees

These lists of budget items assume you're using film equipment (rather than video) in the editing because it's less in demand today and hence cheaper or free. Many people with free access to video equipment have transferred their unedited footage and sound to video tape for editing a final video master. We will discuss the advantages and disadvantages of this approach more in the chapter on post-production. Suffice it to say that you can juggle some budget items by editing in video.

You'll notice that a lot of Hollywood essentials don't appear in this budget list. No big-name stars, no exotic international locations, no sound stage, no insurance, no duplicate negative for safety, no gala premiere, no music-and-effects sound mix for foreign release, no stock footage, no cute little chair with the director's name on it, no toadies to fawn over the producer. There simply isn't enough cash for these non-essentials. So readjust your perspective, and move on.

Here's the final budget for our film "Beyond Bob," which was shot in 1991 and finished in early 1995:

BUDGET - "BEYOND BOB," color, 100 minutes

ITEM	DEFERRED	CASH PAID
Story and rights	$6,000	$60
Producer/SecondUnit-Director	4,000	0
Director	4,000	0
Lead Actors		
Isaac	2,000	20
Bob	2,000	20
Tracy	2,000	20
Supporting Actors		
Neal	1,500	20
Augie	1,500	20
Kris	1,500	20
Ginny	1,500	20
Day Players		
Head Biker	200	5
Pops	200	5
Minister	200	5
Bathroom Woman 1	50	5
Bathroom Woman 2	50	5
Bathroom Woman 3	50	5
Bathroom Woman 4	50	5
Woman at Bar	50	5
Bar Geek	50	5
Waitress	50	5
Band at Bar (and musicians)	100	0
Biker Extras	0	0
Skater Extras	0	0
Skater Boy	50	5
Skater Girl	50	5

Crew, Equipment and Supplies

Unit Production Manager	2,000	20
Asst. Unit Production Manager	1,000	20
Stunt Coordinator (hang gliding)	1,000	10
Art Director	500	0
Set-Construction Coordinator	0	0
Set-construction materials		100
Model Builder	0	0
Model-building materials		50
Wardrobe Supervisor	500	10
Wardrobe rentals/cleaning		60
Makeup-and-Hair Supervisor	500	10
Lighting Gaffer/Boom-		
Mike Operator	1,000	20
Light rental		615
Lighting supplies		240
Dir. of Photography/		
Camera Operator	2,000	20
Asst. Camera Operator/		
Camera Loader	1,000	20
Eclair camera, fluid-head tripod,		
filters, zoom lens, light meter,		
batteries, slate rental, changing		
bag, extra film magazine		800
Lightweight camera dolly		0
Second-unit camera and tripod		0
Sound Recordist	2,000	20
Nagra tape recorder, microphone,		
boom pole, windscreen, batteries,		
cable rental		710
Magnetic tape stock (1/4")		180

Vehicles (on-camera and production)		0
Meals on location		500
Locations		0
Film-stock negative		2,500
Processing and one-light work print		4,615
Sales tax on processing and printing		300
Shipping to film lab		110
Productions stills (film, processing, prints)		75
Sound Transfers from 1/4" tape to 16mm fullcoat		1,300
Film vault rentals (4 years)		800
Film, Sound, Music Editor	3,000	20
Edge numbering for film and fullcoat		410
Flatbed editing table		1,875
Repairs to editing table		525
Video dubs of work print for composer, dialogue looping, sound effects, special effects		20
Slug for editing		15
Splicing tape for editing		25
Composer/Music Supervisor/Songwriter (synchronization rights)	3,000	5
Songwriter (sync rights)	500	5
Songwriter/Singer (sync rights)	500	5
Session musicians	0	0
Back-up vocalists	0	0
Music, sound-effects, dialogue-looping recording		250
Transfer of post-production sound to 16mm fullcoat		835
Post-production sound mix		2,050
Titles		50

Negative cut to 16mm A/B rolls	1,500
Black leader for A/B rolls	250
Answer print	2,525
Video transfer master&submaster	1,325
Sneak preview	935
20 Preview cassettes	280
Publicity photos (5x7)	125
Publicity-packet costs (20)	45
Publicity-packet writing	0
Photocopying 20 scripts	135
Miscellaneous photocopying	100
Postage for publicity packets and preview tapes	100
TOTAL BUDGET	26,775

(Note: As with most budgets, we were off on our estimates for some areas, so we've corrected our original budget to reflect our actual costs. But we've clearly learned something in the process. "Beyond Bob" cost less than "Resident Alien" and looks like it cost more.)

If you have priced out any of the services or products listed in this budget, you're probably saying, "Impossible! There's got to be a trick." Yes, lots of them.

Pinching The Pennies (Unitl Abraham Yells)

There are a several basic principles to use when whittling down your budget so it fits your bank account: You have more time than money. Use what you already own. Make it or borrow it if you don't have it. Use other people's waste or surplus. Dicker for everything you have to buy. Use crew with their own equipment. Rent equipment when business is slow.

Because you're going to spend a lot of money renting and purchasing budget items, we'll start with some general thoughts about these activities.

This budget assumes that you are shooting your production over four weekends, the times when no one else is renting the equipment. Most rental houses will give you an entire weekend for the cost of 1 or 1 1/2 days' rental; you can improve that rate by picking up the equipment late on Friday afternoon so you can shoot some night shots that evening.

You may be able to get better rental deals if you ask for a bid on the whole package you want to rent for four weekends. You might get an even better deal if you use their favorite four-letter word, CASH. Some rental houses have cash flow problems while they wait 90 days for their invoices to be paid. They may trim your bill to put some cash in the till. Sending out a formal bid form will make them think you're getting bids from their competitors even if you're not. However, it's a good idea to get multiple bids. No matter what the rental or purchase price, plead poverty and ask for a deal. A painful wince at the price and saying "We're on a really tight budget. Can you do any better?" will get you an almost-automatic five to ten percent discount at all but the most hard-hearted businesses. And from there you can bargain for better. You've got to have the chutzpah to keep pushing for more and more or, in this case, less and less. ("Chutzpah" is best defined by the old joke about the kid who killed his parents and then pleaded for mercy in court because he was an orphan.)

If you can be very flexible and if you're feeling really lucky, make a deal to rent the equipment dirt cheap if no one else rents it for the weekend. When you offer this, be sure you're talking to the owner, who is going to recognize extra income. The sales people don't necessarily care if they rent anything or not. They're not paying the overhead. Odds are that most of the equipment sits idle on the weekend, so this is a pretty safe rental deal, and one the owner is likely to consider.

Remember, only suckers pay list price.

One advantage of working in the 16mm format is that you don't necessarily have to deal with the rental houses. Many professionals own their own equipment and may be willing to rent it to you for prices well below the going rates. They have a lot of money tied up in their camera or lights or sound gear, and often it's just gathering dust, not income. Before they rent to you, you'll have to demonstrate to them that you are conscientious and won't trash their $5,000 camera. If they agree to rent it to you, be sure to get instructions from them on how to take care of and use their equipment. And then follow their instructions. You will soon be colleagues with these people, and you want only good things said about you. So don't burn any bridges.

You also might find while you're arranging a rental that this professional becomes intrigued and excited about your project. Since you're working weekends when these professionals usually aren't working, they may be willing to join your crew for the experience and the fun of working on a feature film. We called up a friend who runs an audio studio to get recommendations on people who could be sound recordists. He suggested himself and recommended a friend of his to be our gaffer and boom operator. Feature films are infectious.

You also can get some equipment and supplies for lower prices from retailers outside the film industry. For example, we bought photoflood bulbs for $1.70 from a wholesaler that sells all types of bulbs; photo supply stores wanted $3.00 for the same bulb. Instead of renting a boom pole for $10 a weekend, consider buying an adjustable painter's pole for $15 at the hardware store. You'll have to modify the screw fitting (a two-dollar roll of duct tape will do this if you're not handy), and you'll save $25 for more essential supplies. Filmmaking gives you all kinds of opportunities to use your imagination.

Squeezing The Budget

Let's get down to specifics on the budget. We'll go point-by-point through our budget for "Beyond Bob," which is a 100-minute feature film shot and edited on 16mm.

Story and Rights

This area is important in budget trimming for two reasons. The first we've already discussed in the chapter on designing the script. What you write in the script is going to affect what you have to include in the budget. Hopefully, you'll write or have a script written that showcases what you have at hand and limits your expenses. But when you get to really creating your budget, keep in mind that changing the script will change the budget. If you find yourself trapped in a financial corner in the budget, you may need to look at revising the screenplay. This may be an affront artistically, but it's the kind of ruthless act that is needed to get a small story to the big screen. It's painful, but look on the bright side — at least you get to do it and keep control. If someone else were producing this story that means so much to you, they'd make changes, too. Ones you probably wouldn't like. It takes courage to keep your freedom, so if there's no way out of a financial corner, write an escape route.

The other budget-slimming aspect of story and rights is limiting your cash payment for the script. As screenwriters, we can tell you this will be easy to do, especially with writers who haven't been produced. We've said this before, and we'll say it again. It would be great to pay all the people on your project what they are worth, and you will. Just not in cash. Your currency is experience and credentials, and for people new to the film business, these rewards are worth almost as much as cash. Your screenwriter (who may be yourself) will be thrilled to see her or his words brought to life. Other than a token cash payment, that will have to be enough.

Cast and Crew

We made sure that all of our cast and crew got just enough cash so that they didn't feel like it cost them money to work on our production (basically, gas money). For ourselves, as director and producer, we took no money. Since we were financing the production, it would have meant paying ourselves.

We had contract arrangements that gave people a portion of any profits, but we made it clear that profits were a long shot, at best. We also arranged it so we, as producer and director, would share in profits only after everyone else did. This made it very clear to everyone that we weren't out to make a profit off their almost-volunteer labor. This helped create an atmosphere of camaraderie that was needed to get us through the tough spots.

Just as we did, you will probably feel embarrassed that you can't offer real payment to these talented performers and technicians. You're probably thinking that you'd be too ashamed to ask anyone to work so hard for so little in return. Don't underestimate the value of the experience and credentials you are offering.

One of the most gratifying parts of producing your dream film is that you can also help other people realize their dreams in the process. So don't worry if the money is small; the opportunities are large.

For example, one of our lead actors was called by her actor friends in Los Angeles. They couldn't believe they'd made the trek to Hollywood and were still struggling to break into movies while she had stayed in the midwest and had gotten the lead in a feature film.

Our unit production manager, who had been the assistant to John's agent prior to working with us on two films, now makes her living in Hollywood and has worked on an Emmy Award program, the "America's Funniest Home Videos" television series, the World Cup final-game ceremony, the Super Bowl half-time show, and other low-budget feature films, to name a few. She's a very talented person, and having two feature films on her resume didn't hurt when she was knocking on doors.

Another of our lead actors has gone on to perform lead roles in Hollywood low-budget films (meaning million-dollar budgets) and a repeated role on the prime-time television series "Sisters."

Our composer, who had never done a film's music score before doing our two films, has gone on to score several more low-budget Hollywood films and has gotten work with some of the industry's top composers.

We're not saying that their work with us paved the way. But it didn't hurt.

Of course, even the small money that we paid our cast and crew is not inconsequential when added up. We kept our cast as small as the story allowed, and we worked with the absolute minimum crew size in order to reduce the cost of personnel. Also, the smaller crew could keep up with our fast schedule. (Ironically, the more helpers you add to your crew, the slower it moves.)

You may have a story that calls for extras. A contraction and two words of advice: Don't pay them. Amazingly enough, even after a hundred years of movie making in this country, people are still thrilled to be in a movie, even a crowd scene. Just put their name in the credits. We had dozens of people who volunteered to skate for hours in the middle of the night on a July-Fourth weekend for "Beyond Bob." It was far from glamorous, but only a handful went home before we finished our shots. For budget purposes, the one thing you have to remember about extras is that you can't afford to feed them, at least not much. You can provide lemonade and cookies, but that's it. So when you are preparing your shooting schedule, plan to have extras start right after a meal and to be finished with them before the next meal. It's crass, but necessary.

Finally, don't be discouraged that you can't afford a big-name star. You can afford lots of actors who may become stars. The pre-stardom films of Kevin Costner and Jim Carrey are making money for somebody. And you might be able to get the services of a celebrity from outside the entertainment field who will do your film as a lark. Lee

Iacocca doing a cameo as plaid-jacket used-car salesman would be a hoot. A little creative thinking might find you a recognizable name without paying for a star.

Set Construction

Looking over our budget, you may be asking, "How the heck did they do set construction for just $100?" Our secret is "We didn't build any." In truth, we did do some limited set construction on both of our films, but we usually used an existing location and just created a false wall to change the look of the interior. In the case of "Beyond Bob," we wanted to divide a combined kitchen and sitting room into two separate rooms. We built a quick and crude wood framework to support a couple of sheets of wood paneling that had come loose from our director of photography's basement wall. If you've ever seen a Hollywood set, the pressure is off. You can get away with murder. Even the crudest sets look 100 times better on film.

If you have to do some set work, look for borrowed or discarded materials. Haunt the dumpsters at construction and demolition sites. (Yes, you will sink this low to get your movie done.) Commercial construction sites are the best because they often discard items that still look new, such as lumber, sheetrock, paneling, carpet, cabinets, bathroom fixtures, and electrical wiring. Much of this material still looks good enough to serve on a film set. Routinely check dumpsters at businesses for many of your furniture needs, too. Tons of repairable furniture are thrown out every time the office staff decides it looks too old fashioned. You can even find computers and other high-tech looking trash for those science-fiction projects. Dumpsters are a do-it-yourself set-building kit for low-buck filmmakers. Just add nails or sheetrock screws. (Our preference is Sheetrock screws. Using screws and an electric drill, you can assemble and disassemble sets in minutes.)

A word of caution: When dumpster diving, be sure to wear good solid boots, heavy gloves, and even a dust mask. Watch out for hazardous items; this is garbage after all. A small step ladder can help avoid the embarrassment and danger of leaning too far into a dumpster.

Model Building

We didn't budget any money for a model builder because Dale's not bad at it. And we didn't spend much on materials because he's a pack rat. The man just can't throw away anything that looks potentially useful. (Guess who had all the information on dumpster diving?) This is a trait that has kept his marriage lively. We'll talk more about models in the chapter on special effects, but for budgeting you should know that live-action shots that are difficult to set up can sometimes be accomplished as miniatures, saving lots of time and money. This is how we once created and lit a night scene showing a line of jets on the tarmac at an Air Force base, something we couldn't have afforded to do for real even if we had permission.

Wardrobe

You only need a fistful of dollars to get the wardrobe you'll require, especially if you've written a script that doesn't call for Halston designer gowns. There are several methods to pay little or nothing for your costumes. Use what you have, borrow, buy cheaply, make it, rent it, and be slightly unscrupulous.

If you've written the script yourself, it will be easy to use what you have. You should have written in your old prom dress or that beekeeping hat Uncle Jim bequeathed to you. Also ask actors if they can provide their own costumes. If they are working actors or just the wild-and-wonderful people that actors usually are, they probably have a closet full of interesting clothing that fits them.

Borrowing opens up a world of attire to you. Friends and relatives of anyone connected to your project become sources of clothing, uniforms, and professional gear. We literally got the shirt off the back of Dale's minister, and our most dramatic costumes in "Beyond Bob" were borrowed from friends of the actors. Think of it as thousands of dollars of wardrobe just out there for the begging. You can even ask local stores and local designers to loan clothing in exchange for screen credit and any publicity that it will garner. We've found that independently owned stores get in the spirit of the project more than chain stores, which discourage most initiative and independent thought in their employees. You also can find fledgling designers, who are happy for the exposure, at technical colleges or by asking around at fabric stores and funky clothing shops. We got some unique costumes from an up-and-coming designer recommended by a sales person at a clothing boutique. Screen credit and any publicity that mentions the clothing designs can return the favor for the designer's career. You can also approach suppliers of professional gear and people working in a profession to borrow specialty clothing and accessories. It's called product placement, and Hollywood overdoes it daily. We got some name-brand roller skates (Oberhamers — we're still repaying the favor) this way for no cost, and they even let us keep them after the shoot. You can thank businesses by sending them a photo of their clothing or equipment being used in the film for their company bulletin board or newsletter.

Borrowed wardrobe at work on "Beyond Bob."
Pictured, Kathryn O'Malley.
Photo courtesy of Granite Productions, Ltd.

If you are forced to spend actual money on some of your costumes or accessories, head to the thrift shops, garage sales, and used-clothing stores. In most cases, your costumes don't have to look brand new and an imperfect fit can be made presentable for film with safety pins, needle and thread, or even gaffer's tape. By doing a little hunting, you'll find that you can buy more than a pocket for pocket change. Before you go bargain hunting, strip off those preconceived costume ideas, and be open to finding some surprising and stunning new concepts in the rag bin.

For technical and scientific costumes, consider disposable coveralls, gloves, footwear, and head gear from safety equipment suppliers. This disposable clothing is the real stuff, but it's meant to be cheap. We needed the science-nerd look for two characters in "Resident Alien," and we got the desired look by buying orange disposable coveralls for three dollars each. To this costume we added a fifty-cent used belt, borrowed safety glasses, and inspired casting of nearly-identical bald guys (taunting our producer), and, voila!, we had convincing techno-weenies for only $3.50 each.

Specialty costumes, like the alien space suits we used in "Resident Alien," can be hard to find in friends' closets or at the neighborhood tuxedo shop. However, if there's a modicum of sewing talent handy, you can make specialty costumes. You can even do it without sewing talent. Our alien space suits were made from thrift-shop long underwear, foam rubber, cardboard, and spray paint. Sure, the spray paint tends to rub off. Sure, the costumes deteriorate pretty quickly. Sure, the actors don't have a full range of movement. But the space suits lasted long enough to get the shots we needed, they cost less than $10, and they looked like hundreds of dollars on the screen.

You can rent costumes, but this is an avenue of last resort and only permissible when a particular costume is so critical to your project that you are willing to sacrifice other resources for it. Since an $80 costume rental costs the same as 12 minutes of film stock, ask yourself "Am I willing to shoot 12 minutes of my film with only two takes?" This should tell you how important the costume is. Presuming you do need a costume badly enough to rent it, you'll need to get the best deal possible. Actual costume shops are probably too expensive unless you can get the owners to give you a deal in exchange for publicity and screen credit. Theater groups will sometimes loan their costumes for a reasonable fee. You can also try making arrangements with a local high school or university drama program. We found that uniform and specialty-clothing shops sometimes are willing to rent items they stock, but their prices were often high, and their willingness to strike deals was low.

The last method for getting costumes free is not without its own type of payment. Being unscrupulous can allow you to buy clothes on your credit card, use them, dry-clean them, and return them. We did this. We still feel guilty.

Initially, we approached a large department store chain's headquarters to trade screen credit for costumes. They were not interested because they felt it was too much work to review the screenplay for appropriateness. However, we needed an extravagant (and expensive) peignoir for a 30-second scene, and we were out of time to make arrangements to borrow the costume. So we took advantage of the store's generous return policy and put it on the plastic. We shot the scene, knowing full well that if we damaged the lacy item, we'd own it. We dry-cleaned it and returned it. Picture a balding, 30-year-old producer returning this racy getup to the sales woman with the sad phrase "It didn't work out." That's a film scene in itself.

The problem with this method is that you continue to feel guilty, especially if you were raised Catholic as we were. (We probably mention it here out of need for confession.) If we ever get a big-budget project, we'll buy our costumes at this store to make amends, and we try to do our personal shopping there to assuage our guilt. It's about the only thing we've done on our productions of which we are not proud. There's no such thing as free lingerie.

Selecting your wardrobe may or may not require a wardrobe supervisor. If you have very limited costumes — such as two characters lost in the desert wearing just shorts and T-shirts — the director, producer, and production manager can select costumes. A more extensive and fashionable wardrobe benefits from the attention of someone with a flair for clothing. Even if you have a wardrobe supervisor, you don't need this person on the set, except to deliver the proper wardrobe to the location and maybe to stay around for repairs if there are delicate items being used. Otherwise the production manager can supervise wardrobe changes, which helps you avoid having one more crew person to feed, move, and keep out of the way.

The time you spend getting good costumes will pay off in the finished film. Costumes play an important part in creating the screen image of every single scene and the overall look of your movie. You can easily add $100,000 to your apparent budget on the screen by using these free methods to get a top-notch wardrobe.

Makeup and Hair

We've done one production with a makeup-and-hair supervisor and one without. Whether or not you need one on your set depends on the unique needs of your production. If you have a very small cast, simple hair and makeup that doesn't change, and experienced actors, the cast can do their own makeup and hair styling.

If you have a larger cast or makeup and hair that need changing during the shooting day, you'll probably need this crew position. It is a comfort to the actors to have someone else watching these details, but you have to weigh it against adding another crew person who will slow down the march of your little rebel band of filmmakers.

The first thing you must do is discourage your makeup-and-hair supervisor from tweaking and primping the actors before every shot. When you're trying to shoot up to 100 shots each day, a minute to do makeup on each shot wastes 100 minute of production time. And the difference is rarely discernible in the end. Except for makeup effects (bruises, bags under the eyes, and fragile hair styles), makeup and hair can be spiffed up after lunch break, and that's good enough. On the finished film frame, hair styles gone wild are more noticeable than lip blush wearing off, so concentrate on hair the most. This advice will insult makeup professionals, who do an important job well. But remember you're operating in subsistence filmmaking. Only the vital elements. You can only get 90% of what you want, and you have to be willing to sacrifice the other 10%. Touching up hair and make-up definitely falls into the 10% category.

If you have professional actors or a professional makeup-and-hair person (or beautician or hair stylist), they likely can supply the make-up you need out of their basic makeup kit. Everyone on the production should be in the "My uncle's got a barn, and I've got footlights" mode, so ask if they can scrounge or donate the needed supplies. Only pay for what you have to, and definitely don't pay for a shopping spree at the cosmetic counter. It's okay to say you can't afford something. This will cause the makeup person or any crew member to use their creativity to find a solution. Our makeup supervisor scrounged a lot of the makeup for "Beyond Bob" from the set of a made-for-TV movie that shot in town. Their crew was routinely throwing out barely used makeup supplies — another example of Hollywood waste and how to profit from it.

Also, don't make it a secret that you're throwing your personal resources into the project. This will encourage everyone on the crew and cast to add what they can for the benefit of everyone.

Lighting and Lighting Supplies

You can't have enough lighting. That is to say, you can't have as much lighting as you want or need because you lack the necessary money and power (the electrical kind). You won't be working on a sound stage equipped with its own electrical substation, and you probably can't afford a portable generator, much less the truck and the time to pull it around. So accept the situation. Your power shortage actually works well with your money shortage. You couldn't afford to rent more lights even if you had more electricity.

Fortunately, you can get by with a small, lightweight, not-too-expensive lighting kit when you use some of the faster film stocks (500 to 320 ASA/ISO under tungsten light).

The kit we worked with included four 1000-watt lights (called "1Ks") that can be flooded or spotted, such as Arriflex or Lowell DP lights. The kit contained barndoors for blocking the light's spill, stands, and extra lamps.

A good addition to this basic kit is a 2000-watt Lowell Softlight, which works well for lighting larger locations. We were able to light an entire roller rink using only existing light and two softlights. These lights are an extra expense, so try to group all of the large locations together so you don't have to rent this light continually.

For outdoor daytime shooting, the only lighting equipment we used was a 38-inch silver-white Flexfill, which is a collapsible reflector. It's great for filling in harsh shadows when shooting outdoors.

Now you may be tempted to skimp on other equipment and add more lights because your director of photography really wants some 5Ks. Forget it. Here's the math: Most residential and commercial circuits are 15 amps or 20 amps. At 120 volts that means you have 1800 watts (15 amps x 120 volts = 1800 watts) or 2400 watts (20 amps x 120 volts = 2400 watts) of power available. It's easy to see that a 15-amp circuit can only support one 1000-watt light reliably. A 20-amp circuit can handle two, or it can handle one 2000-watt softlight, but not both. In most locations, you'll be running a lot of extension cords just to make three or four circuits available. You see that four lights will max out your power.

Our budget also included some expendable lighting supplies: a roll each of black, white and gray gaffer's tape, a dozen "practical" bulbs (150 to 200-watt tungsten bulbs that fit standard light fixtures for brighter light sources within a scene), a 2' x 3' piece of daylight-correction gel to color the tungsten (incandescent) light to match sunlight (3202 Full Blue CTB from the Rosco company), a 2' x 3' piece of 105 Roscolux tough spun (a fabric-like material similar to tissue paper but without the same flammability) to soften and reduce the intensity of the lights, and a 16' x 58" length of 3401 RoscoSun 85 for correcting daylight coming through windows to match the tungsten lights. This last item is only needed if you are dead set on seeing out windows when you are shooting interiors. This is a $115 choice because gels are not cheap. The other pieces of gel and spun were cut into smaller sizes to be used on several lights at the same time.

From our personal supplies, we scrounged other important lighting gear: wooden spring-type clothes pins to clamp gels and spun to the barndoors, black construction paper to make flags for blocking light, leather gloves to avoid cooking hands when moving hot lights, extra 15-amp and 20-amp screw-in fuses, and three-prong to two-prong electric-plug adapters.

We also built some lighting gear. For locations that were hundreds of feet from the nearest power outlet, we built some 100-foot extension cords from 12- and 10-gauge copper cable used in home construction. They were wired to fiberglass electrical outlet boxes, which were nailed to squares of wood for stability. We used (and recommend) the cable that's intended for wet locations. You'll need heavier-gauge cables for longer runs (otherwise you'll overheat the cable, blow fuses, and not get enough power to the lights). These cables were not designed for use in the rain, but that's the least of your troubles because neither are your lights or camera equipment.

To weight down lights and other equipment, we made sandbags rather than rent them. We put a plastic bag three-quarters full of sand inside the legs of worn-out jeans and sewed the ends shut. This was better than spending $20 a weekend to rent them, and it made decisions on what to wear easier.

As with all the equipment rentals, you can get a substantial budget savings on lighting if your crew person owns the equipment you need. This allows you to limit your costs to replacing burned-out lamps and buying the gels and spun. This approach also gives you an efficient lighting person who knows and cares about the equipment.

Camera Equipment

Your best deals on this equipment will come from people who own their own cameras. You probably won't see an Arriflex in someone's basement, but an Eclair, CP-16, or Bolex are not so hard to find.

If you don't know anything about these cameras, don't worry. They all make images on film. They all have good features and drawbacks. Just make sure you are renting a model with a crystal-sync motor that runs the camera at exactly 24 frames per second for synchronized sound recording. Then ask the owner if there are problems you should know about — problems common to that type of camera and ones unique to the camera you're renting. If your director of photography owns an American Cinematographer Manual, there is a detailed description of virtually every camera in it. You can probably read the three-page description at a photo supply store that sells the manual, borrow it from a professional camera operator, or get it as a Christmas gift as we did.

The key thing is to get the camera package as cheaply as possible. If you're renting the camera and rechargeable battery packs from someone, they'll usually include the lenses, extra film magazine, and maybe even a tripod and light meter with the deal.

Make sure you have enough batteries for the long hours you will be shooting — 14 to 18 hours — and an extra camera magazine. The extra magazine can be reloaded while you are shooting with the first one. That way you'll never wait 15 minutes for the camera to be reloaded. You'll get another shot done instead.

Make sure the tripod has a fluid (not friction) head. Fluid heads don't give you the jerky motion that a friction head does. Don't even consider the gear heads that Hollywood uses. These give a smooth motion by turning gears to move the camera. You can't afford one of these heads, your crew is unlikely to know how to use it, and it's too heavy to move easily or to use on lightweight tripods.

We recommend using a zoom lens for almost all of your photography. While cinematographers will correctly tell you that you lose some image clarity with a zoom lens, you also pick up a lot of production speed. You can reframe a shot in seconds without having to change lenses. And you don't have to clean the film gate between lens changes or carry boxes of lenses with you. Even Ingmar

Bergman used this technique for speeding up production. Good enough for us. Besides, you only have to pay rental for one lens.

If your rental package doesn't include a camera slate, don't bother renting one. Instead get someone with a little carpentry skill to spend a half hour making one out of scrap lumber for you. Don't even bother making the slate part out of slate. Hardly anyone writes on them with chalk. They usually write the numbers on white gaffer's tape, stick them on the back of the slate for storage, and paste them on in different combinations for the scenes and takes as needed. All that matters is that they are legible when you get to editing and that the clapper can be seen when it makes the clack sound for synchronizing sound and picture.

For efficient shooting, you should rent or borrow several important filters. Because your film will be balanced for tungsten light, you need to have a tungsten-to-daylight correction filter. We were generally working in much brighter light when shooting in daylight, so we rented daylight filters with different levels of neutral density in order to cut down the intensity of the sunlight. The specific filters we rented were 85N3, 85N6, and 85N9 (85 is daylight correction, N3 through N9 are increasing amounts of neutral density). These filters will let you shoot both outdoors and indoors without taking time to change to a film magazine loaded with slower-speed film. One drawback is that on most cameras these filters also darken the viewfinder image so it may be harder for the camera operator to follow motion during the actual shot when you're shooting outdoors. For static shots, our operator would remove the filter, frame the shot, lock it down, and then put the filter back on. If you're doing a lot of outdoor photography, it's a good idea to include some slower-speed film in your film order.

A good safety filter to rent, if it's not included with the camera, is an ultraviolet haze filter. This filter is virtually clear glass and doesn't noticeably affect the image. However, it's a cheap filter, and if something accidentally hits the camera lens, the filter will take the blow, not the lens itself. It's easier to live without this filter than without a lens during the shoot. Get one, and leave it on the lens all the time.

A film-changing bag is also worth buying. They're cheap to rent, but they have lots of uses during second-unit and post-production photography. Well worth the $25.

You're probably a little surprised to see us list a second-unit camera in the budget. Why spend precious money on two cameras? Because it saves you money. We used a spring-wound 16mm Bolex on a borrowed tripod as our second-unit and special-effects camera, and it saved us a fortune. You often can buy a good used one for under $400, and chances are that someone in your crew of filmmakers or their friends owns one that you can borrow.

The spring wind and the 100-foot film rolls put a lot of people off the Bolex as a "student" camera. Unfounded prejudice. Footage from our $300 Bolex is virtually indistinguishable from shots done by the $5,000 Eclair we rented. As a second-unit camera used for picking up insert shots and establishing shots, we found that we never needed more than the 30 seconds of run time allowed by the spring motor. And best of all, the rental clock wasn't ticking as we did trick shots and special effects using the Bolex's variable-speed, backwind, and single-frame capabilities.

Being a lightweight camera without the "mouse ears" film magazine on top, the Bolex also made us look like amateur photographers. Consequently, we rarely dealt with curious passers-by and didn't get hassled about permits and other such nonsense. We could also set up our shots, shoot, and disappear before anyone really noticed us. If you need to, the later-model Bolexes (anything less than 30 years old) can accept crystal-sync electric motors, a whole range of lenses, a 400-foot film magazine, and a sound blimp to make it a full sync-sound camera. Dang clever, those Swiss camera makers.

You may have considered using stock footage to cover some tricky shot or distant location that you can't get. After all, that's what big productions do all the time. Good idea, wrong budget. Stock footage costs between $500 to $1,500 a shot. That's cheap footage for a big production. But for that kind of money, you can pack the Bolex in the Ford Escort and drive to the location yourself.

Sound Equipment

There aren't many corners to cut on the sound-recording equipment you'll need. Even big-dollar features don't get a lot more elaborate than what you will be using. We're always amused to see behind-the-scene shots of the latest high-tech production using the same sound-recording techniques we used on our films. Rent a Nagra crystal-sync recorder. There are various models, all which record beautiful sound. Older models will cost less, have fewer confusing bells and whistles, and do a fine job. Be sure that the model you are planning to use has a crystal-sync motor to ensure a frame-by-frame match with the crystal-sync motor on the camera. There are several new digital audio tape (DAT) recorders that can put your sound on a cassette rather than on open-reel 1/4-inch tape, but do some checking before you rent. Not all transfer houses are equipped to work with DAT tapes. Besides, you're more likely to find deals on 1/4-inch tape stock. There's nothing wrong with being behind the times if it saves you money.

You'll need a good shotgun microphone, such as a Sennheiser ME-80. You'll want to put that microphone in a shock mount to prevent picking up noise from the boom pole. As we mentioned earlier, you can find substitutes for the boom pole, but make sure any alternative poles are light enough for your boom operator to hold overhead all day. Whenever you are shooting at outdoor locations, rent a "zeppelin" windscreen to cut wind noise. They work much better than foam windscreens, so pay the extra dollars. It's worth it. You can save money by not renting the windscreen if you know the entire weekend will be shot indoors. The last things you'll need are headphones for the tape recorder, 200 feet of mike cable, and at least three sets of batteries for the recorder and for the microphone. Sometimes you can have another set of headphones for the boom pole operator, but don't spend any extra money for it. We never used them, and our boom operator still knew where to point the mike with a little advice from the sound recordist.

A word about using wireless microphones: Don't. It may seem like a great idea. You don't have to follow the actors with a microphone. And you can cut out the boom operator, saving a crew position. Unfortunately, these systems use tiny lavalier microphones that are more apt to sound tinny than other microphones. They are super-susceptible to sibilance, so they sometimes hiss on "S" sounds. (This last sentence would be a good test.) Clothing and chest hair rustle against the mikes. They are hard to hide when the actors are wearing brief attire. The radio-receiver units for these microphones sometimes pick up truckers' CBs and radio signals from the French underground. In short, they are not worth the trouble. You'll get better sound with less interference, more quickly using a boom mike.

As with other equipment, you may find a person who personally owns a crystal-sync recorder and mikes. Try to rent cheaply from them or get them to join your crew and bring along their equipment.

When you buy your tape stock, you can save a bundle by not getting prepackaged reels. We bought our tape in 2,500-foot "pancakes," meaning the tape comes on a hub, with no reel. We bought off-brand reels and boxes (usually the Nagra recorders use 5-inch reels). Then we borrowed a recorder and a split reel to put the tape and hubs on and spent a couple hours winding our own. You can get four 5-inch reels (625 feet, 16 1/2 minutes each) from each "pancake." The 5-inch reels roughly match the 11-minutes of film on each 400-foot roll of 16mm film. By putting the tape on reels ourselves, we cut our costs in half, at least.

Vehicles

We didn't budget anything for vehicles. We used what we had. John needed to buy a new used car shortly before we began shooting "Beyond Bob," so he bought the kind of car we wanted the main character to drive. Our director of photography drove a van which served as an equipment-hauling vehicle and was used on camera as well. If you've done your scriptwriting well, you'll be using vehicles that are available to you free. If you need something exotic, try to find someone with a car compulsion who owns one. They are as excited by cars as you are about films, so they are usually glad to drive theirs in the movie for you as long as it's not a crash scene. You may be able to talk a local car dealership into providing a vehicle, but beware if they start talking about insurance. You'll be buying film stock instead of insurance.

As for larger vehicles to haul equipment, you'll soon discover you don't need any. The equipment you can afford will fit in the trunks of cars.

Meals

Don't skimp on the quality of the food, just the price. You can easily put together meals that are good, hot, and substantial using ingredients that are affordable on a tiny budget. You can buy the food in bulk to save costs and prepare it yourself to avoid the extra cost of prepared food. Fortunately, Dale's wife Kathy is a very good cook and a tolerant woman. She, along with her sisters and in-laws, prepared and served meals for the cast and crew on both films. These days few people actually make meals from scratch, so even the simplest homemade meals taste like Mom's finest to them. For the cast and crew, these meals almost made up for the meager pay and long hours. In fact, some cast members from our first film agreed to work on the second film only if Kathy was making the meals. Others said it was the best they'd eaten in years. Now don't be thinking we made gourmet meals. This was just standard fare prepared by human hands rather than extruded from vats in a factory.

Basically our budget included a snack for the Friday-evening shoot and three meals a day for the Saturday and Sunday shooting days. Six meals and a snack for about 20 people for $125. Or about 89 cents per person per meal. This may seem like a miracle, but it's not that hard to do if someone makes it.

The snack and breakfasts can be simpler, so you can save some money there to add a little to the lunch and dinner meals. If you plan menus for your entire production ahead of time, you can buy larger quantities of food at lower prices. For drinks, fruit-juice concentrates and generic-brand pop are cheapest (though we ultimately bought some name-brand pop because of crew complaints). For the non-perishable items (canned goods, chips, pop, coffee, tea, baking supplies), buy them as they go on sale during the months ahead of the production. Meats, cheeses, and fruit-juice concentrates can be bought on sale and frozen until needed. Frugal shopping, filling but inexpensive menus, and home cooking can make these meals a high point of your production and a low expenditure in your budget.

Locations

We found it pretty easy to get use of private locations for nothing. Most people are thrilled to see a movie in production, though they quickly learn that it is tedious, hard work, even on fast-paced productions like ours. It's fun for them to tell the neighbors about hosting the movie crew. If you live in a town where film productions are common, you may run into more people asking for money to use their property. You can't afford it, and tell them so. They may relent. If they still want money, move on. Sometimes losing your first choice leads to a better, more interesting choice. At least, try to look at it that way because you lose a lot of first choices making a feature film with no visible budget.

We found small towns to be very accommodating. They don't usually ask for permits to shoot in public areas, and we even were allowed to work on some residential streets after a casual conversation with the police chief and notifying the neighbors who might be inconvenienced. Friends, neighbors, and relatives are also good sources of locations, as are state and federal parks.

Be mindful of distances when you plan your production. You probably can't afford to put up your cast and crew overnight, and if you drive a long distance to a location, the rental dollars you spent on your equipment will be ticking away every minute you're on the road. It's best to select sites that are near to your cast and crew and clustered together for easy grouping on the production schedule. We're fortunate that where we live there are landscapes ranging from rocky cliffs to secluded woods to city skyscrapers to urban decay to suburban yuppie-dom to cows in the fields all within one hour's drive. If you look at your own hometown area with the eye of an outsider, you'll probably discover a great variety of unique settings for your film as well.

We believe a cardinal rule of using locations is to be courteous and careful. Don't use things without asking. Take great pains not to damage anything. Clean up when you are finished. And be friendly to the owners and neighbors. When actors are waiting for their next scene, encourage them to chat with the natives. This is part of the thrill of having a movie crew shoot at your home, and it builds good will that allows you to come back for retakes if necessary. We think it is irresponsible of filmmakers to leave property owners unhappy. This poisons the waters for future productions and gives a bad name to all independent productions. To our knowledge, there aren't any locations that wouldn't welcome us back.

Film Stock

To get good prices on film negative, you have to know where to look, you can't be squeamish, you have to be flexible, and you need to be patient.

Don't buy film from a photo store or a company that sells movie supplies. Their markups are high, and only suckers pay list price. Instead, check with the film-stock exchanges we've listed in the "Other Resources" section of the appendix. They buy leftover film from other productions for dimes on the dollar and then resell it to you cheaply.

Film exchanges usually have three categories of film:

SURPLUS - film that has been bought for a production but never opened.

RECANS - film that was loaded into the camera magazine, never used, and repacked into the film can.

SHORT ENDS - the unexposed ends of film reels which are cut off and put back in a can.

Surplus film usually costs the most, recans less, and short ends the least.

Now here's where you have to not be squeamish. Sure, some of the recans and short ends could have been accidentally exposed. All of these films could have been exposed to excessive heat and moisture. The cans could be dented, creating tiny light leaks. Over-juiced X-ray machines at the airport may have imprinted the Shroud of Turin on the film stock. All this and more. Take deep breaths and pray. Independent filmmaking is not for the faint of heart, and buying surplus, recans, and short ends will test your mettle. Fortunately, most film-stock exchanges hedge your bets for you. They process test strips of film from cans that have been opened. They don't want to sell you inferior stock, so they check history of refrigeration, condition of cans, and the dates on the film before they buy it. This is no guarantee, but it reduces the risk. After buying more than 80 reels from film-stock exchanges for two productions, we only had one reel with some minor, but acceptable, imperfections.

Now film-stock exchanges are constantly shifting stock, and their supplies depend on what other people have as leftovers. This is where flexibility and patience get you most of what you want at a price you can afford. Figure out as far in advance as you can what types of film stock you can use, how much of it you need, and what you can afford to pay per 400-foot reel. Also figure out some second choices of film stock speeds and types. They may not have the Kodak 7292 (ASA/ISO 320) you want, but they may have Fuji 500 (ASA/ISO 500). Don't worry about which brand of film stock you use. Eastman Kodak, Fuji, and Agfa are all good film stocks. Kodak is most commonly used in the U.S., so it is most available; however, you'll get better deals on Fuji and Agfa when they're available because they're less popular. We ran into an over-stock of surplus Fuji 500 on our first production and bought our film for less than one-third the going rate. These types of bargains are not uncommon, but finding them requires patience and speedy decisions on your part. If you end up with several brands of film stock, don't sweat it. Most differences are imperceptible to an audience after lab corrections are made.

In order to get the best prices, you may have to accumulate your film stock a few reels at a time over several months, so clear out the refrigerator, and call the supplier every week or so for an update on what's available. If they quote you a price per can that doesn't fit your budget, ask if they can give you a better price if you take 30 or 40. These suppliers are wheeler-dealers and are used to dickering. Dicker right back, and you might lower the price a few bucks. In our case, the prices they quoted were low enough that we recognized the bargain, took the film, and ran.

There are some other low-cost places to buy your film. We were buying film for "Beyond Bob" during a slump in film production, so the film-stock exchanges weren't getting much stock. So we looked for alternatives. Currently Agfa film is about 25 percent cheaper than other stocks. It's not as popular, but it's fine film. We also found a film supplier that routinely sold new stock for about 30 percent below list price; we've included the name in the "Other Resources" section of the appendix. There are lots of prices out there, so check with your local production community and labs to see if they have other suggestions.

We've also heard of an approach that we didn't try. You can contact companies that do commercial and industrial film productions and try to make a deal to buy their surplus, recans, and short ends. This is where the film-stock exchanges buy their stock, so you may be able to get some very good prices. Finally, some of the Independent Feature Project (IFP) chapters around the country have their own "short ends" programs. They receive recans and short ends from local production companies and offer it free or at greatly-reduced rates to area filmmakers on a project-by-project basis. Check with your local IFP chapter for program specifics and film availability.

In order to figure out how much film stock you actually need, count script pages. Each full page works out to one minute of screen time. You'll be amazed how accurate this is if your script is written in one of the standard screenplay formats, but be cautious of lines like "We see the Crimean War begin." This may require more than a few seconds of screen time. Count how many pages and partial pages worth of interior and exterior scenes you have.

Let's assume you have a perfect script meaning 90 pages long, 90 minutes in length. Each minute of 16mm film is 36 feet long, so 90 minutes of film equals 3,240 feet of film (90 x 36 = 3,240). You'll be shooting in a three-to-one ratio (3:1), meaning you'll expose three feet of film for every finished foot of film. So at a 3:1 ratio, you'll use 9,720 feet of film stock (3,240 x 3 = 9,720). Since you'll be buying 400-foot rolls of film, you'll need just over 24 rolls (9,720 ÷ 400 = 24.3). By the same calculations, a 4:1 shooting ratio will require just over 32 400-foot rolls of film. You'll obviously need more film if your script is longer. (If your script is longer than 100 minutes, it requires cutting to fit a $30,000 budget. Trust us; this surgery is much easier and cheaper to do now.)

For the exterior scenes, it will be best to get a slower-speed film stock (ASA/ISO 100 to 125 under tungsten), so you won't need the neutral density filters on the lens. Just add up the number of pages of exterior scenes, and use the calculations above to get the number of rolls of film you'll need for these scenes. Or you can buy all high-speed stock (ASA/ISO 320 to 500), put on the neutral density filter when you move outdoors, and just put up with a darker viewfinder image during daylight shots. We've done it that way when we had a limited number of outdoor shots. The advantages of using only high-speed stock are that you won't end up with too much or too little of one speed of film stock and the extra film magazine is always loaded with the right film stock.

Processing and One-Light Workprint

You can reduce this budget item if you decide that you're going to edit your film on video. You'll get your best transfer to video directly from the negative, so there is no need for a work print. However, unless you have access to broadcast-quality (Betacam, 1-inch "C", D-2, or D-1 tape formats) editing for free, your best deals will be renting 16mm editing equipment. For this you will need a work print.

Film laboratory prices vary a lot, and most of them are willing to bid on a feature film project such as yours, even though you will be processing less than half the amount of film of most feature productions. We got our best prices by sending out letters requesting bids. In our letter, we requested a bid price for processing and work print for the number of feet of film we anticipated using. We also specified the time period over which we would shoot the film and about how much would be processed each week. Bid prices from a lab are usually good for up to 90 days, so you may want to budget the list prices for processing and work print, and then get real bids shortly before you begin shooting. It will be harder to get a good deal if you are shooting over a long period of time, so planning an intensive month of weekend shooting will save you money.

Don't feel like you have to use the closest laboratory. Get bids from any lab with experience, and just add in the shipping costs. We accepted a bid that offered return shipping free by express mail for our negative and work print. In the end, we saved at least $1,000 on processing by getting bids. There is a list of film labs in the appendix, but check with the yellow pages, your local film office, the local Independent Feature Project chapter, and film periodicals to find other labs that might offer deals to the independent producer.

We've found that Canadian labs are currently very competitive with U.S. labs, and the currency exchange rate shaves 30 percent off their bids in U.S. dollars. Even when you add in shipping and customs-broker fees, the price is a real deal. Also, because most Canadian television productions are done on 16mm, they don't treat you as a second-class filmmaker the way some U.S. labs do.

If you use an out-of-country lab, try to pay by credit card. The card company will do the currency conversion on your bill for a nominal fee, less than a bank will charge you to exchange currency. Also, don't forget that your state may require you to pay sales tax even on out-of-state processing and work prints. That's a nasty surprise to discover later, so check into it now.

Production Stills

You'll be sorry later when you do publicity, but you're going to be giving short shrift to still photos of your production. As the director and producer, we've taken photos during the shoots, but the results have been lackluster because we were busy helping with the movie magic when the interesting photo opportunities happened. We had thought of getting someone who wanted to take photos for the experience and having them click away, but we were concerned about having another person to feed on the set and one more body to slow down a crew that needs to be lightning fast. We opted for one less person, knowing we'd regret it when it came time to assemble a publicity package, and we did.

We recommend picking one day in your production schedule that promises to be photogenic and having a volunteer paparazzo tag along for the day. Another approach is to shoot your publicity stills later as staged shots. We did this to get poster shots for our films. Any way you do this, only budget enough for 5 rolls of 35mm film and processing. There's not money for an extravagant publicity kit, so there's no sense in having hundreds of photos to choose from — all you need is a handful of good ones.

Sound Transfers

Getting bids from more than one sound-transfer company is your best way to get a good deal for converting your 1/4-inch audio tapes into 16mm fullcoat magnetic stock for editing. You're most likely to get the best results from people who specialize in sound work, rather than from a film lab that specializes in pictures. However, some labs do have a division that does only sound. If you go for a whole package of sound transfer and then mixing of the sound track later on, you might get a better price. It's also helpful when you get into the mix, and the inevitable sound problem comes up. There's more incentive to fix the problem if the sound transfer was done by the same company. Professional pride replaces blaming the competition.

Film Vault Rental

We felt the need to safely store our negatives and master sound-tracks in a film vault. It costs about $200 a year. If you want to save this expense, at least store the negative and sound masters at a separate location from your work print and fullcoat sound tracks. If fire or pestilence should strike one site, you could still salvage something of your $20,000 uninsured investment. If you don't put your negatives and master sound in a climate-controlled film vault, be sure to put all your master footage and sound in double plastic bags inside sturdy containers. Make sure the audio tapes are well away from magnetic fields, such as refrigerator magnets, electric motors, and coils of electrical cord. Steel drums buried in the backyard are pretty secure if the Environmental Protection Agency doesn't dig them up for analysis.

Film and Fullcoat Edge Numbering

After you've made your work print and transferred your sound to fullcoat sound tracks, you'll edit them to synchronize the sound and picture. At this point you'll need edge numbers printed onto the fullcoat sound and work print so you can keep sound and picture synchronized when you start cutting them up in editing. You can't skip this step. Yes, there are edge numbers on the film stock, which will be used when the negatives are cut to match the edited work print, but you need another set of numbers that corresponds to ones on the soundtrack for editing. No way around this expense. Just check for the best price. (See appendix.)

Flatbed Editing Table

A flatbed editing table is a joy to edit on and a commodity that you can afford. Most post-production of television commercials and industrial films is done on video these days, even when shot on film originally. The same shift in production techniques that has made 16mm cameras cheaper to rent is working for editing tables. Many professional editors and filmmakers have these tables lying dormant and are willing to rent them for extended periods for low rates. (We think reclaiming that office or home space is one of their motivations.) We negotiated a flat rate for a set period of time. A word of advice: make sure the owner will pay for any maintenance or service during the rental. Parts for these babies can be pricey, as we learned the expensive way.

If you're willing to sacrifice editing convenience for equipment independence, you can buy a used editing system of hand rewinds, viewer, sound reader and gang synchronizer (the type most of us learned on) for about the same money as renting a flatbed table. Editing will be a slower process, but you won't be under the time pressure either. Editors strongly prefer the flatbed editing table, so work it out with whomever will be doing the editing. If that's you, don't let anyone hear you talking to yourself. They already think you're loony for making a feature film, and you don't want to give them more evidence for the commitment hearing.

Video Dubs

You'll need video dubs of your workprint for doing post-production special-effects shots, for your composer to write the music score, for actors to loop lines that were badly recorded, and for timing sound effects not recorded on location. All this for $20 or less? Sure. Just buy VHS tapes, and borrow one of those ubiquitous camcorders to tape a copy of the edited workprint right off the editing viewer. Don't try to use a patch cord to connect the sound from a flatbed editing table into a camcorder, though, unless you really know what you're doing. That's the way we learned how expensive editing tables are to repair.

Slug For Editing

Slug is the film stock you put into the audio tracks when no sound is occurring on that particular track. You can spend good money for this or find a ready supply of discarded 16mm films with long segments of good sprocket holes. We actually cannibalized the work-print outtakes from our first film to edit the second one. However, even with scrounging up old films, we were forced to buy 1,000 feet of blank film from a lab to get enough. So start collecting dead films now, and you might be able to eliminate this budget item. You'll need two to three times the finished length of your film, depending on how many sound tracks you use. So from 7,000 to 10,000 feet. Where will you find all this valuable slug? Make friends with the nearest film librarian, and offer to take out the trash at professional film production companies.

Music, Sound Effects, Dialogue Looping

You'll need to include recording studio time in your budget for the music sound track, sound effects that you are adding, and for looping (rerecording) dialogue segments that are missing or poorly recorded during shooting.

You can cut some of these costs by thinking small and looking for special arrangements. We recorded our sound effects, foley work (sounds synchronized to action), and dialogue looping in one of the smallest sound booths in existence. This was the basement studio of a freelance audio engineer. It was tiny and the cheapest in town, and the results were as good as with a larger studio. As they say, size does-not matter. It's the quality of the microphones and the recording and mixing equipment that are important.

When we needed to record an orchestra and a big band, our composer arranged for free use of the studio and recording equipment at a technical school for audio engineers and musicians. Good connections and lots of friends can help with these expensive items.

Transfer of Post-Production Sound

It's generally best to have all of your sound (both the location sound and the sound you created during post-production) transferred to magnetic fullcoat by the same audio house. That way the procedures will (hopefully) be consistent, reducing surprises during the sound mix.

Post-Production Sound Mix

This is a ridiculously-small budget for a sound mix, but you have no choice. The key to keeping the cost low is working fast and efficiently. We will talk more about this during the chapter on post-production, but basically you figure out how many hours you can afford (at about $125 an hour), and then calculate how many pages you have to mix every hour. And then keep to that schedule. For comparison purposes, the soundtrack for "Beyond Bob" was mixed in 14 hours. We did it in eight hours for "Resident Alien."

Sure this means you'll make some compromises, but that's life in the ultra-low-budget lane. Remember that your audiences most likely will be seeing your film on video, which means sound from a 3-inch TV speaker. Great sound is wasted there. Good sound is fine.

Titles

We were contacted by a company that just makes titles for feature films about doing the titles for "Resident Alien." Mind you, what they were proposing was nothing fancy. Just your basic title cards at the beginning and some text scrolling by at the end. They offered us a special low-budget price: $15,000 to $20,000. After we were done choking, we politely declined. Obviously, we couldn't and you can't go this route. We're talking do-it-yourself with only small expenditures on materials. This is where that second-unit Bolex camera can come in handy. More details on techniques are in the special effects chapter. For budget purposes, just know that you can't pay to have someone else do it, and you can't spend more than a few dollars on them.

Negative Cutting to 16mm A/B Rolls

The cutting of the original camera negatives to match your edited work print is one step where your limitations become your advantages. It's a lot faster to find and splice together negatives when there's only three times the footage that will end up in the finished film (3:1 ratio). This means fewer hours and lower costs. Bigger budget productions may have as much as ten times their final footage. You can also control and trim the budget at this step by negotiating a flat fee for the whole project. Offer to let the cutter do the work during slack times, and you may get a better price. Most free lancers will give up a part of their fee to be sure they'll have jobs when their usual sources of work dry up. Patience can save you cash that you don't have anyway.

Black Leader for A/B Rolls

When your negative is cut, it's on an A roll and a B roll with scenes alternating between the rolls. When a scene is on the A roll, there's exactly the same length of black leader on the B roll in the same spot. When the film is printed, the A roll is printed first and then the B roll is printed over the same length of negative, leaving no splices visible. You'll need the same number of feet of black leader as the final footage of your edited work print. Your negative cutter can probably get you a good deal on this leader. It currently runs about eight cents a foot.

Answer Print, Video Transfer

Heads up. Another tough decision coming. By this point, your budget bucket is just about empty. You have enough money to pick one path for your film and push it out on the road. The two main paths are releasing it on film or releasing it on video. We chose video because films as small as ours have a hard time even making it onto the screens at art houses these days. We knew that any potential distributor would preview it on video and that it most likely would be distributed in the home-video market. This might have been a bad decision; we honestly don't know. If we'd chosen the other path, we would have spent the rest of our pennies getting a release print with an optical soundtrack. Then we could have gone to more film festivals and tried to talk independent theaters into taking it on for limited engagements. But then we couldn't have afforded a high-quality video transfer. We felt more buyers would be judging us on a VHS video cassette than would be seeing it in a theater. We made our choices, and we're living with them. So will you. Study the cards carefully, and then pick the one that you think will be the winner.

Bids again are the key to getting good prices at the film lab no matter what route you take. We got bids on an answer print that varied by $1,000. Pick a lab that seems to have good credentials, experience with 16mm feature films, and a low price. Again, the favorable currency-exchange rate helped us get a great deal from an experienced Canadian lab, saving us about $1,000.

If you're going the video route, you'll want an answer print without a soundtrack. You'll use this print with your fullcoat mixed soundtrack to transfer to video. Not having an optical sound track done and not having a release print done will save you about $2,500. Then you'll take this savings and spend it on the video transfer.

For your final transfer, go for the highest quality videotape format you can afford, such as D-2 or even the digital D-1 format. That way you can make a 1-inch "C" format sub-master for making 1/2-inch VHS dubs. You can get bids for your video transfer to lower the cost, but you may be able to get an even better deal by asking for a flat price for transferring to video when the transfer house has no other business. This approach saved us about $1,000.

If you really trust the transfer house, you can often get a further deal on an "unsupervised" transfer. It's like the old service station adage, "If you help, we charge double." If you can hold your tongue, you may be able to get the "unsupervised" rate while sitting there with the colorist to answer any questions that might arise. You can trim your costs further by buying your mastering videotapes from a wholesaler instead of paying the transfer house's price (ours even advised us not to buy the tape stock from them).

If you have decided to get a film release print instead of the high-buck video transfer, pretty soon you'll discover that you still need video copies for festival submissions and for distributor previews. You can get a "one-light, unsupervised" video transfer for $400 to $800 dollars. No frills, but it will get you a video master for duplicating cassettes. If you have a friend at a television station, you might be able to get a free transfer using their telecine chain. The results won't be as good as with an expensive transfer system, but you will have decided to make your fortune in the theatrical arena, and your video version won't matter as much. However, if you do get a home video sale, you'll probably want to go back and pay for a high-quality video transfer.

Sneak Preview

In order to test how the humor in "Beyond Bob" worked with an audience, we did a sneak preview of our edited work print. We did a quicky sound mix (five hours for $500) and a low-buck video transfer ($400) to videotape ($35 for evaluated tape). This wasn't great quality, but it allowed us to test the film with a real audience.

Preview Cassettes and Shipping

You're going to need video copies for a couple of purposes. For any TV previews, such as talk shows or news interviews, you'll need a 3/4-inch U-matic video or a Betacam SP video version. You can buy your tape stock cheaper from a company that sells recycled, evaluated tapes. They take used tapes from TV stations and production companies who don't use a tape for more than one pass. They erase and evaluate the tapes, or they reload the cases with new tape. Look to the ever-informative "Other Resources" section of the appendix for a listing of these companies and some other low-cost tape suppliers. You can get these tapes for about half price.

You might also try getting free discarded tapes directly from a television station or production company. Then to further reduce this duplication cost, wheedle a freebie 3/4-inch U-matic or Betacam transfer from a friend at a TV station or video production house.

You're also going to need at least 20 VHS cassettes of your movie for festival entries and distributor previews. You probably are going to have to pay a duplication company to make these cassettes. It's hard to spend 40 hours dubbing one tape at a time in the video edit suite at your friend's company without some uncomfortable questions. These will cost about $14 each for this relatively small number of cassettes. The prices drop as you order larger quantities, but that won't be happening on a $30,000 budget.

Publicity Photos and Packets

Patience is a virtue. It also saves money in a world of "we can get it there overnight if you pay $20 more." For our publicity packets, we selected photos from the ones we'd shot on location. While not a sterling collection, they were interesting enough to get them published in more than a dozen newspapers and magazines. We recommend "modest but pithy" as the theme for publicity packets. Don't waste money on 8 x 10s. Most publications can do everything necessary with a 5 x 7 color glossy photo. It will also cost extra to do them in black-and-white, so don't. We had several magazines and newspapers use them in color, and it presents no problem for publications using black and white images. The patience comes in when you get them printed. Forget the labs who serve studio photographers. Go for the mail-order labs. Check the "Other Resources" section of the appendix to find our favorite one. We got our 5 x 7s for $1.25 each. A couple had poor color balance, so we sent them back for a free reprinting, which turned out fine. Sure we had to wait two weeks to get them all, but time was something we had in large supply.

The publicity packets themselves consisted of slick-covered pocket portfolios (bought at a discount office supply store) with the film's title on the front. This title art was photocopied onto full-sheet adhesive labels (same store) and then cut to size and pasted on the folders. We hand colored some of the title text with highlighter markers. Inside we included the publicity photos and photocopied sheets with synopsis, cast list, and a feature article on the production for reporters to plagiarize. We wrote these ourselves and copied them at the cheapest duplicator we could find. Each of our 20 packets cost less than $9.00: five photos ($6.25), folder (.25), about 20 pages of text ($1.40), mailing envelope (.50). Add to that the $18 we spent on the box of 50 label sheets. These looked professional and got us as much publicity as we could get from a packet.

Photocopying Scripts, Miscellaneous Photocopying

You'll need one full copy of the script for each main performer and supporting role. You may be able to trim script copying costs if your cast is small. The bit players only need the pages they are in. You also need copies for director, producer, unit production manager, assistant unit production manager, director of photography, sound recordist, art director, wardrobe supervisor, makeup-and-hair supervisor, editor, and composer.

Miscellaneous copying will include maps to locations, call sheets for the shooting days, release forms, camera and sound log sheets, and dozens of items that will crop up before, during, and after production. Try to get a photocopying shop to do all of your copying free or for a reduced rate in exchange for being listed in the screen credits. Your local IFP office may also have a deal with a local photocopy shop; check with them for details.

Postage for Publicity and Preview Tapes

The publicity packets you'll want to send by first class mail. Don't get sucked into the "send it express" or "fax it to me" syndrome. Planning ahead or waiting until the next printing deadline for a publication will eliminate these unnecessary costs. Everybody wants the material today so it can sit on their desk for two weeks until they get to it. First class postage and a mailing envelope will cost about $1.25 per publicity packet if you keep the size small, totaling $25 for 20 packets.

You're going to need to mail your preview cassettes around to distributors and festivals. We recommend U.S. Postal Service's Priority Mail. A VHS cassette and protective padding costs about $3 to ship, and it will arrive in 2 to 3 days. You can save about 50 cents by going Parcel Post, but you give the disgruntled postal workers a week or so to devise a way to mangle the cassette. For 20 preview cassettes, mailing will cost about $60. What's left in your postage budget will be chewed up easily by remailing the few preview cassettes that are returned and in sending out those bid letters. Eventually you'll find yourself dipping into the grocery money for postage.

* * *

If you've done all the begging, finagling, dickering, and short cutting we recommend, you now have a budget of $30,000 or less. Congratulations. You've just taken one of the biggest steps towards making your feature film a reality. You've set realistic expectations for the kind of movie it can be and created a plan for making it happen. You're on your way to a successful production. Savor the moment after you've completed your budget. Sit back, and just visualize what it will be like shooting your film, what it will be like to see the story you love up on the screen in front of an audience. Spend at least five minutes with this vision so you can remember it well because you're going to need it. This vision of your goal has got to last when the realities of funding, organizing, and launching your production come crashing in.

We hit those realities right after finishing our budget. We couldn't raise $30,000 in time for our planned production start. We could only come up with $12,000. Our solution? Figure out how to shoot it for $12,000. And that's what we did.

How to Shoot It For $12,000

We found that if we threw out all the post-production costs except for the ones that let us begin editing the work print and soundtrack, we were getting rid of more than half of our budget expenses. We couldn't do post-production sound effects, dialogue looping, music track, sound mix, titles, negative cutting, answer print, video transfer, or publicity. But we wouldn't be ready for those steps for months after production anyway. So we shot "Beyond Bob" for $12,000 and then spent more than three years scraping together the money to finish. We did essentially the same thing on "Resident Alien." It would be a luxury to actually start with the $30,000 in hand.

If you have even less money available and lots of refrigerator space (you're going to be living on carrots and bread anyway), you can trim another $5,000 by not processing and printing your negative, except for one roll from the first day of shooting to make sure you have images on the film. Shoot, and put the cans in double plastic bags in the refrigerator. Bag up the sound reels, and put them safely in the back of your closet. The suspense will make you crazy. The cast and crew will hound you. You will have demons whispering to you that the film is blank. And you will have powerful motivation to find the five grand to get a look at your baby.

This has probably given you an inkling of how films like the much-mentioned "El Mariachi" was made for a reputed $7,000. The shooting may have been done for that much, with a bunch of lab bills deferred. The word on the street is that it took another $250,000 of post-production to complete the "El Mariachi" that arrived in the theaters and the video store. The reported budget is the usual movie-business hype to generate interest in a film, but hey, it worked. And the approach used by those filmmakers is one worth noting: They shot a film that was interesting enough that someone else paid to finish it. Not bad work if you can get it.

THE BUSINESS
Ultra-Low Budget, Inc.

When we first dreamed of making our films, we never dreamed of becoming accountants. We never dreamed of becoming corporate officers or contract lawyers or corporate tax preparers.

To us, these weren't dreams. They were nightmares. That's not to impugn any of these professions; they're just not ones to which we aspired.

But just as your dreams at night sometimes cast you in unusual roles, the dream of making your own feature film may put you into some unexpected professions. We found ourselves pushed, pulled, and thrown into all of these jobs as we got into the business end of making feature films.

Now if you're as passionate about making films as we are, you're probably thinking about skipping this chapter and saying to yourself "I don't want to be in business. I just want to make my movie." We said that too, but it didn't help. We still ended up in business, and you will too if you plan to have your feature shown somewhere other than your basement. This is one of the dark chapters of making a feature film, so you might as well come to terms with it now because it's not going away.

Here's the bad news of this book for anyone in love with making movies. It's a business.

During the more than five years that we've spent producing our two feature films, at least three years of that time has been drained away running a business. Sometimes it seems like producing and shooting movies is just a sidelight. But no matter how grisly it is, this work has to be done. Even gourmet cooks have pots to wash. And since you're going to be a gourmet cook working at a diner, you probably can't afford to have someone else do your dirty work.

Now, we're not saying we've got the inside track on the business of business. In fact, it remains the one area we are least certain about. However, we've avoided having any really scary discussions with tax collectors or other people's attorneys, so we make the bold presumption that we've done okay, at least so far.

What follows is how we took care of business, but it comes with a warning: "results may vary." The bad news is that almost every state has different rules related to business issues. The Internal Revenue Service (IRS) has consistent rules, which may be interpreted differently by individual IRS personnel. The good news is that we work in Minnesota, which has some of the more stringent rules and most aggressive tax structures. (We're not complaining, mind you — both lead to an above-average quality of life.) This means that some issues we faced may be non-existent where you work.

The details of our experience aside, you can't ignore business issues without repercussions later. You will have to investigate to find the best solution for your personal situation under the current laws and tax structure. Our approach is only one possible strategy. It might not be the best one for you.

Trust us on this point. You'll be glad you took care of business issues when the distributor who wants your movie asks, "Are all the rights clear on this film?" It may be the difference between making the sale and not.

Business Decisions

There were four main factors that motivated the business choices we made:

1) Money: As always, we couldn't afford to spend any money that wouldn't show up on the screen somehow.

2) Rights: We wanted to produce films that were ready to be sold as professional productions, meaning we clearly owned all rights to our films and could sell them.

3) Legal Liability: We owned houses and cars that we didn't want to lose in a lawsuit.

4) Tax Obligations: We didn't want to spend the rest of our days in tax jail (where you can either make license plates or produce films that explain tax laws).

Because these four factors are often joined at the hip, please excuse some repetition in our ramblings. It's important to know how each of these factors will affect other decisions you must make.

Money

If the point hasn't been made already, let us reiterate. Money and the lack of it are going to be the undercurrent that affects every decision you make. To complete a feature film for a paltry $30,000, you can't spend a penny that isn't going to somehow improve the look or the sound of your film. This means a big list of people you can't hire (but need) and things you can't buy or rent (but need).

Professional Help

At the business end of film production, lack of money primarily translates into not being able to afford lawyers, accountants, and tax preparers. This means you'll need free help to set up your business, develop your contracts, keep your books, and prepare your tax statements. Since we didn't have friends who could do this work for us, we had no option. We learned to do it ourselves.

There are a number of how-to books that were immensely helpful, everything from basic accounting to incorporating a business. We've listed the ones we used in the bibliography, but don't let this list limit you. There are many fine works out there in your local library. Keep in mind that most libraries can borrow from bigger or more specialized libraries if they don't have what you need. Library books are one resource that fits your budget.

We also asked other people who had done this before for their ideas, warnings, sample contracts, release forms, articles of incorporation, and such. We learned that we could take the work of other people's expensive lawyers and tailor it to our needs. We also learned that being a lawyer doesn't mean you can write a good contract. We've seen some contracts with serious holes that could really hurt both parties. Personally, we believe that complex legal language creates more misunderstandings than it prevents. We feel that plain language will make it less likely that you'll have contract problems.

Lack of money will probably force you to do your own accounting, bookkeeping, and tax preparation, too. But they're not so bad when compared with being trampled by stampeding wildebeest. Truly, these tasks are the most boring, confusing, and terrifying work on a film production. Do whatever you can to find someone who loves doing these jobs, and get them to take on the task. Dale, as producer, reluctantly took on these duties and learned basic corporate accounting and tax preparation in the trenches. We think this is what caused his hairline to retreat and go AWOL. Even if you hand over these duties, be sure to learn enough about the books to know where the money is going. (There are too many stories of accountants flying off to Rio . . . not that they don't deserve the break.)

If you're forced to do your own taxes, take heart. Surveys of tax preparers have shown extreme differences in the final tax returns they prepared. Just do your honest best, and hope the IRS treats you kindly.

As for the accounting, it's one of those mystical arts, but it is learnable. If you start with a basic accounting text the way we did and spend a few evernings studying it, you'll soon understand the basic principles of accounting. Many of these textbooks also include helpful examples of lists of accounts, general ledgers, ledger entries, and year-end reports.

Insurance

Working on an ultra-low budget also means your production will probably do without liability insurance, completion bonds, or errors-and-omission insurance. Although you can't afford them, it's a good idea to know what they are.

Liability Insurance: Liability insurance is the basic coverage that pays for damage or injury you cause, such as dropping an electrified klieg light into a hot tub full of bathers. Not having liability insurance has prevented us from using some locations and has caused us to lose more than a few minutes of sleep. But when we looked into getting it, we found it would cost as much as our entire shooting budget. (Recently, prices have decreased for this coverage, so it is now only a significant percentage of your budget and may be worth considering.) However, if you happen to work in the audiovisual-production field, you may already carry annual production insurance that you can apply to your film, or you may be able to add a cheap rider to your existing policy. Unless you have one of these policies in your pocket ("Is that an insurance rider, or are you just glad to see me?"), you'll be on the high wire without "the good hands" to catch you. That's what we did. You just have to be very cautious, safety conscious, and careful with borrowed props, costumes, and locations. The one liability insurance we could afford was a low-cost damage option on our rental equipment. Given the value of the equipment, it was worth doing.

Completion Bonds: Completion bonds are essentially insurance policies that will pay over-budget costs in order to guarantee investors that you will complete the production. Forget it. Anyone putting money into a $30,000 feature film had better recognize that this is a high-risk proposition. There are a hundred minor things that can cripple a fringe production like yours, and only two things that will get it finished — good luck and the kindness of strangers. And you're depending on both of these. You and everyone on your production are rolling the dice that your skills and creativity are going to win big. There are simply no guarantees.

Of course, the biggest reason you're not getting a completion bond is that you can't afford it. Even if you could, the completion-bond company would probably shriek with laughter. It's the equivalent of smoking unfiltered cigarettes, flying home-built jets, and cliff diving . . . and then applying for life insurance. Completion-bond companies don't want to pay to finish your film, so the only way they will give you a completion bond is if your production uses the safest, time-tested production procedures. Get real! You're going to do something that is completely alien to completion-bond companies. You're going to break most of the rules to make something out of nothing. And that's only going to happen if you and your investors close your eyes really tightly and repeat "I believe. I believe. I BELIEVE!"

Errors-and-Omissions Insurance: Errors-and-omissions insurance is liability insurance that protects you in case you failed to get all the necessary rights and releases from performers, used copyrighted material without permission, included libelous material, didn't get location releases, infringed upon a famous title, or based your screenplay on someone else's published work. Simply put, it's insurance to protect against you — the producer — having not done your job.

There are three reasons we didn't bother with this insurance. First, we did our job right and got all the necessary rights and clearances. Second, no one will issue this insurance to you unless you have done your job right. ("Sure, we'll insure you against dying while deep-sea diving now that you've given up diving.") Third, this primarily protects the distributors, so our feeling was, let them pay for it if they are so nervous. If someone is insisting on errors-and-omission insurance, give them copies of your paperwork, and make it part of the contract that they will pay for the insurance.

Employees

Lack of bucks also will prevent you from having employees, especially union ones. You can't afford employees because you have to pay them minimum wage — except for corporate officers, sole proprietors, and partners, who can forego salary. If you were a union production, even at the union's low-budget film rates, you'd have to pay union scale to cast and crew. That alone would use up most of your production money. So if you come from a long line of union activists, either give up this ultra-low-budget movie idea now, or steel yourself for some tense family reunions.

We dealt with the employee salary issue by hiring all cast and crew — including ourselves as screenwriters, director, and producer — as independent contractors. All salaries were deferred and paid only if profits were made. To accomplish this, we wrote contracts that were specifically designed to meet the criteria that were used to determine that a worker was an independent contractor under state and federal rules.

If these people had been classified as employees, we would have had to pay minimum wage, withhold income tax and social security tax, and pay for worker's compensation insurance. We had the state jobs department that regulates these matters review our contracts before we started production to make sure we had independent contractors who were exempt from these requirements.

But there's bad news for you and us on this front. We couldn't do it this way again. The IRS uses 20 job characteristics to identify independent contractors, which we considered when we wrote our contracts. Unfortunately, the IRS now interprets these characteristics more strictly to make sure income and social security taxes are being paid. The result is that our contracts will no longer pass muster for all the workers on a film production. Undeer current policy most film workers would be employees, and only a few jobs, such as screenwriter, director, and producer, might be independent contractors.

This means that you can't be sure that the state and federal revenue departments will view someone you hire as an independent contractor, so you could be asked to pay back taxes on that person's income. Now granted, our kind of productions are small potatoes, and the IRS has primarily been looking at the records of ongoing production companies, not ones that do sporadic productions. But you shouldn't count on being overlooked because you really don't want this type of trouble.

The best idea we have for working around this problem is completely untried, so this advice falls in the WAG (wild-ass guess) category. Since some of the jobs on your film production can be independent contractors, we'd recommend presenting a list of your cast and crew needs along with a sample of your contract to your state jobs department for their interpretation. You may even want to talk to your regional IRS office to get their view since it may be different from the state's interpretation.

Once you have a list of who has to be an employee, you can then take those people on as unpaid student interns. They are on your production to learn and earn resume credentials. This is really true of your entire crew and cast, so you might want to consider this for the entire production company if you can be sure they will show up for the shoot. (Thousands of dollars of rental equipment and film do you no good without the cast and crew to use them.) Also be sure that these student interns sign release forms, liability waivers, and an agreement to show up on the set when needed. Be sure to feed them well, and then give them a big Christmas present if you make money.

One downside of this approach is that your workers will usually work harder and better if they see this as an entry-level professional production. If you're asking them to volunteer their time and effort, it will affect how they view the project, and working professionals are less likely to sign on. This means your crew and cast will be less experienced. But that can be an asset. They won't know that you can't make a feature film for no money.

Rights

The next major factor affecting your business activities is the securing of rights.

Not securing all necessary rights for your film is going to put you at a severe disadvantage when you try to distribute it. It might even tie up your production in legal actions. And it's a problem you can avoid.

Rights are a business matter that you'll want to pay attention to from day one. A lot of decisions you make will relate to getting rights to present your finished movie, and you'll need to diligently gather them as you wend your way through pre-production, production, and post-production. So fire up the photocopier. There are forms to copy.

Contracts, release forms, and letters of approval are the three ropes you're going to use to hog tie those pesky rights. The performance rights you're looking for include the screenplay, the performances of your cast, the work products of your crew, the music and sound effects (if they come from a recorded library) in your sound track, any copyrighted material used in the film (images —such as photos or prints that are more than just background, readings or dialogue from other sources, snatches of music or images on the radio or TV), and the locations you use (excluding public property, but be aware that seemingly public areas such as shopping malls are privately-owned). Get the approvals before you commit these items and performances to film. If you don't and can't get the rights later, you've wasted precious time and film stock.

We started securing these rights as soon as the first crew person joined us. We used a performance-rights clause in our contracts to take care of the cast's performances, the crew's work, the screenplay, and the music created by our composer. The sample contract in the appendix includes all the necessary rights. Our composer, who wanted to potentially use the music again, only granted us synchronization rights. Synchronization rights mean you can do anything you want with the music as long as it stays connected to the movie images. If you want to release a hit single, you have to get more rights. Given that we were getting thousands of dollars of original music for next to nothing, it seemed like a fair compromise. We also bought some previously recorded music for a few scenes, and for this we also used a contract for synchronization rights only.

Release forms will take care of the rights to use the images of extras, unpaid performers, and locations. If you're shooting in a public place, you technically don't need to get permission to use the images of people who could have been seen by anyone in that public place, as long as you don't highlight them (close-ups of people adjusting their undergarments will just buy you trouble). Some productions post signs that warn people entering the area that they may be included in a movie, but that presumes the filmmakers have gotten permission to shoot in that area in the first place. Guerrilla productions like ours only get permission if there's no permit fee from the city or whomever, so this may draw too much attention to your work. If you decide to feature someone in particular, you better get them to sign a release form or make sure they're not identifiable. Also get signed location releases for every privately owned site you shoot on or shoot at. Do this in advance of your shoot dates to avoid those ugly high-stress negotiations with cast and crew waiting. Samples of group release and location release forms are also included in the appendix.

Approval letters are all you need to get use of various copyrighted items. For example, we featured an existing hang-gliding book in one of our films. To obtain approval, we just wrote to the publisher, explained the film and the context to them, and they sent a permission letter.

Sound effects from recorded libraries didn't require any forms. We just bought the sound with synchronization rights from a production house and got a receipt. Be sure to tell them you want it for a feature film because some libraries aren't licensed to be used for feature productions. The company that mixes your final soundtrack will probably have a sound-effects library, too. Of course, if you're getting into the proper low-budget mindset, you're already thinking of where you can borrow a 1/4-inch tape recorder to record wild sound effects.

If in any situation you can't get the rights you need (worldwide, exclusive, without restrictions, in perpetuity), stop. Do not pass go. If you can't persuade that performer, crew person, landowner, or copyright owner, don't even think about using their stuff. Find another solution. Otherwise, you'll regret it when you have to go back and beg that person for the rights so you can sell your film.

The last point you need to consider about rights is holding on to them once you've gotten them. A lot of people don't realize that you can give all your rights away if you publicly present your film without a copyright notice. You retain all ownership of your movie until you present it publicly. At that point, you need to indicate that it is a copyrighted work, or it becomes public domain. Public domain means anyone can use your film any way they want.

You don't need to do all the formal filings with the copyright office before your presentation, but you must have a title or a statement in a program or even a verbal statement to the audience before the showing that the work is copyrighted. "Copyright (year) (the copyright holder)" is all that needs to appear.

Legal Liability

Nobody wants to be sued. As a result, many of your business decisions will be aimed at reducing your potential value as a lawsuit target. For a business on the razor's edge of viability — which we guarantee you'll be if you're trying to make a feature film for 30 grand — a lawsuit could mean the untimely demise of your dream. And don't be foolhardy enough to think that it couldn't happen to you. Law schools are graduating more lawyers than ever before, so many so that their employment possibilities are getting almost as poor as those for filmmakers. But lawyers do have one advantage: A town that can't support one lawyer can support two. They know how to make their own work.

Because of the diminishing job possibilities in established companies and law firms, lawyers are now forced to do what screenwriters and other underemployed professionals have always had to do, which is work on speculation. Just as we have written entire screenplays with the hopes of selling them, lawyers without work will undertake lawsuits just for the possibility of getting a percentage of any settlement. The upshot: anyone can get a lawyer to sue you today. And lots of people do.

You do have some automatic advantages in this area. For the most part you'll be in the turnip category, as in "you can't get blood out of a turnip." However, people who automatically smell money around movie making may mistake you for a worthwhile candidate, and frivolous lawsuits are as costly to defend against as valid ones. The other advantage is that you're small, fast moving, and out of sight quickly — at least one good thing about not being able to maintain a high profile. Because none of these factors will guarantee your safety, it's wise to build in whatever protection you can. There are three steps we took.

1. Incorporation
    If you're going to make this movie for professional sale, you'll end up with some business structure eventually, and by default if you don't actually decide. Basically, you have five choices: individual proprietorship, partnership, limited partnership, S corporation, and C corporation. Don't go to sleep on us now. There's going to be a test at the end of the chapter.

Now if you embrace inertia and ignore business concerns, you'll probably end up being legally classified as an individual proprietorship, which means that you'll personally own the business and all its assets. A partnership is very similar, except that two or more people personally own the business and divide the assets. Now, even these simple business structures have legal and tax requirements, so ignoring business will put you into some trouble with local, state, and federal authorities. Though these business structures have simplified accounting and tax requirements, they didn't meet our main criteria: protecting homes, cars, and personal assets from being taken to pay business liabilities. So we reluctantly rejected these simpler forms of business.

Limited partnerships are used to finance many independent film productions. These businesses are made up of two groups of partners. The first are general partners, usually the filmmakers, who run the business and have all the duties and liabilities of a regular partnership. The other group is the limited partners who are just putting money into the project for a share of the profits. Because their participation in business decisions is limited, so is their financial risk and liability risk. Different states put different restrictions on how these limited partnerships can be set up. (Apparently, the United States are not as united as we thought.) There are also federal limits on the number of limited partners you may have and how you invite people to become limited partners. Too many partners or a general public invitation to become partners will land you in regulations governing securities (stock), and your business won't meet the requirements of a limited partnership. Limited partnerships are complicated beasties that should probably be set up with a lawyer's help. Unless that help is available free to you, forget it. Also, as a general partner who runs the business, you'll find that this structure won't protect your personal assets.

The S-corporation is a corporate structure under which the business' assets are included in the shareholders' personal coffers for tax purposes. This simplifies the business income and tax reporting, but complicates your personal taxes. This was a tempting choice for us, but because it intermingles the business assets with your personal assets, a lawsuit or bankruptcy might also be applied to your personal assets ("Sorry about losing the house, Honey."). Too risky for us.

So we bit the bullet and became a real C-corporation, just like GM and Warner Communications, but without the medical plan and the golden parachutes. This means that all government agencies view our film business as a "person" or entity that is wholly separate from us. As a result, if we want to put personal money into the film production, we have to loan it to the corporation, in spite of the fact that we are the sole shareholders and the corporate officers. It's a little hard to get into this mindset, but you catch on eventually.

As a C-corporation, there's a significant amount of record keeping and tax reporting required (and federal corporate tax instructions are not a pretty sight), but you are afforded almost complete personal protection from lawsuits, bankruptcy, creditors, and the like. However, this doesn't mean you can act irresponsibly. In extreme cases of corporations flagrantly violating the law or endangering employees or communities, the corporate officers have been held liable, even sent to prison. But if you act in good faith and take steps to protect people's safety, the beat-up Toyota in your garage should be safe from seizure. Fortunately, we're writing this chapter before tax time, or we might have trouble remembering why incorporating was such a good idea.

Now, becoming a corporation may seem like a daunting task, but it's actually pretty easy. We had to file some boilerplate articles of incorporation with the state's Secretary of State Office, apply for state and federal tax numbers, and set up stock ownership. (In our case, we own all the stock. If you don't sell stock outside of your state and you don't publicly offer to sell the stock, you are exempt from the rules of the federal Securities and Exchange Commission. In our state, if we don't make more than ten stock sales within a 12-month period, we're exempt from state security rules as well. Check your local requirements.) We found a great little guide book prepared by a state university that gave us all the steps in lay person's terms. It's called "Simplified Business Incorporation: A self-help manual," and it's listed in the bibliography. It's specifically designed for Minnesota businesses, so you'll want to look for a similar publication for your state.

There are small business assistance offices in most states and the federal Small Business Administration to help you get started. Some of them even publish free guides to setting up a business and may even have financial assistance, though filmmakers are not usually considered a good investment risk. The Feds and some states offer free training programs on taxes and other business issues. So do universities, business schools, and vocational technical colleges, but not for free. And don't forget the public library; that's where we found the incorporation guidebook. Ask the reference librarians for help. These people love ferreting out information the way you love filmmaking, and they're usually delighted to be asked to use their skills.

If we haven't been too specific about the actual details of incorporating here, it's because it constitutes its own book, and you'll undoubtedly have more, less, or different steps to take where you live.

Now one last thought on incorporating: Delaware. You may have noticed that lots of companies that send you direct mail or that run late-night TV ads for greatest hits albums are listed as Delaware corporations. That's because Delaware has proclaimed itself the "corporation capital of the world."

You can become a Delaware corporation for about $100 within 24 hours, or you can pay extra for two-hour service. (Would you like fries with that Certificate of Incorporation?) If you call the State of Delaware Division of Corporation (see the "Other Resources" section of the appendix), their computerized phone system will be happy to send you a complete incorporation kit, including boilerplate articles of incorporation for several types of corporations (stock, close, non-stock, foreign, unleaded, low-fat, etc.), forms for creating a limited partnership, fee schedules, a description of the corporate franchise tax (which is simpler than most states' corporate taxes), and a tasteful photo of their governor. All that's missing is the decoder ring.

The Governor of Delaware's photo
— one of the benefits of incorporating there.

If you're considering going the Delaware route, there are a couple of points to consider. First, you must have a registered agent in Delaware. For an annual fee, you can get one from the convenient list included in the incorporation package. Check the going rate before you get in too deep. Second, there's a minimum annual franchise tax and filing fee for your annual report whether you make any profits or not. (In our state, we don't have to pay income tax if we haven't had any income.) Third, you'll be subject to Delaware business laws, so you better become familiar with their requirements. Fourth, to operate in your home state, you'll probably need to file some legal notices as a foreign (out-of-state) corporation. You may even be required to do some type of tax filing as a foreign corporation. Fifth, if you have legal troubles, you may have to handle them in Delaware. And sixth, we've never done this. It only cost us $150 to incorporate in Minnesota. We did it ourselves without legal help, and when we didn't make profits, we only had to pay sales tax. And there's no minimum annual fee. Delaware is home to many corporations, but make sure you know the obligations you will have in that state and in your home state before you make it your business home.

Now if your mind works like ours, the urge to run and hide under the desk is becoming overwhelming about now. Regulations, taxes, legal notices, thumbscrews, and charging mastodons are all listed deep in our primitive brains as things to avoid as fast as our legs can carry us. It's your basic fight-or-flight decision. We could have chucked the entire project when faced with this business stuff, but the rewards from making a movie were great enough that we turned and fought our way through the paperwork and legal language, and we're glad we did. So take heart; success comes to the brave. On the bright side, the remaining steps to protect yourself from legal liability are all easier.

2. Liability Waivers

The second step we took to protect ourselves from lawsuits was to include liability waivers in all our contracts with the cast and crew. This was to avoid lawsuits from inside our production group. Of course, we still took steps to minimize risks of injury, but there's always a chance of an accident. These waivers are not iron clad by any legal definition, but it puts the people you're working with on notice that they are responsible for their own medical and accident insurance and that they have acknowledged that they are accepting any risks of injury. If nothing else, they will all think twice before they ask a lawyer about suing you, and therefore won't be advised that they could sue you anyway. If they do sue, that's when your turnip status comes into play.

There are a couple of secondary benefits to this waiver. When you get location releases signed by property owners, some ask about insurance (which you don't have). It helped us to be able to say that we had this waiver in the contract of every person on the production crew to avoid lawsuits for injury. Of course the waiver won't absolutely prevent legal actions, but lawsuits would probably involve the production company first and the property owner second.

By this point, you're probably beginning to realize that the only real protection from lawsuits that you can have is to make sure nothing happens that anyone can sue you over. To ensure this, take precautions on the set to make sure risks are limited. If you have dangerous-looking scenes, do everything you can with special effects, film tricks, and safety equipment to prevent real injury. In our film "Resident Alien," an important scene takes place on a roof at night, which worried us a lot. The first thing we did was find a one-story building with a roof that had a low pitch, almost flat. We assigned one person to hold the ladder whenever someone went up or down, and Dale, as the producer on the set, spent all night reminding people they were on a roof and warning them when they got too close to the edge. Because of technical problems, we had to reshoot this sequence, so we actually did it twice without mishap. We were very, very careful and very lucky.

Shooting for safety on the roof for "Resident Alien." Pictured, l to r, actor Patrick Coyle and director of photography Scott Lee Dose.
Photo courtesy of Granite Productions, Ltd.

3. Copyright

Our third step to avoid legal entanglements was scrupulous attention to copyright laws. We're always amazed how many professionals in the media business ignore the laws which protect their own work. In case you have any doubts, YOU CAN'T USE ANYTHING YOU DIDN'T CREATE WITHOUT GETTING PERMISSION! No, you can't borrow that music; no, you can't use video footage running on TV; and no, you can't just lift a few lines from a novel or another screenplay. Granted, there are some gray areas in satire and parody, in public domain material, and in documentary or scholarly usage of material, but you aren't likely to have the lawyerly resources to make sure you have clear rights to use these items. So don't.

For low-buck producers such as ourselves, there are only two feasible options (unless you have free use of a copyright attorney). Create something original or get written permission to use it, which often comes at a cost. Creating something original is easiest. There are lots of creative people looking for outlets for their work. They will love you for asking them to create music, artwork, or poetry for your movie. For example, we had at least six composers ask if they could do our music tracks for free. You can also ask these people to give you permission to use music, art, or writing they've already done.

For minor items, like a newspaper masthead with a column by one of our characters, we just made up a bogus newspaper on the computer. When we wanted our characters pictured on *Entertainment Weekly* magazine, we asked permission, and the publisher granted it after reviewing the final layout. (Of course, this was when the magazine was just starting out and looking for publicity. *Rolling Stone* turned us down flat.) Often pleading poverty and being friendly will get you permission for free if it's not something that's normally sold for performance.

There's one detail that you must not forget. For all the wonderful original writing, music, and pictures, be sure you have a contract or release form signed by every artist, stating that you own all rights to that material or at least all rights to use it in your movie. Get these from the composers, painters, musicians, photographers, graphic artists, and everyone else. And then file them away safely. We've never had to pull these out, but we can if there is any question about rights. So don't overlook this essential task.

If something is copyrighted and is identifiable on your set, get permission or replace it with something you have created (and photocopying it is not creating it). It will save you lots of worries in the future.

Even being careful, we got a scary letter on our first film, "Resident Alien." It was from an attorney for a larger docudrama by the same title. In stern legal language, it warned us that our title infringed on their production. It urged us to select another title.

This was not a pleasant letter. Our production money was gone, titles were done, and our title fit our story perfectly. We also knew that you can't copyright a title unless that title is so famous that you would instantly be stealing sales that rightly belonged to the original production (so you can forget about calling your film "Casablanca"). We definitely couldn't afford an attorney to respond, but we wanted to resolve the issue.

This is where being writers and people who know the value of humor came in handy. We mustered our best legal language and wrote back a letter thanking them for asking whether <u>they</u> would be infringing on <u>our</u> film's title. We went on to say that since our films had different audiences and since we couldn't copyright titles, we felt we could co-exist in the marketplace. We closed by wishing them good luck with their "Resident Alien."

Fortunately, the attorney and his client appreciated the ironic humor and the validity of our arguments. We got back a cordial letter that parroted our language about co-existing and wished us luck with our "Resident Alien," which proves that the pen is mightier than the lawsuit.

Our point is don't mess with copyright. Every distribution contract that's come across our desk has a clause in which you cross your heart and hope to die if you don't own all rights to the material in your movie. This is when you'll be glad you didn't borrow that shot from "Star Wars" and that you remembered to get all those release forms signed.

Tax Obligations

Swallow hard kiddies, and hold onto those armrests. Ready to hear some really terrifying tales? We're going to talk about federal, state, and local taxes and how they affect the business choices you need to make. This is scarier than anything you'll see on "Tales from the Crypt."

Actually, the scary part about taxes is the not knowing. Not knowing if there's a tax out there that you've forgotten to pay. Not knowing if you've filled out the forms properly. Not knowing if the IRS swat team is going to kick in the door and seize the paltry gains that you've managed to wring out of your creative efforts. Our advice is to relax and ask questions.

Like most things governmental, there's a lot of fear about taxes that is unnecessary and unwarranted. Dale has worked in government for more than 15 years, and he's not very threatening (unless you ask him to spend money wastefully). And he promises that zombies don't suck the souls of civil servants every morning as they come to work. Government work is just like any other work. Some people are good at their jobs, some are poor. Some are friendly and helpful, some are cranky and officious. The point you need to remember is that the tax man (notice that there's not much clamor for equal gender access to this term?) and tax woman are people you can ask for help.

There are three main types of taxes that may affect you, presuming you don't buy real estate as part of your production: sales/use tax (and this may not apply to out-of-state sales, sales for resale, or when you buy something for your film that will be taxable when it's sold later); employee taxes (social security, worker's compensation insurance, state and federal income tax withholdings); and state and federal corporate income tax.

Taxes have mainly affected our business in three ways: Where we do business, whether we have employees, and what type of accounting we do. We live in and on the fringe of the Minneapolis and St. Paul metropolitan area in Minnesota. Our filmmaking business is incorporated in the fringe community where one of us resides because there were no extra sales taxes to pay for a domed baseball stadium (also it was where there was a corner in the basement for an in-home office).

We operate with no employees except corporate officers, who are the two of us. And the corporate officers have declined any salary until the company is profitable (probably not in the 20th century). With no employee salaries, we avoid having to track and pay employee taxes, such as worker's compensation insurance, social security tax, and withholdings for state and federal income tax. Keep this part in mind especially. Taking on that first employee will probably generate enough paperwork to require at least another part-time employee. We've decided if we ever reach the point of taking on employees, one of the first to be hired will be an accountant/bookkeeper/tax preparer, and if they can sew costumes, that's all the better.

The third taxing effect on our business is accounting. You will be dealing with large enough sums of money that the state and federal revenue departments will want to know what you're doing with them as a business. Even if you've decided to go the individual proprietorship route, you'll still have to keep records for tax purposes. So surrender, and learn how to speak the victor's language. We set up an accounting system that was designed to keep track of our loans and to tabulate the end-of-the-year information we needed to report on our corporate income tax. This system will become your best friend or your worst enemy or both.

Beyond this basic tax advice, you just need to get the forms and read the instructions. It's all right there in gobbledy-gook. If you thought personal income tax forms were incomprehensible, wait until you get a look at business tax forms. They don't even try to make them friendly. But take heart, at least you won't be paying a professional tax preparer to make your mistakes for you. So relax, be honest, and do your best on the forms. That's what everyone else is doing.

It also can be helpful to call the IRS or your state department of revenue for advice when you get stuck. They don't want you to do it incorrectly, so they'll usually help if they can. And be sure to keep a record of the helpful person's name, because surveys have shown that the advice from the IRS tax person is wrong a lot of times.

The problem is that special interests and political deals have made our tax system into a combination labyrinth and morass that no one fully understands. So where the rubber meets the road in the IRS office, there's some poor soul like us just trying to figure all of this stuff out. When you call her or him up, express your fear and your desire to do the right thing, and treat he or she as a person. You'll likely be pleasantly surprised by the results. We were. Time for an example.

We had dutifully applied for a state sales tax number when we incorporated, but were told to wait until we had a product for sale. So we went into production for three years and reapplied when we had a finished film to sell. We got the forms, and as we read through them, we realized that the film stock and processing we had been buying out of state was taxable. This was a hefty chunk of sales tax (about $800) since film was one of our major expenses. Worse yet, some of this tax was three years overdue with a 20% per year penalty. Dollars were mounting.

With faint hope that we could avoid some or all of this tax, we called the state sales tax office and found compassion. The tax guy was actually impressed that we had discovered our oversight (their oversight, too, since they wouldn't send us the information we needed at the beginning) and that we wanted to do it right. He advised us to just pay the tax as if it wasn't overdue. We took his name and thanked him, and avoided more than $500 in tax penalties. This just goes to show you that tax people are human, too, and they respect people who try to do the right thing. They also like it if you don't scream and spit at them.

Now just a word about grants for those of you who are able to pry loose some free money. Remember that even though someone gave you this money to do all or part of your film, you'll still need to operate as a business if you want a salable product in the end. First you'll probably have to report the grant on your personal income taxes and give some of the money away in taxes right off the bat. Because grants are usually given to one or two individuals, not to companies, you are probably going to be an individual proprietorship or a partnership. Even though the money was free, as soon as you hire people, you get into the employee or contractor issue. You'll still need talent and location releases; you'll still need clear rights to music, performances, and images; and you'll still be a target for lawsuits. And if you have the good fortune to make sales of your film, you'll likely have to pay sales tax and income tax. Sorry. No escape from the business demon or the tax incubus.

We know this business stuff is a big turn off. But no art comes without suffering, and this is just part of your penance. Hopefully, our experiences can help alleviate some of your pain in going through the process. Also, keep your eye on the goal, a finished and sold feature film. Knowing your destination makes a bumpy trip more tolerable.

Just to summarize, here's a quick checklist of the business decisions you need to make and tasks you need to do to set up and run your filmmaking business.

Decide:
  *Business structure: individual proprietorship, partnership, limited partnership, S corporation, C corporation

  *Worker status: independent contractors, employees, student interns, volunteers

  *Location of business

  *Cute, funny, or suggestive name for your company

Tasks:
  *Read up on starting a business, basic accounting

  *File necessary business start-up papers with a state

  *Set up partnership agreement, limited partnership agreement, or articles of incorporation if these apply

  *Divide and issue stock to your shareholders if incorporating

*Get tax and employer identification numbers from the state and federal governments

*Set up company accounting books, and begin keeping accounting records

*Prepare contracts, liability waivers, and talent and location release forms, and get them signed

*Get state and federal determinations to find out if your cast and crew are independent contractors or employees

*Get rights to all music, sound effects, images, performances, and work for your film

*Request the appropriate sales tax and income tax returns from state and federal governments

*Pay sales, income, and (if necessary) employment taxes on both state and federal level

*File for copyright protection on script and film

*Lie down in a dark room with a cool washcloth over your forehead

THE MONEY
"Hello, Uncle Burt? You Don't Remember Me, But ..."

This chapter is about raising the money necessary to make your film, which may seem incongruous because one of the major reasons people produce a feature for $30,000 is that they don't want to raise money. They don't want to grovel. They don't want to beg.

Additionally, the best filmmakers aren't necessarily the best money-raisers. And vice versa. Hence, the choice to make a feature film for peanuts. But, no matter how you slice it, that $30,000 has to come from somewhere.

Of course, to Hollywood, $30,000 is nothing. It's less than nothing. It's the WonderBra budget for "Melrose Place." It's the hot tea and crackers budget for "Murder She Wrote." To the average Hollywood insider, $30,000 in hundred dollar bills isn't even worth the effort it would take to carry it around. That's how cool they are.

However, in the normal course of most people's lives, $30,000 is a heck of a lot of money—unless you're buying a house. (If you're buying a house, it's still a lot of money, but at least with a house, you can see what you're getting, and you can even take showers there.)

As you're probably already painfully aware, most people don't have $30,000 just lying around. In fact, if you know someone with $30,000 just lying around, we recommend that you shower that person with compliments and open doors for them and send them sweet little gifts for absolutely no reason. Why? Because you are a person without $30,000 and you need $30,000 to make your dream come to life.

Yes, you've reached that point. You have the idea, the script is written (or percolating), you've worked out your budget, set up your business structure, and now the next big step looms before you. And you're asking yourself, "How the heck do I come up with the money?"

A darn good question. A tough question. A question with many possible answers. Most filmmakers follow one or more of the following well-worn paths: Investors, Grants, Credit Cards, Scrimping, Borrowing, Favors and Found Money.

Investors

The biggest problem with investors is that they generally want their money back. It's annoying. Some of them even want their money back plus a profit.

Apparently they don't understand film investments.

While as a filmmaker you're in a position to offer your investors many things — the thrill of being an integral part of an artistic experiment, the joy of watching talent bloom, the sheer excitement of being involved in the filmmaking process and seeing their names in lights — a guaranteed payback is, sadly, not on your list of deliverables.

So when you begin scouring your hometown for investors, you'll want to seek out people who are clearly much more excited about the process of making a film than its actual outcome, profit-wise. If an investor is simply looking for a fast or hefty return, it's best to suggest that they look elsewhere.

However, if they're committed — to you, to your idea, or to a local asylum and have granted you power of attorney — they can become some of your strongest allies.

The other problem with raising money via investors is that, in many cases, it actually costs money to raise money. And on an ultra-low budget feature, there is no loose change jingling in your pockets for such shenanigans.

Limited partnerships have historically been the financial vehicle of choice for independent feature films, and with good reason: They're sleek, they're relatively fast to put together, and they keep the filmmaker firmly in the driver's seat. In a limited partnership, the filmmaker is the general partner (the one who makes the decisions) and the investors are the limited partners (the ones who put their money in and sit quietly). However, limited partnerships require voluminous paperwork, and with voluminous paperwork come lawyers, and with lawyers come fees.

You see the problem.

So while a limited partnership may be an efficient way to raise your money, it's usually not a cost-effective method because it can also siphon off your resources at the same time.

The concept of spending five to ten thousand to raise 30 thousand may work on Wall Street (where they'll spend a million to make 20 million), but if you've got ten thousand bucks already, why are you blowing it on lawyers and boilerplates? That's enough cash for you to get either a chunk of your feature shot or a stack of paperwork and an invoice from the law firm down the street. Take your pick.

If you're determined to take the limited partnership path, the best advice we can offer is to find a lawyer who will take care of all the above, aforementioned voluminous paperwork for free or on a deferred basis. (You can write a deferred-payment contract for this work, or ask your new friend the lawyer to put one together for you -- also on a deferred basis!)

Once you've figured out how you're going to set up your money-raising apparatus, the next step is to go out and actually start knocking on doors to find your investors. Doctors, dentists, business people with a love of movies, women who've outlived their rich husbands, old rich guys with young second wives who are dying to get into films . . . these are the traditional supporters of independent filmmakers. And the beauty of funding an ultra-low-budget film is that it doesn't take a large number of investors to pull together

$30,000. Thirty friends with $1,000 each will do it, or 15 friends with $2,000 each. Six friends with $5,000, or one really good friend with $30,000. The money is out there; you just have to go ask for it.

Of course, not all filmmakers are natural-born salespeople. You may be a shy, retiring artist. If this is the case, you'll need to find yourself a money-raiser.

Yes, there are people out there who relish the challenge of raising money. They live for it. Just as you are passionate about your film, they are passionate about their potential for rounding up investors. Someone who is truly good at raising money is someone who can do you and your film a lot of good. If you find this person, treasure him or her.

But a word of warning. As with investors, you'll want to work with someone who is excited about you and excited about your project. Money raising is not an end in itself. The film is the end. Everything must be directed toward that goal. Be wary of someone who wants to raise money simply for the sake of raising money. They may get you what you need. Or they may up and leave for a more lucrative project if they aren't totally committed to your project, leaving you without a finished feature or a film can to put it in.

Another word of warning. Sadly, there are people out there who would gladly take advantage of your desire to have someone else raise the necessary money for your film. They will cheerfully offer to raise all the money you need — even more than that. How about enough for two films while we're at it! But with one proviso: They need cash up front in order to get the job done. They will say this is only fair.

We will say this is only nonsense.

No one else is getting paid up front for their contributions to the film. In fact, you don't have to be an MBA to deduce that making money is clearly not the driving force behind the project; it's a nice bonus, but not the reason for the voyage.

There are many more lucrative ways to make money these days than making an ultra-low budget film ... such as charging filmmakers for your alleged services as a money raiser extraordinaire.

As the Romans used to say, Caveat Filmicus. Filmmaker beware.

* * *

Once you've found your investors, and their money, don't abandon them while you dive into production. Keep them apprised of your progress and give them an opportunity to share in the few moments of glamour and excitement that are part and parcel of the process.

If they want, they should be allowed to visit the set, and if extras are needed, they should be asked if they'd like to take part. If you're sending out updates in the form of a newsletter to the cast and crew during post-production, the investors should be added to the mailing list. All the investors should certainly be invited to preview screenings, and they should be given a place of honor at the premiere. In short, you should involve them in the filmmaking process so that they can get something out of it other than a profit (if even that).

Grants

Grant money can be a great financial resource for the ultra-low-budget filmmaker, particularly if your project is out of the mainstream or focused on a particularly unique niche of our society. Granters are always looking for non-commercial, personal films that examine or celebrate cultures, population segments, or lifestyles generally ignored by the commercial media.

While you may not be able to raise your entire budget this way, a grant can help you get started or help you finish, depending on the grant program. Some programs are devoted to supplying seed money, giving you the dollars you need to get your project off the ground but not necessarily enough to complete it. However, one person's seed money can be another person's entire budget. Twenty thousand dollars may be only enough to help a $500,000 feature film set up shop; it's more than enough to get you all the way through production and well on your way into post-production.

Other grant programs are designed to help people finish their films. Usually you can't apply for these programs until you have something that actually needs finishing, such as a rough cut workprint of the film.

Regardless of what kind of funding you're asking for, we should point out that there's a trick to getting grant money. Now, this is a secret, so please don't spread it around because then everyone will know about it, and it won't work anymore. In fact, after you read this section, you may want to tear these pages out and eat them, just to be on the safe side.

Ready for the secret? The trick to getting grant money is this: Follow the grant instructions.

Seems obvious, doesn't it? Yet, every day filmmakers submit grant proposals that blithely, even blatantly, ignore the grant instructions. And not just the fine print. Often the big print and the straight-forward stuff as well.

In most cases, these grant requests are turned down. Ignored. Or even mocked. Yes, it's true. Grant panels will openly mock incorrectly filled-out grant proposals (behind closed doors) and then unceremoniously discard them. It happens every day in foundation board rooms across the country.

It's a shame, isn't it?

Well, no, actually, it's great. Because if <u>you</u> fill out the forms correctly and others don't, it will be <u>their</u> applications piling up by the dumpster and <u>yours</u> that gets moved ahead for further review. That's the second secret of getting grant money: Grant committees are just itching for a reason not to give you money. It's not because they don't like you. Or your project. It's because there are so many requests for grant money — and so little money to go around — that they need an easy way to wade through the piles of plastic binders and find those proposals that are completely and totally deserving of their largesse. And the easiest criteria for eliminating contestants from this pool is to toss them out for rules violations.

Let's say they ask for a one-page project summary, and you, in your foolish arrogance, submit a three-page project summary — well, you're outta there! Kiss your grant hopes good-bye! They can now move on to more deserving candidates. Or perhaps their pedantic instructions insist upon three letters of recommendation. And you submit only one. Heads up! Another grant proposal headed for the wastebasket. They shoot, . . . and you don't score!

Submitting your proposal late. Failure to include an innocuous piece of paperwork. Your name at the bottom of the page instead of the top. Who knows what will set off the finicky grant people?

You do, that's who. You now know how to get the edge over most of the people applying for grants. Read the instructions and follow them to the letter! Not everyone will. Filling out the paperwork correctly doesn't guarantee you success, of course, but it does put you head and shoulders above the rest of the crowd.

At that point, your project and its merits will have to speak for themselves. But at least they'll have an audience.

Credit Cards

Yes, we've all been tempted.

You get one or two or five mailings a week with a simple form to fill out that will make any number of delightful and convenient credit cards wing their way to your abode. And you look at the generous credit limits — $1,500 here, $2,000 there, trusting souls offering you $5,000 — and you do the math. Before you know it, you've got a plan.

Here's one word of advice: Don't.

Here are two words of advice: Forget it.

Here are four words of advice: It's a bad idea.

Sure, you've heard the stories about filmmakers who put their films — and their credit ratings — on the line. They rolled the dice, and they won!

Yeah, sure. And we've got some prime real estate in Florida that can make you a fortune. You can have it for a song. And the song goes something like this: Dum, dum, dum, dum, dum.

It's not just the risk factor that concerns us. We all know that filmmaking is a crap shoot. We actually like risks. It's that it just isn't a smart plan.

Let's say that you decide to finance a portion of your film with credit cards, about $15,000 worth. If it's the $15,000 you need to finish the film, you're in trouble. Why? Because even if you can finish the film in a month — mix the soundtrack, conform the negative, and strike a print, cutting great deals at every point — it's going to be at least another month before you sign with a distributor (and that's being very optimistic). And then there's a minimum of three months before they work it into their distribution schedule (again, wild-eyed optimism). And then there's another four to six months before exhibitors send in the money they owe you (optimistic doesn't begin to describe what <u>that</u> is).

That's ten months. You're paying 18% interest (if you're lucky) on $15,000 for ten months — minimum. And what if you can't get the film finished that quickly? And what if you can't find a distributor? And what if, what if, what if, what if?

Of course, if you want to put yourself in some deeply serious trouble, use the $15,000 to <u>shoot</u> the film. That will tack on another six months to a year to that ever-mounting interest monster you've created.

The stories that have circulated about filmmakers charging entire feature films on their credit cards are good copy, but they're also simply bad business, grossly exaggerated, flat out not true, or about filmmakers who like to play "chicken" with freight trains.

If you want to boast that you charged your entire feature on your Bloomingdale's card in your press releases, go right ahead. We won't let on. But the next time you get one of those "You are already pre-approved" mailings, do the smart thing. Just say no.

Scrimping

Scrimping is an unpleasant word. Say it out loud once, and you'll see what we mean. *Scrimping*. It has an unpleasant ring, doesn't it? It sounds like a particularly demeaning part of a fraternity hazing. "Yeah, first we're going to shave their heads, then they have to climb down into the sewers and spend the night scrimping."

Scrimping is not fun. It requires sacrifice. It requires discipline. It requires saying no to common urges, such as the urge to eat out, the urge to buy extravagant non-necessities, the urge to get a new pair of sneakers when your current sneakers are only five years old and the holes in the bottom aren't really all that big as long as you stay out of puddles and wear two pairs of socks, which also have holes in them.

Can a person really scrimp together $30,000? That depends on the person, their income, and the willingness of their significant other to join in the festive mood of scrimping and living like a pauper. As Ben Franklin said, "Two can live as cheaply as one, but they have no idea how cheaply they can live until they try to scrimp together the money for a feature film." We're paraphrasing, of course, but you get the idea.

You may not put together your whole budget this way, but diligent, concerted, and ongoing scrimping can put an extra wad of cash in your pocket every month. And this cash can come in really handy during those down periods when the film isn't draining a lot of money out of you, but a minimal amount of cash flow is still required (such as the middle stages of post-production).

Scrimping can take many forms. You can bring your lunch to work instead of eating out. At two to four dollars a day, that gives you an extra $500 to $1,000 a year. You can stop buying meat regularly and instead find protein in other foods. You can buy food in bulk at co-ops. Or you can stop buying those expensive breakfast cereals and treat yourself to oatmeal, the breakfast of scrimpers!

Even when you're scrimping dutifully, money can still slip away incrementally — a few dollars here, a few dollars there, adding up to a big part of your income. You can use this incrementalism to your advantage, however, by having an extra $50 or $100 deducted from your paycheck every two weeks as part of your tax withholding or simply increase your W-4 tax deduction (creating a sort of forced savings plan). At the end of the year, your refund will include an extra $1,200 or $2,400, which can be enough to get your negative cut, to get your sound mixed, or even to strike a print.

Of course, many would argue that letting Uncle Sam hold your money for a year doesn't earn you an iota of interest, while even the worst bank savings account will pay you something for the honor of holding your money. True enough. The value of the Uncle Sam savings plan, though, is that once you fill out the form, it's out of your hands. The money is taken out every two weeks, whether you think about it or not. Most people don't have the discipline to set aside money every month; if you do, then skip the tax deduction step, and do it yourself. The result is the same — a bit more money toward making or finishing your film.

Another scrimping method is to join a car pool to cut down on parking costs. Changing your own oil in the car will also save you some cash. If your climate (and commute) permits, you can simply get rid of the car and ride a bike to work. You'll save on gas, auto repairs and insurance, and as an added bonus, you'll start to get yourself in shape for the grueling rigors of film production.

They say art is sacrifice. And they also say that scrimping sucks. They're right on both counts.

Borrowing

Another method we employed successfully was borrowing money. Not from banks, of course, because banks aren't foolish enough to lend money to ultra-low-budget film producers. Few sane people are. So we turned to relatives and friends.

Loans allow people who are interested in supporting your efforts an easy entry into the process, without the hassle and cost of going public or establishing a limited partnership.

Our loan process was simple: Each person who lent our company money (ranging from $200 from some nice people, up to $5,000 from some exceptionally swell folks) signed a loan form (a standard promissory note with a few additions) which spelled out the generous terms of the agreement.

The terms were as follows: Each loan was "due" in three years, which meant that at the end of a three-year period, the lender received back their money (plus interest) if it was available, or they could extend the loan, or the value of their loan could be converted into a part ownership in the film.

This arrangement worked well for both parties. For the lenders, it gave them a generous return on their investment — if the film sold and money came in. At the same time, it allowed us to raise capital and to offer a good return on an investment.

Keep in mind, it takes a special sort of lender to make this arrangement work. A patient lender. An understanding lender. A person with disposable income. While there isn't a one of our lenders who wouldn't be tickled pink to receive a repayment check (with interest), they all went into the deal with their eyes — and their wallets — wide open.

Favors

Favors are the currency of independent filmmaking. They're the oil that keeps the gears running smoothly. They're the sip of cool water in the middle of an arid dessert.

Favors can come from anyone and anywhere. A filmmaker with a camera package lets you use it on weekends. A relative gives you the key to their empty cabin, a perfect location for your film. An old friend from junior high who now works at a rental house cuts you a great deal on lighting equipment. Your ex-brother-in-law who has access to some editing equipment comes to your rescue.

While you probably can't produce an entire feature on favors alone, regular trips to the favor bank can save you oodles of cash along the way.

Of course, building up an account at the favor bank doesn't happen overnight. You must invest in the favor bank, just like a savings account at a regular bank. You do favors for other people in your filmmaking community by helping out on a shoot, lending some equipment or advice, and offering your talent and your services. All of these favors and more are an important investment for you and for the rest of the filmmaking community.

By the time you're done with your feature, you'll undoubtedly be overdrawn at the favor bank in a big, big way. So be sure to get back out there and start investing again, offering your help to those who helped you. Your filmmaking community needs you. And, with any luck, you're going to need them again as well.

Found Money

Found money is great. It's that sudden influx of cash that you didn't expect which suddenly makes it possible for you to get your film off the ground.

Found money was a great asset on both our features. The trick with found money, however, is to quickly invest it in your film before you realize that you have some actual need for it — like home repairs, car repairs, or a new pair of sneakers and some new socks.

Found money comes in many shapes and sizes. Here are some situations that could best be described as found money.

• An ailing, distant aunt dies, leaving you $30,000 (after probate and taxes, bless her heart).

• You win the lottery with a ticket you found on the sidewalk while picking up a nickel because you've been scrimping lately to get a film project off the ground.

• The hours you spent diligently preparing and mailing in all those Publishers Clearinghouse Sweepstakes entries finally pay off when your mailman proposes to you, and you discover that he's really an eccentric millionaire with a penchant for independent filmmakers.

Of course, there are moments during the money-raising process that may cause you to feel panic or even desperation. During these moments, you may feel as though you would do anything for money. Anything. There are a few situations that do not qualify in the strictest sense as found money, and we recommend that you don't succumb to these temptations when money gets tight:

• Your distant, ailing aunt asks for a second opinion, and you arrange an appointment for her with Dr. Kevorkian.

• You enter a convenience store wearing a ski mask and carrying a prop pistol, and the goofy night clerk inadvertently gives you all the money in the safe.

• You tell a naive but desperate filmmaker that you can raise the money for his film, but only if he gives you $15,000 cash up front.

* * *

No matter how you slice it, getting the money is one of the hardest parts of the filmmaking process — whether your budget is $30,000 or $30 million.

Needing only a mere $30,000 for your budget provides you with a slight advantage, but on those dark days when no one is returning your calls and your friends and relatives turn icy when you enter the room, it is little solace. And no longer mere.

Along with distribution hell, the money-raising phase of the filmmaking process is one where you feel the least in control. It follows, then, that this is a time when you are the most vulnerable — to compromise, to inertia and entropy, to complete and total surrender. Resist these feelings with the full force of your psyche because giving in to any of them spells death for your project — and for a bit of your soul.

As Winston Churchill so stoically put it, "Never give up. Never give up. Never give up." If the Prime Minister gig hadn't panned out for him, he was a man who had what it takes to be an ultra-low-budget film producer.

So hang in there. You never know when you're going to find that lottery ticket, persuade that investor, or receive a knowing wink and a smile from your mail carrier.

PRE-PRODUCTION
"Being Compulsive Is Not A Bad Thing.
I Know. I Double-Checked."

He's making a list and checking it twice. Yes, Virginia, Santa Claus would be a welcome addition to any ultra-low-budget film's pre-production team. He's cheerful, leaves nothing to chance, gets things done on schedule, and is able to perform miracles.

On our films, we found that the producer, director, and unit production manager formed a triumvirate that was the guiding force of the production. These are the only three people who see all aspects of production, so it's natural that they do the pre-production planning and follow through. These three members of your production team should be as compulsive as possible.

It's a pity that therapists around the world are trying to control compulsive behavior when independent film makers are looking for that very talent in their crews. (Hint: look for people with clean desks and neatly stacked paper clips, organized by size, color, and age.)

You may want to add the director of photography to this team because so much of the planning is around creating an image on film. You may want to include the screenwriter, who can offer insights into the vision and the intent of the story. In our case, we served as producer and director and were also the screenwriters, so we always had screenwriter input. We included our director of photography in some of our pre-production meetings, but not all because there are hundreds of logistical details that we didn't want the director of photography to think about. She or he will have more than enough to worry about on your production just trying to make sure you've gotten usable and, hopefully, artistic images on the film.

These compulsive three, four, or five people have some basic production decisions to make before the meat of pre-production begins.

Film or Video?

The first big decision will be largely dictated by money, so it may have been decided in the budgeting process. However, debate about video or film may still continue at this pre-production stage. It did on our first production. We were both very familiar with working on video, and John as director felt it was important to be able to check performances, image composition, lighting, and such on a video playback. Working on film requires a lot of faith in what happened on a piece of film that you won't see for days or weeks. It's rather nerve-wracking when you have your life savings invested. We also had access to some video equipment, and tape is cheap. The video sirens continually called to us.

We ultimately decided on film when we gave serious thought to distribution. John had experienced total rejection of a previous feature film done on video when he took it to distributors. You just can't get in the door with distributors for a feature film unless it was shot on film. There's a perceived professionalism that comes with a film production. Even if you spent as much money and creative effort on your video, it will be viewed as an amateur effort. ("My granddaughter uses a camcorder, too. She's only seven.") At this budget level, you're already hanging onto the ragged bottom fringe of the film industry. You can't afford to have any extra disadvantages. Shooting on film turned out to be the right decision. Almost without exception, the first words from a potential distributor's mouth were "Was it shot on film?" It was the secret password that let us in the club house door. Without it, we would have been automatically blackballed. If you're serious about breaking into feature films, don't even consider video. The best you will get is a showing on your local cable-access station.

We even rejected using video-assist playback equipment on the 16mm camera. It was expensive to rent, and production grinds to a halt while the video is checked. We couldn't afford either one.

Having decided on film, you'll now get to face a couple of other format decisions. We'll tell you what we decided, but you'll have to assess your personal situation to decide what's best for you.

Film Formats

At the time we were starting "Resident Alien" in 1989, the Super-8mm film format was being resurrected from the grave by some upstart filmmakers. They shot in this format and then used top-of-the-line video transfer technology to put their edited productions on video. Films like "Jet Benny" and "A Polish Vampire in Burbank" had some real success with this approach, and they are well done. Music videos were also incorporating Super-8mm footage. This resulted in the availability of some low-cost cameras and fullcoat sound recorders that gave Super-8mm productions many of the professional production and editing capabilities of 16mm and 35mm. Even Super-8mm film frames have more image information on them than the highest quality video frame, and the film-to-video transfer technology was for the first time able to get that information to the video image.

We gave serious thought to Super 8mm. It's pretty enticing to buy the production equipment for the cost of renting 16mm or 35mm equipment. But after talking the Post Group in California, which was doing most of the Super-8mm video transfers at that time, and speaking with film people who had worked with the new equipment, we decided not to do Super 8mm. The reasons: 1) At that time there was no negative form of Super 8mm available, so you had to edit on your master footage, unless you transferred to video for editing. 2) The small size of the Super 8mm frame means that you have only one to two f-stops of latitude for errors in exposure, and you need more light to get usable images. 3) At that time there were problems keeping the sound in sync with picture during video transfer unless the sound was edited on 16mm fullcoat. 4) During production, it is harder to get a cast and crew to treat a production professionally when working with Super-8mm equipment.

Because we didn't want to subject our original footage to scratches during editing, because we knew that there would be exposure errors at our demonic production pace, because out-of-sync sound was unacceptable, and because we needed a cast and crew who gave us their professional best, we decided to shoot on 16mm film. It gave us all the professional capabilities of 35mm, and as a format falling from favor for production, we had access to cheap equipment. The lighter and smaller equipment allowed us to pick up and move to the next shot rapidly. And it fit our budget. We have never been sorry we chose this as our working format.

It should be noted that Super-8mm negative is now available, and the sound-sync problems are solved. However, the exposure latitude and the perceived "amateur" status of the format would still cause us to choose 16mm.

The Super-16mm format has also ascended after many years of limited use. While this format creates a larger frame area for better image quality, it's not a good fit with a $30,000 budget. Super-16mm production and editing equipment is scarce, and therefore will not likely be rented for bargain rates. Inexpensive second-unit cameras like a Bolex need expensive modifications to shoot Super-16mm frames. And ultimately, the improvement in the final video-transfer image is marginal, considering the extra costs.

Despite the changes in Super 8mm and in the availability of Super 16mm, we still think 16mm is the most cost-effective professional format for our purposes.

Shooting Ratio

Coupled with this decision was the shooting ratio for the production. It was pretty much a no-brainer. We couldn't afford to buy or process more film than a 3:1 shooting ratio. We also didn't have time to do more setups for shots than that in a day. We knew that we'd get some shots in a 2:1 or 1:1 ratio which would allow 4:1 coverage for a few scenes.

Publicity

Another decision was to publicize or not to publicize. Whether tis nobler to suffer the questions of reporters and spectators or to work in relative obscurity and peace. We chose not to publicize our project locally while we were in production for a couple reasons.

Our budget demanded a non-union production, and we were up front with our cast and crew about this. Several good people who were with the union chose to join us, and we did not want to get them in dutch with the union reps by getting a lot of attention while shooting. (Once you're done, nobody really knows if it was a union shoot or not unless they watch for the union "bug" at the end of the credits.) Most union reps realize that non-union work is where many union actors get their beginning credentials, allowing them to get bigger union work later. So they usually won't interfere if you don't call and ask them if it's okay to use union people on a non-union shoot (they have to say no) and if you don't rub their noses in it with a lot of publicity (they'll feel obliged to interfere; it's their job).

We also decided not to seek publicity because it invariably attracts reporters asking questions and taking photos, both of which take the time of a cast or crew person who needs to be working. Reporters and other spectators also can create sound problems and get into shots. Suddenly, you need to have someone controlling the public, too. You may even get the attention of official types who will feel the need to ask you for permits to use a public location you're shooting in. Now, whenever you're shooting out of doors, you can expect visits from the curious. Usually it's just the neighbors or a couple passers-by who'll get bored soon enough and move on. If you publicize it in the local paper, you could see dozens or hundreds of visitors. That's not a good thing for a production that doesn't have time for interruptions. And since we were in editing for more than a year after shooting, we wouldn't have benefited much from that early publicity anyway.

However, you can benefit from a little national publicity. The two major industry trade papers, *Variety* and *The Hollywood Reporter,* both feature weekly "Production Listings," which highlight all the films currently in production, including their title, start date, primary cast, and major crew positions. Listing your production in the trade papers provides a number of benefits:

- It establishes a start date for your film, which can come in handy when someone challenges the legality of your title. This happened on "Resident Alien," and it was nice to be able to point to a published start date when someone questioned who had the title first — even though you can't copyright titles.

- It alerts distributors and sales representatives to your existence, and the more aggressive of them will begin contacting you about when they can see your film.

- It introduces you to other film professionals, such as composers, editors, and actors — many of whom are looking for work. While the vast majority will be turned off once they learn what your budget is, you may still find one or two who are looking for the experience or are simply turned on by your enthusiasm.

- Finally, it's a kick to see your little film listed along side the latest productions starring Hollywood's biggest guns.

To get your film listed, simply call the papers and ask for a production guide listing form. We've put the information under "Other Resources" in the appendix.

Time For A Breakdown

After struggling with all these pre-production decisions, you may feel ready for a breakdown. That's okay. Pre-production is the only place it's allowed. In fact, it's required.

We're talking about the next pre-production step, the script breakdown. This is where your carefully crafted script, with its interwoven story lines and its fully integrated characters and its gradually building emotional content, is brutally dissected. When the script breakdown process is done, the script will be lying there in front of you sliced and diced into its most elemental parts, all carefully labeled so you can plan your shooting schedule.

Actually, this process is a peaceful task that's perfect for the detail-oriented personalities on your crew, in our case the director, producer, and unit production manager. This is sitting-at-the-kitchen-table work that requires five distinct steps — four if you cut corners. As usual, we made a few changes to the standard Hollywood technique for breaking down scripts; some steps were simply unnecessary for such a small production. We've listed a very good reference source in the bibliography if you want to learn the Cadillac of script breakdown. We're giving you the Geo-Metro version.

Step 1: Marking Script Segments

To start this process, you'll need a shooting script with scene headings that list scene number, interior or exterior, location, and day or night. You may have read or been told not to put scene numbers on a script you're trying to sell. True, but now that script is sold to you, and you need those numbers. Scene headings should look like this: "23. EXT. ROCKY CLIFF -DAY" or "125. INT. SHERIFF'S CAR ON ROAD - NIGHT." If you've never understood why this was the required format for scene headings, you will after you've finished breaking down a script.

"Okay class, pencils up, ruler in hand. You may work in groups." Draw pencil lines across the page at the end of each scene that occurs at the same location and the same time. (Use pencil unless you never make mistakes. Wait, you're the one planning to make a movie for pocket change, aren't you? Definitely use pencil.) Now look at the length of this scene, and mark in the margin next to the scene number how many eighths of a page this scene takes.

We know there's a lot of math anxiety in the world, especially when it comes to fractions. Far be it from us to make this a more anxiety-ridden world. Brief math refresher: A whole page would be eight eighths (8/8). Two pages would be 16/8. A half page is 4/8. A quarter page would be 2/8. And an eighth of a page would be 1/8. Anything less than an eighth of a page is still considered 1/8. Example: A scene running two-and-a-quarter pages is 8/8 + 8/8 + 2/8 = 18/8. Write "18/8" in the margin. (Math wizards, thanks for your patience. Just in case you're feeling smug, remember how many dates this skill got you in high school.)

As you break your script into scenes, watch for hidden scenes lurking within scene descriptions. Read the following scene description, and look for the hidden scenes.

24. EXT. BOX CANYON -DAY

Joe leaps from his horse and leads it to a sheltered spot among the rocks. He then scrambles up the loose rocks to the rim of the canyon. Removing his hat to avoid detection, he peers over the rocks. In the distance, there is a column of dust rising from the surrounding desert. Joe pulls a telescope from his saddle bags and looks again. Magnified, the dust column reveals itself to be Texas Rangers riding single file to hide their numbers. Joe quickly closes the telescope and runs for his horse.

Did you spot them? The first hidden scene is the distant shot of a dust column rising from the desert floor. The second is the closer shot of the Texas Rangers. Because these shots are actually at a different location than the main scene, they need their own scene heading. This is a common oversight in scriptwriting, and you should be watching for it. For the purpose of planning your shooting schedule, hidden scenes may happen on completely different days and locations than the main scene, so you need to break them out separately.

We've found hidden scenes in a variety of places: Shots of a television showing an image (the image needs to be shot separately); point-of-view shots of distant scenes; audio voice-overs on radios, phones, and intercoms (no image to shoot, but you'll need to record the sound of the performers somewhere during your production schedule); and scenes that occur in doorways or looking out windows. This last item may not seem to fit, but consider the situations of using different locations for the interior and exterior of a building in your script. If a scene is viewed from inside the doorway, it is an interior at one location. If it's viewed from outside the doorway, it is an exterior at a different location. Unless you know that you'll be using just one location, list two scenes, an interior and an exterior.

When we found these hidden scenes without scene numbers, we just added a letter to the main scene number to designate them. In the scene above, the dust column shot would be "24a." and the Texas Ranger shot would be "24b."

After you get into it, this is pretty easy, restful work. Enjoy it while you can. It helps to have more than one person working on it so you can discuss and decide how to shoot any ambiguous hidden scenes. Just plug ahead at this task until all script pages are broken down into scenes and lengths.

Here's an example:

```
                    FADE IN.

   1/8              1.  EXT.  CLIFFS - DAWN
                    The sun is just beginning to cut into dawn's haze.  The only
                    sounds are the WAVES HITTING THE SHORE and the occasional, QUIET
                    CALL OF A SEAGULL.  PERIOD MUSIC is heard faintly from a car
                    radio.  A red Mustang, with a hang glider strapped to its roof,
                    pulls off the road.  MUSIC STOPS as the car's ENGINE SHUTS OFF.

                    BOB gets out of the car.  He is twenty-two, and dressed in old,
                    faded jeans and a baseball jacket.  He fumbles with an
   1/8    1A        instruction manual, tosses it aside, and begins to assemble the
                    hang glider.  He pulls some tools out of the trunk.

                    On the Mustang's bumper, a bumper sticker that once read, "Honk
                    If You Love Jesus."  It now reads: "Honk If You Love Bob."

   1/8              2.  LATER:  The glider is assembled and straped to Bob's back.
                    Bob pulls out a large paperback book, still in its shrink-wrap.
                    He tears it open.

                    The book's cover reads, "Hang Gliding For Beginners."  Bob pages
                    through the book, rapidly.  He quickly loses interest and tucks
                    the book under his arm, takes a deep breath, then he runs to the
                    edge of the cliff ...

   1/8              3.  BOB'S POV:  We leave the cliff, soaring over the water,
                    gliding, smoothly and elegantly.

   1/8              4.  Bob, in the air.  He dips, he turns, he glides. He pages
                    through the book, getting the hang of it.

                    He looks ahead and registers an expression of sudden concern.
                    He flips to the back of the book to check the index.  The book
                    slips out of his hands.

   1/8              5.  The book falls, tumbling end over end, down and down, faster
                    and faster.  It lands roughly on an outcropping of rocks.  The
                    torn PAGES FLAP OMINOUSLY in the breeze.

   1/8              6.  We return to a wide-shot of the cliff, showing Bob's red
                    mustang patiently waiting his return.

                    FADE OUT.

   1/8              7.  The screen is black.  A title comes up:  "Ten Years Later."
                    The title fades out.  A door is opened and we see that we're in:
```

PAGES FROM SCRIPT, WITH SCENES BROKEN DOWN

Step 2: Script Breakdown Pages

Almost all Hollywood films do this next step, though it's one that we skipped. We were so compulsive and detail conscious as a team and our scenes were simple enough that we felt this step was work we wouldn't use. Turns out we were right. But that was us. If you don't have the kind of production overseers (producer, director, unit production manager) who ask each other three times if they remembered the yellow sweatshirt for scene 16A, then you might want to consider doing this step. It will help you keep track of the myriad details when you get to the set.

This step is more simple, slightly tedious work. You will go through your script again, marking the key elements of each scene. You can underline these elements with colored pencils or highlight them with colored markers. Pick a different color for each of the following categories:

- Cast - speaking roles
- Extras or stunt performers
- Action props - cars, planes, go-carts, horses, etc.
- Props
- Wardrobe
- Special effects, animation, special camera gear
- Atmosphere - raining, foggy, sunrise (These are all difficult to achieve on a limited budget with limited time. Your script should have avoided these items or used them only as scenes that can be shot by the second unit. Day and night by themselves are going to pose enough problems for you.)

You already have scene headings that designate interior or exterior, location, day or night, and length of scene so there's no need to mark these items.

At the same time you are marking these items, you can be filling out the information on the actual script breakdown pages. A breakdown page lists all these pertinent details about each scene. When they are all done, put them in a three-ring binder for your unit production manager. On the set when the shooting schedule calls for doing scene 16a, the unit production manager will flip to the breakdown page for that scene and be able to see that the yellow sweatshirt is needed. All in all, a useful organizational tool. We didn't really need it ourselves, but there was at least one occasion when it would have saved us some clothing confusion.

Here's what a script breakdown page should look like:

Page # __1__

Scene Breakdown

Production Title __"Beyond Bob"__

Scene # 1	Script Page # 1	Length In Pages $1/8$
Location / Set Cliff near river	Sequence Bob hang gliding	Time Period 10 years ago
Day or Night Day	Interior or Exterior Interior	Season Summer

Scene Synopsis
Bob drives up in his car with hang glider tied on top. He removes hang glider and gets tools from trunk. We see "Honk if you love Bob" bumper sticker.

Cast Bob — Michael Levin	Extras / Stunt Performers None
Action Props (Vehicles, Etc.) & Animals Bob's car (without rust) Hang glider	Props Tools Bumper sticker Ropes to tie on hang glider

Wardrobe (Cast and Extras)
Bob's costume:
    Letter Jacket
    T-shirt
    Jeans
    Tennis shoes
	Special Effects, Animation,
	Special Camera Gear
	
	Second-Unit Camera (MOS)

Atmosphere (Rain, Fog, Etc.) Early morning sun	Set Construction None

In addition to filling out the script breakdown pages, some people total the number of pages (in 1/8ths) for which major elements are needed: cast, locations, day, night, props, wardrobe, etc. It was less work for us to do this in a later step. The only reason to do it now is if you need to know how long you'll be using some specialty wardrobe. Wardrobe won't show up on the production-scheduling items that are next.

Step 3: *Making The Strips and The Production Board*

This is nothing like cruising the strip. It's much more fun. Here's where you begin to put every single scene of your movie on little strips of tag board, so they can be sorted into a production schedule. The first thing you could do is waste $100 to $150 buying a commercially-produced production board and strips. Unless you are being paid more than $50 an hour during your free time, don't do it. You can make your own for about $20 in materials (which you may be able to scrounge) and two hours' time.

Yes, it's arts-and-crafts time, class. The materials you need are 15 full-page plastic sheet protectors (top loading); a ruler; a fine-point permanent pen; double-faced adhesive tape; lightweight, white tag board stock; a paper cutter (optional); a penknife and straightedge; and enough dimes to make a couple photocopies.

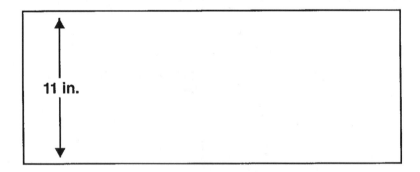

A. Cut the tag stock into 11-inch widths. Keep it as long as possible to save time in the next step. You have enough tag stock if you could make about 14 pages that are 8 1/2 inches x 11 inches.

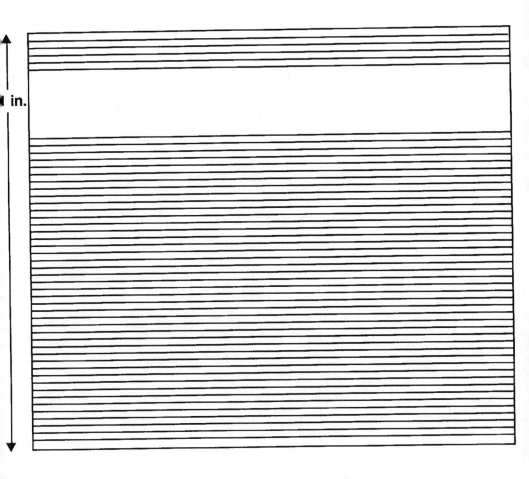

MARKING LINES ON THE TAG STOCK

B. Next you need to mark lines on the sheets of tag stock as shown in the illustration. Starting from the top, measure down and draw five lines 3/16 inches apart. Next measure down two inches from the last line, and draw the next line. Then continue drawing lines that are 3/16 inches apart for the rest of the page. This will be about 40 more lines.

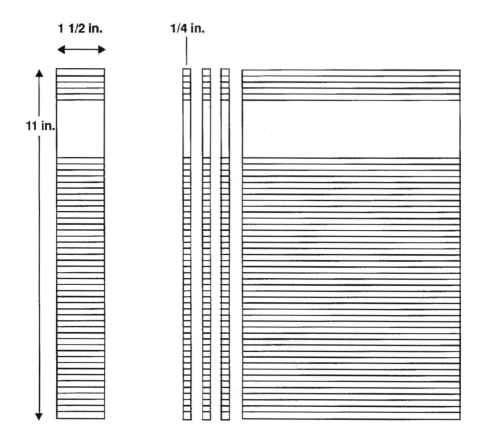

"CUTTING STRIPS FROM LINED TAG STOCK"

C. As shown in the illustration, cut off one strip from your tag stock that is 1 1/2-inches wide and 11-inches long. This will become the header for your production board pages. Now cut up the rest of your tag stock into strips that are 1/4-inch wide and 11-inches long. These will be your scene strips. You can use a pen knife and straight edge to do this, or you can use a paper cutter. Either way, this task is a little mind numbing, so don't daydream and trim off any appendages. You'll end up with a big pile of little strips.

D. It's time to create the header for each page of your production board. (Actually, this should be call a "sider" because it goes on the left side of the page.) You'll make this by labeling major elements of your film on the 1 1/2-inch x 11-inch strip you just made. These elements will then be used to breakdown the scenes in your script. Start out by labeling the top five slots as follows (see illustration):

- Breakdown Page Number
- Day or Night
- Location or Studio
- Exterior or Interior
- Number of Pages

The next slot on the header is a wide one. On the scene strips, this will be used for scene descriptions. However, on the header strip, use this area to list the title of your production and the names of the director, producer, and unit production manager. That way if you lose your production schedule on a bus, the person who finds it will know who is in deep trouble.

The next narrow slot should be labeled as follows:

- Scene Number

Follow this slot with the important

Breakdown Page #	
Day or Night	
Location or Studio	
Exterior or Interior	
# of Pages	
"Resident Alien"	
Dir. J. Gaspard	
Prod. D. Newton	
Prod. Mgr. K. Erickson	
Scene #	
Cal	1
Leslie	2
Allen	3
Davis	4
Jack	5
Bunson	6
Verner	7
Joyce	8
Doris	9
Deputy	10
Tish	11
Naom	12
Reporters	13
Action Props Cal's Truck	14
Leslie's Car	15
Jack's 4x4	16
Davis' Sedan	17
Locations Motel Ext.	18
Roof Ext.	19
Leslie's Apt.	20
Cal's Apt.	21
Allen's Apt.	22
Newton's Land	23
Sheriff's Office	24
Laundry Rm	25
Vacant Lot	26
Bathroom	27
UFO Detector	A
UFO Debris	B
Alien Spacesuit	C
Geiger Counter	D
Metal Detector	E
45° Effects Box	F
Second Unit Shot	G
Miniature-Animation	H
Monster Head	I

scene elements from the next list. These slots should be numbered from top to bottom on the right-hand side of the header strip. To the left of each number, write the name of one of the important scene elements. Don't repeat any numbers because they will be used as shorthand identifiers for each individual item. Fill in these slots with the following:

- All character names
- Extras (this is just one slot)
- All action props (cars, motorcycles, hang gliders, etc.)
- All locations

The next list of items should be identified with letters from top to bottom on the right-hand side of the header strip. Write the name of the item to the left of the letter.

- All specialty props
- All special effects, animation, or special camera gear

If you found yourself uncertain about what to list under some of the categories on the header strip, you may want to go back and do Step 2: Script Breakdown Pages. As you mark the key elements of the script, keep a list of every new item, and use that list to fill out the header strip.

Now you have the completed header strip for your production boards. Make about 15 photocopies, cut them out, and use double-faced tape to attach them to tag stock the same size as the header strip. If you're really into wasting time, hand write 15 more of these header strips instead.

To finish your low-cost production board, use the double-faced tape to attach a header strip inside each plastic sheet protector along the left-hand side. Save out a couple header strips for holding alongside the scene strips as you fill them out. Now that you've completed your production board, you're ready to move on to making the scene strips that will fill the board.

E. The tag-stock strips in the pile you made ultimately are going to represent every scene of your movie, so pick up your script, and get ready to write. This is another good group activity for the leaders of your production. Just make sure everyone is filling out the scene strips the same way, and make sure you don't skip any pages or miss any scenes that cross multiple pages. (And for you punsters, yes, you do need a scene strip for a strip scene.)

Hold a scene strip next to the header strip, and you'll see that the top five slots on each strip represent the information that's in each scene heading and in the information that you marked on your script. For the Breakdown Page Number on your scene strip, write in the script page where the scene begins. Write in "D" or "N" for Day or Night, "L" or "S" for Location or Studio, and "I" or "E" for Interior or Exterior. (For our productions, the only shots that weren't location were credits and special-effects shots that we did in a studio.) Next write in the page length that you've written down by each scene heading on your script,

Breakdown Page #		41
Day or Night		D
Location or Studio		L
Exterior or Interior		I
# of Pages		¹¹/8
"Resident Alien" Dir. J. Gaspard Prod. D. Newton Prod. Mgr. K. Erickson	Leslie looks at Cal's books	
Scene #		90
Cal	1	1
Leslie	2	2
Allen	3	
Davis	4	
Jack	5	
Bunson	6	
Verner	7	
Joyce	8	
Doris	9	
Deputy	10	
Tish	11	
Naom	12	
Reporters	13	
Action Props Cal's Truck	14	
Leslie's Car	15	
Jack's 4x4	16	
Davis' Sedan	17	
Locations Motel Ext.	18	
Roof Ext.	19	
Leslie's Apt.	20	
Cal's Apt.	21	21
Allen's Apt.	22	
Newton's Land	23	
Sheriff's Office	24	
Laundry Rm	25	
Vacant Lot	26	
Bathroom	27	
UFO Detector	A	A
UFO Debris	B	B
Alien Spacesuit	C	
Geiger Counter	D	
Metal Detector	E	
45° Effects Box	F	
Second Unit Shot	G	
Miniature-Animation	H	
Monster Head	I	

such as "3/8." Don't forget to fill out scene strips for those hidden scenes you've found, too.

As you're filling out these strips, you'll want to color code them with a highlight marker to make the upcoming sorting easier. Pick four different colors to represent day-exterior, day-interior, night-exterior, and night-interior. Common practice is to do day-interior as white (uncolored), night-interior as blue, day-exterior as yellow, and night-exterior as green. Just use the appropriate marker to color the long slot where you'll be writing the scene description.

Next move to the long slot, and write a short phrase that describes the main content of the scene, something like "Cal wakes up" or "Davis' car drives up to motel." Then write in the scene number in the next slot down.

Now that you've gotten the basic scene setup coded onto your strip, you need to identify its component parts. Follow down the strip and mark the number of each character who appears in the scene in the appropriate slot on the strip. Use the number rather than just a check mark, so you can tell at a glance that character #3 is in the scene. This is also the reason not to repeat any numbers. When we had a scene where a character was only present as an off-scene voice, we still wrote in the character's number and added a V.O. for Voice-Over or O.S. for Off Screen so we were sure to record this dialogue. Many times you'll want the same room ambiance for the off-scene voice, so you'll want to record it at the same time as, or immediately after, you shoot the scene.

Continue on down the strip, listing the appropriate number or letter for extras, action props, locations, specialty props, special effects, animation, or special camera gear needed for that particular scene. When you get to the bottom of the first scene strip, move on to the next 200 or so strips you have to do. It's not gene splicing, but you have to concentrate and envision the scene and how it's going to be shot.

When you finish going through the entire script, you'll have a pile of tag-stock strips that looks like shredder residue at the CIA. The next step is to make some sense of these color-and-number-coded strips. (Time-saving tip: If you share your dwelling with a pet or child or roommate who likes to chew cardboard, lock the door.)

Step 4: Sorting The Strips

Here's where the hours of tedious coding start to pay off and those enigmatic steps are recognized for their brilliant usefulness. You're going to sort through your strips several times, so clear some table space or shovel the debris of life from the living-room floor.

Begin by sorting your big pile of strips into smaller piles for each shooting location you will be using. Because you have a separate number for each location, you will be able to just glance at a strip and see if it has a number 20, representing "Leslie's apartment." After doing this sorting, you should have a pile for each location and one additional pile for studio shots. Already that mass of unshot scenes should be starting to look more manageable.

Next, sort the scene strips for each location into three piles, Interiors (both day and night), Exteriors/Day, and Exteriors/Night. Moving outside to do exterior shots will require several changes in camera and lighting setup as well as time to move the equipment, cast, and crew, so you will want to group these scenes for your location together. For scheduling, you'll need to know how much of your exterior shooting has to be done before the sun goes down and what scenes can't be started until after sundown, so day and night exteriors are separated. We didn't separate the interior scenes into day and night on "Resident Alien" because we avoided showing windows and modified our lighting to create either circumstance. If you want to or need to show windows with day or night outside, as we did with "Beyond Bob," you should sort for Interior/Day and Interior/Night also.

Now that you have each location separated and divided up by lighting and equipment changes, your next step will be to figure out the most efficient shooting schedule. Now is a good time to put the strips into the production-board pages that you've made (the plastic sheet protectors). Later you'll put a strip of double-faced tape inside the top of the plastic sheet protector to hold the strips in place, but for now, you want to be able to shift them around. Just lay the sheet flat so things don't slide around. Start putting the strips in the production board pages, grouping them by location and Interior, Exterior/Day, Exterior/Night. You can turn over a blank scene strip to use as a divider between sections.

Step 5: Laying Out The Shooting Days

This is the point where your director and unit production manager must be involved if they haven't been so far. You want to organize the shots in your production schedule 1) so you don't waste time setting up scenes or moving equipment, 2) so you move efficiently from one location to the next, 3) so cast members aren't sitting around for long periods waiting to do scenes, 4) so you help the cast give the best performances possible, 5) so you get the necessary number of pages done each day, and 6) so you accommodate any outside scheduling issues.

It's time for some examples.

Scheduling for scene setup: For our film "Resident Alien," we used a single motel room to represent the three different motel rooms that were about one-half of our shooting schedule. It made sense to set up shop at this motel room and shoot all scenes there before moving on, so we spent two entire weekends shooting at this location. In redressing the room for the three different settings it represented, we started with the setting that required the most changes to the room. We shot every scene that occurred in that setup before we changed the look of the room. Each subsequent redressing of the room removed more props and furniture until we got to the final redressing in which the room was virtually bare.

Scheduling for location: "Resident Alien" called for a variety of short outdoor scenes at different locations, some of them 50 miles apart. To avoid wasting a lot of production time driving to locations, we would shoot major scenes that were closest to these locations for most of the day. Then towards the end of the production day, we'd hit the road with the cast and crew to pick up these short scenes. That way when we finished, we were already packed up for the day and ready to go to the next day's shooting location.

Scheduling for actors: We scheduled our shooting so that we started the day with all the scenes using just one of our principal actors, letting the other actors sleep late. We did scenes that called for six actors toward the middle of the day, and then shifted to scenes involving a different principal actor at the end of the day. This way, actors could leave earlier, when their scenes were done, allowing them to get more rest in a weekend of 14-hour shooting days. (The crew was fried, but they didn't have to look good on camera.)

If possible, it's nice to shoot scenes in their actual order as much as possible. Try not to have performers jump from a tense, angry scene directly into a humorously romantic moment.

Also consider the time for makeup changes between scenes. It's hard to go from a bed-head look to knock-dead glamorous in a few minutes' time. Generally, wardrobe changes can be quick, so the only ones we considered much during scheduling were those requiring elaborate costumes or major makeup changes.

Scheduling to stay on schedule: You'll need to consider how many pages of script you have to shoot each day. This is easy to calculate. If you have a 90-page script in standard screenplay format and you know that you'll be shooting on four weekends (eight days) and four Friday evening (figure 1/4 day each), you have to shoot 90 pages in nine days. You need to plan for at least ten pages of shooting per day . . . and 11 or 12 would be better, so you don't get squeezed at the end if production gets delayed. Just count up the page lengths on the scene strips to see how many pages you're placing in each day's schedule. Be sure to consider how many are night shots and how many are day shots, so you don't schedule yourself to do 14 hours of night exteriors on the heels of a full day of daylight shooting.

Set a fast pace early on so the crew and cast know how quickly they must work. Hollywood productions average two pages per day, so you're going to be working in a very fast lane doing 11 or 12. It's best to make the scenes early in your production schedule some of the easier ones. This lets your cast and crew get used to working as a team at a break-neck pace before they face the more challenging scenes.

Scheduling around other schedules: If you have problems with the availability of an actor, a prop vehicle, a location, or even a time of day such as sunset, be sure to consider this when setting up the shots you'll do each day.

As you're probably understanding, setting up the actual shooting schedule is going to require trial and error. Just take a try at it, and have your director, unit production manager, and producer look it over and make changes based on problems they see. We set up our shooting schedule in an evening. We also hit some weather problems during production, so we had to move some shots to different days in the production schedule. Using a production board, this was an easy matter of moving a few scene strips to another page.

Once you've settled on your schedule, put a strip of double-faced tape inside the top of the sheet protector to hold the scene strips in their order. Now you can take these pages and make photocopies for your production crew.

"Resident Alien"
Dir. J. Gaspard
Prod. D. Newton
Prod. Mgr. K. Erickson

10/1/89

Field	#	90	91	94	11B	2	39	106	106	106	106	121	127	151	128	175	178	180	182	176	110
Breakdown Page #		41	42	44	54	1	17	53	53	53	53	63	67	76	89	89	90	90	92	89	54
Day or Night		D	D	D	N	D	D	N	N	N	N	D	D	D	N	N	N	N	N	N	N
Location or Studio		L	L	L	L	L	L	L	L	L	L	L	L	L	L	S	L	L	L	L	L
Exterior or Interior		I	I	I	I	I	I	I	I	I	I	I	I	I	E	E	E	E	E	E	I
# of Pages		11/8	9/8	14/8	22/8	13/8	7/8	3/8	3/8	3/8	3/8	12/8	14/8	4/8	1/8	1/8	4/8	2/8	1/8	1/8	1/8
Scene description		Leslie looks at Cal's books	Leslie and Cal discuss UFO's	Leslie's come on to Cal	Cal and Leslie on Phone	First view Cal's Apt, Leslie Bursts in	Leslie's bandaged hands dial phone	Cal's POV – Alien attack	Leslie's POV – Alien Approaches	Cal bursts through door	Alien POV – Attacking Cal	Cal on Phone – L & A enter	Cal's Apt – Manuscript	Cal, Leslie, Allen in Cal's Apt.	Allen on Road before UFO	UFO over Alien – still cut out – Still photo	Allen greets Naom & Tish	Allen with Naom & Tish	Allen, Tish, Naom leave	Allen's arrive	Faces for Allen's dream
Scene #		90	91	94	11B	2	39	106	106	106	106	121	127	151	128	175	178	180	182	176	110
Cal	1	1			1	1				1	1	1	1	1							
Leslie	2	2	2	2	2	2	2					2	2	2							
Allen	3							3	3			3	3	3	3	3	3	3	3		
Davis	4																				
Jack	5																				
Bunson	6																				
Verner	7																				
Joyce	8																				
Doris	9																				
Deputy	10																				
Tish	11																11	11	11	11	11
Naom	12																12	12	12	12	12
Reporters	13																				
Action Props Cal's Truck	14																				
Leslie's Car	15																				
Jack's 4x4	16																				
Davis' Sedan	17																				
Locations Motel Ext.	18																				
Roof Ext.	19																				
Leslie's Apt.	20						20	20	20	20	20										
Cal's Apt.	21	21	21	21	21	21						21	21	21							
Allen's Apt.	22																				
Newton's Land	23														23	23	23	23	23	23	23
Sheriff's office	24																				
Laundry Rm	25																				
Vacant Lot	26																				
Bathroom	27																				
UFO Detector	A	A	A	A	A	A						A	A	A							
UFO Debris	B	B	B	B	B							B	B	B							
Alien Spacesuit	C																C	C	C	C	
Geiger Counter	D																				
Metal Detector	E																				
45° Effects Box	F																			F	
Second Unit shot	G															(G)					
Miniature-Animation	H															(H)					
Monster Head	I							I	I												

A production schedule obviously can't be done in complete isolation from your other pre-production tasks. To really set a schedule, you'll need to know where your locations are, when you can use vehicles and major props, who the cast members are, and when cast members are available. You can try to get these items figured out before you begin your production schedule, or you can set a tentative schedule and make modifications as these details are settled. We did a bit of both. We had found some locations and knew our cast's schedules, but we didn't arrange for some locations or vehicles until after we'd set a tentative schedule. Sometimes it's easier to get permission to use a prop or a vehicle if you can say specifically when you need it. This leads us to another task that you'll have to undertake sometime during pre-production — a treasure hunt.

Props, Action Props, Locations, and Assistance

The kind of treasure you're after is free, photogenic, and convenient. In the next chapters, we'll describe how to find a cast and crew made up of diamonds in the rough. Right now your task is to find several hundred-thousand dollars' worth of personal goods and real estate, just to borrow for a while. This work will have a lot of bearing on the final quality of your film. We were given full access to a beautiful suburban home as the major setting for our film "Beyond Bob" by a tolerant and gracious homeowner (John's sister). This completely furnished, attractive, multiple-room location easily added $200,000 to the apparent production value of our finished film. And it didn't cost us a dime. You can get the same kind of screen value for vehicles, props, and wardrobe that you borrow. This is part of the reason distributors thought "Beyond Bob" cost $900,000 to make.

So where do you find these hidden treasures? And how do you get permission to use them? Answers: Lots of places and by asking.

There's a theory that you are no more than six relationships removed from anyone in the world. This means that a friend of a client of an uncle of a girlfriend of the mailman of a neighbor of your lead actress owns the lime-green Corvette you need to borrow. We found vehicles, houses, wardrobe, camera gear, specialty equipment for props and effects, and furniture just by asking the friends and relatives of our cast and crew.

Start by making a master list of all the locations, vehicles, wardrobe, and props that you need, and then put the word out. You'll be pleased and surprised how willing people are to help you find what you need to make your movie. Feature films are the conjurings of modern-day wizards like you, and people want to catch hold of your cloak in hopes of feeling a bit of the magic. We even received unexpected help from other film professionals who knew all about the tricks behind the magic. Your vision of your finished movie has the power to bring to you the people and the resources you'll need to finish the project. So spread your vision around, and let people know that they can be part of it by loaning you the things you need.

The people affected by your magical vision are not just friends and family. Complete strangers who happen to own businesses that are perfect locations for your filming will succumb to your spell. Just say the magic words, "We're making a movie, and your business would be an ideal setting." Our experience is that business people don't agree to help with a movie because of the potential publicity. They agree because they personally want to be connected with a feature film. In Hollywood, filmmaking magic is so common that it's lost much of its power. Elsewhere in the country, it still fascinates the crowds. Most people are thrilled to be associated with a movie as long as it's not too much trouble.

If you've been a good neighbor in your local film community and helped out other people with their projects, you'll have a much wider group from whom you can ask favors. Many filmmakers own props and have access to locations that will be useful to you. Similarly, you have access to things and places that can help in someone else's film.

A well-connected group of local filmmakers may have at their beck and call resources that rival that of a small film studio. So get on the team.

Other willing participants are local artists, ranging from musicians to clothing designers to painters. Their work can give your movie a piquant local flavor with a unique look. Showcasing their talent won't hurt the artists, and it may actually help them succeed with their own dreams. Look around for interesting additions to your film, and offer the chance to participate.

When searching for exterior shooting locations, don't overlook public areas, such as parks, wilderness areas, and the local scenic vistas. Bigger film productions pay lots of money to shoot on locations that are in your neighborhood. These are free and, if you shoot quickly, you can avoid any permits or location releases. Now, if you need to be at one of these sites for an extended period of time with lots of cast, crew, or equipment, you better seek formal permission. It's awkward to have your entire day of planned shooting halted by a park ranger with a demigod-complex. Don't forget that you need a location release for using any property that isn't public land.

If you need help finding or getting permission to use a particular local vista, your state or city film office may be able to help. While you're out exploring for that pink adobe bungalow for a location and scavenging for that brass seaman's compass for a prop, there are also technical preparations to be started.

Choosing a Look

This is the point where you'll want to start talking to your director of photography about the production and how you're going to achieve the look you want for your film. As you learn more about locations, the director and director of photography should be discussing the types of shots they want to do, especially if they involve specialized equipment. This is the time to determine the look you want for your film because there won't be time for this to evolve on the set. You need to know before you roll film what kind of images you are trying to achieve and what techniques will be used to create them. Viewing other films and looking at their techniques is a good way to get ideas and to select the look for your production. Movies on video are great because you can stop and study how particular images were achieved.

Recognize that you have to create your look with 1/100th the money and 1/6th the time of almost any film you watch. So consider what time, resources, and money you can commit to creating the look you want. It may be enough to create the visual tone of your film in a few key scenes and use a simpler and faster-to-shoot style for the remaining shots. Often an audience's memory of a film is linked to a few monumental scenes. "The Wizard of Oz" has hundreds of gorgeous scenes, but most people's memories gravitate to a few: the tornado; the Munchkins; meeting the scarecrow, tin man, and lion; the audience with Oz; the flying monkeys; melting the witch; and unveiling the wizard. You can't possibly rival the overall production values of a film like this, but you can create a half-dozen memorable scenes that will stick in your audience's heads.

For example, in our film "Resident Alien," we knew that we needed to make the crucial collision and climax scenes the visual high points in the production. Even though we were unable to achieve much style in 90 percent of the scenes we shot, we took extra pains to make sure these key points in the story set the visual tone for the movie. They also had our most elaborate special effects. The result is that most people recall these, our best scenes, when they think of our movie, not the lackluster images our budget forced us to accept for much of the production.

Technical Preparation

In addition to planning the look of your film, you need to do considerable technical planning. It's no good to get to the location and find that you can't use your lights because you need two-prong adapters for the electrical cords. As you find and get approval to use your locations, do location inspections. If you wish, you can draw a diagram of each room, its windows, doors, and electrical outlets to help you plan your shots on paper. If the number of locations is small, which will probably be the case for your film, you can just do a walk-through with the director and the camera and lighting crew. They can see the conditions they will be working in and decide what equipment will be needed to adapt to it.

For example, if half the living room you're shooting in is floor-to-ceiling glass windows, you're going to have a hard time avoiding showing the out-of-doors. This means you'll probably need to shoot day scenes during daylight and night scenes at night. It also means that you'll have to color correct the windows with large gels (expensive!) or balance the lights with daylight gels (less expensive). You'll need more lights and electricity to compete with a bright sun, so you'll have to figure out if you have enough electrical circuits to handle the load. This is the kind of thinking you need to do on the walk-through.

The most important item to locate and examine for every indoor location is the circuit box. Find out if it has circuit breakers or fuses. If it has fuses, note the type and size so you can buy some extras. It's almost guaranteed that you'll blow a breaker or fuse somewhere during your shoot, so you want to be able to find the circuit box and reset it as quickly as possible.

Other things to look at while visiting the location are room modifications that will be needed, where your crew is going to work, and where meals will be prepared and served. Make sure the owner of the location is comfortable with any changes you wish to make, such as moving the furniture around, temporarily removing a light fixture, laying down dolly track, bringing in furniture and equipment, and demolishing the odd wall here and there. Keep in mind that you are allowed to work at this site only because of the generosity of the owner. Make their wishes and concerns a priority, and be willing to change your plans to make sure they are happy. If they aren't happy, they can pull the plug on you during the middle of shooting. And common decency demands that you treat their property with care and respect. If you can't work within their restrictions, it's better to learn that early and find a different location. As we've said before, we have made it one of our guiding principles that we don't leave behind any owners of locations who wouldn't allow us to come back.

Besides looking for where you're going to shoot your scenes, consider the other work areas you'll need. Where will the hair and makeup supervisor work? It can't be on the set. Find a laundry room, bathroom, kitchen, or utility room with a sink for them to set up their stool and makeup and to plug in the 47 hair curlers, fluffers, and whippers they need. Make sure it's a room with a door, so they won't interfere with sound recording.

Where will the cast change costumes? A bathroom, spare bedroom, or office space will do. If you have a lot of wardrobe, the dressing room should be near the room or hallway space where wardrobe is stored.

An absolute must is an equipment and film-loading room. In public areas, this is where you corral your equipment so it doesn't walk away with pedestrians. Even more importantly, this is where your assistant camera operator will be loading and unloading the film magazines. This is work that must be done correctly to make sure the camera doesn't jam, the right film gets loaded, and the exposed film gets properly labeled. You want this to be an area free from distractions. An interrupted film loader is one who can accidentally reload the film you just shot, creating an artistic double exposure. An interrupted film loader can forget to put the film in the can before opening the changing bag, creating 400 feet of black leader from your morning of shooting. Send chills down your spine? Good. Pay attention to this advice, and find a separate room for film loading on your location.

You'll also need to find accommodations for the creature comforts (even if you're not doing a monster movie). Input and output are two major issues. Where will you prepare, deliver, and eat food? What bathroom facilities are available? The kinds of meals you can provide for your cast and crew will be controlled by the kitchen equipment available. If you don't have running water, electricity, a refrigerator, and a microwave oven or stove available, you'll be in camping-food mode: coolers, water jugs, camp stove, grill, sandwiches, and such. If you have electricity, you can bring electric fry pans, crock pots, and coffee pots to create a mobile kitchen.

Limitations in the bathroom area are much more problematic. You need to find something nearby, especially at lunch time. If your location is in a building, this can usually be arranged. If you're going to remote locations, you better give some thought to this issue. If the best you can come up with is a pit stop behind a bush, you better make sure the people you select for cast and crew can work under those conditions. Otherwise, you'll have some very unhappy campers complicating your shooting days.

When you're working indoors, you need to find a place to store actors when they are not being used. You'll be keeping crew people working pretty much non-stop, but the actors are going to have breaks in their work. The last thing you need on a busy set are people who have time to chat. It erodes the work ethic you need, they get in the way, and their talking and horseplay ruin takes. You need to find a reasonably comfortable "green room" for the actors to spend their time away from the set. It doesn't have to be fancy. An unused patio area, a recreation room, or a television room will do. Just a place where they can relax and talk or read while waiting for their next scene. Having a specific room will also help you know where to find them when it's time for their scenes. We suspect that the Hollywood tradition of the star's trailer is not just for pampering the star; it's also to keep them from roaming. (A producer of early Marx Brothers films actually chained them in their trailers to keep them from wandering away, or so the legend goes.)

On the technical front, there are a few more tasks to complete. You need to talk about the locations and the scenes that will be shot at each with your sound recordist so that she or he understands the sound-recording situations that will be encountered. You will realize that even the quietest location becomes much noisier when you actually want to record sounds in that spot. You easily ignore that airplane passing overhead as part of your daily routine, but it becomes a challenge when you start the tape recorder.

The sound recordist doesn't necessarily need to walk through the locations, though this can be helpful. The main thing the recordist needs to know is what equipment will be available and how many people will be speaking in each scene. Location sound recording equipment is pretty lightweight and portable, so the sound is usually the last consideration on the set, to the perpetual annoyance of sound recordists. That's what they get for being flexible.

With all of the technical crew, make sure they understand how to operate borrowed or rented equipment. Get a copy of the operating manual for them to read, or get the owner of the equipment to give a quick lesson on operating it. Try to get the crew a little hands-on experience (for free) before they get on the set. Even with this, do a little looking over their shoulders on the set. Ask to hear a little sound playback and have a peek through the camera lens after a shot is framed and focused. Take a look at the film magazine, and ask which side of the film is the emulsion side. Asking the crew people to explain their equipment to you is a subtle way to check their technical proficiency without insulting them. If you think someone is unclear about what they are doing, ask more questions and keep checking their work.

Another important part of pre-production is making lists and lots of them. Most of this obligation falls to the unit production manager, but if the director and producer duplicate this effort, there's less chance that something critical will be overlooked. Each weekend will be the equivalent of a separate production from the logistics viewpoint, so these lists should be done separately for each weekend of shooting. You'll be picking up rental equipment each weekend and checking that every item on your equipment list is included and in working condition. You'll be packing up supply boxes each weekend and making sure the necessary production supplies are inside. Wardrobe will have to be organized and transported each weekend. Props will have to be gathered and delivered to the locations. And each weekend, food will have to be arranged for and served on the set. The only way you'll keep this all organized is with lists for equipment, production supplies, wardrobe, props, and food. Hopefully, your makeup and hair supervisor has a list for his or her supplies, too.

The director, producer, and unit production manager should have lists with the names, addresses, and phone numbers of all the members of the cast and crew, just in case someone oversleeps. We also gave these lists to all the principal cast and crew members so they could call each other for help if necessary. You'll also want to carry a stack of forms to use while shooting: camera log sheets, sound log sheets, group release forms, and location releases. It's a pain to run out of these forms when you need them, so make sure you have plenty on hand at all times. We've included samples of these forms in the appendix; however, having a computer with a word processor will let you customize these forms, make legible lists, and create other useful production documents.

The other documents you'll want are the business version of nagging. For instance, make maps to each location for everyone. We simply photocopied the appropriate sections of a street map and highlighted the main travel routes. We also included the address and phone number at the site in case someone got hopelessly lost. If you have cast or crew members who are always losing stuff, pin the maps to their shirts. If you have a schedule that has the cast or crew changing a lot from day to day, you might consider doing a call sheet that lists who is needed for each day of the shoot. Give this out before the start of the production weekend. In our case, the major cast members and all the crew were needed every day, so our production manager just told the supporting characters when to show up. We only had a problem with them not arriving on time twice in two feature films.

A useful memo for the cast and crew is one explaining the conditions they will experience on the shoot and a recommended list of personal supplies to keep them comfortable. Because we were working indoors and outdoors in variable weather, our recommended supply list included hat, long pants, shorts, socks, tennis shoes, sunglasses, sunscreen, insect repellent, jug or other water container, and rain jacket. We advised people to avoid bringing along valuables to reduce the chance of losing them. We also let people know that there would be food and drinks provided on the set. In general, try to anticipate problems and annoyances that will make your production company unhappy, distracted, or uncomfortable.

And don't get cocky. Just because everything goes smoothly one weekend, don't assume the next one will. Use your lists. We slacked off for a minute when checking the list of rental equipment, and we ended up using a spare light stand as a makeshift microphone boom pole all weekend. About the only thing you can do to reduce some of your checking and double-checking is to write the contents on the outside of the production supply boxes (spare fuses, black plastic, duct tape, clothes pins, spare batteries, etc.), and then repack and replenish them at the end of each production weekend. On the following weekend, we always checked these boxes before loading them and then made sure they got loaded.

Don't assume anything has been done unless you've seen it with your own eyes, and just to be safe, make sure no one has undone it when you weren't looking. Your major tasks in pre-production are planning, finding, planning, listing, planning, nagging, planning, checking, planning, double-checking, planning, shopping, planning, and waking up in the middle of the night to write down something you left off the list. If at any point you feel like you've gotten it all organized and ready, get nervous. You're probably forgetting something.

We still haven't talked about one of the biggest pre-production jobs, selecting the cast and crew for your film. So read on.

CASTING THE CAST
To Be Or Not To Be For Free

Unless you're working on an Andy Warhol-type film (an eight-hour static shot of a skyscraper, two hours watching butter melt, ninety minutes of your computer's screen saver), odds are your film is going to be populated by characters that need to be brought to life by actors.

So, with both the script and the budget in good shape, it's time to tackle one of the truly enjoyable parts of the process, casting your film. This is the occasionally magical time when you'll see your film's characters start to come to life before your eyes.

There's a truism that says that casting is 90% of a film's success. For ultra-low-budget films, this figure may be on the low side. Due to your budget limitations, you won't have miles of film allowing for take after take until each word and action is perfection itself. Instead, you must have well-drawn, involving characters who are beautifully interpreted by skillful actors — in one or two takes.

And where will these skillful actors come from? How will you pick the best and the brightest? And how will you get them to work for what could charitably be called a less-than living wage? Read on.

Finding Actors

If you live in one of the major film or theater centers in the country (New York, Los Angeles, Chicago, Minneapolis/St. Paul, Seattle, San Francisco, Orlando, and so on), you may find yourself with no shortage of excellent actors. If you live elsewhere — and let's face it, most of the best people do — there are still excellent actors to be found; you may just have to dig a little deeper.

Talent Agencies

Talent agencies may seem like a logical starting point, and in some cases, they are. However, a talent agent's primary mission in life is to earn money from their clients' <u>paid</u> work. This may explain why they're not returning your calls.

Plus, because your film will be decidedly non-union, those agents who work with the unions, such as the American Federation of Television and Radio Actors (AFTRA) for television and the Screen Actors Guild (SAG) for feature films, may be reluctant to work with you. While both unions have created low-budget options for their members, these costs are still way outside your budget range.

With some luck, though, you may find one or two far-sighted talent agents in your area who see the value of getting their actors on film — any film, short of a skin flick — and who don't mind bending the rules a bit to do it. Good actors can learn a tremendous amount about their craft while working on a film, and smart talent agents recognize that fact and do their best to get their clients in front of the camera.

However, in order to get talent agents on your side, you have to persuade them that your project has merit, is going somewhere, or at least will be completed.

A good starting point is your script. Don't be shy about sharing your script with talent agents who are willing to look at it. They generally know the best actors in your area, and the more they know about your project, the better their talent recommendations will be.

It also may not hurt to give agents some references if they're unfamiliar with you or your work. Good agents protect their clients and want to be sure that they're sending them out on reputable assignments.

The agent may also want a look at your contract. While they understand that the project doesn't offer money to their client up front, they'll want to ensure that if the film becomes even a modest hit, their actors will see some recompense (minus a ten-percent agent fee).

These are all reasonable requests and will help to get the talent agent on your side and excited about your project. If no talent agents are available in your area, don't lose hope. There are other sources of actors available to you.

Local Theaters

If you aren't already seeing a lot of plays in your community, put this book down right now and go see a play.

Okay. Are you back? How was it? Did you have good seats?

The point here is that you should be seeing local performers perform. A lot. You should know who's who in your area, and who does what, and how well they do it. Local theaters — both community theaters and professional theaters — allow you to see a wide range of performers in an equally wide range of plays. They help you to see who has "star quality," who knows how to move well, who seems naturally funny, and who shouldn't quit their day job just yet.

With this information, you'll be in a good position to invite actors to audition for your film. You'll already be familiar with their work, their style, and at least some of their skills. And in casting, that's half the battle.

Cattle Calls (a.k.a. Open Auditions)

Cattle calls are about as fun as they sound, which is not very. They're insane and noisy and exhausting for everyone involved. But they can be a good way to discover unknown talent.

If you can't get the local talent agents to help you (or if your area doesn't have any talent agents) and if you haven't scoped out the local theater scene (or, worse, you don't have any local theaters), then an open audition will be your best tool for finding actors.

A cattle call involves bringing in a herd of actors (usually through an announcement in the newspaper), making them mill about for a while in a tight space, and then releasing them into the audition arena (one at a time or in pairs), and having them read short scenes from the script.

Finding the right actors in a cattle call is like finding your spouse-to-be in a singles bar. It does happen, but you may have to dance with a lot of duds to find a winner.

The disadvantage of cattle calls is that there has been no pre-screening. Using talent agents or going to theaters to find actors is an excellent winnowing process. Cattle calls, on the other hand, throw you into a mass of actors who have a widely varying range of skills and experiences, leaving you to sort the wheat from the chaff.

It really isn't fair to you or to the actors.

In an audition, you want everyone to get a fair shot. That means adequate time to prepare for the audition and adequate time to perform the audition. When you have fifty people in the lobby, and you only have the room at the community center for two hours, nobody wins.

The solution? Start your open audition through the mail. Ask people to send in pictures and resumes first, well in advance of the audition date. Wade through the material, and get a good sense of who should audition for which parts. Then schedule the auditions so that each actor has adequate time to do their stuff, as well as enough time for you to mix and match actors in different combinations.

This prescreening, while time-consuming, can turn the chaos of a cattle call into a well-organized and — with any luck — fruitful casting session.

Auditioning Actors

When it comes time to audition the actors, there are a few things you're going to need to make the day successful:

A Place To Audition

This doesn't have to be anything fancy. It can be the rehearsal space at a local theater, a classroom at the nearby school, or even someone's nicely furnished basement. Some people hold their auditions in conference rooms or suites at local hotels; as long as you get the space for free, more power to you.

There is one requirement, however. You will need two spaces that are adjoining or at least relatively close together; a room for the actors to check in and wait and a room for the actual auditions. These must be two separate spaces; the people waiting to audition should not be watching the auditions. How would you like to have a job interview with the competition sitting around watching? Get the two rooms and give the actors their best chance to do well.

A Traffic Manager

This can be anyone — your mom, your brother, a friend. Anyone, that is, except you.

You have much too much to do to spend time checking people in, giving them scenes to study, pairing up actors, and handling all the other business of the auditions. This is not your job.

There's an advantage to having someone from your production team handle this task (we used our production manager). Afterwards, you can get reports on how the actors were to work with when they didn't have on their best audition face. We also got interesting insights into who had good chemistry in the waiting room.

So find someone to handle this chore, or get a couple people to share it. It will keep your auditions running more smoothly, and it will keep you where you need to be, in the other room, watching auditions.

Sides

Sides are simply scenes from the script that have been photocopied and given to the actors to study and read for the audition. There should be at least one good scene for each of the characters you're trying to cast. Each scene should be two to three pages long; anything longer won't tell you much more about the actor and will slow down the proceedings; anything shorter doesn't really give the actor a chance to get up to speed.

Take some care in choosing which scenes you want to use for the auditions. You'll want to pick a pivotal scene for each character: a scene that is dramatic or funny or telling and that really gives the actor something to play. The scene should have a good mix of talking (dialogue and short speeches) as well as opportunities for the actor to simply listen and react to another character.

For "Resident Alien," we tried to pick scenes that revealed character. To audition the role of the not-as-unsophisticated-as-he-seems sheriff, we picked a scene in which he encounters our hero, Cal, in the woods and off-handedly reveals his theory about the government, UFOs, and his responsibilities as a law officer. It wasn't as showy as later sheriff scenes, but it showed us which actors could play the subtleties of the scene. We figured if they could do that, they could handle other more obvious scenes.

On the other hand, when it came time to have actresses read for the pivotal role of Leslie's mother, there was no argument as to which scene to use — the painful phone call scene between mother and daughter. Not only did this scene establish the characters' relationship quickly and dramatically, it was also the only scene Leslie's mother had in the film. As you can see, some decisions are easier than others.

You should also try to pick scenes that have a small number of characters, preferably two. This will allow you to audition two people at once and get a sense of how they'll play together. Any more than two turns the audition into a crowd scene and usually doesn't give each actor enough to do.

Often people will ask actors to read with someone from the production staff, but we prefer to let actors audition with other actors. It provides a better balance and allows for more spontaneity between the performers.

Finally, be sure to make enough copies of each of the sides so that there are enough to go around. Plan on having one for each person auditioning and some extras. Don't expect people to share or to leave their sides after their audition. They usually don't.

A Schedule-Conflict Sheet

In addition to providing you with a picture and resume, you should ask each actor to fill out a schedule-conflict sheet at the audition. This document lists the planned shooting dates for the film, with spaces for the actor to fill in their name and any work commitments or other conflicts they have with the production schedule.

Conflicts are a good thing to discover up front, particularly if a performer is available only for a few days of your shooting schedule. There's nothing worse than finding the perfect actor to play your lead, and then discovering that she'll be touring with "Nunsense!" for half of your shoot.

Video Camera and Operator

Videotape all the auditions. Any standard home video camera will work, preferably on a tripod. As with the traffic manager's role, you shouldn't act as your own video operator. Your focus should be on the auditions.

Rather than using a locked-down wide shot, instruct the camera operator to zoom in on the talent in order to get a better idea of how they'll look on film.

Review the tape before making any final selections because people come across differently on camera than they do in person. We've been surprised to see seemingly vibrant people lie lifeless on tape while performances we thought were lackluster absolutely sizzled on the TV screen. You'll be amazed to see how the camera really loves some people.

Finally, it's a good idea to hang onto this audition videotape well into production, in case you need to cast a replacement for a part.

The Audition

Auditions can be tremendous fun. You'll get to see some wonderful actors, you'll start to see the story come to life, and you'll begin to move one step closer to making your vision a reality.

However, for actors, auditions can be a real pain. They want to do a good job, and they want an opportunity to really shine, yet time after time producers and directors sabotage the process. This is very frustrating for actors because the audition is their entrance exam. If they don't pass, they don't get to move to the next level.

With that in mind, we humbly offer the following rules to make auditions good for you and for the actors:

THE TEN COMMANDMENTS OF AUDITIONS

I.   Thou Shalt Not Be Rude

Put yourself in the actor's penny loafers. You've got a two-page scene from a movie you know very little about. You're about to go into a room full of complete strangers and prance around, doing your best to breathe life into a scene. Then, in the midst of your best efforts, you see the director or producer yawn, whisper, start to dig into their lunch, or worse yet, doze off.

Wouldn't exactly encourage you, would it?

During the audition, actors are using all of their skills to demonstrate the level of their talent. The very least you can do is be polite. And if you can't be polite because it's the right thing to do, be polite because in the end it will save you money. "How?," you ask, your ears suddenly perking up. Here's how: If you like what the actor does, you're going to ask them to work for almost nothing. And if you were polite during their audition, they just might do it.

So don't do anything during their audition — talk, eat, whisper, sleep or anything else — except glue your eyes and your total attention to their performance. A little politeness goes a long way, and it can net you a great performance for a price you can afford.

Another important politeness tip is to introduce the actors to everyone in the room so that they know for whom they're performing. As one actor told us, "I like to have an idea of who's who in the room, so I know which people to suck up to."

Who can begrudge them that? So make introductions before you start making magic.

II. Thou Shalt Put Actors At Ease

Auditions can make actors nervous. Why? Because it's their one shot. If they don't impress you in the first two minutes, the odds are against their working on your film. At least, that's the way they look at it. As a consequence, many actors, even experienced performers, come into an audition a tad nervous. Hyped up. Scared to death.

In order to get the best performance out of them, it's up to you to put them at ease. Converse with them for a couple of minutes before they read. Ask them what they've been working on lately. Ask them about their past experiences. Ask them if they have any questions about the script or the production. Go over their schedule-conflict sheet, and confirm any problem dates.

Then, after they've had a few moments to relax and to just be themselves, ask them to be someone else for a couple minutes and let them read from the script.

III. Thou Shalt Not Close Thy Mind

Let's say that you wrote a great part in your script for Billy Crystal or Meryl Streep (probably not the same part, but who knows? That Meryl's one talented gal). And let's say that for some reason — a mix-up, a time conflict, or they didn't have bus fare — neither Billy nor Meryl show up at the audition.

What do you do? You open your mind, that's what. You'll be doing a disservice to your film and the acting community if you don't.

The odds are against someone walking in who is a dead ringer for the character you pictured in your mind. The purpose of the audition is to find the actors who are best-suited for the parts, not to find people who merely look like what you had in mind, or who can imitate a well-known personality.

For example, we recently came across this audition notice in the newspaper: "Actors for student film needed. Black male, 23 yrs, 6', fit, short hair; white female, 28 yrs, 5'10", slim, long red hair; black male, 40 yrs, 6', strong, natural hair; white male, 35 yrs, 6', short hair. Unpaid." The odds of finding good actors who fit these exacting specifications are extremely slim. Plus, by requesting such exact types, the filmmakers are ignoring hundreds of talented performers whose height or hair length don't fit these unnecessary standards.

For "Resident Alien," Dale had always pictured the lead character, Cal, to be tall, dark, bean-pole thin, and a classic nerd, like Jeff Goldblum. We saw people during the auditions who came close to that description, but the actor who had the best interpretation of the character was of average height, average weight, fair-haired, and didn't look at all geeky. So we chose him and "geeked" him up when it came time to shoot.

Keeping an open mind also means considering actors for different parts than the one for which they audition. When you're watching auditions, remember all the roles you need to fill, not just the one that's currently being read.

However, if you decide to ask an actor to read for a different part, give them a few minutes alone to go through the new material. Asking them to read it cold isn't fair or productive.

IV. Thou Shalt Not Discriminate On The Basis Of Race Or Gender

There are a lot of things you can't afford at your budget level, and one of them is to let good actors get away. This can happen if you're too narrow in your casting search and you ignore entire populations swimming in the talent pool.

In very few instances, such as when it's a plot point in the story, is race an issue in casting. If you're remaking "Guess Who's Coming

To Dinner?," then race becomes a consideration. Otherwise, you're simply looking for the best actors, and their race should be of no consequence.

You can also overlook great candidates for your cast if you make stereotypical casting choices based solely on gender. The kindly old doctor in your film doesn't necessarily have to be male; the helpful young nurse doesn't necessarily have to be female. Not all lawyers are men, and not all teachers are women. The person installing the phone can easily be a woman, while the owner of the perfume shop could be a cranky, old man.

In fact, the perfume shop owner might be more interesting if he's a cranky, old man.

On an early feature movie John produced, several auditions were held to cast the part of a tough, no-nonsense cop. The auditions were fruitless — until someone suggested that they try casting the part with a woman. The perfect actress walked into the next audition and walked out with the part. And not one line of dialogue was altered in the script. In fact, it improved several scenes, such as the one where she followed the police captain into the men's room to finish an argument. It added to the scene, and to the movie, and it wouldn't have happened if the casting had been narrow-minded.

V. Thou Shalt Offer Direction

Actors may be many things, but they're not mind readers. (Although, many mind readers are darn good actors, but we digress.) All that most actors know about the part they're auditioning for is what they read on the page — unless you tell them more, which is what direction is all about.

If time permits, we let the actors perform the scene once without direction. This gives us a chance to see where their instincts take them. Seeing them work without direction tells a lot about their natural skills (and the clarity of our scriptwriting).

Then we offer direction and try it again. At this point, we're not looking at their instincts; we're looking to see how well they can take direction. Of course, this presumes that the directions you've given are good ones. In our case, we never tell an actor how to read a line. If you want someone who can imitate your every word, hire a parrot. Instead, we suggest the intention behind the line or the action, and then let the actor interpret it as best they can.

For example, "In this scene you're angry at your wife for forgetting your birthday," or "Right now, your character has not slept for thirty-six hours, but he's trying to cover it up." These are more helpful directions than telling an actor to say one word louder than another.

In some rare instances, the first read will be perfect without direction. You'll be amazed. The actor will say every word right, every intention will be clear, and every motion will be poetry. You'll be ready to sign the contract and send everybody else home.

Not so fast.

Never hire an actor just because they read all the words right the first time. Instead, take some time and experiment with them. See if they can take direction. Ask them to play the scene in a less obvious way. If it's a romantic scene, have them play it for laughs. If it's an argument, tell them to make it into a seduction.

Remember, you're not looking for someone who can read just this one scene well. You're looking for flexible actors who can take direction. You want to see how they read with other people. Do they listen and respond to other actors in the scene, or are they acting in a vacuum?

If you still love everything the actor does after that, then bring out the contract, and break out the champagne (assuming it was donated in exchange for screen credit).

VI. Thou Shalt Look For Simplicity

There's a technical term for the type of acting you probably don't want in your film. It's called "Big-Face Acting." (All right, maybe it's not the technical term, but it's what we call it.) It's the kind of acting that plays to the balcony and works great if your audience is a hundred feet away and squinting.

Stay away from Big-Face Acting. Don't just stay away from it; run away from it.

The best way to avoid hiring Big-Face Actors is to videotape all the auditions. Then, after the auditions and before you offer anyone a role, review the tape and compare it to the notes you took while watching the actors live. You may be surprised. Some of the performers who looked great in person, from ten feet away, will seem overblown and unrealistic on tape. That's Big-Face Acting. However, other actors who didn't seem to be doing much of anything at all during the audition may come across as more compelling and interesting on tape. That's film acting. Those are the ones you hire.

VII. Thou Shalt Give Them A Chance To Do It Their Way

After you've given the actors direction, and they've done it your way, ask them if they want to try it again and do something different. Some actors will jump at this opportunity, with good reason.

At this point in the process, they've done it for you twice: Once just on instinct (the way they think you want it) and once with your direction (the way you think you want it). This third shot lets them combine the two approaches or try something entirely off the wall. They can take the scene right to the edge or even over the edge. They can give it a twist that you had never considered.

These "whatever you like" readings of the scene can be terrific. They give you and the actor a chance to really have fun with the scene and start to see all the possibilities. It's these "off the wall" readings that often give you a sense of whether or not you can bond with the actor and trust them to bring the character to life on screen.

Usually the approaches used during these readings don't make it into the film, but they can be a great creative springboard for getting deeper into scenes and bringing them to life in unique and memorable ways.

VIII. Thou Shalt Take Blame

It's happened to everyone at one point or another, and it's nothing to be ashamed about.

You'll have twenty actors read the same scene and none of them will make it work. Your natural instinct will be to blame the actors. "If we had some decent actors in this town, this scene would be working. It's not the script. It's those darn actors."

No. It's the script. It needs more work.

However, don't think of this as a negative; this is simply part of the process. It's far better to realize script problems during auditions and rehearsals, rather than during shooting or — worse yet — during editing.

So make notes during the auditions about which lines are consistently duds and which moments consistently don't work. Since you'll only be using a few scenes for auditions, problems with these scenes should spur you to give your entire script serious, objective scrutiny. If you're too in love with the script to see its warts, get help from people who will call a wart a wart, and listen to their advice.

Each stage of production teaches you a lot about your script, its good points and its bad. It's best to learn to listen and to use what you hear to make your script and your film better.

IX. Thou Shalt Use As Many Actors As You Reasonably Can

This commandment doesn't mean we want you to turn your three-character story into "It's A Mad, Mad, Mad, Mad World."

It does mean that if somebody really good has auditioned for a role and they don't get it, you should consider them for other smaller parts in the film. As we've said earlier, actors live by their credits, and even a tiny walk-on part in a small, regional film has value.

On "Resident Alien," the final casting for our lead female character came down to two excellent actresses. It was a tough choice. The actress who ultimately didn't get the part was offered the much smaller role of a social worker, which consisted of two short scenes. But she made the most of those two scenes, creating a strong, memorable character and making the film that much better because of her work.

So when you find good actors, give them parts in your film. It gives them screen time, work in front of a camera, and a couple minutes of film for their reel. And it gives you performers who really want to be part of your project and who turn tiny roles into small, sparkling gems. Everybody wins.

X. Thou Shalt Not Lie

We don't need to tell you that lying is bad. You're an adult; someone must have mentioned it to you before now.

But often otherwise mature adults, such as film directors and producers, will tell "little white lies" and even "big ugly lies" during the audition process in order to entice skillful actors to ply their trade in the filmmaker's latest opus.

A word of advice: Lying will come back and bite you on the butt. Every time. And your reputation as just another low-life filmmaker will be posted on verbal bulletin boards throughout the acting community for years to come.

<u>Don't lie about money</u>.

We were very clear with the actors we auditioned, and even clearer in the contracts they signed.

We told them how they would get paid. We told them when they would get paid. We told them, in no uncertain terms, that the only money they could reasonably expect to see from the project was the "signing fee" (read "gas money") for their contract. The rest was wishful thinking.

So don't turn wishful thinking into promises you can't keep. It may get you through this project, but people will be less inclined to work with you later when they find out that you were lying earlier.

<u>Don't lie about the nature of the film</u>.

If the film involves nudity, the actors need to know this before you cast them and not on the set just before you yell "action!" If the film will use graphic language or will be explicit in its portrayal of sex or violence, the actors also need to know this before they commit to doing the film.

Lying to the actors the very first time you meet them, in the auditions, is not going to enable them to trust you where you need trust the most, on the set. So be honest about what kind of film you're making and start building that trust early.

<u>Don't lie about the prospects for the film</u>.

Like all of us, actors are hopeful people. In fact, they're often more hopeful than the rest of us. Theirs is a business built on hope.

With that in mind, it's a good idea to muzzle your bounding hopes for the project and try to pull it back into the realm of the probable or at the least the possible when you're talking to the actors.

Don't tell them that the film will be released by a major studio. The odds are against it. You might get a limited theatrical release. You might make it to cable. It could go to home video. But a major studio release? Probably not.

Don't tell the actors that the film will make them famous. The odds are against it. One of the best-known low-budget films of all time, "Return of the Secaucus Seven," produced only one actor who could be considered famous (David Strathairn), and his fame didn't grab hold until several films later. Almost every major actor started out in a low-budget film in a now-forgotten role. It didn't make them famous, but it did get them a step closer to the film that did make them famous.

What your film will give the actors is some experience working in film and in a role larger than they would be offered if a big Hollywood film came to town. It will look good on their resume. It will look good on their reel. But it won't make them famous, yet. Sorry.

Don't lie about the budget. Don't talk about luxurious Winnebago trailers and fabulous costumes and multiple retakes. The actors need to know from the start that this is an ultra-low-budget film, and they need to know that means a short shooting schedule and few takes. They need to know all the project's limitations, so they can begin planning how to effectively use their talents under these circumstances.

Of course, there are lots of things you can tell the actors. You can tell them that this is going to be an educational experience that will help them grow as a performer and that they will gain valuable acting credentials. You can tell them that you hope this will be the greatest film in the history of time. That you hope it will revolutionize the motion picture industry. That you hope it will change the world as we know it. That's your dream, and it's good to share it.

But don't say that the film will open in New York and LA in time for Academy Award consideration, before going national in 2,500 theaters. Talking excitedly about your dream is fine. Lying is not. Be sure you know the difference.

Casting The Cast

Now that the auditioning is over, it's time to officially cast the film. With any luck, you'll have a problem: Too many good actors, not enough parts. This is a good problem to have. A few pointers:

• Don't cast look-alikes. By this, we don't mean celebrity look-alikes. We mean actors who resemble each other. Unlike a Hollywood film, with big-name, recognizable actors, your film will be filled with unknown faces. Don't confuse the audience by casting unknown faces that look similar.

If you are forced to cast actors with similar builds, hair color and features, then be sure to distinguish them with unique costumes and hair styles. On "Beyond Bob," because we had to replace one actress right before shooting began, we ended up with two dark-haired, beautiful actresses who could have caused confusion for the audience. However, by using different hair styles, makeup, and totally different costumes, we were able to prevent any confusion about who was whom.

• Tell the people you choose for your cast before you tell the people you didn't choose. You need to offer the parts to the actors and have them accept the roles before you let the other contenders go. Once all the parts are cast — and accepted — you can then start calling the contenders and breaking the news to them.

• Thank the contenders, but don't go into details about why they weren't cast. Don't tell them that they were too tall or too short or too fat or that their nose was the wrong size. Don't critique their acting (unless it's a compliment and unless you really mean it).

If you were impressed with their work, tell them that you'll keep them in mind for other films and that you'll hang onto their picture and resume (and then really do it).

The results of a successful audition, the principle cast of "Resident Alien."
Pictured, l to r, Mark Patrick Gleason, Nesba Crenshaw, Patrick Coyle.
Photo courtesy of Granite Productions, Ltd.

Asking People To "Work For Free"

Years ago, John worked as a writer on a trailer for a proposed low-budget feature. Early on, the producers decided to pay the crew and not to pay the cast. Their reasoning was that the crew would be working for the duration of the four-day shoot, while most of the actors would only be working for a day or two.

This saved them money. They thought it was a good idea. It wasn't.

The problem with their approach was that it sent a message to the cast. The message said, "We don't think your time and skills are worth as much as those of the kid holding the light stand." This was a bad message to send.

Did it hurt the film? Probably. Did it hurt the chances of the producers putting together another project? Definitely. Because the word was out that those guys aren't just cheap; they don't care about the actors.

Well, we're happy to report that the word is out on us as well. We're cheap. We're known for it. Maybe even renowned for it. But we're also known for caring about our actors. For treating them fairly and honestly. And for paying a paltry pittance. Of course, we don't pay the crew any more than that. We pay ourselves even less. We're nothing if not fair. Maintaining equity such as this is a key component in making your project work. It makes it a project fueled by hope, not by mere money.

Initially you'll probably feel guilty about not being able to pay the cast or crew what they are worth. Trust us, you'll get over it, and we're not being cynical when we say that. You may not be handing out paychecks each week, but the fact is that you're offering everyone involved in the project a great opportunity. You're offering them a $30,000 professional study course that will look great on their resume. As long as you're honest and don't promise things you can't deliver, you won't be doing anyone a disservice. You'll be doing them a favor.

Think about it. There are thousands upon thousands of actors and would-be actors in the world. How many of them ever get to act in a feature film? Or, for that matter, play a leading role in a feature film? Very few. But you're in a position to offer that to people, and that really is something of value.

Your film has a lot to offer people besides money. Yes, it would be great to pay people up front. Yes, it would be great to pay people what they're worth. But don't sell yourself or your film short by thinking that the cast and crew are doing you a favor and working for nothing.

Everybody involved in the film is earning and learning. As long as you warn them about what they're getting into, you should have a happy set and a productive shoot.

CORRALLING THE CREW
Assembling The Dream Team

Production Diary: During the last two weekends, the director of photography has been impersonating Dr. Strangelove behind the camera, the sound recordist and boom operator wore bathrobes and hair nets after being teased about taking naps between shots, the production manager stood on a picnic table operating lights to simulate a UFO landing, and we all worked 14 hours a day. Situation normal.

A little crazed, willing to leap conventional job delineations in a single bound, dedicated to the project — that's the description of a super crew person for your film. This type of crew member is critical to the success of your production. Finding these people is just as important as finding the right actors for your cast. Without them, brilliant performances by the actors can be lost in a muddle of unusable film and audio tape. Fortunately, there are many people eager to fill this bill.

Some of the steps you'll take to find these wonderful people are similar to the ones for getting a great cast, but it is a different process that is best approached separately.

Finding Crew People

Before you begin your quest, you need to know what the holy grail looks like. Who do you need for your crew? The crew positions have already been identified in your budget. The essential ones are:

- Unit Production Manager
- Director of Photography/Camera Operator
- Assistant Camera Operator/Camera Loader
- Sound Recordist

- Lighting Gaffer/Boom Operator
- Makeup and Hair Supervisor

A screenwriter is also essential to your production, and we've discussed how to select one in the script chapter.

Some crew members don't need to be brought onto the project until post-production. We'll talk about selecting people for the following positions in the post-production chapter.

- Composer/Music Supervisor
- Session Musicians
- Film/Sound/Music Editor

Some crew positions are optional and will depend on the nature of your specific project:

- Assistant Unit Production Manager
- Art Director
- Wardrobe Supervisor
- Song Writer
- Singers
- Stunt Coordinator
- Special-Effects Coordinator
- Model Builder
- Set-Construction Coordinator
- Animal Wrangler

We haven't mentioned director or producer in these lists because most people who are foolish enough to produce a feature film for a song (or merely a verse) are just crazy enough to direct or produce it themselves. Just in case you've retained a sliver of good sense and want to get someone else to direct and produce your film, we'll give you some guidelines after we talk about the rest of the production crew.

So where do you find a crew that's strong of back and keen of mind? We found our people largely by word of mouth. We spoke to people who had worked on short films and other low-budget feature films in our area. Most of them told us it was impossible to shoot a film on our budget and then gave us recommendations for crew people. When we called these prospective crew people, they often suggested friends and acquaintances for other positions on the crew. We also watched local productions and contacted people who had done good work on them. Generally, working film professionals were afraid of doing a project that broke so many of the rules, so the best recommendations were for people who were just breaking into the film business. You may find people who are trying to advance to the next level in their professional career and who will join you to get experience they can't get in their day jobs. You can also place ads on the bulletin boards at local colleges and film schools and notices on the Internet or in the newsletter of the closest Independent Feature Project chapter. The state or city film office in your area may also have job listings for film crews. Even film-equipment rental houses may be able to tell you who's looking for the kind of opportunity you're offering.

Cast your net widely to get names of many possible crew members. Don't be bashful or apologetic because you can't pay real salaries. The type of experience you are offering is rarely available to fledgling film-crew members. You're taking a chance doing this production in order to fulfill your dream. They will happily join you in realizing your dream because their own dreams are attached to yours.

This is a good point to remind you to put on your blinders, the good kind. The ones that don't see color, gender, age, or body type when looking at a candidate, only abilities. There are many good people looking for film jobs who get these biases thrown in their faces daily. You can use that to your advantage by scooping up those candidates with great skills who have been rejected for irrelevant reasons.

The first positions that you should be trying to fill for your crew are the unit production manager, the director of photography, and the sound recordist. These are your key crew members, and they should have some input about who will be their helpers — the assistant unit production manager, the assistant camera operator, and the lighting gaffer/boom operator. In several instances on our production, the key crew people recommended people they had worked with before who turned out to be great additions to the team. So you can save yourself some work by starting with these three key positions. If they don't have any suggestions, then it's a good idea to have them involved in interviewing the other job applicants.

Once you have a list of potential candidates, you're ready to start panning for the gold.

Interviewing The Crew

Your first contact with crew people will probably be a phone call. "Uh, I'm (your name), and I'm making a low-budget feature film. I got your name from (an acquaintance, someone they worked for, their response to your ad, the editing-room wall at a film school). Are you interested in working as a (mouth-watering crew position) on our production? By the way, there's no pay, the hours are long, and we work on weekends." If they don't hang up laughing derisively, they will probably ask what type of film, what format, and what your goals and dreams are for the production. Sell your project to them. As far as you know, they are going to win an Academy Award for their next film, and it could be yours. You need their interest to find out if they are right for your movie. They'll only consider joining you because your dream is catching, so tell them enough to capture their imagination.

If they are interested, ask them to send you a list of work experience, some references (unless they've already been referred to you), and a schedule of availability. For the sound recordist and director of photography, ask for samples of their work. For these people on your crew, you need to know they can deliver results. Be sure to ask what their role was in the sample they send you. For example, a candidate for director of photography who just loaned the camera for the film sample you see may not even know how to focus the camera. Once you have some paper records or samples of a person's work and a little bit of conversation on the phone to start sizing up the candidates, you're ready to arrange for interviews. Be sure to look at two or more candidates for each position. That way, the person you ultimately select will give their best work to keep this plum assignment, knowing there are challengers out there just waiting for them to stumble. You'll also get a feel for the range of candidates that is available to you.

Your interviews don't need to be elaborate. They can be done at the kitchen table. You can also do them by phone though you'll usually get a better sense about personalities by talking face to face. Keep it informal, and start by telling them honestly about your production. It's a waste of time to give the impression that this is a bigger production than it actually is. Crew people will find out the truth as soon as the discussion turns to technical needs, and you point out that you can't afford more than three rolls of gaffer's tape. Don't forget to mention hard work, long hours, minuscule budget, small crew, unconventional techniques, token pay, non-union, and slim chances of the final film being a financial success. If they're going to be scared off, now's the time to do it.

After laying out the grisly truth of your project and your commitment to it, let them do some talking about their education, experience, their goals, their dreams, their ideas, and why they're right for your crew. You should be listening for the characteristics and attitudes of a good crew member. They apply to post-production crew as well as production crew:

Desired Characteristics and Attitudes
- Good humor
- Can-do, problem-solving attitude
- Enthusiasm and respect for your project and ideas to make it even better
- Good work ethic
- Willingness to help with other aspects of the project (loan props, paint sets, find equipment for free, etc.)
- Technical proficiency and basic skills needed for their duties or the ability to learn them fast
- Cooperative, willing to follow directions
- Aware of the challenge, but not afraid to try
- Good vibes. You should have a good feeling about these people and be genuinely excited to work with them.
- Actively trying to improve their skills by volunteering on other projects, working on their own films, or taking classes

- Owns equipment and uses it. These people are serious about their avocation and could bring equipment they are familiar with to your production.
- Has connections and is willing to call in favors to enhance the project
- Anti-establishment, let's-make-an-end-run, who-says-we-can't-do-it attitude

Granted, it will be rare to find every one of these characteristics in every crew person, but try to find the people who best match this list and you'll end up with a dynamite crew.

Specialized Skills or Attitudes

In addition to these general characteristics, you'll be looking for some specific skills or attitudes in the positions of unit production manager, director of photography, assistant camera operator, and stunt coordinator.

Unit Production Manager

As we stated in the chapter on pre-production, you want this person to be very organized and conscious of details. If a candidate for this job shows up late for the interview saying they lost the address, look further. This is the one person who has to double-check every step of the project, so make sure she or he is up to the job. You also want a take-charge kind of person, not someone who doesn't move without direction.

Director of Photography/Camera Operator

This person will be your image expert, so the candidate for this job must have a vision of how the movie can or should look and the ability to make it happen. This may not match the producer's and director's vision initially, but if this person can see how to create different looks for the film, then you have a starting point for some serious visual discussions. A person who can only create gothic-horror lighting is only useful for that type of film. You want someone who's familiar with the sorcery that can be performed using lights and lenses and filters. Someone who relishes the challenge of making art from nothing. Someone with ideas on how to create a big look with no money or time. If you can't find such a person, then you at least want someone who can properly compose, focus and light a shot.

We found that this position became the leader of the production crew, setting the mood and the work pace for the others. Sure the director is in charge, but if the director of photography is always grousing about the working conditions, you'll have a surly, disgruntled crew. We were blessed with a "good humor man" as our director of photography, and, with rare exceptions, we had a happy crew even when working past midnight in a 100-degree motel room. Our director of photography had a "we can do that" attitude for every challenge, and that made our crew invincible in the face of technical challenges. They didn't know it was impossible, and we'd be the last people to tell them.

Just a word about video experience versus film experience. Video experience doesn't guarantee competency with film. The equipment is very different, as is the experience of filming a shot and not being able to check playback to see if it worked. It's useful to have someone who knows the limits of video because that will likely be the ultimate distribution format for your film. It's good to know how much lighting contrast video can take, so you aren't shooting film that will fall off into black shadows on video. Taking on someone with only video experience means that person better be the type who will educate themselves a lot before you start production, including doing some actual film shooting. Your best choice, however, is a person with film experience.

Assistant Camera Operator/Film Loader

For this job you want the perfect man or woman Friday. Someone who will anticipate the next task and be ready for it. You want a neat, tidy, meticulous person whom you can trust to clean the camera magazines and the film gate and to be sure every roll of film is loaded correctly. Labeling and sealing every can of exposed film and filling out the camera log during shooting will also be part of this person's duties, so you need someone who's very responsible and reliable. Obviously, this person should be able to work with the director of photography very closely.

Stunt Coordinator

You may have no need for this position on your film, but if you do, you don't want a devil-may-care risk taker. In fact, the stunt coordinator should be the most cautious and safety-conscious member of your crew. The right person for this job is someone with a magician's mentality. How can we trick people into believing a stunt is dangerous as heck, without risking anyone's safety? We know of would-be stunt performers who just like the idea of jumping from moving cars for real. Unless you want your production known for its toll in human lives, steer clear of these gonzo types.

Once you've found your top one or two candidates for each position, it's a good idea to have a second interview to check your perceptions and to see if they are still interested. (Polite people may not tell you that they think you're crazy, at least not while you're in the same room. Crazy people have been known to snap, you know.) This interview can be done by phone if you wish. This is a good time to talk about how this person would approach the production tasks ahead if you add them to the crew. Be especially impressed by those who have started preparing for the job. They've done research, they've gotten connections for low-cost equipment rentals, they've learned how to use the equipment, and they've come up with good ideas that will help the production. These are the go-getters you need.

Choosing The Crew

After a couple of conversations with your prime candidates, you should be getting a feel for their personalities and getting some vibes about each person. We've learned to pay a lot of attention to vibes. It's that nagging sixth sense that a person will be a problem, that vague uneasiness about the person that belies their skills and what they say. Pay attention to these gut reactions. Sure, they could just be that burrito from lunch, but we've found our vibes about people to be pretty reliable. We also get good vibes about people, that euphoric sense that this person will do great things for your film, and some of those people have become friends who have worked on many of our projects.

Just as when you select your cast, call your first choices for crew members first and get their acceptance before you turn down anyone.

If your first choice declines to join you, you can ask your second choice. If you're lucky enough to have two great candidates for a position, consider giving one of them the assistant position. You're likely to create a work team that will have even more good ideas to add to your production. Now, don't expect that you will have a list of experienced people for every position on your crew. In reality, a small production like yours may not have any experienced people who are interested in working on it. Don't be disappointed. There are many wanna-bes out there who want a chance to work on any kind of professional production. Every experienced professional had a first production, and often it was a low-budget project much like yours. Sure, they didn't know everything they needed to know that first time, but they knew enough and learned enough to do a respectable job, and it led to more productions.

If you don't have a list of experienced crew people to choose from, you have to be on the lookout for promising people. That describes many of the crew people we had on both of our productions. They were people who had worked on films in lesser jobs and were ready to move up. In fact, some of them had never worked on a film before.

There are lots of diamonds out there languishing in the rough. You just need to recognize them and give them a chance. You won't be sorry because they will give you their very best work, to your mutual benefit. So consider giving the director of photography position to that assistant camera operator or the sound recordist position to that boom operator.

Selecting a Director and Producer

It's likely that you have decided to be the producer or director of your film. Retaining control of the project is why most of us decide to make independent films in the first place. If you happen to be a screenwriter in search of a production company, then you may need to find a producer and director.

Finding a producer won't be that hard. Finding one that's right for your project may take a little more effort. You need someone with experience developing budgets for films, and someone who can pinch a penny until it bends. Many people in the video and film production business know how to do these things. If the person only has video experience, he or she will have to become familiar with film production techniques in order to create a realistic budget. You need someone who will be the guardian of the budget and will calmly and insistently say "no" when the budget doesn't allow for that camera boom. A good producer will then come up with three ways that you can do just as good a shot for no extra money.

Producing is a job that can be learned. In fact, you can do it yourself after having read this book. Dale's experience had been in budgeting and shooting videos for government projects (contrary to popular belief, most government projects are decidedly low-buck). By going to producers' telephone school, he learned enough to serve as producer on both of our feature films.

What's producers' telephone school? Basically, you call people who know the business, say a camera rental house, and try to get a price for camera rental for your budget. You'll sound like a moron during the phone call when they ask "Do you want an Arri, Eclair, or a CP-16?," and you've never heard of these cameras. Your cheeks will be red as you ask them to tell you the difference and they patronizingly do. You hang up and note how glad you are that you did this by phone. You go back for your next lesson by calling another rental house and asking for their price on an Eclair. Those cheeks of yours start heating up again when they ask if you need crystal sync and what kind of lens you want. You swallow your pride again and ask them to explain the options. More patronizing education. You hang up, let your cheeks and pride recover, and then call rental house number three. This time you ask for the rental price on an Eclair-NPR with crystal-sync motor and an Angenieux 12-120mm zoom lens. In three easy lessons, you know what you're talking about.

Actually, most businesses that supply film equipment and film services are happy to give you an education about their services. They know a potential customer when they hear one. Some reading and some discussions with knowledgeable people can give a would-be producer enough information to do an adequate job. If you can get someone with experience, you're likely to get better than adequate. Dale's experience producing videos and his own films meant he could offer many cost-cutting ideas that a less-experienced producer might have missed. If your producer is inexperienced, try to talk over your plans and budget with other producers who have done low-budget projects. You'll get suggestions that will help you control costs on your film.

If you're not going to direct your project, finding the right director is a much harder task. The director has fingers in every one of the production's pies in order to provide the vision that will guide the project. And that's the challenge. Is it the same vision you have? If your director is seeing how to get laughs from the scene that is your dramatic pinnacle, you've got a double-vision problem, and the two of you won't be seeing eye-to-eye throughout the project. You may even be at each other's throats before you're finished. This is not a good way to work. This is the reason many independent films have screenwriter/director listed in the credits. It can be very difficult to find someone who respects and shares your vision.

Selecting a director is a type of marriage. You have to have a similar vision if you are going to be able to work as a team to realize that goal. That doesn't mean that there won't be disagreements in this marriage, but it does mean that there's a shared respect for the vision you're trying to achieve. If so, your arguments will only be about the best way to achieve that vision.

Obviously, good "vibes" are essential in selecting a director. Some lengthy discussions about film in general and your project in particular will help you figure out if your director candidate is the one. Don't decide until you're sure you've found a person you can trust to take charge of your baby.

Your best choice is also going to be someone who has managed big production projects before because a feature film has almost-endless details that must be remembered while directing. It's usually best if your director has had experience getting actors to do dramatic performances for the camera. Experience directing training and industrial films is useful, but different. If you decide to use a director who lacks this experience (maybe yourself), there are a number of good books on the art of directing which are listed in the bibliography. Read them. It would also be good to practice directing some scenes for a video camcorder. This will help the director see what the results on the screen look like.

First-time directors can do a good job if they've done their homework. (Orson Welles on "Citizen Kane" for example.) Sometimes they even bring a fresh vision to the screen because they haven't been trained to think in conventional ways.

Letting Your Crew Do Its Best

Once you've selected your crew people, encourage them to make suggestions and give ideas on how to improve the production. This can be hard. You've probably been living with this dream for a long time, and it's hard to let go and share it. It can be even harder to let other people change your dream. Be brave. One of the most important lessons we've learned while making our films is that dreams grow stronger and more beautiful when other people add to them.

We found that every actor and every crew member brought a little bit of themselves to the dream and added to it. The screenplay that we started with was only the seed, and each person who came to the production made it grow into something better. The actors brought depth to the characters that hadn't existed on the printed page. The director created compelling scenes that crackled with energy. The camera crew created images that strengthened the messages of the story. The editor created pacing that propelled the story forward. The composer amplified the emotional content of scenes with music. In the end, our films were much more than they started out to be on paper because we let others embellish our dream.

PRODUCTION
Lights, Camera, Chaos!

When most people imagine making movies, what they're actually picturing is just one element of that process — production. They envision beautiful actors and actresses in costumes, huge lights, dollies, cranes, cameras, and egomaniacal directors with monocles and megaphones, yelling "action!" and "cut!"

In reality, the production phase is just one element of the overall filmmaking process, though a vital one. Making a feature film doesn't begin when you yell "action" for the first time on the first day of production or end when you yell "cut" after the last scene is shot. However, if you do your job correctly during the production phase, you can save yourself lots of money, time, and headaches during the subsequent phases.

With that in mind, we've assembled the following production notes to help the director and producer through the production process. This list is by no means exhaustive — the circumstances surrounding your own production are bound to be as unique as the film you're making — but there are certain common elements and concerns that have a tendency to pop up in all productions.

Training

No, we're not recommending film school. Why spend $15,000 a year to go to a film school (where you'll be lucky to make a couple short films), when you can create your own feature film using only two years' tuition? And without having to take 12 credits of a foreign language.

No, by training we mean getting in shape, physically and mentally. Make no mistake, directing is a grueling undertaking. Some people have compared the experience to running a marathon. Of

185

course this is ludicrous because a marathon is over in a measly 26 miles, while you've got an arduous eight or ten days of production to survive. Take it from us, your average marathon runner would be begging for mercy after the first half day of shooting, collapsed by the craft services table, whimpering for Gatorade and aspirin. You must be made of stronger stuff.

The best advice we've ever heard about directing was to "wear comfortable shoes." Directing requires intense concentration and stamina. You'll need to be on your feet most of the day and on your toes at all times.

Taking care of yourself before production (eating well, exercising often) is important; taking even better care of yourself during production is just as important. This means eating regularly and well (not junk food) during the day and getting as much sleep as you can reasonably get each night.

We also recommend staying away from artificial stimulants like sugar and caffeine because while they will make your highs higher, they will also make your lows lower. And there's nothing worse than finding yourself staring at the ceiling at 3:00 a.m., your brains cells screaming with a "Mountain Dew" buzz, while you curse your inability to sleep and your 5:00 a.m. alarm setting.

It's also a good idea to get off your feet at least once during the day. You can call it meditating; you can call it power napping; you can call it whatever you want; just do it. It will clear your head and increase your energy for the rest of the day. This break isn't just for the director and the producer, either. In all likelihood, your director of photography will be on her or his feet just as long (particularly since this person's also acting as camera operator). With setting up the lights, shooting the scenes, tearing down the lights, and preparing for the next set-up, your director of photography rarely gets a chance for a break throughout the shooting day. So find a way to give the director of photography a break whenever you can. This may slow you down for a few moments, but it will pay off with more energy throughout the day and better results.

20 (Thousand) Questions

As a film director, you will be asked more questions and will make more decisions during pre-production and production than you have throughout your entire life. That includes from the moment of your birth until the instant of your death, which will seem like it could be at any minute when you're directing. Director Edward Zwick ("Glory" and "Legends Of The Fall") has said that each day of production involves so many decisions that "I open a menu and try to think about what to order for dinner, and I'm ready to burst into tears."

You will quickly find that the questions are constant and they all demand answers: "Do you want him to wear the white shirt or the off-white shirt?" "When you say 'close-up,' how close do you mean?" "Do you want to break for lunch now or in ten minutes?" "Are we going to see that wall or not?" "Is the car needed in this scene?" "What do you want to do next, scene 112 or scene 4?" "Do you want a normal view or a wide angle?" "Do you want to do a retake?" "Does it matter that he moved?" "Are there any other shots you need or should we send the actor home?" "Are you going to intercut on this shot?" "Are we doing a reverse?" And the question you dread the most, "How did you get this job, anyway?"

You will be expected to have the answers to these and 19,987 other questions on the tip of your tongue at all times during production. In most cases, if you've done your homework (such as knowing the script inside out), the answers will be within easy reach.

However, in some cases, your mind will be blank, and you simply won't have an answer. That's when it's best to fall back on those three infamous words that some people find difficult, if not impossible, to say: "I don't know."

There is no shame in not knowing, particularly if you follow up immediately with, "What do you think?" Keep in mind that the person asking the question is usually someone you hired for their knowledge and skill. They may already have the perfect answer to the question they've raised.

Another good answer, after "I don't know," is "What are my options?" This gives you choices, which are always easier to deal with. The truth is, as a director, you may not always have the answer. But if someone gives you a choice, you will always have opinions.

Just because you don't have all the answers, though, doesn't mean you aren't in charge. The director is the captain of this ship, and this concept must be communicated throughout the staff. This doesn't mean you have to run your set like you're Mussolini on a bad day. But it does mean that all suggestions and instructions should flow through the director — and this includes comments from the producer. The entire cast and crew should look to one person for direction, and if you're the director, that person is you. This is especially important on a fast-paced production like yours. You can't afford the miscommunication and the confusion that result when more than one person is giving instructions.

The Big Lie

You may remember that a couple chapters back we told you lying was a bad thing.

Well, we were lying.

There is one occasion on an ultra-low-budget production when lying is not only permitted, it is required. That's when it comes time to "psyche up" the cast and the crew. To do this you must lie. Just this once. Actually, twice.

Here's how it works. Before you start your first day of shooting, take the members of the crew aside, sit them down, and give them a pep talk. It goes something like this, "Listen folks, you're the best. I know you can do this. With your help, we're going to make this the greatest movie of all time ..."

(So far, it's just hyperbole, which is always acceptable. Here comes the lie.) "The thing is, though ... well, it's the cast. A lot of them are pretty new to movie making, and some of them are going to screw up. So all of you on the crew, who are more experienced, have to work extra hard to make sure that you don't make any mistakes because the cast is bound to. So when they get it right, we don't want to miss it for technical reasons." Thus ends Lie Number One.

For Lie Number Two, you sit the cast members down, give them the hyperbolic spiel, and then say (here comes the lie), "The thing is, though ... well, it's the crew. A lot of them are pretty new to movie making, and some of them are going to screw up. So all of you in the cast, who are more experienced, have to work extra hard to make sure that you don't make any mistakes, because the crew is bound to. So when they get it right, we don't want to miss it for performance reasons."

With two little lies you have psyched-up both the cast and the crew, built up their egos, and persuaded them that the success or failure of the film rests in their capable hands — which is true. Of course, once you've finished this, you have to go back to telling the truth full time. Or, at least until you start dealing with distributors.

Read-Through and Rehearsals

The odds are that your film will be shot out of sequence; that is, all the scenes that take place in one location will be shot at the same time, regardless of where they appear in the story. It's the most efficient way to plow through the 12 pages a day that you'll need to shoot to stay on schedule.

While this is great for your budget, it puts an extra strain on your actors, who must be able — on nearly a moment's notice — to accurately portray their character at any given point in the story.

In a play, actors have the luxury of following the arc of their character's emotional, psychological, and physical changes from beginning to end, both during rehearsals and in performance. No such luxury exists on a film set, where actors are routinely required to play widely disparate scenes in quick succession, such as a violent argument followed immediately by a tender love scene. What makes these dramatic leaps possible are a thorough read-through and comprehensive rehearsals.

The Read-Through

A complete read-through of the script is an invaluable resource for the cast and crew, as well as for you. What were once just words on paper come to life during the read-through, and everyone gets a chance to see how the story develops from beginning to end.

Due to the fractured nature of film production, this is possibly the only time the cast and crew will hear the entire story from start to finish until the night they take their seats at the film's preview. As such, it's a good idea to gather everyone together for this event. If that's not logistically possible, then the principal cast members and all the department heads should be required to attend (production management, sound, camera, and hair and makeup). Knowledge is power, and the more knowledgeable everyone is about the film, the more powerful the end result will be.

As with every other facet of your production, the read-through doesn't require any extravagance. Schedule a decent block of time (three to four hours), secure a space big enough to hold everybody (a good-sized living room will do), provide some food and beverage (cheap pop and homemade cookies), and then start reading from page one.

You may want to tape record or videotape the proceedings, so that you can refer back to moments that caught your attention, either positively or negatively. Otherwise, just sit back, shut your eyes, and listen, imagining the movie while you hear the dialogue and directions. (It's a good idea if someone besides the producer or director reads the directions so that they can concentrate on just listening.)

At the end of the read-through, you can solicit comments from the group: what worked, what didn't, which parts seemed confusing, and so on. If time permits, you can also go back and have the cast re-read troublesome scenes to help you locate problems and get some ideas for solutions.

The read-through is a very valuable tool because it provides you with yet another opportunity to make changes and adjustments before the meter starts ticking and the money starts flying out of your wallet.

Rehearsals

The best feature of our shooting schedules for "Resident Alien" and "Beyond Bob" (four consecutive weekends each) was that they provided plenty of rehearsal time and recovery time. We'd shoot like demons all weekend, then have a full week to regroup and recover. For many of us, this included sleeping at our desks at our day jobs.

Here's how a typical week would go: Monday night we'd look at dailies from two weekends before. (Since the best bid we got was from an out-of-town lab, we called them "weeklies" due to the delivery lag.) Tuesday, Wednesday, and Thursday night were spent rehearsing the scenes for the upcoming weekend's shoot. Friday night was spent picking up equipment and, in most cases, shooting. Then we'd be back in the thick of another frenzied Saturday and Sunday of shooting until we dropped.

Unlike the read-through, which was a sit-down affair, the rehearsals allowed us to put the scenes and the actors on their feet. Rehearsing is, without question, one of the best parts of the production process because it allows you to do all kinds of experimenting and to take all sorts of risks, without spending a dime.

You'll need an empty space for rehearsing, a location where the owners and the neighbors won't mind if you get a bit noisy or work a little late. Chairs for sitting and for use as props are a must, and a bathroom is always a nice perk.

We scheduled rehearsals using the same approach as scheduling the production. For example, if an actor had three scenes to be shot over the course of the upcoming weekend, all three of those scenes would be rehearsed on the same rehearsal night. This was the best use of the actors' time and also eliminated the inconvenience of having actors sitting around waiting to rehearse.

For each scene, we let the actors do it once without direction to see where their instincts took them, just like in the audition. Then we gave them direction and started to refine the blocking (the movements within the scene). As we worked on the blocking, we started thinking about our shots, noting how we were going to cover the scene. Will it need a master shot showing all the characters together? If so, does it have to be a complete master shot? What sort of shots can we do to get the most out of the scene, to make it as visually interesting and effective as possible?

We recommend moving around while you're watching the actors rehearse, observing them from all sides to help find the most cinematic way to execute the scene. If you plant yourself in front of them and watch their actions like a play, you're more likely to shoot the scene like a play, which, although a workmanlike approach, is hardly an effective use of your cinematic tools. So, just as you've put the actors on their feet during rehearsal, you should stay on your feet as well, circling the action and beginning to make some decisions about how each scene will be shot.

Unfortunately, your budget will require you to make decisions about how a scene will be edited together during rehearsal and shooting rather than in the editing room. You don't have that luxury because to delay those decisions you'd have to shoot more choices. And choices cost money. Very little money = very few choices.

In order to make it on your shooting ratio, you'll have to "pre-edit" the film while you shoot it, providing yourself with exactly the shots you need to make each scene work. On a few scenes, you'll also provide yourself with a little "insurance" — an extra close-up, a cutaway, or any other shots that allow you to change your mind (and the scene) in the editing room.

The challenge that you face is making your film as cinematic and visually interesting as possible while still staying within the restrictive 3:1 shooting ratio. Don't despair. It can be done, with proper planning and with actors who are completely rehearsed.

Well-rehearsed actors are a godsend that allow you to accomplish a lot using very little film. For example, we had a six-page seance scene in "Beyond Bob," which involved seven actors seated around a circular table. With our 3:1 shooting ratio, a master shot would have been a waste of film; half the actors would have had their backs to the camera. Shooting the entire scene from three different angles wasn't the answer either because a mere three shots spread over a six-minute scene would have been deader than the ghost the characters were trying to summon.

Instead, John's shot list for the scene had twenty-six camera setups: two-shots, three-shots, a couple wide shots, close-ups, and so on. However, each of the twenty-six camera setups was only designed to cover a small portion of the scene. Each time the camera rolled, the actors went through just a short section of the scene, sometimes performing as few as one or two lines.

However, because they were well-rehearsed it played beautifully and came off without a hitch. The actors knew the scene backward and forward, and they could pick up at any point in the scene. They knew the lines, and they knew the pace, all because the scene had been thoroughly and rigorously rehearsed. Without this level of preparation, the shots would have had to be simplified enormously, diminishing the drama and humor in the scene.

Of course, you do need to walk that fine line between being adequately rehearsed and over-rehearsed. You don't want the scenes to sound rote or become flat. The key is to rehearse each scene enough so that you and the actors are comfortable, but then stop rehearsing so it doesn't lose its freshness.

Shot Lists

Using your notes from the rehearsal, you can assemble your shot list for each scene. The shot list tells you and your director of photography how you're going to cover each scene. This can be a list of shots ("two-shot of Bob and Isaac, Bob's point of view of the eagle, single shots of Bob and Isaac") or crude storyboard drawings that detail each angle.

As we learned with our seance scene, don't get trapped into thinking that your 3:1 shooting ratio limits you to only three shots. The 3:1 shooting ratio allows you enough footage to shoot the equivalent of three complete takes of the scene. You can break that up any way you want.

For example, let's say that — based on the rehearsal and the pre-edit you've done in your head — you know that you want the scene to begin and end on a master shot. You also know that during the middle of the scene you want a two-shot of two characters as they stand face-to-face. You also want single close-ups of each of the characters for this dramatic moment. And you want a close-up of a prop that one of the characters points at.

That's five setups: A master, a two-shot, two close-ups, and a cut-away. But that doesn't mean you need to shoot the scene in its entirety five times. You only need to shoot those portions of the scene you know you'll be using in the finished, edited scene. You need to shoot a master shot of the beginning and the end of the scene, a two-shot and two close-ups of the middle of the scene, and a cut-away to a prop. If you add up the length of these shots, this works out to about a 2:1 ratio, meaning you shot the equivalent of two complete takes of the scene. With the take you saved from your 3:1 ratio, you could do a second take on a shot or use it to help shoot a more difficult setup later.

While this approach is both demanding and restricting, it allows you to stretch your film ratio and get a lot more than just three camera setups from your painfully limited amount of film. Be aware that this technique should only be used on scenes that require it. If you double the number of setups for every scene, your 14-hour shooting day may turn into a 28-hour marathon. As with everything on your film, do what's necessary, and then move on.

Long Takes

Of course, no one ever said you have to intercut shots with masters and close-ups. You can compose your scenes as long, continuous takes with the actors moving artfully within the frame.

Cinema history is filled with revered examples of this technique, from Orson Welles' fluid opening shot in "Touch Of Evil" (which was parodied in Robert Altman's "The Player") to Jim Jarmusch's achingly static camera in "Stranger Than Paradise." Mike Nichols pulled off some remarkable long takes in "Carnal Knowledge," and directors as diverse as Alan Arkin and Michelangelo Antonioni have made them work in films as diverse as "Little Murders" and "The Passenger." Even Woody Allen has used this approach, to greater and lesser effect, in many of his films.

There are, however, drawbacks to this technique. The first is that if it isn't staged properly, it can become visually boring. If that's your point, then fine. Otherwise, the trick to making a long take work is to keep the frame energized by moving the camera, moving the actors, or presenting a very dramatic moment so that you hold the audience's interest without turning the shot into a filmed stage play.

The second drawback is that long takes are risky. A long take requires that the actors and the crew get it right — absolutely, flawlessly right — from the beginning of the take right down to the very last frame. If someone blows it halfway through the shot or even in the last few seconds, you've lost all that film. If someone blows it on the second take, you can kiss that film good-bye as well. You can then imagine the kind of pressure that puts on everyone during the third and final take. At this point you may become scared and just shoot some other angles and close-ups to cover the flawed portion of your long takes. You'll have lost the power of the long take without gaining the advantage of truly varied camera angles.

Long takes are also risky because they give you no options in the editing room. Often a long continuous take will seem great while you're shooting it, but when it's edited into the film, it will slow the pace or even bring the movie to a dead stop. If you haven't shot any other additional shots (known as coverage) of the scene, you'll be left with no options, which is always a bad place to be.

On the positive side, if you have performers who can do a scene perfectly and a crew who can execute a camera move flawlessly, long takes can save a lot of time and film during your production schedule. It's just a question of weighing the risks and the advantages.

Abandoning Your Shot List

Of course, the best-laid plans occasionally go awry. You may find when you're on location that the scene you rehearsed and story-boarded so meticulously simply can't be shot the way you intended. You may have lost your original location, it may have changed, or you may not have remembered it accurately. There may be technical problems, or you may simply have run out of time. Whatever the reason, you are now faced with a serious problem in need of a speedy solution.

The best solution that we've found in this situation is to go back to the basics. Ask yourself what your original intention was. What ideas were you trying to convey with the shots you planned? Rather than forcing your shots into a room or a schedule that can't hold them, you need to rethink your plan, using your original intentions but finding a new way to reach your goal.

Often you'll find that the best solution is the simplest. Of course, the simplest solution is sometimes the hardest one to discover. It may not be the one that will make future film students "ooh" and "ahh," but if it gets the job done and keeps you on schedule, it's the right solution.

For example, the script for "Beyond Bob" had always called for an opening title sequence that followed our protagonist's car — from above — as it moved from an urban to a suburban to a wilderness environment. The plan was to shoot the sequence from a helicopter and do a number of matched dissolves so that the car would always be in the same position on screen and the locales would change around it.

Great idea, but not possible, at least not on our budget. This "simple" shot would have required a special camera mount, radios between the car and the helicopter, and a pilot willing to donate his time and his aircraft. None of which we could find.

Our initial rethinking of the shots had us looking for tall buildings, towers, cliffs overlooking highways . . . anything really high that we could shoot from to get the overhead shots we were looking for. This, we soon discovered, was the wrong approach. Our initial idea had been to show the car moving deeper and deeper into a wilderness environment, not just to shoot it from overhead. So we rethought the shots, going back to this original idea and finding a new way to do it that got the idea across and still worked within our budget.

The new approach, which featured the car zipping past a series of city signs (all with the word "lake" in their names, like Ham Lake, Crystal Lake, and so on) didn't cost anything but time. Our second unit made a 12-hour trek through neighboring cities (Minnesota has over 10,000 lakes and nearly as many cities with the word "lake" in their name) to capture the requisite images, and we got what we needed on a virtually 1:1 ratio. The end result is a much livelier scene, and one that's guaranteed to get a laugh (at least in Minnesota) as the audience catches onto the "lake" theme.

Continuity

The key to continuity at this budget level is to keep a keen eye on the big things and make sure that they match from shot to shot. Try to make the small details match too, but don't sweat it if you miss. That's because you don't have the funds to go back and fix the big things, and odds are nobody will notice the small stuff.

For example, if you have a character exiting one room wearing a blue shirt and entering an adjacent room wearing a red shirt, you have a big continuity problem that you need to correct. That same character exiting one room wearing earrings and entering another without them is less of a problem, unless the earrings are the size of hubcaps.

In general, the continuity issue is the domain of your production manager, assuming it gets past the actor. (Most actors are remarkably adept at remembering which costume goes with which scene.) To prevent these potential snafus from happening in the first place, the production manager needs to take a Polaroid photo of each of the actors during their final costume fittings or the first time they wear each costume during production. Each photo should show the actor wearing one of their costumes for the film. If the actor has six costume changes during the course of the film, the production manager will have six Polaroid photos of them. On the bottom of each photo should be noted the scene numbers in which the costume appears, listed in chronological order. This technique can also be used with special makeup or hair styles.

It becomes a simple matter then to check the photo against what the actor is wearing before each scene to ensure that continuity is being maintained.

Some small mistakes are bound to slip by given your shooting schedule. This will be much more noticeable to you than it will be to the audience. However, there is one area where continuity errors always seem to appear and where audiences always seem to notice — eating scenes.

Even in big-budget movies, watching eating scenes can drive you crazy. In one shot the glass will be half full, in the subsequent shot it will be completely drained, and in the following shot it will be full again. Food disappears from a plate in one shot, only to re-appear magically in the next. Silverware pops in and out of actors' hands from shot to shot, like Uri Geller on acid.

There were a number of eating scenes in both "Resident Alien" and "Beyond Bob." Rather than suffer the humiliation of this gaffe-prone continuity nightmare, we came up with a solution. We rewrote all the scenes so that they took place <u>after</u> meals.

In these scenes, the plates are mostly empty, the glasses drained, and the dirty silverware rests safely on the table. By the looks of each scene, the characters have finished a fine, perhaps even sumptuous meal. When we got to the editing room, the scenes cut smoothly, with no continuity gaffes — at least, none that we've noticed. This technique also released the actors from the difficult task of trying to talk and eat simultaneously.

Placing the scenes after the meals instead of during them also saved us some money because we didn't need to provide actual food for these scenes. The scraps of food remaining on the plates were always leftovers from the most recent lunch or dinner break.

It should be noted here that your production is missing one important crew person, the script supervisor. This is the person who makes sure the lines in the script are said correctly and that continuity — at least the major stuff — matches from shot to shot and from scene to scene. Our unit production manager performed this function during takes. She read along with the script as the actors said the lines, and she noted details like which hand the actor used to hold the carving knife. Script supervisors on big productions keep very detailed notes, but your project will probably be simple enough that the unit production manager and the actors can keep track of continuity issues.

Touch-Ups

We mentioned this before, but it bears repeating: Tell your hair and makeup person to keep the touch ups that they do to the actors to a minimum. Primping and fluffing before each shot wastes time and generally makes no appreciable difference on film.

That's not to say that the makeup people shouldn't be alert to makeup problems and be prepared to jump in and correct them. You simply must establish up front what you consider to be a problem and what you can live with.

You may not even have a full-time makeup person. Instead, the makeup and hair supervisor may stop by in the morning, do the makeup for your key actors, and then disappear for the rest of the day. If this is your situation, it's a good idea to get your part-time makeup person to create makeup kits for the key actors. Each kit can be as simple as a baggie filled with the materials each actor will need to repair his or her own makeup throughout the day. Because different actors may be using radically different shades or types of makeup, creating these individual kits makes it easier to keep all the makeup elements straight and in a place where the actors can find them.

"Action," "Cut," and Slating Scenes

Nothing makes you feel more like a director than yelling "Action" and "Cut." Saying those two words tells you — and the world — that you have arrived. You are THE DIRECTOR.

Of course, once you've said them once or twice, you'll realize that nobody ever just says "Action" or "Cut." Everybody draws it out, saying, "Annnnd . . . action." Or whispering, "Annnnd . . . cut." After the first couple tries, you'll find that you do it as well.

Welllll . . . get over it. You need to get over it because you're wasting film and, consequently, wasting money. Remember, you're in charge. The actors don't start acting until you say "action." The camera operator doesn't stop the camera until you say "cut."

It's not so bad if you do it once or twice, but over the course of an entire production it adds up. If you've got one hundred scenes in the film, and you shoot each one three times, that's three hundred extra pauses during "action" and three hundred extra pauses during "cut." At one second per pause, that's one 400-foot roll, or about 11 minutes of wasted footage and $200 of film and processing. So, don't draw out the words. Just spit them out and save yourself some film.

Another excellent way to save a lot of film is to start rolling sound before you begin rolling film. Traditionally, both the sound person and the camera operator start their equipment when they're given the direction to "Roll 'em." The sound person waits until the recorder is up to speed, saying "speed" when it is. Then the camera assistant holds the slate in front of the camera and calls out the scene and the take number, "Scene four, take one!" The camera assistant then claps the slates' sticks together, the director yells "action," and the scene commences.

This approach works fine in big-budget films where they have film to burn. However, a more economical approach is to start the sound recording first, record the slate information ("Scene four, take one!") and then start the camera, just before the slates' sticks are clapped together. This technique still gives the editor all the information needed to sync the sound to the picture, and it saves film. In fact, over the course of your entire shooting schedule, it can save you quite a lot of film, at least 20 or 30 minutes' worth!

Where To Begin . . . And Where To End

On your first actual day of production, you may find yourself filled with feelings of trepidation and anxiety. Consequently, we recommend that you lessen your burden a bit and start out your shoot with something simple. And that you start off quickly.

Starting quickly establishes a quick pace for the production, and it establishes the director as a take-charge sort of person. Starting simply gives everyone a chance to get up to speed with a scene or a shot that is not too taxing or difficult.

On some productions, due to the logistics of locations or the availability of actors, you have to start your first day with a dramatically intense or technically-complicated scene. In such cases, there's nothing you can do but dive in and do your best. But, as a rule of thumb, don't start with the hardest scene.

The first shot of the first day of "Resident Alien" was of a car driving into a driveway, hardly a taxing beginning. On "Beyond Bob," we started with a character in the shower. Neither scene was difficult to pull off, and they allowed us to start production with something simple before kicking into high gear and burning through setups and pages.

If possible, it's also a good idea to save scenes that aren't pivotal for the last few hours of your last day of principal photography. These are scenes that advance the characters without necessarily driving the plot. If you begin to run over schedule on your last day, you can eliminate these final scenes without doing serious damage to your film. Of course, it's best to have every scene advance both the characters and the plot; however, there are usually a few minor scenes that can be deleted without damaging the logic of the film irrevocably.

The Geography Lesson

The beginning of the film is where your audience becomes acclimated to your characters, to the tone of your story, and to the environment in which your story will take place. Part of your job is letting them know who's who, what the relationships are, and where the story is set so that they aren't asking these questions later.

As the storyteller, you want the audience to laugh when you want them to laugh, to be moved when you tell them to be, and to be confused only when it serves your purposes. To that end, it's best to perform a sort of "geography lesson" early in the film. As the characters are introduced and the situation is established, you also want to teach the audience where everything is located.

In "Beyond Bob," it was important to establish that the primary location was a lake home situated in the middle of nowhere. This was done with establishing shots at the beginning of the film and then reinforced visually during early interior scenes by placing characters in front of windows that overlooked the forest that surrounded the house. (The "forest" was actually several artificial Christmas trees placed to block out the other homes in the suburban housing tract that was our primary location.)

These early scenes were also used to establish where each room was in relation to the others, geographically laying the groundwork for later sequences. The shots established where the kitchen was in relation to the living room, where the deck was in relation to the den, and so on.

Similarly, on "Resident Alien," shots early in the film not only established the motel that was our primary location, but also demonstrated to the audience where the main characters' rooms were in relation to one another.

You need to keep this concept of the "geography lesson" in mind while you're planning your shots, particularly when you're shooting out of sequence. Scenes that take place early in the story — but perhaps late in the shooting schedule — need to present the "lay of the land" more than scenes that take place in those same locations later in the story.

For example, the scenes we just described from "Beyond Bob," showing the windows and the trees outside, were terribly time-consuming to set up and shoot. The light from the outside had to be color balanced with the light from the inside; there were only certain times during the day when the light was right; and the trees and the shots had to be positioned with great care to avoid revealing our actual location.

As a consequence, the only time you see out the windows in the film is at the beginning of the story. Once the location had been established, the windows were not shown or the shades were drawn in most shots. The audience, however, still believed that the story was taking place in a lake home surrounded by trees because this had been established earlier.

This approach also allowed us to shoot most of the scenes that took place later in the story, whether they were day scenes or night scenes, at any time of day because the windows didn't need to be included in the shots. In fact, many of our night interiors were actually shot during the day. By not correcting for color temperature differences between the sunlight outdoors and the tungsten light indoors, we were able to cast bluish sunlight from the windows on interior shots, giving the scenes the traditional "night time" look.

Directors vs. Producers

If you've ever sat through the closing credits of a Hollywood feature film (and thanks to folks like the Zucker brothers, there is often good reason to), you've probably realized just how many people it takes to make a big-buck movie happen. From the Assistant To The Assistant Director to the Good, Better, and Best Boys, there's a big crowd of folks on the average movie set. That's one of the reasons those movies are so expensive.

Of course, your budget is much smaller, and as a consequence, you will have to deal with fewer people. But don't kid yourself; you will need to deal with them. Part of your job as producer or director is managing the people working on the film, getting the most out of them without killing them.

One of the ideas you'll need to communicate right away is the concept that this is a professional production (the absence of pay-checks aside), and everyone is expected to act professionally. That means that we can have fun on the set, but when it comes time to crack the whip and get the work done, everybody does their part.

Consequently, you'll need to decide who is going to be in charge of cracking that whip. Our approach has been a variation of the Good Cop/Bad Cop method, adapted for our purposes as Good Director/Bad Producer. Basically, this means that the producer is the person who ultimately says no. As in, "No, we can't afford that prop," "No, you can't keep shooting," "No, you can't have a helicopter," and our favorite, "No, you can't have a percentage of the gross." This technique allows the director to maintain her or his rapport with the crew and cast.

Of course, making a film is a high-pressure situation, and con-flicts are undoubtedly going to arise. After long hours of intense work, nerves may become frayed, and tempers may flare. As produc-er or director, it's your job to keep those conflicts to a minimum.

One way to do that is to hire funny people who can keep the atmosphere light on the set. We've been graced with some terrifical-ly funny cast and crew members who have helped to keep spirits up and make the long hours move much faster. From joke-telling com-petitions to dueling impersonations, these folks kept their co-workers smiling and the production moving smoothly.

Despite all the jokes and the fun, you may encounter a situation where a crew or cast member is simply not working out. They may be a constant complainer, a malcontent, or someone who is simply incompetent. Whatever they are, they are trouble, and they can do serious damage to morale and to the film.

Just as no one likes to be dumped, there are few people who enjoy the act of dumping someone else. But in some situations it must be done, and for the sake of your film, it must be done quickly and cleanly. We had a situation with a crew member on one of our films who was not only verbally disruptive but who also blatantly and repeatedly disregarded our instructions. Although everyone was essentially working in a volunteer situation, that didn't allow for unprofessional and damaging behavior. So the crew member was asked to leave and not return. The person received credit for work done, but it's the last time that person will be working for us.

Tough to do? You bet, particularly when you're in the midst of a complicated shoot and you're losing a key crew member. But that's when you have to do it. To wait and prolong the inevitable only exacerbates the problem.

The Information Chain

Your production unit will consist of four primary departments (plus the cast): Camera & Lights; Sound; Hair, Makeup, and Wardrobe; and Production Management. Each of these departments needs to work and play well with others. In order to do that, they all need one thing. Information.

If an army runs on its stomach, a film crew runs on information (okay, and on their stomachs as well). People need to know what's happening, when it's happening, and when it will be finished so the next thing can happen. For example, the makeup person has to give an accurate prediction of how long it will take to get the actor ready for the next shot. The director of photography has to give a reasonable estimate of how long it will take to light the next setup. The sound recordist needs to let the director know how long it will take to change the tape reel. The unit production manager needs to be able to forecast the arrival of certain key props.

The momentum of production comes to a screeching halt when people aren't kept informed or when they receive incorrect information. This point can't be stressed enough. The department heads must provide accurate estimates of how long each task will take during the course of production. Delays of 15 or 20 minutes can eat into your schedule and rob you of precious shooting time.

On a larger film, the production manager would have a large staff of assistants devoted to running from department to department, letting people know when things are needed and finding out how long key tasks are going to take. On your production, you don't have the luxury or the need for a large staff of production assistants. But you do need to keep the information flowing. The production manager will have to handle this as well as serve as script supervisor. In the end, though, it's the producer — with one eye on the clock and one hand on his or her wallet — who needs to drive this wagon train.

The producer, in consultation with the production manager, needs to constantly assess what has been accomplished during the course of the day and what objectives still need to be met.

And where is the director during all this? Directing, that's where. She or he is running through scenes with the actors, setting up shots with the director of photography, refining and redesigning the shot list, and begging the producer for a bit more film or five more minutes.

The balance of power between the producer and director is vital. It's sort of a right-brain/left-brain balancing act. The director drives the creative decisions, and the producer handles the logistical and financial concerns. Often the two halves of this brain will clash. The director will want more (time or film or both) and the producer will insist on less (of everything). Both people are working toward the same goal (the best interests of the film), only each is doing it from their particular side of the brain.

Does this create friction on occasion? You bet. Does it have to get ugly? Not necessarily. People can disagree without bringing the film to a standstill. The end result is usually a compromise. More time and film will be spent on one scene, with a later scene being trimmed to bring things back into balance. As with any creative endeavor, each person must be willing to make at least a partial concession or to seek the solution that solves both the director's and producer's concerns. This is not a struggle to see whose position wins. This is two people trying to discover a course of action that best serves the production.

So, you may ask, can I both produce and direct my film? You can certainly try. When John was younger, he produced and directed two Super-8mm sound features. Those productions taught him a valuable lesson. On a low-budget (actually, no-budget) production, you can be both producer and director, but the odds are that you won't do either job particularly well. When facing the obstacles of production, a minimum of two heads are better than one.

Sound Advice

Although you're working in a visual medium, don't ignore your sound recordist and boom operator during the planning process for each scene. They need to know as soon as you do what sorts of shots you're planning, so they can find the best and most efficient way to record each scene. Ultra-wide shots, characters moving within the frame, moving shots, and master shots with characters talking to each other across a wide space can be real headaches for your sound team. So, the sooner you let them know what you're planning, the more likely they'll be able to figure out how to record the best sound.

Of course, in some instances, they simply won't be able to get great sound. There are limitations to recording with a boom microphone, the biggest of which is wide master shots. In "Resident Alien," we had a scene with three characters talking as they walked across an empty lot. Because they were moving and because the lot was empty, there was simply no way to get the boom anywhere near them. The solution we came up with was one we've used a number of times since with good results. We shot the scene pointing the boom at the actors from off-camera to get a reference sound. Then, immediately after the shot, the sound crew moved into position, and we did the scene a couple more times. This time we only recorded the dialogue as wild sound (that is, not in sync with images). Later, in the editing, we were able to use the reference sound to sync this wild sound with the picture. It takes a bit of tweaking, and the lip sync won't necessarily be perfect, but in most cases, it will be close enough that no one will notice.

This technique of recording wild sound for a scene when you can't get decent sound only adds a bit of time to your shooting schedule, but you'll thank yourself when it comes time to edit the film.

A basic rule of thumb about recording sound is that if you're in a pinch and the sound is bad but the picture's okay, move on. You can fix the sound later. This is generally true. Bad sound is much easier to fix than a bad picture; however, that doesn't give you carte blanche to record bad sound. You'll want to record the cleanest sound you possibly can while on location. That's the primary concern of your sound recordist on location — getting clean dialogue. Beware of the sound recordist who makes your track sound like a finished, mixed soundtrack. You don't want that. You want dialogue, spotless, pristine dialogue that's so clean you could eat off of it.

Sound effects are definitely a secondary issue. It's much simpler and often better to add them in post. For example, in "Resident Alien," we had a scene with two characters sitting in a car with the engine running. For this scene, it was much simpler to shoot it with the engine off and add the sound effect of the engine running later. If we hadn't, our poor sound recordist would have had to try to balance the sounds of the voices and the engine every time the microphone was moved, so that the finished shots would cut together. And even then they probably wouldn't have matched.

The same is true of any scenes with ambient sounds, such as crowd noises, doors opening and closing, phones ringing, doorbells, crickets, babies crying, and so on. Save yourself the trouble and add the sound effects later. You may want to record the effects as wild sound while you're on location, but it simplifies the editing enormously if you record them separately from the scene itself.

In "Beyond Bob," there was a scene that took place in a noisy, small-town bar. During the course of the scene, a live band finished playing a song, and everyone in the bar applauded. While they clapped, two characters carried on a short conversation. We wanted the end result to look and sound real, but we also didn't want to give ourselves headaches when it came time to edit the sound. So we concentrated simply on making it <u>look</u> real.

The extras were instructed to talk and laugh and carry on conversations — but they weren't allowed to make any noise. It all had to be done silently, and all the "noisy bar" ambiance was added in post-production. When it came time to applaud, the extras had to clap vigorously — also without making any noise. Try it sometime; it's not so easy. This looked silly while we were shooting, but it allowed us to get a clean recording of the two characters carrying on a conversation during the applause. (We did have to remind the actors to raise their voices in order to sound as if they were trying to talk over the "noise.") The applause was added in post-production and balanced so that it didn't obscure the dialogue. In the end, it both looked and sounded real.

On a related note, make sure that your sound recordist gets you plenty of "room tone" from each location. Room tone is best defined as the sound you hear in a room when you don't hear anything at all. Stop reading and listen. What do you hear? The sound of the refrigerator in the next room, the sound of traffic outside, or the "presence" of an empty room. That's room tone. Your editor will need plenty of this ambient sound to help cover dialogue edits, so don't leave a location without having everyone stand very still while the sound recordist records two minutes of ambiance. This is also a good time for silent prayer; the quieter the better.

Grain, Grain, Go Away

Because shooting quickly with minimal lighting equipment pretty much requires you to use a faster film stock (ASA/ISO 320 or faster), we had some concerns about how grainy our final image would look. We had read about other filmmakers solving this problem by overexposing their images by one f-stop in order to reduce the grain. (The extra light hitting the film's emulsion causes the crystals that make up the grain not to grow as large, resulting in a less-grainy image.)

Our only concern with this technique was that there were bound to be exposure errors when shooting a hundred setups a day. The lab can easily fix an overexposure by one f-stop, but there could be problems correcting more than that. Our solution was to intentionally overexpose our images by 1/2 f-stop to allow for a small amount of error. This approach still ensured that the images were slightly overexposed in order to improve the look of the picture. We were very pleased with the additional clarity that this technique produced.

Throw A Little Light On The Subject

Do like we say, not like we did.

When we shot both of our films, most of the effort was put into creating motivated lighting that looked like it came from actual lighting sources within the setting. We also used simplified lighting setups that would allow us to shoot from several camera angles with only minor adjustments to the lights. While this approach prevented mismatches in the lighting between different shots of the same scene and kept us on schedule, it had a serious shortcoming — dark faces.

When light is supposed to be coming from natural sources, often someone is in the shadows. If you don't adjust lighting, they stay there when they are filmed. We've learned that audiences pay a lot more attention to faces than they do to the scene lighting. In order to avoid annoying shadows that obscure the actors faces, we would recommend a minor modification to our overall lighting scheme. We would still use real light sources to motivate the artificial light and diffused lighting that accommodates several camera angles, but when it came to the actors' faces, we'd throw motivated lighting out the window (so to speak).

We're not suggesting you shoot a 5,000-watt klieg light up a performer's nose. A small 250-watt to 500-watt light with enough diffusion to prevent harsh shadows could be moved along with the camera to fill in those shadows on the faces. If you're outdoors, a well-positioned Flexfill will do the job. Of course, this assumes that you aren't trying for a moody look.

This extra light we're recommending isn't large enough to interfere with the scene's lighting, but it's enough to make sure the audience can see the expression on the performer's face, which is why they paid the price of admission.

Fade and Dissolves (And Why You Should Avoid Them)

There are two reasons to think about fades and dissolves as you're shooting your film. The first is that fades and dissolves require extra film time before or after the main action of the scene to accommodate the time it takes to do these effects. Because you'll be trying to use as little film as possible, you aren't likely to leave this extra screen time at the beginning and end of a scene unless you plan for it. The second reason is because you should be trying to avoid any transitions between scenes that would require fades and dissolves (so if you want, you can ignore reason number one).

The monetary reason for avoiding these optical effects is that it costs a little extra to have the lab produce these effects when they print your film, and it costs a lot extra to fix the problem if they don't do it correctly the first time. This is especially important if you're planning to transfer your trial answer print directly to video as we did. In order to keep the answer print clean, we didn't view it before transferring it to video, so we wouldn't know if these effects didn't work. At the point of the video transfer, you can't really repair the problem without paying for another print of the sequence, transferring the reprint to video, and paying for editing the new sequence into your master video tape. Not fun, not cheap.

We decided that it was more reliable to shoot the scenes so that no dissolves were needed. Lingering a moment at the beginning of a new establishing shot can tell the audience that there has been a transition of time or place just as well as a dissolve can. Music can also be used to signal a transition. As for fades to black or up from black, these are easily done as part of the video transfer, and you can test different lengths of fades before you commit to one.

Even if you decide to make a print of your finished film, you can avoid all fades and dissolves except the usual fade up at the beginning and the fade down at the end. Generally, no one notices the lack of fades or dissolves in a film, and it can save you a lot of trouble by not including them.

You've Been Framed

You may have modest expectations for your film, hoping it will play at some festivals, maybe get sold to cable television, and perhaps even end up in your local video store in the "Manager's Choice" section. These are noble ambitions, but we recommend that you aim just a little higher, if only during production.

There's always the slim chance that your film may end up as a 35mm theatrical release. Don't count on it, don't bank on it, and certainly don't borrow against it, but be prepared for it just in case. That preparation includes framing all your shots so that they'll look decent if your film gets blown up to 35mm wide-screen format. If you don't, all of your wide shots will cut off your actors at the forehead and ankles, and your close-ups will take on the look of a dermatological examination. You also have to consider that when a film is shown on television, some of the outside edges of the film frame are lost, making your film look badly framed.

So what's a director to do? Our advice is to play it "TV safe." The diagram below compares the two most common wide-screen theatrical formats and the "TV safe" format with the actual frame of film you'll be exposing. As you can see, if you frame your action a little tighter than the "TV safe" area you'll also ensure that you don't exceed the limits of the wide-screen formats either. Many 16mm-camera viewfinders show the "TV safe" area as a line within the viewfinder frame. If you're not sure what it is, ask the camera's owner.

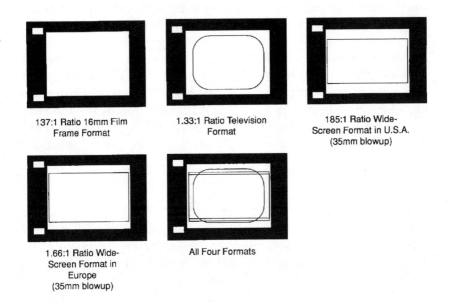

137:1 Ratio 16mm Film
Frame Format

1.33:1 Ratio Television
Format

185:1 Ratio Wide-
Screen Format in U.S.A.
(35mm blowup)

1.66:1 Ratio Wide-
Screen Format in
Europe
(35mm blowup)

All Four Formats

"FRAMING" DIAGRAM

Framing within the television and wide-screen formats also requires that the microphone boom must stay out of this area as well. Generally, we tried to keep the microphone just outside of the film frame, so there was plenty of room for error.

There are many small battles that take place on a movie set, but none is so primal as that between the camera operator and the boom operator (who is being egged on by the sound recordist). Each has turf to protect, and each will protect it to the death to make the film better. The camera operator wants the boom as far out of the shot as possible. Even the next room is too close for some camera operators. Their point is a valid one because when the boom is too close to the top or bottom of the frame, the camera operator loses the flexibility to subtly re-frame the shot during the course of the action.

The boom operator, on the other hand, wants to get the boom as close as possible to the sound source (the actor's mouths) in order to please the sound recordist. That's why, as shots are being set up, you'll hear boom operators repeating their mantras over and over as they (literally) lower the boom: "Am I in? Am I in? Am I in?"

Some boom operators and camera operators bond psychically, signaling their moves to each other telepathically, each working at the very edge of the frame. Others establish a wary, brittle truce with small territory skirmishes throughout the day. You really can't take sides in this issue because both of them are right. It's best to simply acknowledge the battle and to do your best to keep it from producing bloodshed.

Feeding The Masses

There is one thing you can provide your people that's more important than the opportunity to express themselves artistically, and that's food. Hot, healthy food and plenty of it. People will put up with almost anything on a movie set, from long hours to lousy conditions, if the food is good and plentiful. Or even just plentiful.

Regular meal breaks are an important part of your production schedule, as is the easy availability of snacks and drinks. Good food doesn't have to be costly. (In fact, many productions are able to persuade local restaurants to donate food.) So by all means get good, varied food. It shows your cast and crew that you care. We've heard tales of the "great bun revolt" that occurred on a production that repeated too many sandwich menus. Some cheap, varied entrees are chili, sub sandwiches, lasagna, tacos, chicken casserole, and Sloppy Joes.

Extra! Extra!

In order to make you film look like it takes place in the real world (not necessarily the existing world, but a real world nonetheless), you will discover the occasional need to populate your film with people other than your primary actors. This population can be drawn from your family, your friends, friends of your friends, friends of your family, and even strangers off the street. These are your extras.

There are three key things to remember about extras. The first is that you don't want them to look at the camera. Ever. Most of them may never have appeared in front of a camera before, which may explain why they keep looking at it. You must stop them from doing this. Nothing ruins a perfectly good scene faster than some yutz in the lower right corner of the frame who's making goo-goo eyes at the lens. So instruct, order, and threaten them against looking at, around, or near the camera. If they're members of your family, they'll just think you're being bossy and mean. Who cares? Just so they don't look at the camera.

The second point is to be sure to get release forms from every-one who shows up to be an extra. Whether they actually end up on film or not isn't the issue. You need signed release forms from all the people who might appear in the finished film, or they don't step in front of your camera. See the appendix for sample release forms.

And finally, organize any shooting that involves extras for the maximum value over a minimal amount of time. In other words, do whatever you can to avoid feeding them. Offering extras beverages is only fair (we recommend inexpensive bulk drinks, such as lemonade, as opposed to individual cans), but unless you're heir to a food-service business, nothing will chew up your food budget faster than trying to feed ten, twenty, or fifty extra mouths.

On "Beyond Bob," we had one long night of shooting (about fourteen painful hours) in a skating rink, a scene that our actors cheerfully referred to as the "Bataan Death Skate." In order to make the rink look populated, we rounded up all the extras we could find and slapped skates on their feet. We wanted the rink to look full. We wanted the extras to look graceful. We wanted everyone to appear on film, if only for a moment.

We did not, however, want to feed them dinner. To meet that goal, we first filmed all the wide shots that involved the extras and then got rid of all but a handful of them. These few remaining folks — the extra extras, if you will — were sent whizzing past in the background of the close shots to provide the illusion that the rink was still brimming with happy skaters. And we made sure we were done with these remaining extras before it was time to feed the primary cast and crew.

When the wide shots were intercut with the close shots and the sound effects were added, the result was a scene that looked and sounded like a busy skating rink. Although if you look closely you can see some extras looking at the camera as they tear up their release forms, mouthing the words, "When do we eat?" In case you're wondering, these are members of our families.

Photo Opportunity

One of the first things most distributors will ask about your film (right after, "Do you have any name actors, any violence, any sex, or any name actors having violent sex?") is whether or not you have production stills.

Production stills are very important to distributors. They are often a vital part of their publicity campaign. And they're hard to create once the film has wrapped and the actors, costumes, props, and locations have dispersed. Consequently, having decent production stills will make your film more attractive to potential distributors. Of course, if they hate your film, it seems unlikely that they'll distribute it just because you have great production stills, but stranger things have happened.

Most Hollywood films employ a full-time photographer who uses a special camera box to take silent photos as scenes are being shot. Since these photographers are there all day, every day, covering every scene, they burn through a lot of film. As a result, the distributor usually has a treasure trove of photos from which to choose.

Because of time and money constraints, we just kept a 35mm camera on the set and, whenever we had a spare moment, snapped a couple photos. The results were less than stunning.

A rare good publicity shot captured on the set of "Beyond Bob." (Pictured, l to r, Patrick Coyle, Michael Paul Levin, Peter Moore, Leslie Ball, Julie Briskman Hall, Dan Rowles, Kathryn O'Malley. Photo courtesy of Granite Productions, Ltd.

You will get a better set of stills if you have a photographer join you for a particularly photogenic day of production or set up a later date to shoot staged publicity stills. Be sure to get a creative release from the photographer so you own copyright on the photos.

If money is really tight (and when isn't it?), shoot photos, but don't process them until later. Process only one roll, to make sure there were no technical problems. Keep the rest of the unprocessed film in a safe, cool, dry place until a distributor asks about production stills. If they're interested enough in your film to distribute it, they'll welcome the opportunity to pay for the processing of your production stills.

Action and Stunts

We can't emphasize enough the need for planning and safety in anything you shoot that could even vaguely be considered an action scene or a stunt. While we don't expect that you'll be creating "Speed 3" or "Die Hard V" on your budget, you're bound to encounter one or two sequences that could potentially be dangerous. Scenes that involve explosions, moving cars, or even a fist fight are all potentially dangerous scenes and must be approached and executed with the utmost care. To ensure safety, there are two avenues that you can pursue that will help to minimize the risks and still give you great results. You can fake it, or you can get an expert.

In both the films we've done, we had sequences that involved cars speeding down deserted country roads. (Call it a recurring motif.) Although the roads were actually fairly deserted, we didn't want to have the cars zipping by the camera at 85 mph, for the safety of the camera operator, the occupants of the car, and anyone who may have inadvertently wandered onto our "movie set." So we faked it.

By undercranking the camera (from 24 frames per second down to 16 frames per second), we were able to make a car going 50 miles per hour look like it was going 75 miles per hour. (This is the same trick they used on the old "Batman" television series with the Batmobile, which had a top speed of about 40 mph). We then added to the illusion of speed by using a wide-angle lens and shooting from low angles to emphasize the car's movement past the camera. And, voilá, a speeding ticket waiting to happen.

However, when it came to shooting a hang-gliding sequence in "Beyond Bob," we realized that faking it wasn't the way to go. So we got an expert.

The opening scene of the film called for Bob to assemble a hang-glider, strap it on, hold his finger out to check the wind, and then step off a high cliff and glide away across the sky. So we shot our actor doing all those things, until that moment when he was to step off the cliff. That's when we brought in our hang-gliding expert, dressed him in Bob's costume, and filmed him as he stepped off a frighteningly-steep cliff and floated away. Our expert has been hang-gliding for years, so his performance, which was breathtaking to us, was just another day of flying to him.

To further ensure the actor's safety, the shots of assembling and strapping on the hang glider were photographed weeks later, far from anything that even vaguely resembled a cliff. We didn't want to take the chance of a big gust of wind blowing away one of our primary actors.

Scenes that you may not consider action scenes can also have their risky elements. Even something as benign as the skating rink scene we did in "Beyond Bob" had the potential for injury. To prevent twisted ankles and broken wrists, we found a skating instructor to spend an evening with the cast teaching them the basics of skating and the best way to fall.

Fight scenes are another area for concern. Something as seemingly simple as throwing a punch can injure participants who aren't trained in stage combat. Even the simplest fight scene should be choreographed like a tight dance number, with no surprises and little margin for error. If someone in your cast isn't trained in stage combat, it's well worth the effort to seek out an expert who will help stage the scene and keep it safe. The end result will be a well-staged, believable, and injury-free fight.

Finally, there are many things that happen behind the camera that aren't stunts but are potentially dangerous as well. In "Beyond Bob," we had several instances where skylights needed to be covered to block out sunlight, and we had one instance when several lawn chairs needed to be placed on the peak of a two-story house. To ensure the safety of the crew in these situations, we came up with a novel solution. We made the producer (Dale) do it.

While he may not have been the most qualified person for the job, there were certain things we knew about him that made him our first and best choice. He had insurance. He wouldn't sue us if he was injured. And if, God forbid, he fell off the roof, shooting could continue unabated.

Seriously, we feel that's it's often best to do these dangerous tasks yourself. You're in no position to cover someone else's medical bills, nor can you foot the cost of a lawsuit. This doesn't mean that you should approach these tasks cavalierly; however, you can trust the person doing it and you can handle the consequences if something goes wrong.

Intimate Scenes

Unless your day job involves shooting photo layouts for Victoria's Secret catalogs, you may find it awkward doing scenes that involve intimate moments or partial and total nudity. These scenes can be as difficult and as tense as staging a stunt or action scene, with the added pressure of having naked people around.

Your first concern in these scenes should be the comfort and security of your actors. While they may have learned to overcome shyness about baring their souls, baring their other parts is an entirely different matter and should not be treated lightly. To begin with, they must know up front what is expected; trying to coax someone into disrobing on the set is not only unreasonable, it's unprofessional. It's also not kosher to ask them to disrobe under the pretext that you "won't show anything."

The set should be cleared of any unnecessary personnel, and you should be prepared to be very stringent when you define "unnecessary." In many cases, it can simply be the camera operator, the director, the sound crew (if you're recording sound), and the production manager. For some reason, nude scenes attract a crowd like a fire sale, so make sure your production manager clears the set and keeps it clear. During the couple of short nude scenes we had on "Beyond Bob," all of which took place outdoors, we were surprised by how many people "wandered" into the area before we shot. Be both diligent and vigilant about protecting the actors' privacy during these scenes.

It will probably make the actors more comfortable and will better prepare the crew if you rehearse the scene once or twice with the actors fully-clothed. Keep checking with the actors throughout the process to see how comfortable they are with what's happening and what you can do to make it easier for them.

Before we shot a sequence of one character running naked from a lake in "Beyond Bob," the actor broke the tension by saying to the crew, "We're all adults here. We've all seen 'Willie' before." That's the sort of attitude that you should pass onto your cast and crew. They are all adults. They've all seen Willie before. So just shoot the scene and move on.

Viewing Dailies and Weeklies

Depending on where you're located in relation to the lab you've hired for your processing, you may be lucky enough to have "dailies" (footage from the previous day's work) the next day, or you may not see finished footage for a week or more.

If you think that you may not see footage from your first weekend of shooting before your second weekend rolls around, we recommend that you spend a little extra money and get one of the rolls processed and shipped back to you earlier. Looking at one roll from your first weekend allows you to identify any camera problems before you would repeat the same mistake on the second weekend.

Our disastrous experience on "Resident Alien" (where we loaded the camera wrong for the entire first weekend of shooting) would have been an even greater disaster if we hadn't seen the first weekend's work before we started our second weekend of shooting. Paying for overnight shipping or using a more expensive local lab to process one roll of film is cheap insurance and well worth the money.

It's also important to see your first three weekends' work before you wrap the fourth weekend. This allows you to do any last-minute reshooting while everyone is still together and the equipment is already rented. The final day of shooting principal photography for "Beyond Bob" found Dale squirreled away in a small room at our primary location, watching the two previous weekends' footage for out-of-focus shots, low-flying boom mikes, and other mistakes. His mission (and location) was a secret to keep the actors and crew from flocking to the room to see their work and slowing down the shooting that was underway elsewhere in the house.

This raises the issue of attendance at the dailies. Some people restrict who can view dailies to a need-to-know basis (director of photography, camera operator, production manager, hair and makeup supervisor, producer, director — basically anyone but the actors). Their thinking is that they don't want the actors to freak out when they see themselves on film, fearing that it will change the actor's approach and ruin their performance. Or something. This strikes us as a bit silly. As much as anyone else on the shoot, the actors need a chance to evaluate their work while in the process, when it can do some good, rather than at the premiere, where it's impossible to change things.

The only time we've restricted admittance to dailies was when we were in the middle of shooting, as described above. Otherwise, everyone was invited and encouraged to attend. Our reasoning was that once people got over the shock of seeing themselves on film, they would begin to realize that they were involved in making a real movie. This proved to be the case, especially with the more experienced actors who were somewhat skeptical about our low-buck approach. Our sessions of watching "weeklies" turned into a great support group and morale booster with everyone cheering on each other's work. After all the effort — the proverbial blood, sweat and tears — they were beginning to see the fruits of their labors up on the screen. Little did we know that it was only the beginning and far from the end.

SPECIAL EFFECTS
Please Pass The Construction Paper

The goal of movie special effects is to convince the audience they saw something that really wasn't there. We did one step better than that. We convinced seasoned Hollywood distributors that they were seeing $50,000 of special effects when we had actually spent about $1,000. That's fifty dollars of production value on the screen for each dollar spent. Hollywood producers fantasize about ratios like this when they look at their budgets. Ironically, some of the most visually exciting shots were produced for nothing but film costs (and a healthy chunk of our spare time), and some of our most effective special effects went unnoticed, which is the goal of all but the big showy effects, like UFO crashes.

A certain amount of special effects is needed just to make routine movie magic, such as a blender that blasts orange juice into an actor's face, an establishing shot of a building that doesn't exist, or the illusion that day is night and night is day. Some special effects are essential to create a fantasy world called for by a screenplay, such as a UFO encounter or a ghostly manifestation. And most important for all you ultra-low-budgeteers, special effects are used to save on expensive production costs, to let you show images that you can't really afford to film, and to cut costs for routine lab services. And if these weren't reasons enough, special effects are fun to do, and it's fun to trick the audience.

You may not realize that just about the whole realm of special-effects production is available to you. The reason is that most motion-picture special-effects techniques were developed between 1896 and 1933 with technical resources that are within the reach of today's low-budget filmmakers. Even the newest computer digital special effects rely almost exclusively on these seminal techniques. Only the technological method and speed of production have changed. This means that by using older techniques and investing more time, you can achieve many special effects comparable to Hollywood's. We'll tell you about ours to give you some ideas how to do your own.

Miniatures

Miniatures saved us a bundle of money and days of production time. Shots that would have been too difficult or costly to shoot for real were created in Dale's basement for mere dollars. An example of a mundane but completely effective shot is from "Beyond Bob." The script called for a night shot of a stoplight hanging on cables over a secluded rural intersection. The changing lights on this traffic signal were integral to one of the film's funniest scenes; however, this type of traffic light arrangement is relatively rare. We only located one in our area, and shooting it posed some significant problems. First, it was hanging 20 feet in the air, making a face-on close-up challenging. It also hung at a relatively dark intersection with no electrical outlets within reach. Consequently, lighting the exterior of this traffic signal would require powerful lights and an electrical generator. Very expensive for ten seconds of footage in the finished film. So, we used a miniature instead.

Dale built a one-fourth scale miniature of the stoplight out of cardboard, mailing tubes, aluminum foil to reflect heat, a three-dollar can of highway-yellow paint, spare lamp parts, and some colored overhead transparencies. The miniature was shot in Dale's basement using utility floodlights with practical bulbs for lighting. The end result is a shot so convincing that no one has ever suspected that it wasn't real. Sure, it took a day's work to create, but almost no cash. Renting the equipment to shoot this shot for real could have cost hundreds of dollars. Time we have, money we don't.

We also used miniatures built with cheap hobby store materials to create a night shot of a military air base. Cheap plastic jet models were lit by lights shining through hidden holes in the cardboard runway. In the foreground, a miniature chain link fence made from wire mesh completed the illusion for another shot we couldn't afford to light. The key to using these miniatures effectively is keeping their on-screen time brief and making them night shots. Convincing daylight miniatures are much harder to create.

We also used quite a number of miniature signs when real ones didn't exist or conveyed the wrong impression. These signs were usually small so we could take advantage of paste-on letters or computer-generated typefaces on 8 1/2 x 11-inch sheets of paper. For example, Skatedium roller rink is a major setting in "Beyond Bob," but it had an uninspiring soft-drink sign with the rink's name on it. We built our own sign, starting with a piece of white tag board about 8 x 6 inches. We scored it with a knife and damaged the edges to create the look of painted sheets of plywood. Colored adhesive vinyl letters provided the words "Roller Rink," and some salvaged plastic letters from a lobby informational sign were glued on as the "giant" plastic letters spelling "Skatedium." We added a tacky "giant" skate painted on tag board "plywood" to complete the look. A few nail heads with rust stains dripping from them were drawn in using colored pencils, and a grey crayon was used to give the black plastic letters a weathered look. A sprig of juniper branch intruding into the corner of the shot creates a convincing billboard that helps convey the feel of the setting. Cost was zero thanks to Dale's packrat pile of supplies. We used a similar approach to create the sign for a rural sheriff's office. We shaved bark from one-inch tree branches and stained them dark brown to create a convincing frame for this rustic sign.

Miniature signs from "Beyond Bob" and "Resident Alien."
Photo courtesy of Granite Productions, Ltd.

Miniatures seem to work best when they are simple. More detail is not necessarily better. If you look at professional matte paintings that are used to create the illusion of larger scenes or fantasy scenes, you'll be amazed how impressionistic they are.

For example, the matte painting that was used for one of the closing scenes for Alfred Hitchcock's "The Birds" shows a huge landscape covered with roosting white birds. On the actual matte painting, only a few of the painted birds even look like birds. The rest are nothing more than white streaks of paint. However, the short shot in the finished film is totally effective because you expect to see birds. We created a foreground wheat field for one miniature by just making random streaks on a strip of cardboard with colored crayons.

You can check your miniature by taking a Polaroid or some video footage. When filming miniatures be sure to use the same camera angle you would use for the real thing.

Photographs can help you put people in your miniatures. In "Resident Alien," we have a wide shot of a character looking up at a hovering UFO. The person is standing still, thanks to a special-effects-conscious script. We took a still photograph of our character in the actual setting. Minnefex, a special-effects company which offered its services to the film, built a miniature of the real setting and suspended a UFO over it. The actor's photo was enlarged to the proper size on a photocopier, hand colored, cut out, and placed in the miniature setting. The result is a shot worth thousands in street value in the movie capitol. If you don't have a handy special-effects company to build miniature settings, contact the model-railroad crowd in your area. With a few adjustments, their skills adapt well to film production. Also, there are many good library books on miniature construction, again, usually aimed at model railroaders.

Mini-Sets

Many times you need a shot in a setting that doesn't require an entire set. Mini-sets can be easily created that can convey a sense of a larger location, and the audience then fills in the rest at no extra charge.

In "Resident Alien," we needed interior shots of a mysterious spaceship showing an unseen person's hand adjusting the ship's controls. There was no need for the entire spacecraft interior, so a control panel was built from painted cardboard (one of Dale's favorite building materials because it's usually free, reasonably durable, and can be easily shaped). A few lights, plastic parts, colored gels, and a hand wearing a spray-painted rubber glove created the control-panel part of the set. The distant wall of the spacecraft in the background is actually a nearby mini-set constructed of spray-painted egg cartons and cardboard packing material. A little mood lighting created an effective, short scene in the spacecraft.

We've also used realistic mini-sets to save the time of doing special effects during full production. For "Resident Alien," we needed a scene of someone putting bare wires into an electrical outlet, creating sparks. The scene was shot during production without this close-up shot. Later we bought a piece of art board that roughly matched the look of the location's walls and attached it to a scrap of sheetrock wall board. We cut a hole and installed a real wall outlet that was wired to an extension cord. Using this mini-set, the character's costume, and Dale's arm and hand, the second-unit did this insert shot several times to get the proper sparks, without danger to the actors or wasting expensive time with the full production company.

Replacement Shots And Continuity Tricks

Mistakes are going to happen when you're shooting up to 100 setups a day. Perhaps, there's a closeup you should have done for dramatic emphasis, or you accidentally crossed "the line" and your shot is from the wrong camera angle. At this pace of production and budget, you're long gone from the location by the time you see the footage, and you can't afford to take the whole production company back for a reshoot. What do you do? If the shot is of minor importance, you live with what you've got. Those are the breaks in the low-budget biz. But sometimes it's an important shot. In that case, you assign the shot to the second-unit. For us, that was the director and producer wearing different hats. With your inexpensive second-unit camera (such as a Bolex), you can shoot replacement shots quickly, efficiently, and cheaply.

Here's an example. We shot a scene of a character falling asleep at a tape recorder while holding a cup of coffee. In the medium shot, the coffee spilling in the character's lap just looked silly, and we had no close shot. So we took the same cup, a similar shirt, and a different person, and reshot the cup spilling in close-up. This improved the suspense of the gradually-tipping cup, and when we cut to a shot of the tape recorder's VU meter as we hear the character yell, the scene became funny as intended. The replacement shot works great, and it cost us just an hour of time.

Continuity tricks can make the audience believe they are seeing two things together that were never in the same vicinity. An actor on the pitcher's mound can throw a fast ball to a batter at home plate who is filmed months later at a different ball field. Careful use of props for continuity can connect the performances.

We pulled off this kind of trick when we couldn't get a sheriff's vehicle and a performer we needed to an out-of-town motel location during the "Resident Alien" shoot. The scene called for the actor to drive up in the vehicle and have a conversation with a passenger while parked in front of the motel. The motel had a front awning supported by white wooden posts. These posts had been seen in earlier shots of the motel, so we just painted a 2x4 white and stood it within the frame where a motel post would be. The sheriff's vehicle pulls up to a post 60 miles from the motel, but you'd never guess it from watching the film.

It is truly amazing what an audience will believe it saw when it is expecting something. This makes continuity tricks even easier. In the opening title sequence of "Beyond Bob," a character repeatedly walks past a photo on a dresser. With each pass, we jump closer to the photo. However, only the first two passes were shot with the actor in silhouette passing the actual photo. We then cut to an enlargement of the photo which was shot at another time to allow us to see close-ups of the people in the photo. The actor's body still appears to pass the photo, but it is actually Dale's hand inside the sleeve of a black sweatshirt. Because the first two shots established an expectation, no one has ever seen anything but the actor.

Tricks like these can save flawed shots and can do much to simplify scheduling problems during production.

Poor-Person's Process Shots

Let's do a definition first so no one feels left out. Process shots are ones in which a non-existent background is created behind performers or an object, such as a window. This can be done using any of several optical, rear-projection, and digital-effects techniques. An extremely common example is the shot of people riding in the car. Many times the view out the car's rear window is a process shot, and the actors are actually sitting on a sound stage. The image behind them was shot at a different time. When certain methods are used, these shots may be called "matte" shots. No matter what the technique, unless you work for a company that does these shots, you can't afford any of them.

However (you're starting to expect this, aren't you?), you can afford a poor-person's process shot. The riding in the car shot is a little hard to do in daylight, so you'll probably shoot it for real and do what we did, scrunch the camera into the rear seat or the passenger's seat and give the camera operator a neck rub when the shot's over. Night time is a different story. For a night shot, you can just drape the windows that are visible with a black cloth. While the actors take their imaginary ride, just have someone occasionally push down on the bumper to create a little road bounce. You can add to this by panning a light that's spotted to its narrowest beam across the car from front to back to simulate passing headlights. Adding sound effects of passing cars in post-production will complete this illusion.

You can create the illusion of flying during day or night using a similar technique. Just frame your shot so there is a featureless sky with no clouds in the background. You can fly through the air or have an airplane plummet to its doom, and the background view looks okay. We did this with a hang glider shot. The glider was suspended by a rope from a tree, and the actor was strapped to a board on sawhorses. The pilot's cocoon hid the board. Using a low angle shot, all we needed to give the illusion of flight was a wind-direction cloth tied on the glider within the frame. We blew the cloth with a leaf blower. This kind of minor, but significant, detail doesn't really register consciously with the audience, but it creates subconscious supporting data that helps make the shot convincing.

That significant detail helped us do another process shot that is common but hard for us independent filmmakers. We wanted a clean cutaway shot of some actors appearing on a television screen. We didn't want picture roll and other TV artifacts that result from filming a video image, and we couldn't shoot it at television frame rates because the actors had to talk and sing in the shot. There are technologies to synchronize television monitors and film cameras that are shooting at sound speed (24 frames per second), but they were all too pricey. Our solution was to get the front frame of a TV and put clear plastic across the screen. The performances of the actors were shot live through this facade. We just lined them up with the camera looking through the frame. A little bit of light was allowed to reflect on the clear plastic covering the screen area to create that significant detail that says "Hey, this is a real TV." The result looked better than the usual process shot where a film image is inserted onto the TV screen. There was no annoying blue halo around the edges of the screen image, and you could see reflections on the "picture tube."

We've also used a very simple version of a "matte" shot to remove a dock we didn't want in a night scene at a lake shore. The sky, land, and water were essentially black except for the pool of light where our shot would take place. Unfortunately, a nearby dock was also catching the light. To eliminate it, we simply hung a piece of black construction paper in front of the lens so it blacked out the offending dock, making it look like more black lake water. Because the paper was very close to the lens, the edges were out of focus, creating a "soft matte" that was invisible in the final shot.

Specialty Costumes

If you're doing a realistic story set in modern times, your costumes will largely come out of the closets of the people connected with your production. Our first film was a science-fiction comedy romance, so some unusual costumes were pretty much mandatory for the genre. Knowing this, Dale wrote in scenes requiring a monster costume and space suits.

We used one technique to make all three costumes, in part because the script called for them to be reminiscent of each other. The basic space suit was lightweight long underwear from a surplus clothing store. We added foam rubber accessories — chestplate, brief, helmet, footwear — and then spray painted the whole thing with metallic paint. The paint does tend to rub off slowly, but it was quick, looked good, and lasted long enough to get the shots.

Foam rubber is easy to use for these types of soft costumes. Just cut out the shapes you want from sheets of foam that are 1/2- to 1-inch thick, depending on how thick you want the final costume. You don't have to have seamstress skills to design with foam rubber, though it is helpful. Just hold the sheet of foam rubber up to the person you are fitting, and tuck and pinch it into the shapes you want. Wherever you have to pinch the material together, mark the edges that come together with a marking pen, and then cut out the excess in between with a scissors. In sewing terms, you have created a "dart." Usually the 1/2-inch foam rubber works best for this type of fitting.

To assemble the costume, spread carpenter's contact cement (the nasty-smelling solvent-based type works best) on the edges where the foam rubber will butt together. You don't need to overlap the foam unless that's the look you want. Gluing the edges together will create a seamless look. Let the glue dry to the touch on both edges, and just squeeze the butt joints of your pieces together. Voila! Instant seam. If you have the pieces all cut, you can assemble an entire costume in about a half-hour.

For larger shapes that need a support structure, such as space suit helmets and monster heads, corrugated cardboard is our material of choice. It's light, easily cut, easily glued, and usually free. The support structure we used was designed much like the keel and ribs of a wooden boat. The foam rubber is like the outside skin of the ship.

Before you spend time making your real support structure, test your design with a small-scale version that you quickly cut out of tag board (old potato chip or cereal boxes work nicely).

After your support structure is completed, fit pieces of foam rubber over it, cut the pieces, and glue them together with contact cement over the structure.

The beauty of these lightweight and soft materials is that you can easily modify the final shape to better fit the performer, and you can spray paint or airbrush the entire rig when you're done. One word of caution: sunlight and air tend to deteriorate foam rubber and make it crumbly. We've stored our headgear in plastic bags, and many years later they are still usable.

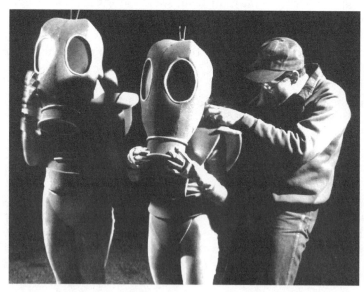

Producer Dale Newton (right) makes some final adjustments to foam rubber costumes on the set of "Resident Alien."
Photo courtesy of Granite Productions, Ltd.

Mechanical and electrical effects can also be added to costumes. For example, we needed a glove with glowing lights in it. We used a painted rubber glove and poked miniature Christmas tree lights through holes in the palm. Wire for the lights traveled down the glove, up the sleeve, and out the back of the costume to the power source. (Be sure this kind of wiring is well insulated to protect the performer; we had to convince our actor that it was safe.) The finished hand glowed nicely on film, and in the medium shot we used, the lights weren't visible until lit.

Specialty Props

We've used many specialty props to add spice to our films and to achieve specific effects. One simple specialty prop was a branch that a pigeon had to walk on for a key shot in "Beyond Bob." We made arrangements to use a racing pigeon as our performer, but we learned that racing pigeons are trained not to land in trees, only at their home roost. So we had trained birds to use, but they didn't like sitting on branches. Our solution was a specialty prop. We used a real tree branch that was attached to a stand. Along the branch we drilled holes out of view and filled them with corn. The pigeon was enticed out onto our branch by the line of corn, and it eventually did a nice little performance for our shot.

"Beyond Bob" also required a couple ghostly floating effects. In the film, we used black string to lift up objects that the ghost was moving. Generally, the biggest giveaway for these kinds of "wire" shots are the wires that the audience looks for overhead, so we put our wires out the sides. We stretched two black strings between two wooden handles. We attached the strings behind a tree branch that the ghost was "carrying." Out of camera range on each side of the branch, two people held the wooden handles. With this arrangement, they were able to fly the stick and give it movements, much as you would do with a marionette.

In the story, the invisible ghost uses the same branch to write in the sand. We did it with some careful editing and a different technique. We drilled a hole in the end of the branch so it would fit onto a large nail. That nail stuck out of a wooden handle and protruded through a letter "S" which had been cut into the top of a box, much like a stencil. By burying the box under a thin layer of sand, we could move the handle and make the stick appear to write a letter "S" in the sand by itself.

Also for "Beyond Bob," we couldn't get permission from a major game manufacturer to use a game board that "mystically" spells out answers to questions. (Hint: The game's name rhymes with "squeegee gourd.") This forced us to come up with our own connection to the spirit world, and the results were much more fun. Our spirit board looked like an oriental roulette wheel with the alphabet and the words "yes" and "no" printed around the edge of the wheel. A dragon-shaped ticker hit nails around the edge of the wheel as it spun. When the wheel stopped, it pointed to an answer or the next letter in the answer. The entire board sat on a cloth, giving the impression that there was no way of manipulating it from below. Actually, a slit in the cloth allowed us to slide a trigger cable up under the wheel. This cable lifted a Velcro pad up to hit another Velcro pad on the underside of the wheel. We just moved the pad on the wheel to match the letter we wanted to stop on. All this was invisible to the camera, and it allowed us to show a continuous shot of the actors spinning the wheel and it stopping on the desired letter. Very convincing, very simple, very cheap.

The Spirit Board created for "Beyond Bob."
Photo courtesy of Granite Productions, Ltd.

In "Resident Alien," we needed to show a rigid chunk of UFO debris become pliable when an electrical charge was applied to it. The debris itself was easy; two prop pieces were used. A rigid one was made from auto-body putty, and a pliable one was made from foam rubber. We painted and decorated them to be identical. The rest of the trick is in planning the sequence in which electricity is applied to the debris. We designed the natural points where edits would occur, such as going to a close-up of poking the electrified debris, as the points where we would switch the props. As long as all the edit points seemed to be ones naturally motivated by the other actions in the scene, the audience didn't realize that we were using them to switch the props. In fact, audiences are so used to this kind of editing, many of them don't even realize an edit has been made. Just ask a non-filmmaker to tell you how many shots are in a fast-paced soft-drink commercial, and they will usually guess about ten. What they actually watched may have been 50 edits. You can use this obliviousness to film editing to help your specialty props create some surprising effects.

A more mundane type of specialty prop was a jail-cell door. We needed one to create the right atmosphere for a small-town sheriff's office, and we couldn't arrange to use any real jail cells. So we made our own cell door by drilling holes through 2 x 2-inch boards and inserting electrical conduit for the bars. A few screws to hold them in place, a wooden box for the lock, and a coat of black spray paint created a convincing cell door that we just slid into a regular door-way. Interestingly, while visiting the set of a television western for which he was writing, John spotted a jail-cell door constructed the same way. The lesson is that specialty props don't have to be elaborate to be effective.

We've also used colored adhesive sheets to good effect. In "Beyond Bob," a car needed to be aged ten years. We considered starting with a rusty car and paying for it to be repaired to a ten-years-earlier look, but that was too expensive. Instead, we painted brown rust on pieces of clear adhesive plastic and applied them to the car's fenders, wheel wells, hood, and trunk. This easily knocked a couple grand off the resale value — temporarily. (The car later rusted in the spots we had predicted.)

Paste-on letters and decals cut from colored adhesive sheets also helped us transform a family car into a convincing police vehicle.

Animation and In-Camera Effects

Optical printer effects and digital computer effects are the standard techniques for creating many special-effect shots in the film industry. However, many times an effect that is achieved completely in the camera is more believable than all but the most expensive lab tricks. Laboratory effects can lose almost-indiscernible bits of reality, a bit of haze here, a shadow or reflection there. While it's hard to put your finger on the specific loss, something in the audience's subconscious sees what's lacking and spills the beans to the conscious mind. Because in-camera effects and animations really occur before the lens, they retain more of these intangible trappings of reality. In the early days of film, most special effects were done in the camera, and it has worked well for us, too. Watch the original "King Kong," which has animation by Willis O'Brien and special effects that primarily were done in the camera. While the animation is a bit choppy by today's standards, hundreds of other special-effects shots still look great. Many times, animation, split screens, rear projections on miniature sets, and glass mattes (scene elements painted on a pane of glass in front of the camera) were all used within the same scene, creating stunningly-realistic special effects. The use of more than one technique can distract and confuse the audience's subconscious minds, preventing them from figuring out any of the tricks.

Some in-camera effects are time consuming and elaborate, others are laughably simple. Here's a simple one that we did.

We wanted to show space travelers being transported by a beam of light from their ship to the ground. To accomplish this effect, we relied on a technique that was pioneered in a 19th-century magic trick called "Pepper's Ghost," which was used to conjure up an apparition. It's a simple effect that uses a thin pane of glass placed in front of the viewer (or camera) at a 45-degree angle. The diagram below will show how it is set up. You've probably seen this effect if you've ever opened one of those casement windows with a hinge on the side. On a bright day, you'll see an image reflected in the glass from the left or right of the window.

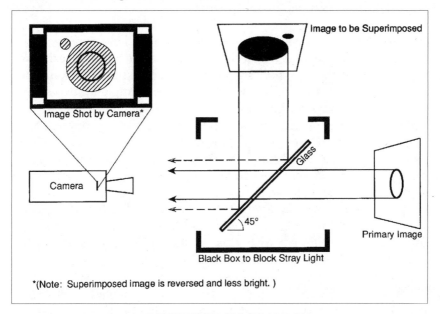

Image to be Superimposed

Image Shot by Camera*

Camera

Glass

45°

Primary Image

Black Box to Block Stray Light

*(Note: Superimposed image is reversed and less bright.)

45-DEGREE GLASS DIAGRAM

We created a light beam that delivered our space travelers by installing the 45-degree-angle glass in a cardboard box painted black inside. The front and the back of the box were open so the camera could look though the 45-degree-angled glass. One side of the box was also open but covered with a piece of black construction paper. The shape of the light beam had been cut out of the paper, and the hole was covered with some Rosco tough spun (tissue paper would have worked too). We put a light with a dimmer behind the paper cutout. Then we covered the cutout with a piece of cardboard hinged with tape to the bottom of the box. We started the shot seeing only the empty location. By slowly lowering the hinged piece of cardboard, the light beam was revealed from top to bottom, so it appeared to drop down from the sky. The light beam's image reflected in the 45-degree glass was brighter than the night location, so the beam couldn't be seen through. At this point, we stopped the camera and brought in the actors to stand behind the beam. The camera was started again, and we dimmed the beam's light source, revealing the actors. We shortened the shot in editing, but other than that, the effect was done completely in camera.

We used simple single-frame animation to help achieve some shots that were beyond our technical expertise to do for real. We wanted a night shot of a military jet landing behind a military air-base sign. The sign didn't really exist, so we made a simple miniature and placed it in front of a night sky that consisted of aluminum foil that was spray-painted black and then attached to a glass window. A light source and some Rosco tough spun to diffuse the light were placed behind the glass. Small holes poked in the aluminum foil created a starry night sky. We used our Bolex camera to shoot a first pass of the sign against a star field background one frame at a time. Across the sky background, we animated a black cutout in the shape of the jet. Its path and progress were marked invisibly in black pen on the black-foil sky. On the film negative, this created an unexposed hole in the starfield so no stars would show through the jet.

After completing this shot, we rewound the footage (a nifty feature of the Bolex) for a second exposure. This time we covered the sign and stars in black so they wouldn't be double exposed. The jet would pass behind the blacked-out sign to add to the believability. A flat painting of the jet was then animated to match the position of the black cutout. The Bolex has a frame counter that allowed for perfect matching of frames, and we kept an accurate log of what happened in each frame.

One of the big problems with animation is that it looks too sharp. Real motion images are slightly blurred in individual frames. The big special-effects companies use special motorized equipment to slightly move models during single-frame exposures to create this blur. For our jet, we just painted it with blurry streaks coming off the trailing edge of the image, so each frame already had this blur. We also cut a few holes in the painting of the jet and put colored gels behind them. Then we opened up the foil from the star field just behind the jet, so the light from behind illuminated the holes in the jet painting, creating landing lights.

The final shot isn't perfect, but because it's short, because it's a night shot, and because there is a jet-landing sound effect to match it, no one has noticed it wasn't a real jet landing behind a real sign.

Our most elaborate in-camera shot involved several levels and types of animation, miniatures, a 45-degree glass, and eight hours of work to complete the shot. The end result was worth it, however. It's a night scene in which a television antenna shakes and becomes electrified by a passing UFO, with sparks jumping from the antenna. This shot was all the more difficult because it had to match live-action shots of actors filmed at the base of the antenna.

To start, the live footage was timed to determine the frequency of the camera's shaking, which had been done by hand for the shot with the actors. Next a miniature antenna was built and placed in front of the same night sky used for the jet landing. The antenna was tipped at an angle to create the look of a shot from below. The 45-degree-glass box was put into position between the camera and the miniature. To create the camera shake, boards of increasing width were placed under one leg of the tripod in each frame and then removed in sequence. This was repeated throughout the shot. The electrification of the antenna was accomplished by a back-lit cutout in roughly the shape of the antenna that was positioned to the side of the 45-degree glass. This created a transparent luminous glow, which was uncovered a frame at a time so it appeared to spread across the antenna. Sparks were added in a second pass. They were also back-lit cutouts to the side of the 45-degree glass. For this second pass, the miniature shot was completely blacked out except between exposures when it was used to align the sparks.

Getting everything lined up and exposed properly was the biggest challenge. The rest was careful record keeping and close attention to what happened in each frame. Even though audiences know that the electrification is an effect, we're especially proud that they've never guessed that it wasn't a real antenna shaking.

Titles

Titles can make or break the first impression an audience or a film buyer has of your film. It's very important to do them professionally, but they can also cost a lot to do professionally — like half your production budget if you go to a title house. So, as usual, you're stuck doing them yourself. We've had pretty good results with an unconventional technique, and we've seen some other approaches that also work well.

The first thing you need is access to a computer with a laser printer and some decent typefaces. You don't need anything too fancy, but it's always nice to be able to find a typeface that conveys the spirit of your film. If that's not available, go for a simple block style that won't clash with your movie's content. If you can't get use of a laser printer, then you will be spending lots of tedious hours with rub-on or paste-on letters, but the results won't differ greatly.

We found that we could produce titles that faded up, did some simple animated changes, and faded down in the camera without expensive lab work. To accomplish this, we used slide projectors with a dissolve-control unit and a black rear-projection screen. (Roscoscreen black rear projection material is under $20 per yard, 55-inches wide. You can just stretch and staple it to a wood frame.) Laser-printer titles, black ink on white paper, were photographed with 35mm Kodalith film to make high-contrast negative slides with white text on a black background. Small pieces of colored gel were taped to the slides to add color to some of the titles. These slides were projected on the rear-projection screen and the camera filmed them on the other side. We kept the image small enough to be bright, but not so small that the texture of the screen was noticeable. Because we had free access to a dissolve unit that could operate three projectors, we were able to take advantage of standard multi-image effects like fading up title and creating glows that popped around the titles.

The biggest challenge was getting the titles aligned properly. First we shot an alignment slide with a box that showed the outside of the frame area. This allowed us to align the camera to the slide projector image. We also manually aligned each title slide to make sure it matched the alignment slide. We taped the title slides to their frames so they wouldn't shift. (You can get the same results with more expensive glass slide mounts.) Even after this effort, we tried to keep titles away from the edge of the film frame so misalignments would not be so noticeable.

A problem we discovered when using multiple slide projectors stacked on top of each other is that the images from the top and bottom projectors would lose intensity as they neared the bottom and top of the frame. Only the center projector seemed to create even light intensity. So, if you're using a multiple projector system, project the main title from the projector that's in direct line with the camera. Use the other projectors for effects only. Shooting titles this way allows you to save the cost of fades and produces professional-looking titles if you work within the system's limitations.

We have also taken our black-text-on-white-paper titles, had 8 X 10-inch Kodalith negatives made from them, and shot these titles from a light table. We had more problems with alignment using this approach. We'd recommend doing it on a back-lit animation stand if you can, so you can do fine adjustment to the alignment.

These techniques require some precise alignment on imprecise equipment, so you can save yourself a migraine by developing titles that intentionally use angled or distorted titles. Turn your problems into your art.

The film "Four Weddings and a Funeral" uses another title technique that is both stylish and less technically challenging. The titles were inspired by the film's subject matter. Title cards were done as wedding invitations and were shot as part of a table-top arrangement of wedding paraphernalia. This approach could be easily adapted to many films. For example, titles for a children's story could be scrawled in colored chalk on the sidewalk along with kids' drawings. Titles for a college-days drama could be written as notes in the margins of textbooks. A film about the tribulations of waitressing could have titles written on restaurant order slips that are clipped to an order carousel and rotated into view. You get the idea. These types of titles can be simple to do and can really help your title sequence come to life.

Camera Rigs and Effects Gear

It's very likely that your script will call for some type of special gear to create an effect or special camera rigs to create a shot. Some of what was once specialty gear is now considered routine equipment. Camera dollies and wind machines are some examples. Sadly, this equipment is often too expensive for ultra-low-budget producers to rent, and it's too cumbersome to fit our hit-and-run shooting schedules. Of course we've come up with some inexpensive alternatives.

We built our own low-cost, easy-to-move dolly after seeing one advertised in a filmmaking magazine. The basic concept was to use light PVC pipe as the dolly track and to attach special wheels to a sheet of plywood to make the dolly. The commercial version cost $500. We built our own for $80. It can only roll in a straight line, and for sync-sound shots, you need to put talcum powder on the PVC pipe to stop squeaks, but it adds a lot of production value by creating some very acceptable dolly shots. The heart of the dolly is the wheel sets that hug the PVC tracks. We made our plywood sheet smaller and hinged so it would fit in our car trunks, but you can add these wheels sets to just about any platform. We cut hardwood on a table saw to create the angled base for standard cart wheels with their own brackets. We made four sets with two wheels each and just bolted them to the plywood base. See the diagram below for creating your own wheel sets.

For the actual dolly track, you can use 10' lengths of PVC pipe. We improved ours by cutting the PVC pipe into three-foot lengths and using connectors that fit inside the pipe to allow the pieces to butt together. This allowed us to carry 24 feet of track in a car. We added some threaded metal rods with wing nuts as spacers to hold the tracks at the same width as the dolly's wheels. The completed dolly and track can be assembled in less than 15 minutes, it can be easily picked up and carried around the location, and it all fits in a car trunk.

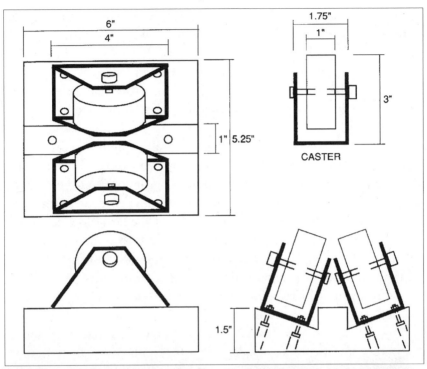

A low-buck but effective camera dolly.
Photo courtesy of Granite Productions, Ltd.

On "Resident Alien," we needed a wind machine to simulate the concussion from an explosion. Our solution was a leaf blower, which is a ridiculous use of technology for removing leaves, but which makes a great portable wind machine for a limited area. We simply aimed it at the actors' faces, turned it on, and we had an explosion concussion that would blow the rug off a Hair-Club member.

We've also seen other slick home-built equipment, such as a skateboard with a tripod head mounted on it for those "I feel so low" dolly shots and simple camera stabilizing gear for hand-held shots. Just look through the equipment advertisements in an "American Cinematographer" magazine to see some of the latest low-cost camera systems. If you're a bit handy and willing to trade chrome and aluminum for wood and PVC pipe, you can build your own versions of these wonders for tens of dollars. True, they won't be quite as streamlined or attractive, but who are you to be picky?

In addition to this general-use equipment, you may need something very specific for a scene in your movie. The first step to designing this type of equipment is freeing yourself from any thoughts of how professional it has to look. The only thing that matters is what the result is on the film frame. For "Beyond Bob," we needed a blender that sprayed orange juice on one of our actors. The actual blender wouldn't throw it effectively, so we built an orange juice squirter. It was made entirely of scrap parts in a half hour. A nozzle of pinched-off copper pipe was stuck in the end of plastic tubing that led to a piston made from two plastic pipes, one inside the other. We taped the nozzle behind the blender, filled the piston with juice, and squeezed the piston together to douse the actor. It was primitive and ugly, but highly effective. You can achieve all kinds of effects with simple apparatus like this. Just remember, it only has to work for the shot, and it doesn't matter how cobbled together it is.

We've also created some equipment that helped us speed up production and trim costs.

In the opening sequence of "Beyond Bob," we needed to show a car repeatedly passing highway signs that are in the same position in the frame. To compose the shots identically, we attached a thin board under the camera that extended in front of the camera lens out of view. To this we bolted a small square of clear plastic that sat in front of the lens. For the first shot of the sequence, we marked the plastic to show the position of the sign and the roadway. We removed the plastic square and did the first shot. Then we composed each subsequent shot using the plastic square, removing it before filming. The shots matched beautifully.

We also saved on film costs for our Bolex by rolling our own 100-foot daylight film spools. You can get better deals on 400 feet of film on a core than you can when buying 100-foot spools; however, you need to find a way to wind the 400 feet onto four 100-foot rolls. We created a rewinder with very primitive materials. A short piece of laminated counter top became the base. Two roofing nails were taped point up to the top with gaffer's tape. The nails were poked through two tag-board circles. In a completely dark room, the 400 feet of film on the core were placed onto the nail "spindle" of one of the circles. An empty 100-foot daylight film spool was put on the other "spindle." Still in the dark, a roofing nail poked through a piece of gaffer's tape was attached to the daylight spool for a handle. The film was threaded into the spool, and the handle was turned to roll off 100 feet of film. (If you buy a daylight spool of film, it's wound to prevent light leaks along the sides of the spool. Your spools don't have this, so load them into the camera inside a changing bag.)

Sure, you can buy professional winding gear, but we spent the money for something we needed more. This unsophisticated arrangement has worked so well that we've never gotten around to improving it. The moral: Don't be embarrassed by any equipment that works.

Chemistry Effects

You can create a variety of interesting effects using simple kitchen and bathroom chemistry. Dale once poured vinegar mixed with food coloring over baking soda to create a sink drain that frothed up with colorful bubbles — a no-cost effect that worked well on camera. By spending a few pennies you can make "bullet holes" in a window and not have to replace it. Buy clear gelatin capsules at the drug store. (Don't wear dark glasses when you do this unless you plan to shoot some scenes of narcotics agents following you.) Fill the capsule with petroleum jelly and a few slivers of black paper. Use a sling shot to launch these at a window, and they will look like a bullet impact. Cheap and safe.

Seltzer tablets and water inside a small container like a 35mm film canister can create mini-explosions. The ever-popular dry ice is great for making boiling brews and mist effects. Mouse traps attached to fish line can jerk objects so they look like they've been shot.

A word of caution: Be sure you know the effect of chemicals you plan to mix together. If you whip up a batch of ammonia mixed with chlorine bleach, you will become the star of your own snuff film. Be careful. There are a number of good books on effects for theater and film that will give you tested, safe ideas. If you're thinking about creating that "Star Wars" explosion, read on to the next section.

Don't-Try-This-At-Home Effects

During our first film, we were very fortunate to be approached by a relatively-young special-effects company called Minnefex. The two owners offered to do our spaceship and explosion effects for cost. Most of the time they were creating effects for television commercials, fun things like break-away bags of charcoal briquettes, and they wanted to do some challenging dramatic-film shots. We struck a deal, and they delivered some great special-effects shots with space-ships, explosions, and miniature sets.

Minnefex co-owner Dave Weiberg puts some finishing touches on a spaceship model for "Resident Alien."
Photo courtesy of Granite Productions, Ltd.

The point is that the people who do special effects professional-ly rarely get to do the really interesting jobs that first attracted them to the business. Most of them have a closet full of "Famous Monsters of Filmland" magazines somewhere. (Our special-effects guys now have John's collection as a thank you for their hard work.) This means that many of them will do whatever possible to help you with your film, just to get a chance to do the neat stuff. So if you need to do some of the dangerous tricks like explosions, ask some of the pro-fessionals. They may be willing to do it for fun. That's a lot better than hoping you won't lose a hand while you learn the art of minia-ture pyrotechnics.

As you can see from our examples, there are many types of movie magic that are available to you on a low-budget production, especially if you have a script that is designed to make good use of simple, well-placed effects. If, as you've read through our examples, you came up with better ways to do the effects we described, you're on the right track. Once again, creativity and ingenuity will greatly enhance your production values where money can't.

POST-PRODUCTION
The Light At The End Of The Tunnel:
Completion Or An Oncoming Train?

Whew! It's finally in the can. You've made it through production in one piece, and the hard part's over, right? Not entirely, sorry to say. Post-production lies before you, and it can be just as grueling and exhausting as production, but in a different way. If production was like an intense, four-week boot camp, post-production is like months of water torture as you move slowly and painfully toward completion or madness — or both.

Of course, there is some fun along the way. Editing is filled with equal parts of pleasure and pain. The process allows you to finesse and perfect your film while at the same time it magnifies all of the film's inadequacies. Your rough cut and your fine cut will let you see your film as you've never seen it before, all together and in one continuous piece. The addition of sound effects and music then take the film to the next level, and by the time you see a finished color-corrected print or video transfer, you may not even recognize the movie that you've only seen as a beat-up work print for months (or years). But we're getting ahead of ourselves. Suffice it to say that the end is in sight, but it's only visible with high-powered binoculars.

The post-production process consists of a number of occasionally overlapping phases: editing the rough cut and the fine cut; sound-effects editing; dialogue looping; music scoring; sound mixing; conforming the negative; striking a print; and video transfer.

Editing

The first decision you need to make before you begin editing is whether you're going to cut your feature on film or on videotape. As with most of the decisions you've made so far, the answer will largely be driven by access and economics. You'll work with what's available and what you can afford.

Editing on film requires using a 16mm editing table and physically cutting your work print (your dailies), which was printed from your original negative. All the sound you recorded on 1/4-inch tape will need to be transferred to 16mm fullcoat, which is 16mm magnetic filmstock, and put into sync with your picture. Your editor will cut both sound and picture, assembling all the material into a rough cut. Further refining and fine-tuning will result in your fine cut. This is the approach that's been used since the beginning of the sound era. It's a tried-and-true method and, best of all, it's often the cheapest way to go.

Another option is to edit your film on videotape. In this scenario, your film and sound will be transferred to videotape, where all the shots and scenes will be assembled into first a rough-cut and then a fine-cut version. The editing can be done on either a linear or a non-linear editing system. A linear system puts the shots together in a linear fashion — one shot after another onto a master tape. Non-linear editing involves digitizing your film footage into a computer hard drive, and then the editing is done on the computer. The term "non-linear" refers to the system's ability to add and subtract shots anywhere in a sequence without having to re-edit everything following your change, which is the major drawback to linear editing. In many ways, non-linear editing is really just a computerized version of film editing. As with many high-tech innovations, it does the same things as the old-fashioned method, only faster, with more flexibility, and at a higher cost.

Editing your film on video doesn't necessarily mean you can never make a print of your film. However, the costs and the equipment associated with conforming your original film negative to video master are probably out of your budget range. Of course, the choice of editing in film or video may be no choice at all if you don't have cheap access to video editing equipment. State-of-the-art equipment generally comes with a state-of-the-art price tag.

But don't despair. The popularity of video editing can work in your favor because it has pushed 16mm editing tables into storage closets and basements all over the country. In most situations, when it comes to renting a 16mm flatbed editing table, it's definitely a buyer's market.

In our case, the choice was simple. With no access to sophisticated video editing facilities, we chose to edit both films on 16mm flatbed tables. Because we think you're most likely to find this same situation and because it preserves your distribution options for both film and video, we will focus our attention in this chapter on film editing. In most cases, the techniques and philosophy are the same for video; only the equipment is different.

Finding Your Editor
In outlining how to find and work with an editor, we're making the big assumption that you're not planning to edit the film yourself. At this budget level, it's a very common practice for the director to wear a couple of hats, sometimes a whole hat rack. Director-writer, director-composer, director-actor — you can find plenty of examples of these combinations working and even working quite successfully. The same can be true of director-editor.

With that said, we'd like to champion the idea of bringing on an editor. Not just any editor, of course. You need to find someone who can work with you in partnership to shape the film and get the most out of the footage you've worked so hard to shoot. On "Resident Alien," John acted as both director and editor, and the results were fine. But sensing that we weren't getting the most out of the editing process, we brought in an editor for "Beyond Bob," and the results were outstanding. As with everyone else who had been involved in the project, our editor brought something extra to the table. That's what a good editor can do for you. He or she can take what was shot and get the most out of it, often finding things in the material that may have slipped past the director.

That's because the editor brings a fresh set of eyes to the film, another perspective that is entirely divorced from the travails of the production process. Good editors don't care how hard a shot was to get; they only care about making each cut and each scene work the best way possible, regardless of what went into shooting the footage. A good editor becomes a partner with the director, helping find the great film trapped within the raw footage.

So, how do you find this partner? The same way you've found everyone else: by grapevine, word of mouth, and networking. Put the word out in your film community and get a sense of who's good, who's great, and — most important — who's interested. Editing a feature film is a major undertaking, roughly equivalent to a second full-time job, so you need to find someone who is as committed to the project as you are -— if such a thing is possible.

An editor who owns an editing table is a plus, but that alone isn't sufficient reason to sign them on. What you're really looking for is someone with a philosophy similar to your own. When it comes right down to it, editing is as much about philosophy as it is about technique. Talk with candidates about what movies they like. Find out who their favorite editors are and why. Start to get a sense as to whether or not you "click" with this person. You're going to be spending a lot of long hours with them, so rapport is required.

Looking at their past work is helpful but also problematic because the best editing is often seamless. If it's done right, you won't recognize how an editor may have saved a scene. Conversely, a beautiful and dramatic montage on their demo reel might be cut exactly as the director storyboarded, with little real input from the editor.

Looking at a number of their past projects will begin to give you a sense of their work; however, the best editor for your project may not have much appropriate material to show you. Instead you may be looking at work samples that include documentaries, industrials, news stories, and student films. In some cases, potential editors may have no dramatic examples on their reels. So how do you know if they'll be right for your film? Again, it comes down to philosophy and rapport. Like everyone else who's signed on so far, the editor may be looking at this project as a way to take a step up the ladder and learn more about their craft. If they're committed to the film and you feel a philosophical connection, you may have found your partner.

Editing Equipment

Your editor may have specific ideas about the kind of editing table he or she wants to work on. If it fits into your budget and the editor can help you find it, give them what they want.

As we mentioned, the video revolution has made 16mm film editing nearly obsolete. Depending on where you live, editing tables may be plentiful and relatively cheap. For "Resident Alien," we rented a flatbed Moviola and the editing suite it called home for over a year for a mere $500. On "Beyond Bob," we rented a similar flatbed table and moved it into our editor's house for a year and a half for $1,875. It would still be there today if his wife hadn't want to redecorate and found that the editing table didn't fit her color scheme.

Though not as elegant or easy to use, a simple editing system consisting of rewinds, motor, viewer, split reels, sound reader, synchronizer, and splicer can also be used for editing. Many people have done it, but it's not as easy to use as a flatbed table. The problem is that the mechanics tend to get in the way of the creative process. However, you can often buy this kind of system for the cost of renting an editing table, allowing you to edit for an unlimited time period. Because working on this type of system will require more time, don't make this decision without your editor's input.

No matter what film editing system you use, your editor will need the following:

• A good splicer. If the person you're renting the table from doesn't have one and your editor doesn't have his or her own, then try to rent one or buy a used one, whichever is cheaper. They're well made, so most used ones are just fine.

• Splicing tape. Buy this in bulk, avoiding the middle-people if possible. It's not cheap to begin with, and the price mark-ups can be high.

•   Spare lamp bulbs and fuses. It's always good to have a spare of each around for those times when the lamp blows out on Friday night and you'd lose a weekend of work if you can't track down a replacement. The person from whom you rented or bought your system will know what their particular table requires and where to find it. If you're renting, try to get fuses and lamp bulbs thrown in with the rental.

•   Edge numbering. This is a process that takes your synced picture and sound and puts corresponding numbers on the edges of the film and the fullcoat soundtrack. This is an invaluable tool because it helps keep your film in sync throughout the long process of cutting and recutting. Before adding edge numbers, you must sync the sound and the picture by matching up the slate's clack and then trimming the sound track and the picture to the same length.

•   Film cores. Once your footage has been put in sync with the sound and the edge numbers have been added, your editor will probably want to break the footage into separate scene reels. This step puts all the footage for each scene on its own reel, which makes finding shots easier as you get further into editing. If your film has a hundred scenes, you'll have a hundred picture reels and a hundred sound reels. As you can imagine, this takes a lot of film cores (the spools that the film wraps around). You can buy these from a film supply store or catalog, scrounge them from other filmmakers, or even borrow them, which is the course we took. When you're finished editing, you can put all the outs (the footage not used in the finished film) on a few reels and return the cores.

•   White grease pencils and black permanent markers. The editor uses the grease pencils to mark where they want to make cuts on the film and on the soundtrack. These are far superior to permanent markers because the grease wipes off and helps to keep your work print relatively clean. However, a couple permanent markers are needed for marking the start points on each film reel and its corresponding sound reel, as well as for general labeling.

•   An editorial assistant. This is a luxury that isn't included in the budget, but you might find one hanging around looking for an opportunity to donate her or his free time in exchange for some experience. If so, it can be a big help. Editing is about 30 percent creative and 70 percent repetitive grunt-work: cataloging, cleaning up, organizing, and putting away outs. To get the best out of your editor, it's great to have an assistant doing the grunt work. As payment, give this person the title of editorial assistant. While the job won't offer a lot of hands-on editing experience, it will teach the assistant the process. It will also teach them what grunt work to give to their assistant when they become an editor.

Working With Your Editor

Often the hardest part of working with an editor is simply letting him or her do the job. The urge to micro-manage the process may be great, but we recommend that you resist it. Leaning over your editor's shoulder critiquing every cut will drive both of you batty and one of you off the project.

Instead, sit with your editor and review all the footage for a given scene, talking about what elements you like and what you don't like. For some scenes, you won't have much to talk about, simply because you won't have many choices — the reality of your 3:1 shooting ratio. Once you've reviewed the footage, let the editor go off and put the scene together using your comments as a starting point and adding his or her own creative "zing" to the process. Then review the work, offer suggestions for changes, and let the editor take another crack at it. Keep doing this until both of you are happy with a scene, then move on to the next one.

We've found that this approach works well for both parties. It allows the director to come in and look at each scene fresh, without any baggage about how difficult it was to edit. It provides the editor with some creative license to work without someone watching and second-guessing each move. Take it from us, you won't get the most benefit from the relationship if you simply look upon your editor as an order taker. Just as you have with the other creative people who have joined your project, you have to let editors stretch their creative muscles a bit. It will be good for your editor, and it will make your film better.

The Rough Cut

As you will quickly learn, the rough cut is aptly named. In fact, you can consider yourself lucky if the first cut of your film is only "rough." For some films, the first assemblage of footage could charitably be called "the dismal cut" or worse. There's an old saying in the film biz that "nothing looks better than your dailies or worse than your rough cut." You're about to experience this firsthand.

For all of its flaws, though, the rough cut does give you a sense of what your film will become. It allows you to get caught up in the story's flow, and — more important — it alerts you to when the story stops flowing. It opens your eyes to the slow segments and the dead ends, flaws you may have been unconsciously ignoring from the early days of the script's development. It may not be an entirely encouraging time, but it's not a time to panic, either. Instead, it's an opportunity to make an accurate assessment of the film. It's a time to really look at what's not working and to figure out why and what you can do about it.

This is the point in the process when you make a real switch in your thinking. You stop trying to make the movie you set out to make, and you begin to define the movie that you've made. All the pieces are there; it's up to you and your editor to assemble them in the most effective way. For some, it's a major overhaul, where the film is quite literally remade in the editing room. (See Ralph Rosenblum's excellent account of the editing-room re-creations of "Annie Hall," "A Thousand Clowns," and "The Night They Raided Minsky's" in his book, <u>When The Shooting Stops . . . The Cutting Begins</u>.) For other films, it's a question of juggling, moving things around, and deciding to add or subtract some elements. (See Charles Grodin's very droll description of the editing of "11 Harrowhouse" in <u>It Would Be So Nice If You Weren't Here</u>.)

Whether the surgery is major or minor, it's important that you keep an open mind and be willing to make the painful cuts in order to make a better film. That said, it's just as important to make sure that you don't throw out good material that simply hasn't been perfected yet. A good example is the seance scene from "Beyond Bob." From the beginning, this was always one of our favorite scenes. It had atmosphere, it had humor, and it also had a couple of powerful character moments. However, in the rough cut, the scene stunk.

The problem started with the sound and just got worse. On the night the scene was shot, there was a problem with dialogue recording that made half of it unusable. The rough assembly of the scene was painful to sit through as sound jumped from bad to indecipherable, making the scene nearly unwatchable. Even if it had perfect sound, it appeared that the scene was clearly a turkey headed for Thanksgiving. John was ready to toss it out and cut our losses. But Dale and our editor argued for it and eventually won out. The scene stayed, and repairs were made.

As it turned out, the only real problem was the sound, but it was such an overwhelming problem that it masked an otherwise good scene. In the end, with a number of the lines in the scene re-recorded by the actors and some terrifically creepy music added by our composer, the scene played great and is a high point of the film.

The lesson here is to use your rough cut as an opportunity to take a cold, hard look at what's working and what's not working, and make decisions accordingly. At the same time, make sure you understand why the scene isn't working before you decide what to do about it.

This process of refining the film — shortening and cutting scenes, moving sequences around, shaping each scene so it has the utmost impact — may take many weeks or months. For some films, it takes years. But after all the pruning and preening, you will eventually arrive at a major destination, The Fine Cut.

The Fine Cut

There's no question that, given the opportunity, some directors and editors would never reach the fine-cut stage. They would instead spend the rest of their lives tweaking and futzing with the film, making imperceptible changes here and there, completely unwilling to throw in the towel and call it done. But at some point you have to lock the film (finish cutting the picture) so that other steps in the process can get started.

One of the best ways to determine if you've actually reached the fine cut is to screen the work print for a small group. The ideal audience is one that doesn't know anything about the film; however, by this point the only way you'll find anyone in your life who's unaware of all the minute details of your film is to pull strangers in off the street. This is the approach we took with "Beyond Bob."

We put together a rough mix of the soundtrack (mixing the dialogue, an early version of the music, and many of the sound effects) and made a quick video transfer of our work print. With the help of our local Independent Feature Project chapter, we then got the use of a local theater with a video projector and advertised a special "sneak preview" of a locally produced film.

To get an unbiased reaction from our showing, we held an earlier, invitation-only screening for cast, crew, family, and friends. This private screening ensured that these people wouldn't show up for the public screening and skew the audience reaction. Although a few of them stuck around for a second look at their work, their reactions didn't seem to affect the crowd.

After the screening, our test audience was asked to fill out comment cards, but this was of marginal value. Most of what we needed to know had been learned simply by watching and listening to the audience while they experienced the movie for the first time. And we learned a lot.

The screening was great because it gave us a better sense of which scenes moved too slowly (too many of them) and which ones moved too quickly (almost none). It also told us which jokes were drowned out by laughter from previous jokes (an enviable problem), which plot points were obscured by laughter, and which scenes got laughs we didn't intend. The screening helped us identify big problems, such as scenes that had to be shortened or eliminated, and little problems, such as sound that needed further repair or music that wasn't quite right yet.

Our showing was more elaborate than most. You can also get good results just by sitting several people in front of the moviola. However, since "Beyond Bob" is a comedy, we were anxious to see how it played in front of a crowd. With the information we gathered at the test screening, we were able to make some final changes and lock the film's picture, meaning we said, "enough, that's it, no more editing." The fine cut was done.

Sound-Effects Editing

Once your picture is locked, you can begin creating the different sound-effect tracks you'll need to give your soundtrack a full, "lived-in" sound. A sparse, hollow soundtrack is a dead giveaway that yours is an ultra-low-budget film, but with a little work and ingenuity, you can spice up the track and give the entire film a bigger-budget sound for very little money.

Before you begin assembling your effects tracks, you need to chat with the sound-recording studio where you plan to do your final mix and find out how many tracks they can handle in one pass. For example, the studio where we did our mixes could handle eight separate soundtrack reels at once; anything more than that required creating a submix of some of the tracks, which in turn required more time in the mixing studio, which in turn required more money, which we didn't have. So eight tracks became our maximum.

Besides the cost of mixing the additional tracks, each extra track also costs money to create because they require that you buy more sound stock and slug (the blank film stock you use between sound effects to keep all the reels in sync). You can see why it's a good idea to really plan your tracks and keep them to an absolute minimum number.

Some sound-mixing studios now have digital systems which allow you to dump a large number of tracks into a computer for mixing. This eliminates the problem of only being able to mix a limited number of tracks at a time. However your budget probably can't afford assembling a large number of sync tracks, nor can it pay for the amount of time it will take to mix all those tracks. So even with new technology it's a good idea to limit the number of soundtracks.

On our films, we generally had seven or eight tracks, depending on the complexity of the scenes on each reel. The first two tracks were reserved for dialogue. Tracks three and four were for sound effects. Some of these were the sound effects that had been recorded on location during the course of the scene, for example, the sound of someone setting a glass down on a table or walking through a room. All these ambient sound effects were separated from the dialogue track and put on their own track once the picture was locked. Separating these sound effects from the dialogue tracks provides the flexibility to mix a foreign soundtrack for the film that includes the ambient sound effects but doesn't include the dialogue. A foreign distributor will add the dialogue in whatever language is appropriate.

Along with these ambient sound effects, these two tracks also contained other sound effects that were recorded after the filming or taken from a sound-effects library. Sound-effects libraries are a fast and cheap way to fill up your film with realistic effects that would require lots of time and effort to create on your own. Most recording studios have purchased licenses for a number of prerecorded effects libraries, and they can put together a tape of what you need for a nominal fee. However, be sure that the library you draw from has the rights cleared for theatrical feature motion pictures (as opposed to industrial productions). The sounds that we bought for our films included effects like cars starting and stopping, doors opening and closing, ambient outdoor sounds, and lots of other necessary or odd-ball effects that we wisely didn't waste time trying to record on location.

Tracks five and six also contained sound effects, but of a slightly different variety. Track five consisted of re-creations of all the sound effects from the dialogue tracks that couldn't be removed without damaging the dialogue, that is, those sounds that occurred while an actor was speaking. In our case, they included sounds like a person tearing lettuce for a salad, the splashes made by two people frolicking in the water, a pencil writing on paper, and many other sundry sounds. Since we couldn't remove these effects from our dialogue tracks, it was necessary to re-create them for a potential foreign mix of our soundtrack. (That's because a foreign mix wouldn't use the two dialogue tracks or the sound effects on them.)

We created these effects by putting together our own little foley stage in a basement recording studio we rented. A foley stage is where sound people create a lot of the simple yet essential sound effects that you hear in big-budget movies. The stage is equipped with all sorts of tools to help them create practically any sound, from a person running across cobblestones in high heels to all the punches and jabs for a fierce fist fight. (If you want to see the funny side of using a foley stage, watch Albert Brooks' "Modern Romance," which presents a fairly accurate view of film editing and how sound effects can change a scene.)

Using a videotape of the film shot directly from the editing table as a visual reference, we listened to the original sound effects on headsets and re-created them using an amusing assortment of tools and props (hammers, cookie sheets, and the occasional body parts). To save money in the sound transfer, the mistakes were edited out, and this recording was transferred to 16mm fullcoat. Then these sounds were edited into the foreign sound-effects track in sync with the original sound effects on the dialogue reels.

Track six was filled with the long, continuous sound effects. For example, a four-minute night scene would have the continuous sound of crickets on this track, just to make the scene sound more real. "Beyond Bob" takes place in a woodsy setting but was actually shot in the heart of suburbia. All of the exterior scenes had "outdoor" effects — birds chirping, wind in the trees, and so on — added to them to aurally reinforce the idea that we were out in the middle of nowhere.

Track seven was reserved for the music, which was either underscore (defined as music that the audience hears but the characters don't) or source music (which is music within a scene coming from a radio, television, a live band, or such). We worked with our composer to keep all the music on one track whenever possible. To do this, he designed each music segment (called a "music cue") so that it would end before another one started, rather than creating overlapping cues which would have required an extra sound track.

Track eight, our spare track, was rarely used unless a scene had an abundance of sound requirements. By judiciously picking and choosing the most important and effective sound effects and then squeezing them all onto the available tracks, we were able to get a lot of sounds in our mix from just seven or eight tracks.

To illustrate the placement of sound on the various tracks, here's an example of a simple scene from "Beyond Bob" with complicated sound. Sound effects are in capital letters. In this scene, the ghost, Bob, appears in a car driven by the film's antagonist, Neal.

It is outdoors as the CAR PULLS UP and IDLES at a rural stoplight. CRICKETS AND OTHER NIGHT SOUNDS are audible. Neal looks ahead and sees that in front of his car is a small group of bikers REVVING THEIR ENGINES as they wait for the light to change. Unbeknownst to Neal, Bob is sitting beside him in the passenger seat. Neal TURNS ON THE CAR RADIO, and he hears A SONG he doesn't like. So he SHUTS OFF THE RADIO. Bob, annoyed, TURNS THE RADIO ON; Neal and Bob engage in an odd battle, in which Neal (mystified that he can't seem to shut off the car radio) keeps TURNING OFF THE RADIO which Bob keeps TURNING ON, each time MAKING THE SONG LOUDER.

Bob notices as the stoplight changes to green; the second it does, he reaches over from the passenger seat and HONKS THE CAR HORN at the bikers in front of them. The bikers turn and glare at Neal, who doesn't know why the horn honked. A second later, Bob HONKS THE HORN again. The head biker gets off his cycle and WALKS TOWARD THE CAR. Neal ROLLS DOWN THE CAR WINDOW, and he and the head biker have a short, pointed, and threatening conversation.

For a relatively simple scene, the biker scene had quite a number of sound effects, some which were recorded on site and some which were added in post-production. Fitting everything on our maximum of eight reels took some careful juggling. As with the rest of the film, all the dialogue was confined to tracks one and two. Tracks three and four were used for sound effects recorded on-site, such as footsteps, the car window being rolled down, and the radio knob being clicked on and off (without the source music, of course). Other sounds that we recorded later, such as the horn honks, were put on these tracks, too.

Track five was normally used for foreign effects. Fortunately, there were none in this scene. Instead, this track was used for the sound of the car engine idling, which ran throughout the entire scene. Track six was devoted to the sound of the motorcycles, which also ran throughout the scene. Track seven contained two pieces of music for the scene, the source music (the song on the radio) and underscore music that was used at the end of the scene. Finally, track eight was used throughout the scene for the sound of crickets to reinforce the feeling that we were outside.

With some planning you should be able to fit most effects on your eight tracks. If it turns out that you can't, then leave out the continuous-running effects (like the crickets or the car idling), and have your sound mixer take them directly from his or her sound-effects library. The sound mixer can run it unsynchronized from a tape or a compact disc during the mixing of your final track.

Looping

While you're recording your sound effects and doing your foley work, you may also need to "loop" or rerecord lines of dialogue that were not recorded cleanly on location.

On "Beyond Bob," we had a couple scenes in which the dialogue needed to be replaced after the fact — the troubled seance scene and another short scene in which the original sound reel disappeared (most likely a victim of mislabeling). In the case of the seance scene, a poor recording of the actors' voices was available for reference. In the second scene, there was no reference sound. In order to loop the scene, the actors had to rerecord the dialogue by checking the script, reading their own lips, and matching their words.

Hollywood films use a fairly sophisticated system for looping lines of dialogue, called an Automatic Dialogue Recording (ADR) system. With this approach, the actor goes onto a recording stage where they watch the scene they're dubbing and hear the original sound on headsets. The system is set up so that they can watch and say the same line again and again until they're able to rerecord it perfectly in sync with the picture. (To see the ADR system in action, look at the climax of the film "Postcards From The Edge," where actress Meryl Streep rerecords a scene for director Gene Hackman.)

You can create your own low-budget version of this system using a home video camera. First, videotape the scenes that need looping directly off the editing table along with the original reference dialogue. Then find the cheapest recording studio you can with a mixer, a 1/4-inch tape recorder, a separate soundproof recording booth with a viewing window, and a skilled engineer.

Set up a VCR and monitor so that the actors in the booth can see the television screen through the viewing window. (You don't want the monitor or the VCR in the sound booth because both make noise.) The reference sound with the picture on the VCR needs to be routed into the actor's headphones so they can use it as a reference. The VCR reference sound also needs to feed through the mixing board and into the tape recorder. This allows the engineer to lay down the reference sound onto the tape recorder at the beginning of each take, and then remove it just before the actors rerecord their lines. The actors, however, will hear all the reference sound to help them sync up their voices with the original track. Just keep rewinding and replaying the videotape until the actors get it right or close enough.

Once you've rerecorded all the lines that you need, edit the audio tape so it contains only the takes that worked. Transfer this tape to 16mm fullcoat, and edit it into one of your dialogue tracks, using the reference sound that you recorded to line up your new dialogue with your old dialogue. Once the new sound is in sync, cut out the reference sound and the old dialogue. Incidentally, you should save up all your post-production sound — looping, sound effects, foley, and so on — and get them transferred to fullcoat at the same time to avoid paying more than one setup charge.

One final note on looping. It's a good idea to have your sound engineer dirty up these new lines a bit when you do your final soundtrack mix. Generally, the dialogue you record in a recording studio will sound a lot cleaner than the dialogue you recorded on location, so your looped lines might not mesh well with your original dialogue. With a little bit of electronic wizardry, your engineer should be able to degrade this new sound so that it matches the original track. If possible, avoid intermixing looped and location sound on the same track, so the sound engineer doesn't have to keep turning the electronic filters on and off. The end result will be a consistent-sounding track, and the audience will be none the wiser.

Music

Few things are as important to the success of your film as music. The right music score might not be able to save a picture, but it can certainly help. Conversely, a bad or inappropriate score can really drag down an otherwise good movie. So plan on giving a lot of attention to this part of the process. Even though it happens toward the end of the line, it is worthy of your complete attention.

It's also going to cost some money. How much depends on the amount of music your film requires and how it is created and recorded. However, at this point in post-production, your checking account has probably dipped into the low triple or double digits — or even lower. Because the creation of the music score usually comes near the end of production, it is the most vulnerable to budget cuts. This is unwise; "borrowing" against your music budget for other production elements will weaken your final product, perhaps immeasurably. So strive to keep money set aside for music, and then make sure that's where it ends up.

Using Existing Music

Through every draft of the screenplay for "Beyond Bob," it was spelled out very clearly — Isaac (our hero) was smitten with Tracy (our heroine) at a young age when he saw her perform the song "These Boots Are Made For Walking." Tracy, who knows this, later sings the song at a pivotal point in the film, leading Isaac to think that she has fallen for him. The song "These Boots Are Made For Walking" was an integral part of the film. It was set in stone. There was no way the film would be made without it.

It's not in the film.

Early in pre-production, as we ran numbers for the budget and looked at the cost of buying existing music, we reached a crisis point and found we had two options. We could afford to buy the rights to the song and not make the film, or we could make the film without the song. It's not such a tough decision when it's presented that way.

The point of this story is that the odds are really against you having the money to put recognizable music into your film. That's because, with the exception of the classical music of Mozart, Bach, Beethoven, Brahms, and that ilk, most recognizable music is not in the public domain. Even "Happy Birthday To You" is owned by someone and will cost money for you to use it, even if it's only hummed or sung a cappella. If you do find music that's in the public domain, you can't just take it from your favorite record or CD; you must pay the people who recorded the music and the people who distributed the recording. This costs money, sometimes lots of money. And at this point in the production, you'll be lucky to have enough money to jingle in your pockets, let alone get a jingle on your soundtrack. Your only option for using public-domain music is to have it recorded by your own musicians.

In our case, the unavailability of "These Boots Are Made For Walking" was actually a good thing because it forced us to come up with a cheaper and better solution. (It's amazing how often that happens during this process.) The solution was to have an original song written and produced for the film.

Creating and using the original piece, "The Last Song That I Wrote For You," solved several problems. The first was financial.

Producing the song was far from free, but a bargain compared to buying the rights to an existing song. As an original piece, the music could be used as often as we wanted throughout the film. Also because we own the song, we can use it to promote the film, which would have been prohibitively expensive with an existing song.

Just as important, creating an original song also helped the drama of our story. With a little rewriting, the song became one Isaac had written for Tracy when they were in college. Years later, when Tracy sings it and dedicates it to "someone special," Isaac understandably thinks she means him. This small change made the movie, the song, and the dramatic moment much stronger — for a lot less money.

Leslie Ball <u>not</u> singing "These Boots Are Made For Walking"
in a scene from "Beyond Bob."
Photo courtesy of Granite Productions, Ltd.

267

However, don't let this story persuade you that using existing music is entirely out of the question. Recordings of the original music of bands and musical groups in your area are excellent sources of music. We obtained five songs for the soundtrack of "Beyond Bob" from local bands who were happy to provide their high-quality songs in exchange for the exposure and a deferred payment. None of the bands are nationally known — yet — but all the songs are professionally produced and provide the film's soundtrack with a nice variety of styles.

If you aren't connected with your local music scene and the musicians in it, find a local critic, club owner, or music fanatic who can introduce you to the right people and the right sound for your movie. It's a win-win situation for everyone. The artists get some excellent exposure for themselves and the music they've already recorded, and your film's soundtrack moves up a couple notches. It doesn't cost the musicians or you anything, and you both might share some profits down the line.

Finding A Composer

As with the other professionals and soon-to-be professionals you'll gather to help make your film, finding your version of Jerry Goldsmith or John Williams may take equal amounts of perseverance and luck.

In our case, we got lucky. We stumbled upon the Hope Diamond in the rough. When our composer joined us for "Resident Alien," he had never scored a film, but he did possess an encyclopedic knowledge of music and a burning desire to compose for feature films — a winning combination. He has since moved out of our budget range and gone on to score several larger-budget features, which is Hollywood's gain but our loss.

As with the other people on your team, you need to look for a composer who is passionate about her or his role and committed to your film. By this late point in your production, it's possible that you've been contacted by composers eager to ply their trade on your film. During our productions, we received inquiries from both coasts and many places in between from composers who were willing to work on a feature project, even one as low-budget as ours.

If you haven't received any inquiries by the time you've begun editing, then it's time to start beating the bushes. Some of the best sources are industrial composers in your area or the nearest large city. These are composers who create jingles and write music for commercials and industrial films and videos. They are working professionals who understand the process, have a lot of the connections you'll need to get the music produced, and who are already doing what you need, albeit on a smaller scale.

It's possible that one of these industrial composers will leap at the chance to do a dramatic music score for a film that doesn't star bug spray or bathroom tissue. Of course, the only way to find out is to track them down and ask them. Once they learn what your budget is, some will lose interest. Be persistent. Make a list of the best composers in your area and go down it until you find a composer who connects with you and your film. Every time you're turned down, be sure to ask if they know of someone who might be interested, a new composer, a promising assistant, or an unknown waiting to blossom (like the one we found). As with every other facet of this production, the more experienced people you can get, the better the end result will be. However, enthusiasm and talent can make up for inexperience, a lesson we've learned many times.

Besides tracking down industrial composers and networking through the grapevine of your film community, you can look to local schools and universities. Schools with a music arts program can be an excellent resource not only for finding your composer, but also musicians to perform the music and maybe even recording engineers. Both students and teachers are candidates.

On "Resident Alien," most of the music was created with synthesizers, with a few real instruments to produce those sounds the computer couldn't effectively replicate. For "Beyond Bob," our composer wanted to create a fuller sound, so he tapped into a number of local sources to get the musicians needed to bring his score to life. The bulk of the score was performed by a 16-piece orchestra he put together, using semi-professional players. Other portions of the soundtrack were performed by a string quartet, and a number of soloists provided their services for key portions of the soundtrack. Finally, for the opening and closing titles, he and our assistant music supervisor gathered together 17 members of the University of Minnesota Jazz Band to create a big band sound. All the musicians worked in exchange for credit in the film and for the experience of working on a film score.

Our wily and resourceful composer also swung a deal with a local music school that provided us with free studio and recording time in exchange for letting their students earn credit by working on our project. With all the deals he put together, and the existing songs we got for deferred payments, we ended up with about 70 minutes of music in "Beyond Bob" for an out-of-pocket cost of about $800 in materials and lab work. A price that was music to our ears and to our checkbook.

What To Give Your Composer

Film composing is a very precise art. In order for your composer to create a finished score that fits your film like a glove, you'll need to provide an accurate copy of your film. By accurate we mean that the picture should be locked, with no further changes. Once your composer has started scoring the film, let she or he know if you make any changes to the film. Even trimming a few frames from a scene can throw off a music cue, so it's essential to provide a new tape of any sequence that you've changed once the composer has started.

You can videotape the film right off the editing table with a home video camera, but make sure that the picture is clear and the dialogue track understandable. The composer doesn't necessarily need the sound effects, but all of the dialogue is essential. The composer needs to know exactly when characters are and aren't talking, to get the right timing for the music.

If you have access to the equipment, burning in a "time code" window is nice; however, a stopwatch is nearly as precise, and if that's the cheaper path, take it. However, if your composer's equipment is set up to receive and lock to audio SMPTE time code, and if you can get access to a video recorder that does this without breaking the bank, it's worth the extra step and the money.

If your composer isn't using SMPTE time code to lock up with the videotape, then precision becomes an issue. Every machine in the process (editing table, video camera, composer's VCR, the recorder for the final music) can potentially run at a slightly different speed. The differences may be tiny, but over a long music cue, it can be enough to throw the music out of sync with the picture. To guard against this possibility, your composer should limit each music cue to less than four minutes. Most machines will hold sync for this long. While this shouldn't be a problem if you're locked to SMPTE time code, it's still best to play it safe and keep the long cues to a minimum.

Working With Your Composer

We've had two experiences with one composer. On "Resident Alien," he came into the project at the point most composers do, as the final edit was being completed. On "Beyond Bob," due to the amount of music that had to be preproduced for lip-syncing on the set, he worked on the film for nearly a year before one frame of film was shot. He continued with the production through the rough edit and right up into the final mix.

This latter approach was an ideal working relationship because it really established the composer as a creative partner on the project. Just as you've done with the writer, the actors, the editor, and all the other creative people who've brought their skills to your film, it's essential that you give your composer some latitude in creating the score. It's best not to dictate musical instructions or give the composer a temporary score filled with existing music and ask them to duplicate what they hear. This isn't a good use of their time or their talent.

The first step you'll go through with your composer is the spotting session. This is where you sit down and watch the film, pointing out where you feel the music should go. Why is this called a spotting session? We don't know. It might be because you're trying to "spot" the best place to put the music, but that's a guess. However, it's an important and fun part of the process.

Before the spotting session, watch the film on your own a couple of times. By this point you've seen the film a million times, but now you're looking at it strictly from the standpoint of its musical needs. Take notes as you think about when, where, and why you want music. What do you want the music to do? What should it accomplish?

A good preparation for this part of post-production is watching other films. Figure out why and where they have music, and see the effect it can have on scenes. Listen to movies, and watch scenes with the sound off to figure out what role the music is playing. Then you'll be ready to sit down with your composer and go through your movie scene by scene and sequence by sequence.

Steve Martin has been quoted as saying "Talking about music is like dancing about architecture." It's true; talking about music can be tough, particularly if you don't have the vocabulary to do it. You may be tempted to give your composer very precise directions ("I want violins to come in here, and then a single clarinet over this part"), but unless you have a master's degree in music, you're really talking the wrong language.

A better approach is to talk about the emotions you're looking for in each scene ("I want some tension here," "The mood needs to be lighter in this scene," or "We need a jolt right now"). It's the composer's job to translate those emotions into music, and they'll know the best way to create what the scene needs.

That doesn't mean you can't play examples for them. We played music for our composer that had the mood, spirit, or orchestration that we were thinking of for certain parts of both films. He didn't duplicate what we played for him, but instead used it as a form of research for the score he produced.

If your budget allows for some extra sound transfers, you can also create a temporary music track with existing music. A temporary score is a fine tool for your editor to cut against, and it will give your composer a strong sense of the mood you're after. The drawback is that you'll get used to the temporary score, and you may want the composer to duplicate it instead of reinterpreting it. That's the situation composer Alex North found himself in after Stanley Kubrick fell in love with the temporary score full of classical music he'd put on "2001: A Space Odyssey." North's finished score was set aside and never used because Kubrick was unwilling to let go of his temporary score. Of course, since you can't afford to pay for the existing music on a temporary score, this won't be a big problem for you.

The Final Mix

Once your music tracks are recorded, transferred to fullcoat, and edited into the music reels, you're ready for your final sound mix. While some mixing studios are more sympathetic to independent filmmakers than others, the odds are that this is going to be an expensive process — even after you've cut a great deal. As much as you'd like to spend days mixing every scene with the care and precision it deserves, the simple truth is that you'll only be able to afford a few hours. You can't afford to make it perfect, so you'll have to live with making it perfectly good.

This is a key concept to explain to your sound mixer. Although yours is a feature film, the odds are that it will only be shown on some form of television — cable, syndicated TV, and home video. As such, the sound mix doesn't require the full theatrical mix with every cricket chirping a different part from "La Boheme." All you need is a competent television mix. If you hit the jackpot and get a theatrical release, the distributor can pay to remix the soundtrack as part of the 35mm blow-up. So carefully explain to the sound mixer the level of quality you're looking for and the amount of time and money you have to get you there. Then get ready for a wild ride.

During this whirlwind process, all of your different soundtracks (dialogue, sound effects, foley, and music) will be mixed together into one master track. During the mixing session, the sound engineer will play all six to eight tracks simultaneously and find the right balance, backing up the film over and over until he or she has found just the right "mix" of sounds. You can speed up this expensive process by coming into your mixing session with a clear idea of what you want and where everything is located.

To do this, you need to create an accurate and complete mixing log. This log will tell you and the sound mixer the location of every bit of sound in your film, its length, and where it is in relation to other sounds. In short, it's a clear road map of your soundtracks. The illustration below shows how we handled our sound logs. Working with six to eight horizontal rows, assign a row to each of the tracks. Then list what sounds appear on each track as they occur, along with a time and the footage count of where the sound starts and stops. The finished log will show where each sound happens in relation to the others, as well as the duration of each effect.

Reel # __8__   Scene # __84__

Track 1		
	Neal: "Oh, I think I've heard quite enough of her for one night." (7:22 min.)	

Track 2		
	Bob: "Don't you touch my radio." (7:25 min.)	

Track 3		
	Radio On (7:18 min.) Radio Off (7:24 min.) Radio On (7:28 min.) Radio Off (7:31 min.) Radio On (7:33 min.) Radio Off (7:36 min.)	

Track 4		
Car Drives Up (7:10 min.)		Horn Honk (7:43 min.)

Track 5		
	Car Idle (7:15 min.) -------------------------------------->	

Track 6		
	Motorcycle Idle (7:13 min.) -------------------------------------->	

Track 7		
	Song (7:18 - 7:24 min.) Song (7:28 - 7:31 min.) Song (7:33 - 7:36 min.)	

Track 8		
Crickets (7:07 min.) -------------------------------------->		

SOUND LOG EXAMPLE

The sound mixer who worked on our two features was a seasoned pro who really didn't need or want a mixing log. His approach was to keep one eye on the film and the other on his mixing board. Signal lights on each of the faders alerted him when a sound was coming up, so he was rarely caught by surprise. The only problem was when several sounds happened at once, and he'd ask which sound was on which track. That's where the mixing log came in handy. This method — a seasoned pro and a couple neophytes with a thorough and accurate mixing log — allowed us to get through both mixes on time and on budget. Plus, the finished tracks are actually quite good and sound like they took longer to mix than they actually did.

In most cases, however, your sound mixer will want and need the log you create. Creating this log can be an eye-opening experience because it can reveal how sloppy or inconsistent you and your editor have been in putting together your sound reels. This includes sound gaps where ambient sound is missing or lax organization that doesn't make the best use of your existing tracks. Don't waste time beating up yourself or your editor. Instead, take the necessary time to get each of the tracks in shape before you walk into your mixing session. It may take a while to put everything together properly, but it will save you hundreds of dollars in the mix.

Consistency is the first important step. If you establish a pattern, stick to it. For example, if you start with all your dialogue on tracks one and two, keep them there throughout the film. If you have some dialogue or effects that require special equalization or filtering, such as looped dialogue or dialogue heard through a phone receiver, always keep that sound on the same track. Swapping it from one track to another — particularly in the middle of a scene — is going to waste time and cost money during the mix.

We mixed "Resident Alien" in eight hours. We did a really quick mix of "Beyond Bob" for the sneak preview of our work print in only five hours. The final mix of "Beyond Bob" had a more complex track than either of these, but we were still able to get it all mixed in 14 hours. To keep yourself on track and on budget during the mix, figure out in advance how many hours you can afford or how many

275

hours you're getting in the deal you've cut. Once you know how many hours you have to work with, take your script and divide the number of pages by the number of hours you've got. This will tell you how many pages you have to get through during every hour of the mix.

For example, if you can afford ten hours of mixing and your script is 90 pages, then you need to mix 9 pages an hour. Of course, some hours may be more productive than others. You may get 12 pages done in one hour, so you'll only need to mix six pages during the next hour. However, don't slow up. The time you gain by moving rapidly through easy sections will be quickly eaten up by the rough spots.

In order to keep up our pace while John directed the mixing session, Dale served as a human metronome, tracking and reporting our progress at 15-minute intervals. Figure out in advance which sections of the film will require the most work, and try to pace yourself to provide extra time during these trouble spots. These can include sections that need a lot of equalization and cleanup or scenes that have a number of precise or tricky cues.

At the end of your mix, you'll want to listen to the entire mixed soundtrack from beginning to end to check for errors. If they'll let you do it for free, do it in the mixing studio. If they want to charge you for the time, politely decline, and take the mixed soundtrack back to the editing table to listen to it there. There's no sense adding two hours of studio time to your bill just to listen to the track. Granted, it won't sound great on the tiny speaker or headphones on the editing table, but you're really only listening for big mistakes and sync problems. Those will be evident on the table, and you won't have to pay for it by the hour.

A word of warning: Use a head degausser to de-magnetize the sound heads on the editing table before you listen to the mixed soundtrack. This will prevent distortions from being created on your brand-new mix. (This is also a good routine procedure to do when you're editing the sound tracks.) Only listen to the mixed soundtrack once. Then pack it up securely, and put it in the film vault or the safest, driest, coolest (but not freezing) place you have. Losing or damaging your mixed soundtrack is not the end of the world — you've still got the original, unmixed tracks — but it's a costly item and a pain to redo.

Conforming

You haven't gotten this far by being a conformist, and we don't expect you to start now. A major theme throughout this book has been that there are many film jobs that don't require hiring professionals. Negative conforming is not such a job. When it comes time to conform your negative, it's not a time for do-it-yourselfing.

The negative conformer's job is to take your film's negative and cut it to match the edits in your finished work print. It's a job that requires great precision, attention to detail, and cleanliness. Your film negative is a precious, almost sacred thing. You must guard it with your life. And you must only hand it over to a professional, particularly when this professional is wielding a scissors. A wrong cut or a scratch on the negative are problems that will take years off your life and haunt you and your film to your grave.

You may be forced to pay the going rate for your conformer's services. The increase in projects shot on film but edited on video may have lessened the need for negative cutting, but there's still a market out there. So the negative cutters in your area may not be looking for work, particularly projects with low price tags.

For once, your budget can work to your advantage when negotiating conforming rates. Due to your low shooting ratio, you can justifiably argue that — for a feature film — the conformer will have very little film to dig through and possibly fewer edits than the average MTV video. This will help to make your project seem less burdensome than other features, and therefore more attractive. In the end, you'll doubtless have to lay out some cash for this procedure, so you might as well bite the bullet and get someone who's a pro.

One final note on negative cutting: In the process of cutting your negative, you will lose one frame on each end of every shot. That is, if a shot in your work print is 12 frames long, 14 frames of your negative will be used in the process. The first and last frames will be used to glue the negative to the black leader between shots on the A roll and on the B roll being assembled by the negative cutter. Losing these two frames usually isn't a problem unless your editor has used these frames later in the film. For example, in an edited sequence you might have a shot of a person's face, cut to what they're reacting to, then cut back to the shot of their face at the exact place you left off. When it comes time for your negative cutter to conform this sequence, you'll be short two frames between the shots.

To avoid this problem, remind your editor to make sure there are always two frames left between shots taken from the same strip of film.

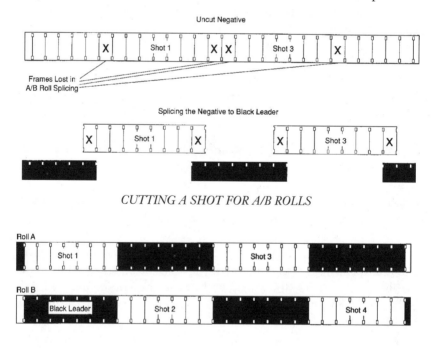

CUTTING A SHOT FOR A/B ROLLS

CONFORMING THE A/B ROLLS

Striking A Print

You're so close to the end now you can taste it. Just a couple more procedures — and a couple more big invoices — and your film will be done.

With your conformed A/B ROLL negative, you're now ready to strike a print of your film. Before you send the film out to a lab, though, it's time to take another cold, hard look at its potential. Do you really need to finish on film? Will you ever need to run the finished movie through a film projector, or is it more likely that all future audiences will be watching it on some form of video?

Making a release print is an expensive proposition, so be sure you really need to have a finished film print of your feature before you lay out the cash. If the festivals you want to attend insist on screening projects on film rather than tape, you may have little choice. But if your market is strictly home video and cable television, you may have no need for a finished print of your film. The choice you ultimately make will determine whether the next step is expensive or really expensive.

Regardless of whether your end product will be film or video, you're still going to need to get a trial answer print made. This print will either be used for your video transfer or as the first step in creating a release print.

To find the right lab to make this print, we offer two recommendations. First, put the job out for bid in order to find the most competitive price (we've listed some of the bigger labs in the appendix). And second, all things being equal, you should go to a lab that has experience doing feature films that have been shot on 16mm. Don't be shy about calling and asking them about their experience with 16mm features, how many they work on in a year, and what ratio it is to the rest of their work.

Once you've picked the lab to create your trial answer print (and subsequent prints, if you're going that route), send them your conformed negative, your work print, and any notes on color and timing corrections you feel are necessary. Include footage counts with your correction notes.

It can be quite nerve-racking to send all this valuable material away to strangers in another city, but there are some things you can do to put your mind more at ease. Be sure to put all the items in plastic bags (in case the package hits a rain storm or worse), and pack everything with plenty of padding to cushion any blows.

Although it's more expensive, use overnight or two-day shipping because the less time the package is traveling the less likely it is to suffer mishaps. If the package is crossing the border, be sure to check on customs requirements and tariffs — they will add to your costs.

For the trial answer print, the lab will take your checkerboarded A/B rolls and create a single strand of film with the lab's best guess at how you want your film to look.

If you're going to take the additional step of striking a release print, you'll look at the trial answer print, make notes about what's right and what's wrong, and send it back to the lab for correction and reprinting. Once they get the timing to your satisfaction, they'll create the final answer print. You'll also need to have the lab make an optical soundtrack from your mixed fullcoat track and have it lined up with the negative so that your final print will have sound. Money will be leaping from your wallet like frogs from a stew pot, but you'll get a finished print you can project.

If you're only going as far as the video transfer, you'll make all final corrections on video. So don't look at your trial answer print when you get it back, because running it through a projector may add scratches and dirt to the print. Instead, wait until you're in the video-transfer suite to view it. Their machines are designed for kinder, gentler projection and won't harm the film.

If you decide to finish on film by making a final release print with an optical soundtrack, don't run it through a projector until you've made a video transfer. Even if you're going the film route, you'll still need to be able to show the film to interested people on video. To get the best sound, don't use the optical track for the video transfer. Go back to your mixed fullcoat track which has much better audio quality.

Whether you go the film print or video transfer route, be sure to ask the lab for the timing-light and footage logs for future reference. You may need these for future prints of the film.

Video Transfer

The final step of the post-production process is making that transfer from a film print to a master videotape. This is the point in the process where everything really comes together and the budgetary restraints (they may be feeling like weighted shackles by this point) finally pay off. Your film, transferred properly to video, will look as good as many of the films people rent in video stores and watch on television — films that were shot on 35mm and cost millions of dollars. You've produced a similar product, at a fraction of the cost. This is a time for true celebration. But don't open the champagne until after the video transfer; you'll need to keep your wits about you.

Getting the quality image that you need requires a particular type of transfer system, such as a Rank-Cintel, a Rank-Ursa, or a Bosch system. These systems are the descendants of the film chains used by television stations years ago to get news film onto videotape. The basic principle behind a film chain is projecting a film image and pointing a television camera at it. The new telecine systems use flying-spot-scanner technology that rapidly scans each film frame as it passes. These systems can "read" much more image information from the film frame than the old systems. Because even the stepsister 16mm film format contains more image information than broadcast-quality video, these systems can produce video images from 16mm that can rival the look of 35mm film transferred to video.

Proving this point, several television series are being produced in 16mm, and they look every bit as good as those filmed in 35mm.

In addition to this high-quality transfer technology, many of these telecine systems include computer systems to correct and manipulate the image as it is being transferred to video.

The people who operate these telecine systems are called the color timers or colorists. They control the adjustments for color, contrast, and brightness of the image, much like the color timers in a film lab, but with more adjustments. They balance each shot with the one before it and the one after it. The colorists you'll work with probably spend most of their days working on 30-second advertisements, making and refining nearly imperceptible adjustments to high-end film commercials. Now, we're not suggesting that your film doesn't deserve that sort of painstaking care. It does, but it won't get it. You can't afford it, and you need to explain that to your colorist.

In our search for the right transfer house, we found that some organizations simply don't like to work at the pace we needed. They were very proud of their work and felt they'd be compromising their standards to do anything less than their best. Unfortunately, we couldn't afford their best, nor did we need it. We thought their "good enough" would be fine. So we went elsewhere.

The transfer house we ended up using understood what we wanted, and they gave it to us — plus more. They spent more time than we asked for and made more refinements than we needed. They just couldn't help themselves. They tweaked. They adjusted. They made tiny changes that we couldn't see, but it seemed to make them happy. As long as it didn't cost us any extra, we didn't complain.

Usually there are two levels of service you can ask for at a transfer facility: a supervised or an unsupervised transfer. The difference is you. For the supervised transfer, they work at the hours you set and under your direction. With an unsupervised transfer, they work whenever they can fit in your project, and you're not there to give direction. Instead, you look at the finished transfer, give them notes, and they make the changes later — again, on their schedule, without you.

We've found that it is possible to meet them halfway on this. You can cut a deal that allows you to sit in and be available for questions while only paying the unsupervised rate or even less. In order for this to work, you have to be willing to show up whenever they're able to work on the film, which may be during their second or third shift. You also have to promise to not slow them down with a lot of special requests. Usually this won't be a problem, because their standards for what looks right are probably higher than yours. In order not to be billed extra for their unsolicited refinements, try to negotiate a flat rate rather than an hourly rate for a transfer.

You may have to shop around to find a place that will cut a deal to let you sit in, but someone will. Nobody likes to have a million-dollar machine and a salaried employee sitting idle when they could at least be doing a cut-rate job with you watching. It's important to be there to answer questions as they make their way through your film ("How dark do you want this night scene?"), but it's also an important part of the process. This is the last step of post-production where your film is really and finally finished. It's a truly great moment and a great feeling. You'd hate to be home sleeping when it happened.

Keeping In Touch

The post-production process we've just outlined can take from three months to three years, depending on your degree of patience and the depth of your pockets. While you may be quite busy working on the film during this time, many of the people who worked on earlier phases of the project may begin to think that you and the film have dropped off the face of the earth. Nowadays, with TV docudramas turning up on television only weeks after the actual event, most people don't realize how long it can take to complete a feature film, particularly a feature film that's darn near out of cash.

In order to keep your ever-growing list of supporters updated on the progress of your film, we recommend creating a regular or irregular newsletter. It doesn't need to be elaborate. It's enough to give a one-page recap of the film's current status, the upcoming steps in the process, and maybe news about what's going on in the lives of the cast and crew.

This is a simple way to keep in touch and it allows the people who've donated their time and talents to follow the filmmaking process to its inevitable (and occasionally interminable) conclusion. The mailing list for this newsletter will also come in handy when it's time to schedule your premiere . . . or find help for your next film.

DISTRIBUTION
Read This Chapter First!

Of course, if we had really wanted you to read this chapter first, we would have put it first. But, as with most other independent film-makers, we're in denial about distribution. After reading the following pages, you may be as well.

As you're about to learn, distribution is the stage of the process where reality begins to settle in, and as they say, reality bites.

The reality is that if you thought it was tough to make your film, you ain't seen nothing yet.

The reality is that you're going to have trouble finding a distributor who wants to market your film. Maybe even a lot of trouble.

The reality is that most independent films never find distribution — and when we say distribution, we're talking about all forms, theatrical, home video, cable, and broadcast. Some statistics suggest that only about 10 percent of the feature films made every year ever find any sort of outlet. That means 90 percent of all the ultra-low-budget, low-budget, medium-budget, and even high-budget films never see the light of day.

Of course, there are those rare few that break through, reach an audience, receive acclaim, and pave the way for the filmmaker's next project. But for every one of those success stories, there are another nine stories with less-happy endings.

The road to independent-film success is strewn with films that got this far and then petered out. What went wrong with these films? Did the makers simply lose momentum? Were the finished films unmarketable? Or did the distributors refuse to take a risk and let these films die before they ever really had a chance to live?

Yes. Yes. And yes. Plus a thousand other reasons.

Distribution is its own special level of hell, different from the raising-money level of hell, the production level of hell, and the rough-cut level of hell. The primary cause of this torment is that when you start looking for a distributor, your film changes from being a personal expression of your own imagination into a mere product, which will be marketed and sold alongside Crest and Spam.

But unlike those well-known brand names, your product is the one and only, a prototype without an audience. Of course, this problem is not unique to independent films. This is true of all films, and that's why distributors love films with presold elements, such as big-name actors, a well-known director, a screenplay based on a famous book, or nearly any title that's followed by Roman numerals. Unfortunately, your film will likely have none of these elements, which will make it more difficult as you make your way through the distribution obstacle course.

The one thing your film can have that will make it attractive to distributors is a great story. An involving story. A surprising story. In talking to distributors about what they look for in films, we heard again and again that the more excited they are about your story, the less concerned they are about big names and big production values. In short, you don't need to blow up buildings, but you do need a story that explodes onto the screen with characters an audience can care about.

So, if you are actually reading this chapter first, double your efforts on your script, and make sure it's the very best it can be. There's usually a long time between when you write your script and when you start knocking on doors to find a distributor, but your early efforts on the script will pay off when it comes time to try to sell your finished film.

The Distribution Stream

Generally speaking, most dramatic feature films follow a similar path through the various levels of the distribution system. First comes a theatrical release in mainstream or art-house theaters. This is followed by an appearance on one or more of the pay-per-view systems. Once this venue has been exhausted, the film moves onto the pay TV channels (that is, premium cable channels, such as HBO and Showtime). At about that same time, the film will show up on video store shelves. Next, it's on to the basic cable networks, network television, and then finally syndicated TV.

A film can jump into this distribution stream at any point. For example, many low-budget independent films never get a theatrical release or even make it to pay-per-view. Instead they start their distribution life on cable channels or go directly to video stores. On very rare occasions a film may swim upstream; that is, it starts on home video or cable and then moves to a theatrical release. Notable examples are John Dahl's "Red Rock West" and "The Last Seduction," both of which were made for theatrical release but which debuted on cable before moving into the theaters. In most cases, though, wherever you dive in is your starting point, and it's all downstream from there.

When Should You Approach Distributors?

There are two answers to this question: As soon as your film is perfect or when it's completely done. Whichever comes first.

Showing your film before it's entirely finished is not a wise move because distribution people are notoriously literal-minded. They see what is, not what might be. As a result, it can seriously hurt your film's chances to screen it for them in rough cut or unmixed form.

Showing a rough cut with a partially mixed soundtrack to an audience to gauge their reaction is one thing. Showing the same, unfinished film to distributors is entirely another. No matter how many caveats you issue before the screening, once the lights go down or they press "play" on the VCR, your film will be judged as a finished product and not for its potential. And once a distributor has looked at a film and passed on it, very few will reconsider the same film later. The demands on their time are just too great.

Of course, if you're desperate for finishing funds, this argument may be falling on deaf ears. It certainly fell on ours. While we were trying to finish "Beyond Bob," we sent a fine cut of the work print to a number of distributors in hopes of enticing them to pony up some cash to finish the film. We didn't get any offers, but at the same time, the work print did win a top award at a large festival, which certainly proves something, although we're not exactly sure what. However, we still believe that it's in your best interest to show potential distributors only the most completely perfect movie you can make.

How To Find Them / How To Be Found

Before you can start tracking down distributors, you need to decide what sort of distributor you want; that is, at what point in the distribution stream are you going to dive in?

To do that, you have to step back and take a cold, analytical look at your film — not the film you set out to make, not the film you hoped to make, but the film that you've actually produced. It's no small task to divorce yourself from your film and look at it completely objectively. This may not even be entirely possible, but you do have to look at the film in realistic terms to determine where it is likely to fit into the distribution stream. Otherwise, you will waste a good deal of money and time barking up the wrong distributors.

Of course, everyone wants their film to receive a big, splashy theatrical release with 1,200 prints opening in multiplexes throughout the country simultaneously. While this is a nice wish, it's not a particularly realistic goal. Even if your film is released theatrically — a darn big "if" — it's more likely to be rolled out with a small number of prints, territory by territory. So you need to establish some realistic, attainable goals.

After looking at your film realistically, you may conclude that it's not theatrical material. Instead, it may be better suited for cable television or home video, and you may wish to concentrate on those venues. Or you may realize that your film has little commercial potential and is better suited to the festival circuit. There's nothing wrong with recognizing your film's limitations. It's a whole lot cheaper (and less demoralizing) to realize this before you spend tons of time and money looking for the wrong kind of distributor.

There's no great trick to finding distributors; most of them actively want to be found because they need a constant flow of new product to keep their doors open. Almost all distributors will look at your film because they're afraid they might miss The Next Big Thing if they don't. Imagine yourself as the person who turned down "Halloween" or "sex, lies and videotape," and you can see why the distribution business is run on paranoia and fear.

So, finding them is no great trick. As we mentioned back in the chapter on pre-production, you can list your film in the trade papers, *Variety* and *The Hollywood Reporter*, at any point during production or post-production. These listings run every week and are a primary source for distributors looking for new films. Call or write to the papers to get a listing form. (We've put the information under "Other Resources" in the appendix.) As soon as your listing appears, you'll start to get calls and letters from the more aggressive distributors, anxious to view your film.

Besides the trade papers, there are four tried-and-true methods of getting your work in front of distributors: film markets, film festivals, the direct approach, and getting someone else to do it.

Film Markets
A film market is like a supermarket for films. Buyers come, squeeze the melons, read the ingredients, and try to find the freshest, ripest produce in the store.

Sometimes a market is attached to a film festival, like Cannes; sometimes its a free-standing event, like the American Film Market.

For an ultra-low-budget feature, there currently is no better venue than the Independent Feature Film Market (IFFM), put on each fall by the east-coast branch of the Independent Feature Project. It's overcrowded and over booked, and in recent years, the event has experienced an overall decline in quality. But that's not necessarily a bad thing. If you bring a good film to the IFFM, it's going to stand out in the crowd.

As of this writing, the market is divided into four categories: feature films (including documentaries), short films, works in progress, and scripts. This wide array of product is one of the reasons the event is so overcrowded and exhausting. Housed in the Angelika Film Center in New York City, the market runs for seven days, screening films from 9:00 a.m. to 5:00 p.m. in all of the Center's six theaters. Throughout the day, the lobbies are packed with filmmakers trying to corner buyers. The buyers, meanwhile, are racing from theater to theater, trying to find The Next Big Thing. It's a zoo, it's demoralizing, and it's exhausting. But most of the buyers are actual buyers, and the reality is that some films do get discovered, bought, and distributed based on their showing at the IFFM.

Several words of advice before you go to the IFFM (or any film market, for that matter):

• Be sure you need to go. It can be an expensive proposition, particularly if you don't live in the city where the market is held. With our usual low-budget approach and free lodging, we still managed to spend around $3,000 at the IFFM on entry fees, plane tickets, and promotional items, money we're not convinced was well-spent. For that reason, we didn't include a visit to this market in our sample budget. So check out other options before making this trek.

• Track down attendees from previous years and get tips from them about how to attack the market. For the IFFM, check with your local IFP office for names of people from your area who have attended. Recent attendees can give you an idea of what promotional tricks seemed to work, who was buying, and what to do (and not to do) to get your film noticed.

• Target the buyers you think would be right for your film and work on getting them to your screening. Don't spread yourself and your resources too thin by trying to get all the buyers to attend. Peruse past market catalogs to get an idea of who buys what.

If you do decide to attend a market, consider the following advice:
• When you're at the market, attend as many other screenings as you can. Talk to the other filmmakers, compare notes, trade horror stories about production, and invite them to your screening. To get the best reaction possible for your film, you'll want to pack the house with as many sympathetic bodies as you can, and for the most part, other filmmakers are a very supportive group.
• Don't make any deals while you're there. Take business cards and phone numbers, pass out cassette copies of your film, and wait until you get home to weigh any offers. And don't sign anything without talking to a reputable entertainment attorney first.
• Don't bother entering a script in the market. We've never heard of anyone buying, much less reading, a script at a film market.
• Keep a firm handle on your expectations. Walking away from a market with several offers would be nice, but you may end up with nothing but memories. As you look through materials from previous years, compare the number of films that have any name recognition to those that don't ring any bells at all. You'll see that the majority of films are in the latter category.
• Be patient. We were contacted about "Beyond Bob" by interested buyers months after the event, simply because there was so much material to go through that it took them that long to contact us.
• Finally, try to have some fun. A film market can be a very intense environment, buzzing with hundreds of people who all have a lot on the line. So relax. See some films. Meet some people. And try to enjoy yourself a bit. A good time may be all you get from a film market.

Festivals

One benefit of the IFFM is that it is attended by many of the big film festivals, including Sundance, and it's a good way to spark their interest in your film and start some buzz about it.

If you're only looking for awards, then it makes sense to blitz all the festivals. If you're looking for a buyer, then you're better off selecting those events where your film is likely to be seen by the right people. Check with a festival's promoters and filmmakers who entered in previous years to see how much buying takes place at the event.

While there are hundreds of film festivals throughout the world (check the appendix for a list of a few of them), only a handful are regularly attended by buyers, such as the Toronto Film Festival, the Sundance Film Festival, the Miami Film Festival, the Berlin Film Festival, and the Cannes International Film Festival (which is out of your league because it only accepts 35mm films).

Currently, the hottest festival ticket is the Sundance Film Festival. Everyone wants to attend, and everyone wants to have their film entered, accepted, screened, and then sold to the highest bidder. It's happened to many other ultra-low-budget films, and there's no reason why it can't happen to yours. All you need to do is get accepted. But that's the tricky part.

As with any popular festival, you'll have a better chance of getting in if you submit your film well before the deadline. Sending in your film at the last minute — in order to give yourself as much time as possible to make final tweaks — will bury your film among the crush of eleventh-hour entries, and you may disappear without a trace. So get yourself organized and get your entry in early, or wait until the next year.

The Direct Approach

The third approach to finding a distributor is the most direct. Find the distributors you feel are right for your film, contact them directly, and send them a cassette copy of your film for review.

Not so surprisingly, this approach — like all the methods we've outlined — has an up side and a down side. The up side is that it's generally faster and cheaper than pouring money into prints, cassettes, publicity and entry fees for markets and festivals. The down side is that there's nothing like screening your film for distributors in a theater with an actual audience. Watching the same film in a nine-by-nine cubicle on a twelve-inch screen under fluorescent lights is hardly an ideal viewing situation. Particularly when you realize that many distributors watch tapes with one eye on the clock and one finger hovering above the "fast forward" button.

Researching distributors is the key to successfully using the direct approach. Don't waste your time and their time by sending your film to distributors who are not suited for your project.

• Look through back issues of <u>Variety</u> and <u>The Hollywood Reporter</u> to learn who is distributing what. Each publication puts out special issues several times a year, right before the Cannes Market, the MIFED market, and the American Film Market, with ads from all the key distributors touting their films.

• If you're looking for a particular venue (such as a theatrical release), make sure the distributors you approach are in that business.

• Learn what types of film they release, and then approach those distributors whose films are the same genre as yours. If you're approaching a cable channel directly, make sure you've watched that channel and understand the kinds of films they buy. The same is true of home-video buyers.

• If you're targeting basic cable channels (such as Lifetime, USA Network, the Sci-Fi channel) and broadcast channels, keep in mind that they present films in two-hour blocks. This means your film needs to be between 90 and 92 minutes long (the other 28 to 30 minutes are devoted to commercials). Sending them a 120-minute movie tells them that you don't understand their business.

• Basic cable channels and syndicated television have standards-and-practices departments (a fancy word for censors) just like the broadcast channels. Consider this if your film's content requires any serious cleaning up before it can be aired. A four-letter word here and there can be cut out, but wall-to-wall swearing, explicit nudity or sex, or over-the-top violence are not what they're buying.

After you've picked the distributors who are most likely to be interested in your film, send each of them a short inquiry letter.

Briefly describe your film and include photocopies of any reviews you've received from premieres, screenings, or festivals. Don't send a preview cassette until they ask for it. It's a waste of your limited money to give cassettes to people who haven't asked to watch them.

It may seem to verge on paranoia, but for your preview video cassettes it's a good idea to have "For Preview Only" superimposed on the picture throughout your film. Usually this text is semi-transparent and placed across the bottom third of the screen so it doesn't obscure too much of your film. Piracy, especially illegal video cassette duplication, continues to be a big problem throughout the industry, and there's no reason why you should make it easier for the thieves.

After you've sent out the preview cassettes, be a little patient. In most cases, you'll be approaching small companies with small acquisition staffs. One person may be in charge of doing all the screening, all the negotiations, filling out the paperwork, and helping out with other projects. It took one distributor a full year to screen "Resident Alien," because he receives hundreds of submissions a year. We just kept a file on him and checked-in every month or so; our approach was friendly instead of high-pressure. Although he ultimately passed on the film, he did steer us toward other resources and has proven to be a great advocate of our work. So be patient but persistent.

Getting Someone Else To Do It

Up to this point, making your film has been pretty much a do-it-yourself affair. However, finding a distributor is a time-consuming process, requiring you to become a promoter, a salesperson, and a negotiator. You may simply not want to do this. Maybe you want to focus on your next project or recover from this one. In that case, you need to find someone else to help you sell your film.

The people who help filmmakers sell their films go by many names: sales representative or rep, sales agent, producer's representative, and others. Often these are people who've spent some years in the distribution business and now are out on their own. Some are people who have spent time selling their own projects. Most work out of their homes using only a phone, a fax, their good judgment and their industry connections to make their living. The best ones are very aggressive and knowledgeable about the business (however, don't ever confuse aggressiveness with knowledge).

As with all professions, some reps are better than others. To find the ones who do the best job of selling, talk to the buyers. Place a couple calls to key theatrical distributors, buyers at cable networks, or large home-video distributors and find out who they know and — more importantly — who they trust.

Sales reps (or whatever they call themselves) generally work on commission. Some have set rates that they use regardless of the project; others slide their commission scale, depending on how much or how little work they think they'll need to do to sell your film. If they like your film (or even if they hate it but think they can sell it), they'll want the right to sell the film in all the territories they cover, and they will want to be able to sell these rights for periods of up to 20 years. As with all contracts that you sign during the distribution process, you should have an experienced entertainment attorney look over any sales rep agreement before you sign it.

The Budget Question

One question you may be asked by most potential distributors is "What was your budget?" If they ask this question before they see your film, they may be trying to determine if it's worth their time to watch it. If they ask after they've seen the film, they may be trying to determine how much to offer you for it, or they may simply be curious.

One thing you should remember going into this discussion is that the viewing public doesn't really know or care about a film's budget. They may be curious about the most-expensive or least-expensive film ever made, but otherwise it's not an issue.

So when a distributor asks the question, you can do one of four things. You can lie outright. You can tell an alternate truth. You can skirt the issue. Or you can tell the complete truth.

Lying

This is a bad idea. It always trips you up somewhere down the line, and it puts you on that slippery slope to becoming yet another Hollywood lowlife. If you insist on lying ("Our budget? A million three, plus deferrals."), keep in mind that most distributors are pretty smart. They've looked at hundreds of movies and perhaps have been involved in the production of some of them. They know what crews, film, and actors cost. And they can add. So, if you lie, you better stay within the bounds of reality.

An Alternate Truth

You can tell an alternate version of the truth by figuring out what your film would have cost if you had actually paid everyone. To do this, add up all the deferrals, and include the actual costs for everything you got for free. Then, when you're asked the budget question, you can say "Quarter of a million, including deferrals," and you'll be telling the truth. Sort of.

Skirting The Issue

We're big fans of skirting the issue by turning the question around and asking, "What do you think the budget was?" With "Beyond Bob," only one distributor came close (guessing "around $50,000, with lots of deferrals"). As we've bragged before, one knowledgeable person even went as high as $900,000, which was obviously way off and which also made our day. This approach can be educational because it will give you an objective assessment of your production values.

The Truth

Telling the unguarded truth about your budget will have more impact if you skirt the issue first and let the distributor guess. The person who guessed $50,000 felt good about himself when we told him the actual cash budget had been under $30,000; he was also impressed by what we were able to achieve for that budget. The person who guessed $900,000 was enormously impressed with us when we revealed our true costs. In both cases, we got the maximum benefit out of telling the truth.

The big fear about the truth is that it will come back to haunt you, particularly in the form of a low offer from the interested distributor. Don't be afraid; simply stand your ground. The production budget of a film has no bearing on its market value. Films costing under $100,000 have been sold for several times their budget; movies with multimillion dollar budgets have been purchased without so much as a one-dollar advance. At this point in the process, the value of your film has very little relation to its budget. It's worth whatever the market will bear.

The Deal & Other Details

Once a distributor makes an offer, you need to do two things: Check them out some more, and if they pass the inspection, hire professional legal talent. We can't overstate this enough: Don't accept any offers or sign any contracts without the aid of an experienced entertainment attorney. Distributors buy films all the time, week in and week out. They write the contracts. On the other hand, this will probably be the first time for you. Who do you suppose has the advantage in this situation? Don't take any chances. Get yourself some expert advice.

Your local Independent Feature Project will have the names of lawyers who are both experienced in entertainment law and sympathetic to your cause. Some work for free or on a sliding scale. Others may accept a deferral or perhaps a credit in the film in exchange for their services.

But before you get to that stage, you need to investigate the distributor a little further. You need to find out how they've dealt with other filmmakers in the past. Ask for the names of people they're currently doing business with who can vouch for their business practices. Call everyone on the list and question them in detail about the deal they got, the results they've achieved, and their overall impression of the company.

Then disregard everything you've heard and dig deeper.

Find out what other films they've released and track down those filmmakers — the ones who didn't make the reference list. Ask them the same questions.

We followed this approach with one distributor and didn't even need to get off the reference list. We sent a letter to one of the film-makers and she phoned us a few days later. She was out of town at a retreat miles away from a phone. But when she got our letter, she drove into town and called us immediately to warn us away from the distributor. Needless to say, we didn't sign with that company, and a few months later they disappeared off the face of the earth.

Just as every film and every distributor are different, so too is every deal. What's a standard contract item in one medium is something you may need to fight for in another. Here are some of the things that are the same and different in each venue:

• It costs money to distribute a movie. In the case of a theatrical release, it can cost a lot of money. With low-budget, independent films it's not uncommon for a distributor to spend two or three times the film's production budget on prints and advertising (P&A). It cost hundreds of thousands of dollars to get the $7,000 "El Mariachi" in shape for its theatrical release. The sound mix alone for "Clerks" was twice the film's production budget. A home-video release also requires considerable capital for advertising, tape duplication, and packaging.

That's why distributors resist giving a film an advance and often offer the producer a smaller percentage of the film's profits, such as a 60/40 split or less. Of course, profits don't happen until they make back their costs, which could take a long, long time. For distributors who are sharing percentages of profits with you (such as theatrical and home video), find out in advance what expenses are going against the revenues.   If all the distribution costs are being subtracted (including distribution staff salaries) you'll probably never see profits. A better deal is one that gives you a percentage of the revenues. In either case, ask for quarterly reporting and payments. They may try to negotiate an annual reporting structure, which basically allows them to keep your money longer. Don't let them do that.

• Large distributors, such as those run by the studios, have lots of ways of burying losses and cross-collateralizing their films. A small distributor can't afford to simply break even on a film; each film must make back its costs plus some more. It only takes two or three bombs to put a small distributor out of business.

In order to protect their investment, both large and small theatrical distributors are probably going to want to hang on to all the other rights as well, including home video and cable. Their argument will be that the theatrical release of the film is the locomotive that pulls the rest of the train, publicizing the film for cable and home-video release. They may want to be able to make cable and home video sales to offset any losses from a theatrical release.

So if you're planning to splinter your rights (sell theatrical rights to one distributor while retaining other rights to sell elsewhere), you may be in for a big fight with your theatrical distributor. If you insist on doing this, you'll be in a better position if you go into the negotiations with these ancillary rights (like home video and cable) already sold. Even then, the absence of these rights may break your deal with a theatrical distributor.

• Depending on the film and the distributor, you may have an easier time holding onto the rights for things like a soundtrack album, book publishing, or merchandising, although you'll probably fight tooth and nail over all that stuff as well.

• For lump-sum deals, such as a contract with a cable network, the distributor or buyer may try to spread out payments as much as possible. For example, you may ask for the first payment to be due upon delivery of the film. They may counter by making the first payment due on the first air date. If they lock up your film with a contract and have no required air date, you could sit around for the duration of the contract and never see payment. Stand your ground and make them pay for the right to tie up your film. They can be pretty tough about this, but it's just another technique for holding onto your money for a little longer.

•   If a basic cable network wants your film, they're probably going to want it exclusively, and they're going to want it for a long time. A five-year exclusive contract is not uncommon. Their reasoning is that they have to be able to offer product that viewers can't find anywhere else in order to stay in business. Otherwise, they'll be swallowed up in the mass of cable channels and eventually disappear. So find which network is right for your film, and don't expect to accumulate sales across the cable dial.

•   As more and more cable channels are added, the prices paid for films go down, not up. Sure there are more buyers of films, but as each network is added, the ratings (market share) go down for everyone because there are more of them dividing up the same audience. As the ratings go down, the budgets shrink proportionally — the pieces of the pie keep getting cut smaller and smaller. The positive aspect of this growth of cable channels is that more channels need more product, particularly exclusive product. Although they won't necessarily be paying as much for the films they buy, it should increase your chances of making a cable sale.

What You'll Need To Provide

Again, the specific requirements of what each distributor needs will change, depending on the company and their venue. But some things are true across the board.

•   Many distributors are going to want Errors-and-Omissions (E&O) insurance; it just comes down to who is going to pay for it. E&O insurance guarantees that you have proper clearance for all elements of the script (title and story), that you have releases from everyone in the film, that you have releases from all the recognizable locations, that you have cleared the rights for the music, and many, many other details. Distributors want it because it protects them from lawsuits by ensuring that you have all your ducks in a row.

Who pays for this insurance is a negotiable point. With their access to blanket policies, distributors are in a better position to put up the money, but since that adds to their overhead they're often resistant to doing it. However, in many cases the deal can't proceed until it's resolved, so if they really want your film they'll cover this cost.

• Foreign distributors (theatrical, home video, cable, and broadcast television) may need for you to provide a music and effects (M&E) track for your film. This is a special mix of your soundtrack which includes all the sound effects and music, but none of the dialogue. (That's why we told you to put all the dialogue on separate tracks, and to create one sound-effects track that replicates any sound effects that were intermingled with the dialogue.) Using this M&E track, the foreign distributor can create foreign-language versions of your film for each country in their territory.

You won't have the cash to create this mix at the same time as you do your regular sound mix, but don't panic. There's really no point in doing it until a foreign distributor shows interest — and that interest should include enough cash to cover the cost of the new mix. Because you've prepared the tracks in advance, creating this new track will be a snap.

In addition to the M&E track, the foreign distributor will also need a continuity script. This is a word-for-word transcript of your finished film, which will be the basis for the foreign language translation.

• Publicity stills and PR material. This will vary from venue to venue. As we mentioned in the chapter on production, theatrical distributors desperately need quality production stills to promote your film in newspapers and magazines. And they have to be smart stills — photos that really capture the tone and mood of the film, not snapshots of actors and crew mugging for the camera (unless that really captures the tone and mood of your film). Not having these professional stills will make your film less attractive to buyers because they'll need to do more work to promote your film.

Home-video buyers also need stills for video-box art, but these photos generally need to be more stylized, with slick, well-lit images and a lot of attention paid to hair and makeup. Spend some time in a video store and look at a lot of different boxes to get an idea of the types of photos used to sell films in this venue. If your time and budget allow, schedule a photo shoot for right after you've finished with principal photography (before the actors, costumes, and locations disappear) to shoot some high-quality images. This will make your film more attractive to the home-video market, where the artwork on the box is often more important than the film inside.

Staged publicity photos from "Resident Alien" and "Beyond Bob."
Photos courtesy of Granite Productions, Ltd.

Cable television has less need for photos, because they usually promote films using on-air promotions (which are short trailers of footage from the movie) and the synopsis that is printed in the cable guide.

• Incidentally, don't expect to have much say about the creative campaign your distributor puts together for your film. Most will listen to your thoughts, but it's not a contractual right that they're likely to give to you. It would mean that if you don't like their campaign, you could hold up the release of the film. In their defense, most filmmakers are not equipped to put together an effective trailer or a powerful poster. That's what distributors are good at doing, so don't be surprised when you're left out of this loop.

• Some distributors (and film markets and festivals) may ask you for a press kit on your film. This is written information about your film — the story, the cast, the crew, the production history, and reviews — that will be given to the press for promotional purposes. Publicity photos are also included. You may also use elements of the press kit to entice distributors to look at your film and to promote any local premiere that you do for your film. In short, it's a selling tool and should be approached as such.

Every press kit has a few basic elements (See the appendix for a sample of each):
- The Cast List. This is a list of your principal cast members, along with the names of the characters they play in the film. In a film such as yours, which will be populated with unknowns, this is how film critics will know who plays which character. This is also where the critics will go to find out how to spell the actors' names, so proofread it twice, and then get someone else to proof it, and then proof it one more time yourself.
- The Production-Team List. Same as above, this time featuring everyone behind the camera: producer, director, writer, director of photography, editor, composer, and so on.
- Story Synopsis. This is a one- or two-page synopsis of the key elements of your story. Some filmmakers prefer to tell the whole story in the synopsis; others use it to set up the story and leave the

reader hanging, so as not to give away the film's ending. This second approach is a better selling tool. It entices the reader to want to watch the film, and if the reader is a potential distributor, that's a good thing.

- Production Notes. This is something of a catch-all where you can highlight the biographies of your key players and present interesting anecdotes about your film. Although every part of your press kit should be professionally written, the production-notes segment needs to shine. The better it is, the more likely newspaper writers are to simply retype it and print it as is, which is exactly what you want them to do. (Newspaper writers are notoriously willing to let someone else do their work.)

Keep in mind that all this promotional material — which will help with your local premiere and may pique the interest of a distributor — may be tossed out and rewritten by your distributor if your film gets picked up. Or, if you've done a really stellar job on it, they may follow the example of the newspaper writer and simply retype it on their letterhead.

Self-Distribution & Self-Flagellation: How To Tell Them Apart

Despite your best efforts, you may not find a home for your film with any of the big or small fish swimming in the distribution stream. You may have been turned down flat at all venues, or you may have received some offers that offered more harm than good. Whatever the reason, you may now feel like the proud owner of a $30,000 paperweight.

Don't despair. You're not dead yet.

Self-distribution is a viable alternative for you and your film. On the up side, it allows you to control how and where your film is shown, and it eliminates that pesky middleman who seems to come out ahead on most deals. On the down side, you have to commit to distribution in the same way you committed to production, recognizing that this is nearly a full-time job, requiring as much faith and stamina as the production process did.

The most likely markets for self-distribution are theatrical and home video. Before you dive into either one, consider the following:

Theatrical
   • Theatrical distribution is the more risky of the two because it generally requires more capital, such as renting a theater, renting 16mm projection equipment or making a 35mm blow-up print, and buying advertising. None of this comes cheaply, so try to think of ways to cut costs. For example, rather than four-walling (renting the entire theater and keeping all the hoped-for profits), strike a deal with a local theater owner. Split the house and let him keep all the concessions, which is where the theater makes all of its money anyway. However, you'll have to persuade the theater owner that you can draw in an audience before he or she will be willing to make that deal. If your film falls in the cult category, you can offer to make it a midnight movie on weekends, so it doesn't cut into the theater's prime time.

   • Use articles and reviews in the local media as your advertising. Don't stop with the major newspaper; do some legwork, and make sure you get mentioned in the alternative press, in neighborhood papers, on local radio, cable and broadcast television shows — anywhere! A press release written in news style will often be picked up by neighborhood newspapers, which are well read by their audience. This sort of publicity is cheap and will pay off with paid admissions at the door.

   • Don't blow the bank on elaborate posters with expensive photography and graphics unless the theater is located in a high traffic area where the poster will serve as advertising. Otherwise, go with a simple, elegant (meaning cheap) poster that lets people know they've made it to the right theater.

Home Video
   Home video is cheaper to break into than theatrical, although not necessarily easier. You can rent space in a movie theater; you can't necessarily buy your way into a video store unless you want to own the entire store. More and more, video stores are only looking for

the "A" titles (big name movies with big name stars) and the "B" titles (exploitation and action pictures with semi-big name stars). This often leaves the "C" titles (small, independent films with no-name stars) out in the cold.

There are some things you can do, however, to get your films into video stores on a local, regional and even national basis:

• Generate interest in your film, so that store owners will see a value in buying your film. Stage a local premiere and get as much publicity as you can. Then approach local chains and dealers about buying copies of your tape, using the publicity and reviews as supporting arguments that prove there is a demand for your film. Dale approached one local video store owner with a copy of "Resident Alien." She was only marginally interested in it. Dale said he'd stop back. After the local paper ran an article about the film, Dale went back to the store. As he walked through the door, the owner pointed at him from across the store and yelled, "I want your film!" It was an easy sale.

• If cast and crew members are from out of town, send video copies of the film (and any reviews you've already gotten) to their local papers to generate publicity. Then use that publicity to persuade video store owners in that area to stock your film. By the same token, if you shot in any towns outside of your own, be sure to generate some publicity in those towns as well, and then start hitting on those local video store owners.

• Work with your area's film commission to persuade all the video chains in the your state to create displays in their stores of films that were made in your state — the big-buck Hollywood films that have passed through the state and the locally-produced films such as yours.

• Create a great, eye-catching box. To find out what sorts of designs work, walk through a couple video stores, and see what catches your eye. For example, when we were putting together the video box for "Resident Alien," we walked through several video stores and noticed two things. The first was that there were very few videos that had yellow covers. The second was that the ones with yellow covers really jumped right out at you. So we used a lot of yellow in the "Resident Alien" packaging to create a video box that people would notice.

• If you're not a graphic designer, don't pretend to be one. You've done a lot for your film so far, but don't feel that you have to do absolutely everything. Find yourself a graphic designer to create the right look for your video box. Get a friend of a friend or a promising student at a local art school, or call ad agencies in your area and see if they can recommend someone looking for the experience. You need to make your box look great, and you may need a professional to do that. Also, try to get them to do it for resume experience with you covering the production costs.

• You'll also need great photos. If you didn't shoot them before, then shoot them now. On both of our films, we ended up shooting photography for the video box long after the films had wrapped. It can be a hassle to get the actors back together. If they have moved on, you'll have to use your imagination. In the case of "Resident Alien," one of our key actors had moved to Los Angeles, so we used a stand-in wearing the large alien "bug head" we had created for the film, which was actually a more eye-catching approach!

• Keep your price point low. If you're charging $70 for your tape, and a store owner knows she can get two "A" titles or four "B" titles for the same price, what do you think she's going buy? To keep your price low, use the same methods you used during production. Never pay full price for anything, cut deals at every turn, and use your networking skills to get the most bang for your buck.

For example, for less than 400 copies it's usually cheaper to create an insert cover (artwork that slides into a clear plastic sleeve that surrounds a plastic video case) than a paperboard cover. And to keep your overhead down make only one copy of your full-color cover, and then color photocopy it. This will cost about the same as four-color printing for quantities up to about 500, but you don't have to spend the money until you get the orders. Make sure your designer knows that you might do this in order to ensure that the design is compatible with photocopying technology. Some colors and designs copy better than others.

• Contact all the libraries in your state. Many buy videos and will be interested in locally-produced films, particularly if those films have garnered some local publicity.

• Be persistent. Be very persistent. This is a hard way to make sales, one to a dozen at a time. You'd probably make more money flipping burgers for the hours you'll invest, but then you'd miss all the glamour of show business.

* * *

We're not giving away any secrets when we say that distribution is perhaps the toughest part of this entire process, primarily because most of the control is out of your hands for the first time. However, you are not without some advantages. The biggest is that, from the financial point of view, you don't have to do a lot of business to be successful.

A producer with a film that has a $500,000 or million-dollar budget has to earn back a lot of money just to break even. You don't have that problem. You don't have to make a killing to pay off your investors.

By the same token, your film can be attractive to buyers simply because it doesn't cost a lot; you don't need to demand big advances and large percentages in order to be profitable.

The final advantage you have is one of patience. Depending on how you raised your money and who you raised it from, you probably won't have high-rolling investors breathing down your neck. They won't be insisting that you unload your film as quickly as possible to get them a return on their money. You can afford to be selective and patient as you look for the right distributor. This is good, because you'll need to be.

HINDSIGHT
It's 20/20

Road trips can get pretty exciting when you choose a dashed line instead of a red line on the map and end up flinging your passengers against the doors as you make mid-course corrections and hit potholes that jar your molars. After you survive without crippling your car or passengers, it's pretty easy to look at that map and identify a superior route. If this kind of hindsight is used to assign blame, it's a great way to beat up your psyche. However, hindsight that makes mental files for future reference can really improve the next trip.

We have plenty of hindsight from our two films, all filed under "future reference." We're not second guessing our earlier decisions. In fact, we stand by almost all of those decisions, given the time and the circumstances when we made them. That's how life is. You can only do your best for the moment, and some of your decisions may not look so hot in retrospect. We acknowledge and accept this, and at some point, you'll probably have to accept your film in the same way, as a love child with a few warts. If you don't, your finished film will torment you because it will have flaws. It's not realistic to think it can be perfect with the money and time constraints you will face. In fact, given the complexity and uncertainties of creating and assembling a feature film, it's probably impossible to create a perfect movie under any circumstances. Don't beat yourself up for what your film is not. Celebrate what it is, a dream taken form by dint of your own tenacity, a remarkable achievement. We look on hindsight as evidence that we've mentally started pre-production for our next film.

However, the fact remains that we've learned some things we didn't know when we started. There are new techniques and equipment that weren't available when we made production decisions for our films. You'll want to consider these ideas and innovations because they can improve your production values and keep your costs down.

Script

Even though we've made this point earlier, it bears repeating as a lesson that was reinforced as we began seeking distribution for our films. Make sure your script starts with a bang. That doesn't mean a chase scene or an explosion. It means making sure you engage your audience in the first minute of your story and that you keep them intrigued, amused or entertained every minute after that. The ideal independent film packs 120 minutes of drama into 90 minutes. Ideally, every scene exists to move the story forward, to reveal a notable aspect of a character, or to present an interesting idea that is important to the story.

When you find yourself in the desert of distribution trying get a distributor to come close enough to grab, the only thing you have to entice that person is your story. Your production values, your cast, and your crew may be uninteresting to someone who's looking for selling points in a film. An intriguing or insightful story is your only chance. Take the time to make sure you've written and rewritten your script to greatness before you start production.

Pre-Production

If we were starting pre-production on a film today, we'd spend more time designing the "look" of our production.

In "Resident Alien," we concentrated on the "feel" or tone of the film and the look of some key scenes, but much of the film "just happens" visually. In "Beyond Bob," we intentionally spent more time using costuming and setting to create the desired look for our film, but we could have done better defining the look of the film through the choice of camera work and lighting. In our next film, we'll work on all three areas: the feel and tone, which are largely the product of the script and performances, the look that's created by the setting and costumes, and the look that's created by lighting and camera work.

Another aspect of pre-production where we might make some changes is the casting. We might spend more time, effort, and even money to get a "name" in the cast. Distributors always ask if there's someone big in the film. However, you'd need a name like Michael Keaton or Darryl Hannah or Glenn Close to really help sell your film. Face it, any "name" actor that we could afford has slid from favor or power to the point that he or she won't really help at the box office or video store. What might be worth considering is adding a personality from another walk of life, who may take the job just for fun, not money. This could add a little box-office draw without exceeding the budget.

Production

During our shoots, we attempted to make some use of the unique geography and scenery of our area; however, this was almost exclusively a sidelight to the main story. The attitudes of people in our area and the environment they live in could have played a much greater role in story motivation and conflict. For example, a movie set in dairy country might feature a romantic rendezvous with a serenade by bovine troubadours. The isolation and danger of a South Dakota blizzard might be the antagonist in a story set there. The sultry pace and the steamy atmosphere of the bayou could be the Cajun spice of a Louisiana potboiler.

Simply put, look around. Start seeing what you long ago took for granted, and celebrate it in your film. This will help make your film unique and notable, and it lets you use the resources you have readily at hand.

Post-Production

In post-production, there has been a relatively recent technical advance that would have radically altered the special effects for

"Resident Alien" and would have helped us raise the production values of "Beyond Bob." It's New Tek's Video Toaster.

This add on for the Amiga computer and for personal computers with Windows software is a low-cost version of the video-effects generators used by the better-equipped video-production studios and most television stations. This system costs between $10,000 and $15,000 to set up, low enough that many cable-TV access centers have added this capability. Many computer hobbyists and video-production companies also own a Video Toaster.

Now, you're probably wondering why we're blathering on about a video innovation after making it clear that we don't think it's a good idea to make your film on anything but film.

The answer is that video footage doesn't have to stay on video. There are a number of companies out there who will gladly convert video to film for you. If you carefully design your video segments to be lit and shot like film, they shouldn't look significantly different than video transfers from film footage, which is what you'll be doing to distribute your film.

This technique will be most effective when the video sequences occur in a different setting or time than the film footage. For example, a dream sequence is expected to look different than other scenes. If you have a segment that takes place in outer space, in a mythical world, under the ocean, at night in the forest, or any other location that's distinctly separate from most of your other settings, there's a possibility of doing those segments in video so you can use video effects. You can then transfer them to film. As long as the entire sequence is done using the same technique, there should be few problems integrating it with the other film footage. Obviously, it's important to keep the limitations of this technique in mind when writing the screenplay. If a scene needs video effects, make sure it's in a different setting. If you need that wizard to transform into a dragon, don't do it in the main character's apartment where you're shooting most of your scenes. Have the main character chase the wizard into the nearby dark alley for the sequence, so the video-to-film footage doesn't have to be intercut with film-only footage.

In addition to regular video effects, the Video Toaster is capable of creating computer-generated animations. These too can be recorded to video tape if the Toaster system has an animation video recorder or if it has a large hard drive to store the animation so it can be transferred to video tape. This tape footage of the animation can then be transferred to film.

Titles in particular offer a great opportunity to use this video-to-film method. The Video Toaster does wonderful titles easily and quickly, much better than you could ever afford on film. Since titles don't really have to match your other footage, they are perfect candidates for being done on video initially. Some television series that are shot on film have been creating their titles on video and just editing those titles into the final video transfer from film. They never even go to film format. This is especially common for end credits. You could do the same thing if you never plan to make a film print. If you are creating a film print, just pay to have these video titles transferred to film. Video-generated titles can greatly enhance the quality of your title sequence, without significantly detracting from the film format of the rest of your movie.

A word of caution. You don't want to pay to have Video Toaster titles "rendered" to film. This is the process the big productions do when they use computer effects. It costs $75 to $200 a second, well beyond your budget. What you want is a tape-to-film transfer, which is much more reasonable — about $80 per minute, including negative, work print, and fullcoat sound track. Still expensive, but affordable for some unique special effects or for title sequences.

Change Is Good

In the years since we began our film-production company, many changes and innovations have occurred. We've seen Super 8mm rise to the level of a professional production format. We've seen 16mm being used increasingly for shooting television series and feature films. We've seen the Video Toaster shake up the video production business. We've seen computer-generated images become financially and technically feasible for film productions, even lower-budget ones. We've seen computer communications offer new ways for film-makers to conduct business and find compatriots. And we don't expect the new developments to stop. These changes will open new opportunities for ultra-low-budget filmmakers in several ways.

New techniques will offer new opportunities. Just as the improvements in film-to-video transfer technology made it possible to do high-quality productions on 16mm, new advances will bring more capabilities within the budget range of those of us who are rich in ideas and poor in cash. Keep an eye on the trade publications for new advances that will make filmmaking cheaper or faster (which can also mean cheaper). Even if the new technology and equipment is beyond your financial reach, you'll still benefit. For every new gizmo that's added, there's an old gizmo that falls into disuse even though it is still perfectly functional. We shot major segments of our films on a 40-year-old Bolex. We did our titles using slides that were programmed on a 20-year-old dissolve unit. We used special-effect techniques that are nearly 100 years old. While most of the film industry is racing to have the fastest and shiniest new equipment, we're happy to pick up the garage-sale items that still help us get the job done. So, look for what's hot and also for what's not.

Technical innovations are also creating new markets. Just as the advent of video-cassette players created the home-video market, which now is the major outlet for films of all types, new innovations are going to create new places and ways to tell stories with images.

We're currently seeing the birth of interactive computer stories, ones with multiple plot lines and the ability to delve into characters' backgrounds. This is a new approach to storytelling and to delivering a story to an audience. The gee-whiz aspect of this new medium is still predominating, meaning lots of mayhem, titillation, and surprises, but is this significantly different than the first motion pictures? The Edison Studio's "The Kiss," a short film of a man and woman kissing, was considered scandalous in its day. Edwin S. Porter's "The Great Train Robbery" featured murder, torture, and guns being fired directly at the audience for shock value. Georges Mèliés' films often had scant story lines that were mainly an excuse to present special effects, which are still the mainstays of film effects today. These early experiments with a brand-new medium helped develop the film language that allowed storytellers to embrace the medium and turn it into an art form that moves us, forces us to examine ourselves, and allows us to experience worlds unknown to us. Given sufficient time, these new media will mature, and with the help of storytellers, they may offer a new and clearer mirror with which to reflect our world.

At the pace of development in the visual medium, it wouldn't surprise us to have this entire chapter seem quaint and humorously antiquated within five years' time. Given that expectation, the most important hindsight we can share with you is keep your eyes open and watch for new opportunities that will allow you to tell your stories to as wide an audience as possible on a budget you can afford.

OTHER FILMS / OTHER APPROACHES

We don't claim to be the final word on ultra-low-budget film production. Far from it. There are plenty of ways to skin this cat, metaphorically speaking, and our one approach is simply that -- one approach. So, to put our experience in a larger context, we sought out other ultra-low-budget filmmakers to learn how they flayed their respective felines.

The filmmakers profiled below come from all across the country (Boston to Santa Monica; Minneapolis to Houston; Chicago to Salt Lake City), and their films are as diverse as the people who made them. What they all share is a persistence of vision. They created a dream and then made it a reality, often under overwhelming circumstances. While some of the methods they employed were the same as ours, we've tried to highlight those ideas that were different, unique, and most of all, successful.

Good Grief: Richard Glatzer On The Making Of "Grief"

Two common suggestions for first-time filmmakers are to write what you know and to surround yourself with good people. First-timer Richard Glatzer followed both those rules but broke many others when he wrote and directed "Grief," an ultra-low-budget feature that went on to win the audience prize at the 1993 San Francisco Gay Film Festival and has since found distribution throughout the world.

At the suggestion of producer Ruth Charny, Glatzer wrote a script based on his own experiences as a writer and producer for the television show "Divorce Court." As Charny recalled, "Richard used to tell me the most hilarious stories when he was working on daytime television. I knew there'd be a lot of great material there if he'd only get around to writing it."

Glatzer agreed, but with reservations. "I had the makings of a good comedy, but I wanted to do more than that. I wanted to make a film for my lover, Donald Berry, who died. And I wanted to use the concept of a week in an office to examine my feelings about surviving him."

He also wanted to make sure that, once written, the film would get made. "I had no interest in doing anything unless it was a movie that we could make on as little money as anyone could make a movie. Otherwise, it wasn't going to get done. I had enough experience trying to get things done through more conventional channels. So I thought if I conceived of a movie that's basically one location and think of it as an independent, independent, independent film, then maybe we could actually do it."

"Grief" takes place during five hectic days in the television production offices of "The Love Judge." The writing and producing staff for the sleazy show are responsible for cranking out tabloid sagas with topics ranging from schizophrenic opera divas to circus lesbians to Tourette-syndrome sufferers -- in short, something to offend everyone.

A strong cast helps make a good "Grief."
(l to r, Carlton Wilborn, Illeana Douglas and Craig Chester.)
Photo courtesy of Strand Releasing

The week begins as Mark (Craig Chester) contemplates the one-year anniversary of his lover's death from AIDS. His boss, Jo (Jackie Beat), announces her decision to quit, leaving her job up for grabs between Mark and his friend Paula (Lucy Guttridge). The office's secretary, Leslie (Illeana Douglas), struggles to be taken seriously as a writer while carrying on a romance with the copy-machine repair-man. To add to the pressure, Mark finds himself attracted to a straight co-worker, Bill (Alexis Arquette), and at odds with his friend, Jeremy (Carlton Wilborn), who also has designs on Bill.

Besides writing about what he knows, Glatzer also surrounded himself with an impressive team, both behind and in front of the camera. Co-producer Ruth Charny also produced "Mistress" and "Search and Destroy" while the film's other co-producer, Yoram Mandel, had previously produced "Parting Glances," "The Big Blue," and "Johnny Suede." As executive producer, Marcus Hu, co-president of Strand Releasing, helped to locate investors and also lent a hand in assembling the film's cast.

The cast had equally impressive credentials:
• Craig Chester made his film debut as Nathan Leopold in the critically-acclaimed film "Swoon."
• Alexis Arquette appeared in "Last Exit To Brooklyn," played Tim Roth's brother in "Jumping At The Boneyard," and appeared with John Malkovich and Gary Sinise in "Of Mice and Men."
• Illeana Douglas experienced a cheeky encounter with Robert De Niro in "Cape Fear," and was also in "Goodfellas," "Guilty By Suspicion," "Alive," "Household Saints," and "Quiz Show."
• Lucy Guttridge played Hillary ("She whose bosoms defy gravity") opposite Val Kilmer in "Top Secret."
• The film also includes cameo appearances by Paul Bartel and Mary Woronov (of "Eating Raoul" fame) and Mickey Cottrell (who played a cleanliness freak in "My Own Private Idaho") as the Lionel Barrymore-inspired Love Judge.

To shoot the film, Glatzer put up $20,000 of his own money, and then the entire team worked to find investors to provide the other

$20,000. The crew was paid on a sliding scale based on what benefit they were likely to receive from the finished film -- the greater the benefit, the less they got paid.

"Line producer Yoram Mandel felt that any department head stood to really gain by having a finished film that they could show," Glatzer recalled. "So the director of photography didn't get paid, anybody whose name was going to be featured, they would not get paid. But their assistants would get paid, something really minimal -- not minimum wage -- but something. You can imagine that if we only had $40,000 that nobody's getting paid very much. Basically the money went to the people whose names barely get noticed. I thought it was really fair, and it seemed to work because everybody had a good attitude about it."

Although the script was completed before shooting began, Glatzer was not afraid to question and tweak the script during production and well into post-production. "It was an ongoing process; I was always scrutinizing it and always fiddling with it," Glatzer said. "We did have a week of rehearsal, and that was really great and crucial, especially for doing a movie that fast. Particularly one like this, which was so character and performance oriented. I felt that was the highest value of the film -- the quality group of people I put together -- and I wanted to make sure that the parts really came alive."

"There was a lot of rewriting in rehearsal," Glatzer continued, "and throughout the whole process -- in the editing room as well. The finished movie is maybe 75% of what was in the original script, but there are little things tweaked here and there. This was especially true of emotional stuff; you'd see it and think, 'wait a minute, there's not enough here, it's not sounding right.' I was just constantly fiddling with it. And I felt really good about that because I think everyone's hesitation about a writer-director is that you're going to think that every word is sacrosanct. I felt like I was very able to put the writing behind me and just listen to it and watch it and see if it was working or not."

The film shot for ten days on one floor of the building that was once the Hollywood Athletic Club. "It used to be this hotel that was adjunct to the Athletic Club," Glatzer recalled, "where people like Charlie Chaplin would rent rooms as members, and if they wanted to spend the night or wanted to just crash or have an affair up there or whatever, they would. And now it's an office building. So it was exactly what I needed, with the sense of history of the building and hookers' ghosts and all that. It was kind of window dressing, but to me it was really significant. I really wanted that feel to the office."

Another half day was used to shoot the short vignettes from "The Love Judge" show on an existing courtroom set. These sequences were shot on film, transferred to videotape, and then photographed off a television monitor to give them the proper low-budget look. "At the time we shot it, I didn't know how we were going to ultimately do it," Glatzer explained. "And I thought if I shoot it on film, I have the option to use it on film or video, but if I shoot it on video, then I'm stuck with video."

Although the courtroom set only cost them $500, one of its drawbacks was that it was only available on short notice. "I never knew from one day to the next when it would be available," Glatzer recalled. "So we only had two-days' notice to get up there. I had Tim Roth and a couple other people who were going to do cameos in those scenes, and they couldn't because of the last-minute scheduling. But I was thrilled that Paul Bartel and Mary Woronov were willing to do it."

Having just one primary location, plus the half-day for the courtroom sequence, may have seemed like a disadvantage, but Glatzer said he thinks it actually made for a stronger finished film. "I set out to make a movie in one location for financial reasons," he said. "I think the whole idea of grieving and the fact that Mark's dealing with the death of his boyfriend, to me, are so much more interesting indirectly. To me, the movie gained its identity and meaning from giving him that sense of privacy and from being limited to the office. It was a budgetary limitation that ended up working in the movie's favor."

Post-production on the film was a much longer, more harrowing process. "It took forever to post it," Glatzer moaned. "We didn't have enough money. The $40,000 was to shoot it, but we didn't have anything left to do any of the post. We were trying to raise money and trying to find freebie stuff. It's so frustrating when you've got this in the can and you want to work on it, and you can't. It took us about a year to edit the thing, getting a few bucks here, a few bucks there, and begging favors everywhere. And really the only reason it ever got finished was because Mark Finch, who was the head of the Gay & Lesbian Film Festival in San Francisco, saw a rough cut of the film and loved it and said he would give us the closing night if we could finish. So then it was this panic to finish it."

Before that point, Glatzer had shown a rough cut of the film to many potential buyers -- a practice he would not repeat. "You get so desperate, and you think your film's so good, and it's like, 'I've got to show it to them, and they're going to love it, and they're going to give us money,'" he recalled. "But I think it's really important to realize that as a filmmaker you are able to see the finished product more than what's in front of your eyes, and other people won't necessarily respond to it. Especially if it's a comedy, you need that kind of audience response to convince buyers that it's working. If you're showing it to them with just a few people in a screening room, they're never going to get it. Or, worse yet, a rough cut on a video tape -- forget it. It would have to be really an unusual film to work as a rough cut on video tape."

Following the film's successful debut at the festival, a positive review from Variety ("Glatzer's direction is perfectly attuned to his lovingly-fostered ensemble rhythms. As 'feel-good' sleepers go, this one is funny, smart and sweet.") helped propel the film further. "We did the show in San Francisco, got one review in Variety, and then all of a sudden we were off and running," Glatzer recalled. "We never made a phone call after that; it was all the festivals calling us."

Glatzer traveled with "Grief" for a year and a half, hitting key festivals around the world: Toronto, St. Petersburg, New Zealand, Jerusalem, Australia, Berlin, Italy, and London. While making the film was an important experience, traveling with it also proved to be just as enlightening.

"It's been an amazing thing to me," Glatzer said, "just really amazing to think how many thousands of people have seen this thing around the world, and that it's really moved some people and really gotten to some people, and that I've gotten to meet so many people through this. I've met so many people who really are encouraging to other independent filmmakers. There's no sense of competition. There's only support. That's been fantastic."

Although the film has been successful on many levels, it isn't a financial success -- yet. "This is the problem with having good actors," Glatzer explained. "They're all Screen Actor's Guild. And so we wanted to pay them. As far as the Screen Actors' Guild is concerned, we should have paid them the week we went into production. It's fifty thousand dollars to pay the cast SAG minimum. I had a pretty big cast when you consider all the courtroom stuff. By the time you pay all the pension and the taxes, it's a huge amount of money. So, we've almost paid the actors what we owe them. And then the investors will start to see some money. And we do have a lot of money coming to us from TV and video that we haven't seen. But it's taken a long, long time and I really don't know if we'll ever even really break even on it."

Despite the lack of financial recompense, Glazter said he is satisfied with his "Grief" experience -- up to a point. "It's hard to be satisfied," he explained. "At one point I would have been satisfied just to finish the film because I thought we'd never get the money to finish the film. I thought, 'Oh, if I can only finish it -- it doesn't matter if it's distributed if only I can finish it.'

"Then you get it finished, and then you see it received well, and you think, 'Oh, well, now I want more.' And then you think of all the films, independent films, that never get finished or never get out there or get to two festivals and then they disappear. I was so much luckier than that."

What's Black And White And Made On A Shoestring?: "All The Love In The World" and "The Usual"

Black-and-white movies are dead, right? They went out in the 1950s, and what life was left in monochrome was bludgeoned out by that electronic version of paint-by-numbers -- colorization. Guess again, grasshopper. One of the advantages of doing a film on an ultra-low budget is that you get to decide to shoot your film in black and white if it's right for your film, and there's no studio executive cajoling you to shoot it in color. Black and white is alive and well and helping breathe life into the films "All the Love in the World" and "The Usual."

* * *

Having finished film school in Chicago and recently gotten married to each other, director-writer Daniel Curran and producer Jennifer Howe were looking forward to a bright future -- but instead they lost their jobs with a local film-book publisher. Unemployment is devastating to many people, but Curran and Howe saw it as an opportunity to begin their first feature film, "All the Love in the World."

"We had done a few shorts together and then pretty much decided once we were both done with school that we needed to start doing features," Howe recalled, "and the only way to really do that was to say we were going to do it."

To that end, the couple set the starting date of their first feature film for the fall of 1989, which was less than nine months away. At that time, they had less than half of the money they needed to shoot their film. Their director of photography and friend from film school, Janusz Kaminski -- who received an Academy Award in 1994 for his cinematography on "Schindler's List" -- was working in Los Angeles. Howe said she finds it hard to believe now just how certain they were that they would begin production. She said, "I remember Janusz calling us from LA and saying 'Do you guys have the money?

Are we really going to do it?' We kept saying 'Yeah, yeah, yeah, we'll have the money,' knowing that we really didn't have the money at all. I really don't know exactly what we were thinking about."

Just before the start of production, the couple received an unexpected windfall from their former employer. Severance pay, vacation pay, and the return of their 401K retirement contributions added up to enough cash to start filming "All the Love in the World" in September, 1989. And thanks to Curran's new job in the Columbia College film department, they had free access to some of the film-production equipment and facilities they needed. They shot for 14 days and then took a break to allow Kaminski to return to Los Angeles to do another job. During that break, Howe was able to get a job in a film-equipment rental house, so when they resumed production in November, they were able to get reasonable rates on equipment for the remaining 14 days of production. Howe jokingly noted that it would have been helpful to work in a film lab during post-production in order to get low-cost printing. However, neither had such a job, so post-production work forced them to resort to paying with credit cards.

Like most independent productions, there were nay sayers telling Curran and Howe that reaching their goal was impossible. "We heard so often that we couldn't do it. I think in some ways it's probably good that people tell you that because it makes you fight even harder to get it finished," Howe said.

"All the Love in the World" is a unique story about a man who falls in love with the idea of being in love. When faced with a violent, loveless world, he strikes out in anger, leaving a trail of innocent victims whom he blames for the death of love. He travels to the depth of despair before he finds the woman of his dreams. One of the elements that distinguishes "All the Love in the World" from many independent films is its strong visual style reminiscent of the German Expressionist films of the 1920s and the Film Noir style of the 1940s. This look was specifically chosen in advance of production.

Actor Tom Blanton in one of the many atmospheric shots from
"All The Love In The World"
Photo courtesy of Nadjafilm Productions.

"Some things I really care about are gorgeous light and moving camera and wonderful composition," Curran said. "It was something Janusz and I talked a lot about before we shot. We sat down and watched a couple movies. Almost as a cliché we sat down and watched Bertolucci's "The Conformist," which I think so many people sit down and watch before they make a movie, in terms of visual style. Janusz and I had both seen a lot of Andrei Tarkovsky films. We both really wanted to do some of the things he had done with black and white, especially in the underground area where our main character lived . . . these pools of water underground, dripping from above. It's all kind of a Tarkovsky world."

Kaminski had not shot a black-and-white film since his days as a film student when he was "just learning to expose emulsion," and "All the Love in the World" was one of the first films for which he served as director of photography. "Dan and Jennifer's movie is the kind of movie that I would like to make more of, labor-of-love movies," Kaminski said. "Also, I was looking forward to creating the look of the entire picture."

Kaminski felt that Howe and Curran were wise to model their filming style on that of the French New-Wave films of the 1950s. "I think the French New-Wave approach was actually very good because those filmmakers shot a lot of movies with limited budgets," Kaminski pointed out. "They shot on 16mm; they shot black and white; they shot very often with hand-held cameras; and they shot in the streets."

In addition to creating a striking visual style for their film, the filmmakers wanted to look at their surroundings with a new perspective. "One of the things we really wanted was to get the side of Chicago that isn't seen that often," Howe said. They did not want to show a lot of the typical downtown, lake-front shots that are commonly used in films set in Chicago.

By seeking out these uncommon locations, Curran and Howe created a world made up of gleaming, sterile subways stations; beautiful but haunting beaches; the rubble of bombed-out buildings; dripping cellars; tenements; and apartments bathed in romantic light. Curran said he is especially happy with one scene that was remarkable for its simplicity. The scene was the result of a last-minute decision late in the shooting schedule at an apartment that figures prominently in the story.

"We had been in the apartment for about a week at that point, and every day around two or three o'clock, Janusz and I noticed this beautiful, beautiful natural sunlight that was pouring through the front window," Curran recalled. "So finally, we just moved one of the scenes into the living room and did the whole thing with the natural light that was coming in. Janusz can really light, to say the least, and it was fun to do a scene where we did nothing. We had, I think, one bounce card and a mirror from the back of a door bouncing some other light. It was exciting to work with a cinematographer who really had a great visual style."

Kaminski pointed out that, despite the low budget for "All the Love in the World" his work was similar to what he later did on "Schindler's List," which had a multimillion-dollar budget. "Whether you have $20 million or $20,000, you still have to light the human face," Kaminski said. "Basically, there's no difference between what I was doing on Dan and Jennifer's movie and what I was doing on Steven Spielberg's movie. I was lighting human faces. Yes, Steven's movie was extremely large and had big night exteriors and thousands of extras, but also there were many, many scenes that were very intimate scenes between two people talking, and the lighting was basically the same. Usually the lighting instruments don't have to be excessive. Whatever you can get for $2,000, that's what you need to light the human face."

Curran said he is also happy with the opening titles of the film, which use photographs of the main characters from a photo booth to introduce the film's theme of love. "I had always wanted to do that with photo-booth photos," Curran said. "The two actors and I went into this bar in Chicago at around noon. We got a pitcher of Leinenkugel's, and we sat there, and we did about 15 or 20 of those little strips. We just kept doing shots over and over again, needing to get a strip of four that really worked." A fellow film student then combined the photo strips with titles that had been designed for the press kit in order to create an inexpensive title sequence that pulls the audience into the story. "Very often in low-budget films, the titles tend not to be very evocative. They're just there," Curran said.

"I think the other big sign of a low-budget film is bad sound," Curran said. "We spent a lot of time trying to do good sound work. It's easy to forget. You spend all your time and money getting your images on the screen, and then there's no money or your don't pay attention to sound."

Because of his connection with Columbia College, Curran was able to get free use of a sound booth for replacing dialogue that had been marred by squeaky wooden floors at one location. He did his own foley sound effects by creating a home-built foley stage, using a videotape of the work print for reference, and recording the sound effects in his living room.

After all the hard work producing the best possible results in production, Curran and Howe were pleased to find a local laboratory that respected what they were trying to accomplish and understood the importance of good-quality post-production work for an independent film. Even though Spectrum Laboratory primarily processed educational filmstrips and rarely did black-and-white film processing, its staff was very interested in doing feature-film work. Curran said that Spectrum did not treat a 16mm feature film as an amateur production the way some labs do.

Even though Howe and Curran are proud of the quality of their first feature film, they wished they had done some things differently.

In retrospect, they said they would have changed how casting was done, spending more time selecting the cast, making use of someone with casting experience, and finding a known performer from stage or film. "Even though you're doing a movie for no money, actors will do it," Curran said. "I wish we would have gotten some 'name' actors. At the time, we didn't want to." Instead, they had wanted to follow in the footsteps of Spike Lee and Jim Jarmusch by using all unknown local talent and shooting in black and white.

Howe felt that more work on their script would have improved the finished film. "Really, really look at the script you have," Howe recommended. "Because we were trying to work in this new avant-garde way -- or we thought we were -- we were really close-mouthed about the script. We didn't share the script and get it out there and get comments from people. It doesn't mean when you get comments from people that you have to change things. It just makes you have to address and defend what it is that you're trying to do . . . even to yourself."

The decision to improvise much of the dialogue on the set is one that Curran now regrets. "This is a movie we made coming out of film school, and you have these Godardian ideas that you can just go onto a movie set and write your dialogue, and it will be great," Curran said. "I really wanted to do that. I wanted to go with what was happening on the set. And if something wasn't working or if another idea hit us, we would just go off for a little bit and rewrite things and shoot it. It was kind of invigorating on the set to do it like that, but not so invigorating on the Moviola."

Howe added, "You know you have your movie, and you start to cut it, and you start to look at it, and you know what you think is wrong with it. Then as people start to notice the same thing, you realize that you can't hide those things. The film's been a good thing for us, but looking back after three or four years you say 'God, it could have been so much better.'"

"I don't want to go into another movie without having the script locked completely," Curran said. However, he still thinks that improvisation is a valuable tool when it's done during the development of the script. They have done this with their current project by inviting actors to do a reading of the draft script and offer their improvised additions. This has given them some new ideas and also identified places where the script has problems.

Like many independent filmmakers with their first feature-length movie, Howe and Curran ran into unexpected difficulties and realities when they sought distribution for "All the Love in the World."

"I think there's some naiveté when you go into a project like this," Curran said. "You're going to take your life savings and your credit cards and make a movie, and it's going to get into film festivals, and it's going to get distribution. And then you realize that film festivals are really only concerned with selling tickets, and they aren't going to sell tickets if the actors don't ring any bells when they put out their catalog. Name actors are a safety net."

Howe felt that a film's story has the greatest effect on its success. She felt that their film's content prevented them from getting the attention they sought at festivals. "For whatever reason, what we had put together didn't quite click with people and didn't really resonate enough," she said.

The choice of black and white caused them problems in distribution, too.

"We wanted to do black and white because we felt it would work for the story and that it would look good," Howe said. "One of the things I heard probably the most from distributors is 'Just forget it, black and white overseas right now is dead.' That was before 'Schindler's List,' and before some other black-and-white features that have been doing well. But still, I didn't expect to hear that at all. Naively, I thought that Europe would want those films. Even if I had heard before we started shooting 'don't do it in black and white,' I don't know that I would have changed my mind. But it would have come as less of a shock, and I might have been able to come up with other ways to push the movie."

Despite his own success filming the black-and-white "Schindler's List," Kaminski said he doesn't see an expanding position for black-and-white films in the market. "Automatically, when you do make a black-and-white movie, you're making an artistic statement, and most movies have stories that don't allow for that. Also, there's reality. I'm sitting here seeing all kinds of colors. We don't perceive reality in black and white, so movies shouldn't be made in black and white." With the exception of an occasional feature film, Kaminski foresees that most of the future for black-and-white cinematography will be in television commercials and music videos.

"Coming out of film school, you kind of think you know what's involved in putting it together, and every step of the way was just starting over in kindergarten practically," Howe remembered. She said that everything about dealing with distributors was unfamiliar. They had to figure out what to say and how to approach distributors. "I would say do some of that stuff even before you start shooting. Talk with these people, and build relationships with them. See what they're looking for," she recommended.

"I went to film school. I've taught in film school for five or six years," Curran added. "But I think the main damage that's done at film schools is that you're a little too sheltered from what goes on in terms of distribution and exhibition. I think it's silly to enter into this with the naiveté that it's all art and no business."

"I wouldn't buy a car for $35,000 without really checking out the market, but for some reason, I put $35,000 into a movie without really checking into the market," Curran said. He recommended reviewing the catalogs from film festivals and film markets to see what type of films are being shown, and then figure out where your project fits.

Even before they completed the final cut of "All the Love in the World," the filmmakers took the production to the Independent Feature Film Market (IFFM) in New York as a work in progress in hopes of attracting the interest of a distributor. They would not do it again unless they had the funds to do a slick presentation to help distributors envision the finished film. Adding to their problems in getting distributors interested, the film was shown in the 4:00 p.m. time slot on the last day of the market. "Every time I talk to people who have gone to the IFFM who aren't from New York and don't know people there, they tell me they ended up with poor time slots," Curran noted.

While they described their experience as "kind of horrifying," Curran and Howe recommended that filmmakers attend the market the year before they take their films to it in order to learn how to get attention to their productions. "What everyone tells me is that no deals are actually made at the IFFM. All it does is get people thinking about you," Curran said. He also recommended creating a very professional press kit, not just putting a label on a folder. "A press kit is what people are going to see before they see your movie," Curran said. "So if you can fool people with a press kit, that's a start. It gets them to return your phone calls."

Their premiere in Chicago in February 1992 was a success and a disappointment. They were successful in getting a theatrical premiere running twice a night for a week. Unfortunately, even though many nationally known film critics live in Chicago, they were unable to get any to attend the screenings. They didn't fare much better with a screening for sales agents and distributors in Los Angeles. They were able to get about ten to attend, but half of them left 20 minutes into the film. They realized that their film was not meant to have a Los Angeles-based distributor and ultimately found distribution through Facet Multimedia in Chicago, which distributes many independent and foreign films.

In spite of the ups and downs experienced in the production and marketing of "All the Love in the World," Howe said she doesn't regret the experience. "It was definitely something that was valuable in terms of learning how to be filmmakers," Howe said.

In Kaminski's view, there are some decided advantages to shooting films on an ultra-low budget. "The great thing about working on low-budget or no-budget films is that the cinematographer can take great chances. If you push the medium -- which is film emulsion -- to the limit, and you mess it up, you say 'I'm sorry, guys. It's too dark.' If you do it on a big-budget film and you mess up, you're pretty much wasting $100,000 to $200,000, and you may be fired."

There is a similar freedom for directors to experiment when doing ultra-low-budget films, something that is not allowed on major films, Kaminski said. "Very often, if the studio is not liberal enough, they will question the director the moment he or she starts making unexpected decisions or unexpected coverage or angles that are more artistic than what's expected." While no-budget filmmakers can shoot just the shots they intend to use, the big-budget director is not given that latitude, Kaminski reported. "You are not allowed to do minimal coverage on a big studio movie because the studio will come to the director and tell him 'Hey, you've got to do more coverage so we can manipulate the pace and the drama of the movie in the editing.'"

Because there is less pressure on the director in an ultra-low-budget movie, Kaminski also felt that the collaboration between the director and cinematographer can be more friendly.

The similarities with European films continue to attract Kaminski to low-budget films. "They're about telling story regardless of the budget, telling very personal stories. And it's very good to work on these movies, just for your soul," Kaminski said. "To me, it's all about story. I love to do movies with good stories, regardless of the budget."

Curran is philosophical about the experience of making "All the Love in the World." "I think we were really trying to make something different and challenge the form," Curran said. "And I think it's just one of those exercises that failed, but it was really great doing it. You have to really enter into it not afraid to fail."

* * *

"I think low-budget film is a chance to take all the risks you want to because really you've got nothing to lose," according to Eric Tretbar, writer-director of "The Usual." "If you fail, no problem. If you succeed, you're really going to succeed completely on your own terms."

And Tretbar has succeeded on several fronts with his black-and-white feature film. "The Usual" tells its story of a woman's transition between two relationships in a style that is Tretbar's own. That honest, patient style is what helped the finished film find an international audience for it's less-than-usual approach to cinematic storytelling.

The story is simple, but it bears witness to many people's experiences as it introduces us to Claire, a student and part-time waitress. Claire is just getting over the demise of her relationship with Aldo when she meets Spike, an aspiring musician who works as the fry cook at her new job. Spike and Claire draw together in a slow dance of food orders, rides home, evenings of TV watching, and joke swapping. Just as they begin to move though life in unison, Aldo's return to town and to Claire's life threatens to change the tune.

(l to r) John Crozier, Lisa Todd, and Steve Epp
try to untangle romance in "The Usual."
Photo courtesy of Periferia Films

Tretbar's exploration of this awkward pause between old love and new demonstrated its universal appeal when "The Usual" was shown at the Independent Feature Film Market in 1991. Representatives of the Berlin Film Festival invited Tretbar and his co-producer Emily Stevens to bring the film to Berlin, where it was selected as the best film of the International Forum of New Films. "The Berlin festival set the pace," Tretbar recounted. "From there, we were invited to a lot of other festivals -- Hong Kong, Vienna, Warsaw, London, the American Film Institute in Los Angeles, Seattle, and Toronto." The film was also shown on television in Germany and Israel and in museums on a tour sponsored by the Berlin Film Festival.

Tretbar began his production in a series of steps, some planned, some not. He shot a 15-minute Super-8mm trailer for the film in 1989 in order to apply for a grant to produce a half-hour version. After receiving the $12,000 grant, a friend persuaded Tretbar that he could shoot a feature-length version instead. Armed with the 15-minute trailer, Tretbar pitched the film to family friends in Kansas

City and was able to get investors to put up the remainder of the $25,000 shooting budget.

While arranging for production funds, Tretbar began preparing an 85-page script for the production. In an effort to reduce the cost of sound recording, 40 of the 120 scenes were to have voice-over narration by the story's three main characters. Tretbar also chose to shoot the film in black and white for several reasons. "I thought it would make the story a little more dramatic," Tretbar said. "Also it would be much cheaper and quicker to light. You can just get away with more in black and white, especially in a no-budget situation. I think color has much more chance of looking gloomy and dumpy in a no-budget setting when you don't have the money to really make sure everything is perfect."

An austere visual style was also chosen in order to work within the limited resources of the production. "I didn't want to try to do something that I didn't have the equipment to do," Tretbar recalled. He also decided to deviate from the classic film technique of wide shots followed by closer shots. Instead, he let his scenes play out in long takes that held a medium or wide shot.

In order to let the actors grow into their characters and to allow for rewriting that tailored the characters to the actors, Tretbar rehearsed the production for three weeks before starting 13 days of shooting in the spring of 1990. The production company was made up of local cast and crew from the Minneapolis area. The cast did have an international flavor, though, because two key roles were played by performers from a French theater company that divided its performing season between Minneapolis and Paris.

During the shooting, Tretbar continued the collaborative relationship with the actors in order to add bits of reality into the film's characters. This approach was used to good effect in a scene in which the old boyfriend is on his way back to town, and the new boyfriend, Spike, knows it. "Spike and Claire are having breakfast together,"

Tretbar said. "But it's this very silent, horrible time when they are at each other's throats, but they're not saying anything. Well, John Crozier, who played Spike, had told these two jokes while we were setting up the shot, and the whole crew was just in hysterics. So, I told him to tell one joke and Lisa Todd, who played Claire, to tell the other joke, and that became the whole scene." The deadpan exchange of jokes served to heighten the humorless undercurrent of the scene.

"I think that was the most fun for me, watching the actors flesh out the characters with parts of their own personalities," Tretbar observed. "I think as a director, you're being given all this fresh vital material to work with on the spot. To me, that's the reward that hopefully I'll get for sitting in my hole writing and writing and writing."

The production was fortunate to have a well-supplied lighting truck and enough film for a 6:1 shooting ratio. Even though Tretbar said he regrets not having the time to make better use of the unique qualities of the black-and-white image, he's happy that they were able to achieve a pleasant look for the film. Despite having a generous shooting ratio for an ultra-low-budget film, Tretbar found that the long-take style could quickly chew up film stock on difficult scenes. Technical problems during the shooting of one four-minute scene consumed two days' worth of film before the crew got a good take. The next day, they made up for the extra film used by shooting eight scenes at one location with only one take each. Tretbar worried later when he realized that there were no back-up takes for those scenes, but the performances and camera work were all fine, and the scenes were all usable.

While production went smoothly, problems with the film began to show up in post-production. Tretbar recalled that when the planned voice-over narrations were added to the film, they were "horrible." The visuals in the scenes gave all the information that was contained in the narration. Fortunately, the sound person had been available throughout the production, so sync sound had been recorded for all of those scenes, making it possible to replace the voice-overs. However, when more than 30 voice-overs were removed, the pace and flow of the whole movie was thrown off. By winter of 1990, editing had bogged down, and Tretbar's first cut was 160-minutes long.

"A friend of mine said to put it on the shelf and forget about it for six months," Tretbar recalled. "I said, 'Six months! But it's done. Can't you see? It's perfect. It's two hours and forty minutes. It's perfect.' He said, 'Eric, put the film away.'"

After heeding his friend's advice, Tretbar cut the film's scene list into strips of paper and arranged and rearranged them on his bedroom window over the next three months, trying to create a whole new movie without the voice-overs. "I even tried doing a Dada trick. I threw them in a bag and shook them up just to see if something good would happen," Tretbar said. Where Dadaism failed, Tretbar's persistence succeeded, and a new film was created out of the old. He said that there were not more than three or four scenes that were still in consecutive order after the re-edit. He also discarded a 20-minute subplot and trimmed the final film down to 80 minutes.

The film's post-production problems were not over, however. One scene of the film had the characters watching television, and the sound of a cartoon was heard. This sound had been taped off of the television and had been included in the film. Tretbar assumed the old cartoon would be in the public domain, but his co-producer insisted that they find out for sure. After speaking with a cartoon expert at a California television station, they learned that the 1938 Warner Brothers cartoon was owned by Turner Broadcasting. Getting rights to use the 40-second sound clip cost Tretbar "more than they had a right to get, and more than I had a brain to pay."

Because of his rush to complete the film before the IFFM, Tretbar missed the opportunity to do a real music score with themes for each of the characters. "It would have been a much richer movie, and I think some of the emotions would have been much clearer." Instead, music from a band that Tretbar played in was used along with some other existing musical pieces. He said he hopes to do a real musical score for his next production.

Reflecting on his own experiences, Tretbar had advice for other filmmakers. "I was too strict. I think that was my greatest mistake, not letting myself be myself. The secret in the end is to be yourself as clearly and strongly as possible. Whatever you care about saying is valid and important. I think everybody has something to show. Their point of view is interesting."

Tretbar acknowledged that shooting a black-and-white 16mm film puts the production at a disadvantage for distribution. It limits most of the exhibition opportunities to film clubs and colleges because the television and home-video markets are not very interested in black-and-white films.

After "The Usual" got international attention on the festival circuit and a review in Variety, the film industry became interested in Tretbar. "A bunch of people called me after that, thinking I was the 'new great thing,' not realizing that 'The Usual' was a very quiet, intimate black-and-white 16mm movie," he said. However, the inquiries did connect Tretbar with a production company for which he worked two years developing scripts, though none passed the development stage. "Strangely enough, movies, which are made out of pictures and live people, involve very little of either in the development process," Tretbar observed.

Another problem that Tretbar said he sees with the film industry's way of working is that it advances promising filmmakers too quickly. "You make your little no-budget film; then they want you to make a $5 million or $10 million film the next morning. I think you still need to make two or three or four or five little films where everything's not at stake," Tretbar said.

After parting ways with the production company for which he was working, Tretbar next spent a couple years trying to raise money for projects himself in Hollywood. "But it takes two or three years for any one movie, so I realized I could be doing this for the next 15 years and never shoot one frame," he said. So he set a new course for himself -- he plans to begin production of another ultra-low-budget film.

"I think the difficult thing is once you are introduced to the film scene, into the film society, then everyone says, 'Well, your next film needs to be a little bigger, and you should have some name stars. Take the next step,'" Tretbar said. "I don't care if I take the next step. I just want to make another movie. I don't think doing your own films precludes having commercial success. Because I think people like Gus Van Sant have shown clearly that it's possible to stay in your own city -- he lives in Portland and does everything in the northwest -- and still deal with Hollywood for money and talent. I think that's an attractive model."

To Boldly Film Where No One Has Filmed Before - "Slack Trek: The X Generation" and "Plan 10 from Outer Space"

Audiences unfamiliar with science fiction often discount this literary and film genre as having a heart of ray guns and rocket ships. However, fans of science fiction know that its imaginative worlds allow the freedom to speculate about and comment on present-day lifestyles and cultures. In spite of the well-known challenges of creating an alternative universe even with a large budget, filmmakers with ultra-low budgets have gravitated to this liberating field of storytelling.

Two films that explore the galaxy on three dollars a day are "Plan 10 from Outer Space" and "Slack Trek: The X Generation" (a working title only, thanks to a cadre of Paramount lawyers, possibly with the support of Klingon warriors . . . or, worse yet, Ferengi business managers).

Grabbing the first flight out to enjoy a dream vacation is the goal of most graduates from MIT's Sloan School of Management after they've gotten a five-figure bonus check for signing on with a new employer. Julie Chang chose to pursue dream fulfillment instead. She used her bonus check as seed money to launch "Slack Trek: The X Generation" in order to follow her dream of making a feature film in the Boston metropolitan area.

Chang's enthusiasm, even in the face of ever-present advice to delay or quit the project, attracted friend Joe Rubin to share writing and directing duties on the film. Robin Alper, another friend who had recently graduated from Harvard Business School, joined on as producer. Chang's apartment became the production office, the six months she had before starting her new job became the production schedule, and Rubin and Alper moved back into their parent's homes to save money and work full-time on "Slack Trek."

Producer Alper saw the work ahead as a unique opportunity. "I basically agreed to do the project without having seen anything on paper, not one written word. I was weighing the options of either working with Julie or moving directly out to Los Angeles and start-ing as an assistant to an assistant to an assistant for someone and doing grunt work for a couple years. So, it was a really a no-brainer decision for me. When else would I have the opportunity to produce a film without ever having done it before?"

"Making an indie film with virtually no money is pretty much impossible," Rubin said. "Add to that two first-time directors with no film experience who've written a completely unrealistic script, and you have a great fantasy. There is only one thing to do in this type of desperate situation. Simply announce that you are doing it. That was Julie's brilliance. That's how she got me hooked."

Alper and Chang had just enough experience with the film and video business to be concerned about their lack of experience at the start of "Slack Trek." Alper said they looked into taking film pro-duction classes, but felt they were overpriced. "We both looked at each other and said, 'You know, we could put this money into making a film instead.'"

"You don't have to have a film degree to do this," Alper asserted. "The proof is Julie, Joe, and me. None of us had ever done this before. There are so many rules that you have to do this and you have to do that to make a film. And we just disregarded all of those. . . . There is no one way to do it. You just have to really want to do it."

The dedication with which the trio launched into production is somewhat ironic in light of the film's central topic, the "slackers" of their generation. The story is propelled by rebels from the future who have fled to 1994 in an effort to prevent the development of technology that will soothe the future into mind-numbing bliss. Beside evading the Futurist Squad sent to capture them, the rebels must recruit slacking members of the X generation in order to change their history. Their best prospects are a perpetual student of chem-istry and fuzzy logic, an out-of-work cappuccino vendor/journalist, and a bicycle delivery man who returns slackers' videos for them. Special effects, one-liners, out-of-this-world costumes, sight gags, and futuristic devices are on hand to help lead the audience on a rau-cous tour of the twenty-something world.

(l to r) William Katzman and Alexander Pak enjoy mindless bliss as Futurists in "Slack Trek: The X Generation."
Photo courtesy of Fish Productions

Chaos didn't reign on the screen alone. The production had its share of challenges and surprises, too. With less than three months to the start of production in August 1994, there was only a one-page story treatment in hand. Chang and Rubin spent six weeks brain-storming and completing a draft script. "We were inexperienced, so we were adding characters all the time. We had no sense of control over our writing, making things very complicated for ourselves," Chang said.

Alper, as producer, was worried about the ambitious script. "I had really encouraged Julie to scale down the script. We had far too many locations and far too many speaking parts, but that didn't real-ly deter her," Alper said. "We did it, but it was really a big pain in the neck."

Because of the six-month production window, there was no time to reflect on the script and edit it prior to production. Chang remembered, "Even during the shoot, our script editor and myself would go through the scenes the night before and just lop off actors' lines. And the next day, we'd tell them as gently as we could 'We're going to change this whole scene around.'"

During editing, scenes were rearranged and titles were added to make sure the film's story was clear to audiences. In retrospect, Chang advised, "If you're going to shoot it yourself, keep the characters and locations to a minimum."

The production company shot for 16 days, taking Sundays off, and used 40 locations with 80 actors and 75 crew members. In addition to this rigorous schedule, the filmmakers had to deal with the usual and unusual production problems.

Chang remembered shooting in busy Harvard Square as the most difficult part of the production. Even though they had gotten the necessary permit to work there (which they rarely did at other street locations), a less-than-neighborly police officer took it upon himself to harass members of the production company because they had not hired their own security officer for the location. At another point, two-bit thieves attempted to steal equipment by offering to "protect" it. (The police officer was apparently no longer in the vicinity.) The Harvard Square problems culminated when two rolls of negatives from the shooting were ruined in processing by a nationally known New York film laboratory.

One early decision plagued the film throughout the production. Wanting to create the best possible film image, the filmmakers selected the Super-16mm production format. They now consider that decision a huge mistake.

"I had to order a special projector from New York, which is more expensive," Alper said. "It was really difficult to find editing equipment that could take Super 16mm, and now I'm stuck with a film shot on Super 16mm that I can't project at festivals. . . . I can't shop this around except on video."

"We could have gotten a free camera if it were on 16mm," Alper recalled. "I would really recommend for people doing independent films to shoot on regular 16mm."

The grueling shooting schedule and the ambitious list of locations paid off by giving the film a bigger look than its small budget would suggest. Chang also found that she could be very creative with locations by using different angles and different set dressings. Locations that she originally thought could only serve as one setting ended up representing as many as five different sites. "Just think really creatively about locations," she recommended, "and try to keep moving to a minimum because there are always little things you don't think about, like parking and how people are going to get there -- all these little issues that end up posing delays and problems."

The filmmakers also met with their share of good fortune. Boston-area restaurants donated food to feed the crew, the camera crew was able to create the future primarily with simple and innovative lighting, local bands gave permission to use their music to help create the film's unique soundtrack, and a talented local composer created a film score that greatly added to the humor of the film. The film's art director, who had never worked on a film before, created unique sets out of nothing and has since gone on to do other films.

Chang and Rubin were also able to add a celebrity to their cast, their friend Amy Carter. The former first-daughter not only portrayed one of the future rebels, but she also constructed the "Super-Smelly Unhygienic Garbage Bombs" used in the film's climax. Carter was also a source of publicity that landed the film's title in "People" magazine and newspapers across the country. Sadly, that publicity also attracted lawyers from Paramount.

Chang felt that they made some very good decisions in picking a cast and crew who offered many suggestions that made the finished film even better. Chang said, "Pick your people really, really well, . . . not just people who are friends. Try to find people you are going to

345

work well with. And be really strong. There are a lot of times when people are going to tell you not to do it and doubt you and be critical. Just know that you've got to get it done."

*   *   *

"I got run out of Hollywood," is the reason Trent Harris gave for returning to Salt Lake City to write and direct his ultra-low-budget feature film "Plan 10 from Outer Space."

After living in Los Angeles for more than a decade, Harris got his chance at a Hollywood production with his film "Rubin and Ed." The film, which has become a popular late-night cult film, never caught on at the mainstream box-office with its story about a quest to bury a frozen cat in the desert. One reviewer even described it as the worst film of the year. Hollywood was not amused. Harris agreed that the film is not for everyone, but he doesn't want to do films for the masses.

"I spent about 12 years in Los Angeles and finally got tired of asking people's permission to make movies," Harris said. "They just were never going to make the kind of movies I was interested in. So I decided to come back to Salt Lake City, which was my hometown, where I had access to a lot of resources and try to tap into those resources to make a low-budget film."

The film Harris made is unusual to say the least. "Plan 10 from Outer Space" turns Mormon history on its ear in a delightfully weird reinterpretation that includes over-sexed aliens, a Joseph Smith sphinx, Mormon hit squads, a panty-thief who hears messages from space, secret alphabets, a grudge-toting wife of a pioneer polygamist, and Mormon statuary being destroyed by spaceships. (The film's advertising tag line says it all: "Just because it's made up doesn't mean it isn't true!") A repressed author serves as the film's Nancy Drew-style protagonist who uncovers "Plan 10" and "the secret of the bees." While the film leaps through time and space, it's also a travelogue for one of the filmmaker's favorite places.

*Mormons, cardboard sets, and Karen Black help to make
"Plan 10 From Outer Space" memorable.*
Photo courtesy of Plan 10 Productions Ltd.

"What I see this film as is really a celebration of Salt Lake City,"
Harris said. "It's all of the weird, wonderful, wacky stuff that I like
so much."

Harris' former career as a television journalist in Utah helped
provide background, locations, and characters for the "Plan 10"
script. "I worked in news here for years back in the 70's, so I had a
background of material and characters and places that had always
interested me," Harris said. "Salt Lake City is one of the strangest
places in the whole country in kind of a wonderful way. . . . I've kept
clipping files and various research materials over the years, and when
I traveled around, I'd run across these places."

The script Harris wrote and filmed is not for everyone, but that's the way the filmmaker likes it.

"I find that most independent films are audition films for Hollywood," Harris said. "My approach has been the opposite of that. I don't want to go back to Los Angeles in the worst sort of way. The whole reason I left and came here was to pursue films that were not necessarily made for everyone, films that have a specific and perhaps smaller audience."

"In Hollywood, they spend such enormous amounts of money that they have to make movies that appeal to a billion people, and the only way to do that is through lack of content. You can't really say anything. Because as soon as you say something, you begin to offend people, and then they don't go to your movie," he said.

To achieve the look of a bigger film, the "Plan 10" production team used a unique approach to filming. The film was shot over the course of 18 months, but production wasn't continuous. They broke the sequences of the script down into "little movies" about ten pages in length, which were shot in about four days. Then they would regroup and begin planning the next sequence. While planning was underway, they would edit the segment they previously shot. Because they didn't lose production time moving the cast and crew, this shooting schedule made it easier to include many Utah locations in the film.

Harris said that getting use of locations was easy as well. "Around here you say, 'Hey do you mind if we shoot in your yard for a couple hours?' and they say 'No, heck, go ahead. Can we make you some coffee? Do you mind if we watch? Can we be in it?'"

A local rave club served as a studio for some scenes in the film. The filmmakers were allowed to use the club during the day to build their sets and props and to film scenes. At night the rave club would use the sets and props in their shows. One of the hallmarks of this film is elaborate fantasy sets, which were built almost exclusively from painted cardboard. "We didn't have any money, but I have a very clever friend named David Brothers who designed and built these sets out of just cardboard," Harris said.

Brothers and fellow set designer Joe Stetich cut and painted cardboard into everything from planets to spaceship interiors. They also scoured junk stores and laboratory-supply shops to decorate the sets. "These guys are really, really good; they can make anything out of cardboard," Harris proclaimed.

Harris was impressed by the number of talented people in Salt Lake City who offered their services and lamented how few of them get an opportunity to display their talents. He was pleased to have been able to offer skilled film technicians a chance to work on something fun and creative rather than their usual mundane assignments. "How many car commercials can you do as a grip? It's just not very rewarding," said Harris.

"Plan 10" also received some out-of-town help to realize its ambitious special effects. Alien spaceships attacking Salt Lake City were created for cost as a favor by Image G, the Los Angeles company that did visual effects for the television series "Star Trek: The Next Generation." The producer for "Plan 10," Walter Hart, had previously worked as an executive producer for Image G.

Harris felt that this type of help is not out of reach of filmmakers with little money. "What does money get you? Money buys you equipment and talent. But you can get equipment and talent without money, too. There are other kinds of deals you can work," Harris said.

Harris is unconcerned about mixing high-tech and low-tech equipment in a production. He said that once you've finished your film, no one can tell whether it was edited on a state-of-the-art non-linear editing system or with a pair of scissors and tape. As production companies rush to buy the latest technology, lots of useful equipment is discarded, and Harris has been happy to take it off their hands.

"I was able to pull in a lot of that equipment because people think it's obsolete," Harris said. "It works fine for me. My office is full of obsolete equipment."

Like most low-budget independent productions, aid came from many quarters. Harris' mother helped cook spaghetti for the cast and crew when shooting a dance scene that included more than 100 performers. The U.S. Forest Service gave the production rolls of film stock. When the actress for a key role backed out fearing reprisals from the Mormon church, Harris' friend Karen Black agreed to join the cast, giving the film a "name" performer.

"We just got more darn support here," Harris said. "Places would let us in for free, supply the power, and come and help. It was really an amazing community effort here."

Harris is also dedicated to the community that embraced his cinematic efforts and would like to continue working there. "I really want to make films in Salt Lake City," Harris stated. "I know I can make films here now. The question is can I market them from here and make enough money back that we pay everyone who worked on it and do it again?"

To this end, Harris has redirected his energies to the marketing of his film. Promotion of the film began weeks before its Salt Lake City premiere in an effort to make sure as many people as possible had heard of the film. The premiere itself was a publicity extravaganza. The local radio and television stations gathered to cover the premiere live among spotlights, limousines, a samba band, Lamanite warriors, and a barbershop quartet wearing hubcap hats. The tickets sold out in advance, and about 10,000 tickets were sold in the four weeks the film showed. Though this was a gratifying response, Harris said he views it as only the start of his effort to market "Plan 10."

"You can't make your movie, make a tape, send it to a distributor, and expect him to pick it up," Harris advised. "You have to build it into a product that can be sold."

For a film like "Plan 10" which doesn't have any obvious selling points, Harris said he feels it's important to build word of mouth, gather quotes from reviewers, and do screenings at selected places. Unlike studio films which are released along with dozens of other films and which disappear after a few months, Harris said that an independent film must build a reputation, a press packet of reviews, and an audience slowly over a year or more before it is even ready to be presented to a distributor.

"You have to give these people permission to like your film," Harris said. "They have to be able to see a handle they can use to sell it. You have to spell it out for them."

In order to prove that Harris' movie has an audience outside of Utah, the "Plan 10" marketing plan includes more than a dozen screenings around the country at theaters that run 16mm films. He's also using the high-tech, low-cost Internet to build word-of-mouth and support for his film. The Internet home page for "Plan 10" includes video clips from the film, scenes from the premiere party, interviews, and an opportunity to order "Plan 10" T-shirts and buttons. The Internet has also been a source of mailing lists for theaters that show similar quirky films.

Though Harris said he hopes that all this publicity and buzz building will lead to a distribution deal, he's not pinning his hopes on that alone. If he can't find the right deal, he will go solo, distributing the film himself one theater at a time. He pointed out that one advantage of doing an ultra-low-budget movie is that you don't have to earn a lot of money to be successful. If you cut out the distribution middleman, you can actually arrange some lucrative deals, such as 50 percent of the door receipts, according to Harris. However, he said he expects to be working full-time for months to come promoting the film.

Even as he looks back on almost two years making his film and ahead to another year marketing it, Harris is undaunted. He's begun planning his next production, and he's working with a long-time friend on an offbeat documentary about Utah's Zion National Park, reputedly Adam and Eve's old neighborhood. Harris' advice to people contemplating creating their own ultra-low-budget movies is "don't be afraid to do it." After all, Trent Harris isn't.

Life As We Know It: "Someone Special" and "World And Time Enough"

One goal of most independent filmmakers is to say something that is personally important to them. So, is it any wonder that these acts of unfettered self-expression often explore the realm of personal relations? The makers of "Someone Special" and "World and Time Enough" used their forays into feature films to examine and comment on humankind's search for love and acceptance.

Key players in the romantic rectangle featured in "Someone Special" (l to r, Lisa Marie Reichle, Layton Payne, Paul Locklear, and Stephanie Delape.

Photo courtesy of Caspian Films.

"Someone Special" pokes a finger in the side of love in the 1990s as its nerdy and dateless protagonist Norman tries everything to find someone special. After exhausting the "standard" methods of finding a date -- group therapy, infomercials for TV psychics, and shopping at supermarkets on Monday nights -- he takes the drastic step of joining a dating service. He gets more than he bargains for when his search for companionship lands him in a love rectangle. Houston filmmakers Soodabeh Babcock and James Babcock, who moonlight as husband and wife, used this story to showcase their city and to have some fun at the expense of modern dating rituals.

James discovered the story as it was being written by a friend of his in a screenwriting class. After he and Soodabeh read the 30-page treatment, they decided they wanted to make a feature film of the story, with her directing and him producing. The final script took about a year to complete, and pre-production efforts were then begun by the Babcocks.

The characters were cast before rewriting of the script was completed. The actors did some stage readings of the screenplay to help test the script, and the results of this activity were mixed, according to Soodabeh. "It was a very interesting process," she said. "Every time you would have a reading you would make more discoveries about what worked and what didn't work." However, she felt the process became a little too collaborative. "You really have to have a completed screenplay before you do a reading," she recommended. James compared it to the old joke about a camel being a horse designed by committee. The director, producer, screenwriter, and actors often had very different reactions to suggested changes. "It created a lot of tension," he recalled. "It was a very painful process."

However, the Babcocks said they feel that a great script is essential to an independent film, and that it is especially important for the filmmaker to write the script or have a significant role in its writing. "I think in some ways for an independent it's even more important," James said. "You're going to put heart and soul into something for a couple of years. It better be your heart and soul, not someone else's."

With a finished script in hand, production began in July 1993 and continued on evenings and weekends for six months, working around the schedule of the cast and crew as they filmed at more than 40 locations. While acknowledging that they were lucky to hold together the principal cast members for such an extended production period, James said that it helped them achieve the look of a larger film. "One of the advantages of the way we did it was that we might spend only four or five hours a night shooting, but because we had so many different days that we were shooting, we were able to get all the variety of locations," he said.

The project also became a family affair, with Soodabeh's mother overseeing food for the cast and crew, James producing and recording location sound, and Soodabeh directing and filling in on other production jobs. "You carry most of the responsibility on your own shoulders," Soodabeh recalled. "As director, I shot about a third of the movie myself. I was also trying to make sure that the props and the costumes and everything else were working the way I wanted, and I was making sure the actors knew where they were going and had all their blocking and lines correct. You feel like you're doing the job of 20 people."

The filmmakers also were responsible for the gargantuan task of organizing the production and making sure everyone got to the many different locations. "What happens when you do that is you end up not having the kind of control you want," James said. "You find there are compromises you wish you didn't have to make just because of the press of time."

While weathering the tempest of production, the filmmakers were gratified to find that local businesses frequently opened their doors to the production company. In one instance, they found a unique solution to the problem of not having a bedroom outfitted with the necessary high-tech furniture. "We just shot in a furniture store," James explained. "We talked them into letting us shoot it in the showroom." Unfortunately, the store was not as empty in the afternoon as the owners had described. "So you have the poor actors trying to do their scene while patrons in the store were wandering by," he remembered. "Try shouting 'Quiet on the set!' to a bunch of people who came in to buy furniture."

Soodabeh was particularly proud of one exterior night scene that they shot. It presented the aftermath of an apartment fire, complete with displaced residents, fire trucks, ambulances, and firefighters. She remembered that they talked nearby residents into providing the electricity for lights to illuminate the street. Many of the homeowners volunteered to play extras in the scene also. Local paramedics helped to provide the needed emergency vehicles and personnel. "If a studio shot this scene, it would have cost a lot of money," she said. "In our case, we were able to pull it off with nothing."

For the post-production phase of the project, the uncut film footage was transferred to Betacam SP video tape for editing. A rough cut of the film was edited on a 3/4-inch editing system that was available at no cost, and then the filmmakers rented a Betacam SP system to make the final video master. James said that they intend to go back and conform the negative, but "it's just a question of getting someone to pick up that cost."

While a film version of "Someone Special" may not be needed for most of the distribution markets they may be aiming at, James recommended finishing on film. "I think, for independents, film festivals are a very important way of getting your name out there," he said. "Even if you have the best film in the world, on video I think it's difficult to get people to take you seriously."

The filmmakers used a high-quality video projector to present their finished production for a sold-out premiere showing at the Houston Museum of Fine Arts in April, 1995. They followed up by winning a bronze award in the category of comedy feature film at the Houston WorldFest International Film and Video Festival. The pair was especially proud of this showing considering that they were the lowest-budget film in the competition, which included entries with the backing of major studios. James observed that the film festivals are no longer solely the domain of independent productions; studios are now using the festivals to get exposure for their films, too.

Reflecting on the production process and their efforts to promote their finished film, Soodabeh and James Babcock have learned what to do better next time and have gained some new perspectives about filmmaking and distribution.

James would like to have more funds before starting production of another feature film. "I'd try to raise just enough money so that we could pay people enough to keep body and soul together, and then just go ahead and shoot all at once," he said.

While promoting "Someone Special," he recognized the merits of the advanced publicity Hollywood does for its films. He recommended that producers of ultra-low-budget films start creating name recognition for their movies at the beginning of pre-production. "With a little planning and a little work, you can be obtaining your publicity stills or advertising literature so that you can start generating interest in the film even before it's finished," James said. He even recommended finding a publicity person to be a member of the core production team because many independent filmmakers don't pay enough attention to sales. "They think of themselves primarily as artists and don't realize you also have to be a salesman," he said.

He also warned against having unrealistic expectations for a first feature film. "A lot of independent filmmakers have this illusion that they're going to get picked up right away for distribution," James said. "But there's a fierce competition out there, and you have to have either a very, very unique point of view or genre of film to get distribution."

"My fantasy is that a first film makes somebody a lot of money so that the next time around you'll be in a better bargaining position," James said. "A lot of people have the attitude that you make one film, and you strike it rich. It just doesn't happen that way. Even if you are wildly successful, all you get is a ticket to the next ride."

* * *

"World and Time Enough" differs from many ultra-low-budget productions in that its crew was primarily made up of working film professionals. While it was the first feature film Eric Mueller had ever written or directed, he and his producers Julie Hartley and Andrew Peterson all had years of experience working on commercials and industrial films in Minneapolis and other cities, and they had worked on several Hollywood movies that had been filmed in Minnesota, including "Drop Dead Fred" and "Equinox." This experience helped them entice a crew of professionals to work with them on "World and Time Enough."

Through the eyes of the film's narrator, David, the story follows the lives of his gay friends Mark and Joey. Mark is an artist who creates guerrilla performance art to state his political and social views. Joey picks up litter for the city and saves his favorite discards for his personal collection. A different side of Midwest life is seen as the two boyfriends face AIDS, a search for Joey's birth parents, the death of Mark's father, the rejection of Joey's adoptive parents, and Mark's obsession with building a cathedral in his father's honor. All challenges are faced with humor, wit, compassion, and the help of an eccentric parade of friends and family.

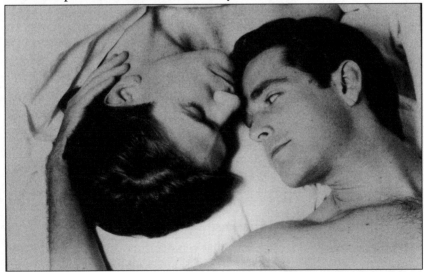

(l to r) Gregory G. Giles as Joey and Matt Guidry as Mark star in
"World And Time Enough."
Photo courtesy of Strand Releasing

"The script started with the idea of a guy who is HIV positive who wanted to build a cathedral," Mueller said. "And as he was thinking about making this cathedral, that the audience saw these images of real cathedrals, and when the film was finally edited together, they would be some kind of visual counterpoint to the dramatic narrative."

With this idea, Mueller was able to get a Minnesota State Arts Board grant that allowed him to go to France to shoot the cathedral footage that appears at several points in the film. At this stage Mueller did not yet have a completed screenplay. He applied for and received a fellowship that allowed him to take enough time off work in 1991 and 1992 to complete the screenplay.

"Like all first-time screenwriters, I thought I had to make a very serious sort of dramatic film," he explained. "Then I started drawing more from everyday life to flesh out the script." Mueller said that the finished script was much less linear than the edited film ended up being.

Co-producer Peterson recommended that the screenwriters of independent films put in extra effort to create a well-crafted script that suits the project's budget. "You can't work on the script enough," he said. "For a first feature, you have to have it tight. You have to limit the number of locations. You have to realize that everything you write has a price attached to it." He added that by limiting the locations and the number of actors, filmmakers actually gain more opportunities to explore their characters and settings because they aren't racing to get everyone to the next location.

In 1992, Mueller was able to get a National Endowment for the Arts grant, an American Film Institute grant, and a grant through a local film organization which was distributing National Endowment for the Arts funds. Hartley said that the production had a final budget of about $60,000, with $50,000 of that coming from grants. She said Mueller asked her to join the project to help with the financial end of the production and because she had low-budget-film and public-television experience that had taught her "how not to spend money." But the dollar amount of the budget didn't reflect the true value of the production, according to Hartley.

"We had an enormous number of things that were in-kind contributions, and I don't mean people's moms making dinner," she said. "I mean equipment houses, gaffers, grips, not your brothers, your aunts, or your uncles. These were movie professionals who were willing and able to donate their time to us. We've heard the comment that our film has very high production values, and there's a reason for that because, for example, our gaffer was a professional in the industry. It wasn't somebody learning. Every single person, with the exception of our two production assistants, came from the film industry."

Peterson recalled, "We were very organized from the start, and that's what brings professionals in for 18 days with no pay. They're not going to waste their time if you don't know how to set up, at the low end, a craft service table or, at the high end, a shot list." They also attracted industry professionals by offering people positions they might not normally be able to get. All crew members signed paperwork stating that they were volunteering their services, and no deferred salary payments were arranged.

With the help of a casting director, the three chose their cast from the ranks of actors doing professional theater and commercial productions in the Minneapolis-St. Paul area. In order to use Screen Actor's Guild (SAG) actors at a price that fit the budget, the producers entered into a limited-exhibition agreement with the union. The New York office of SAG approved the agreement only after reviewing Mueller's previous work and after determining that the script was an artistic endeavor, not a commercial one. The producers also had to meet several other requirements and pay a $2,500 worker's compensation deposit. The agreement wasn't completed until just two days before shooting began, something that Hartley and Peterson did not tell director Mueller. Under the agreement the actors were paid $75 a day, and paperwork such as call sheets, sign-in/sign-out reports, and production reports had to be done daily. The final agreement did not permit video distribution, and it limited exhibition of the film to the "art houses."

"I would recommend that people think very carefully about signing a limited-exhibition agreement because it does work out to be quite a substantial amount of money that you are then obligated to pay," Hartley advised. She noted that the union can put a lien on the finished film to prevent distribution in violation of the agreement. When a distributor later picked up the film, an advance had to be negotiated for the sale of foreign rights. All of this money was paid to SAG in order to get the rights for wider distribution of the movie.

The production also incorporated and purchased insurance in the event that there might be a mishap during production. Even though they never used the insurance, Peterson felt it would be false economy to try to save money by not spending the $3,000 for it. Hartley added, "One production assistant smashes into someone's car, and there it goes." They were able to get equipment-rental houses to loan them a dolly, lights, and a generator because they had the insurance to protect the equipment.

Mueller credited Peterson and Hartley with raising the overall quality of the project. "When Julie and Andrew came on board, all of a sudden it became a professional production," Mueller said. "The absolute smartest thing that I did in the whole movie was to give away all that power and control to the two of them. I remember saying to Julie one day, 'Wow, this is almost like a real movie.' She said 'I am working on a real movie.'"

Mueller felt that giving control away is the hardest thing for first-time directors. But if they don't, they will ultimately lose control of their productions. Peterson added, "You have to concentrate on the directing. Our goal was just to make sure all Eric had to concentrate on was the actors."

Hartley said that one thing that she and Peterson brought to the production was the ability to get things for free. "I think that for people who don't have any experience, the first thing they should do is to get somebody who does. Our film was made on favors because it sure wasn't made on money. If you're going to do it, you better find people who have favors. And every one of us called in every favor we've ever had in our professional careers." Mueller cashed in one of his own favors to get their director of photography to come in from Seattle for the shoot, bringing his own equipment and assistant with him.

Peterson also advised, "Don't burn any bridges because ideally, you're starting your career, and you want to do this again."

The actual 15 days of shooting and one day of second-unit shooting in May, 1993, were largely uneventful, according to the trio, because everyone was working for the good of the film. The production company shot at more than 20 locations with more than 30 speaking parts. However, this large cast was manageable because most of the roles were only involved in one or two days of shooting, and there were only a few principal characters.

However, the going got rockier once the film entered post-production, with which none of the three had much experience. One problem was that their first choice of editors wasn't the right match for the film. After further searching, they found an editor with whom they were very pleased. Unfortunately, editing problems didn't end there.

"We put the film together, and we looked at it, and we realized that there was a lot of basic exposition that was just not covered correctly," Mueller remembered. "The characters were not set up the way they needed to be, and there were a lot of facts that the audience needed to know in order to have the payoff we wanted to have. So we said, 'Okay, what's the least painful way we can get all this exposition out there to the audience and make the film more intelligible?' Also the film was kind of a downer. More of a downer than we wanted it to be. So we were looking for a way to bring a little levity to the film and try to position it more as a comedy than as a drama."

The solution that the production team arrived at was to use the supporting character of David as a narrator who could comment on the events and could fill in the needed exposition. The character also could add more humor to the production. An important benefit of this solution was that it could be filmed in one day at one location using one actor. The resulting narration helped tie the film together in the more-linear form that it took on during editing.

The film was edited on video, and more problems appeared when the final cut was completed. There were difficulties converting the time code from the video to match the numbers on the film negative. This delayed the cutting of the film negative and the final printing of the film. Consequently, the print was not finished until just before its first scheduled screening. Mueller, Hartley, and Peterson watched the film for the first time with the audience at the festival screening.

Music rights also became an unexpected headache for the production. Hartley had used a demo tape from a crew member's band as background music for a party scene after receiving the crew member's assurance that the rights were clear for use. Later, during post-production sound mixing, Hartley discovered that part of the rights to the music were owned by a major record label which wanted $10,000 for the use rights. After much persuasion, the record company relented and gave Hartley two-year limited-exhibition rights. After distribution was found for the film, the record company wanted $5,000 for the exhibition rights. Not being able to afford this amount, the filmmakers ultimately had to remix the sound track with original music, remake the film print, and destroy the old prints.

The challenges of post-production were all overcome in the end, and the film premiered to good reviews at the 1994 San Francisco International Gay and Lesbian Film Festival. "World and Time Enough" won the Audience Award for Best Feature and went on to be picked up for distribution by Strand Releasing.

Hit The Road: "Highways" and "Criminals"

Conventional wisdom suggests that road movies and ultra-low-budget filmmaking shouldn't mix, but breaking conventions is a big part of the appeal of this small-budget art form. Still, there are barriers to overcome when you're trying to tell your story at sixty miles an hour, as well as plenty of opportunities for your project to stall, crash, or simply die along the side of the road.

"Highways" and "Criminals" are two ultra-low-budget road pictures that overcame those obstacles, discovering some profitable detours and short cuts along the way.

The idea behind "Highways" is a simple one: Take five strangers, put them in a 69 Lincoln Continental convertible with suicide doors, add a mysterious hitchhiker, and send them all on a trip of self-discovery across the United States. Although a promising dramatic device, director Sean King said he and his partners came up with the story for more practical reasons.

"We wanted something that would take us away from permits," he said. "We thought we were getting off easy by using a car on the open highway. That was the premise. If we're out in the middle of nowhere and we're shooting, we pretty much have a free reign. The two things that we hadn't planned on was a car that wouldn't run, and the noise factor."

Repairs on the car during the course of the production totaled nearly ten percent of the film's $50,000 budget and extended the production schedule from 20 to 30 days. And the sound problems -- the roar of wind in an open convertible -- required looping nearly all of the dialogue that occurred in or around the car. In fact, King figures that nearly 60% of the finished film is looped.

Besides directing, King also wrote the script (based on a story by King, Robert King and Michael Brillantes) and produced the film with Brillantes. On top of that, both Sean King and Michael Brillantes played major acting roles in the film.

"I would put Michael into any film I make," King explained. "I cast myself only because, having so much car stuff, there was no place to direct from. Unless I was part of the action, I would have no idea what the end result would be of any scene in the car. And since my ego has now grown to such large proportions, I'll be in every film I ever do."

Egos aside, King recommended that you don't race through the casting process. "There are so many good actors out there that want to work. Really spend your time on casting, because it costs you almost nothing -- except your time -- to audition these people, and you might find someone who's just fantastic who really needs film on himself or who really wants to work."

The team also hit upon an innovative money-raising technique. Because so many struggling actors are desperate for film of themselves for their demo reels, King and Brillantes required the actors in the film's six major roles to invest $1,300 each -- including themselves. This sum got the ball rolling. The rest of the budget came in the form of investments from family and friends.

Then they hit the road. Although they started production with a completed script, circumstances often required some fast thinking and quick changes. "About forty percent of the script was re-written on location," Brillantes explained. "We just had to go with what we had as far as making the scenes come together."

That flexibility allowed them to create or delete scenes on the spot, depending on the car's willingness to run. "When a problem came up, we dealt with it, and we moved on," King said. "There's nothing worse than having crew standing around when you're arguing, trying to figure out what to do. And we had very little of that. When the car broke down, within ten minutes a decision was made about what we were going to do -- either we were going to go back or we were going to shoot an alternative, and within 15, 20 minutes, we were shooting something."

This decisiveness also helps build morale with the cast. "The moment that the cast begins to sense that things are really unorganized, you might have problems," said King. "But if you can keep it organized, and show that you have a focus on what you're trying to do, they'll stick with you through some pretty adverse conditions. We had some real bad wind storms and everything else. The cast just grabbed a blanket, and they huddled up and didn't say a word."

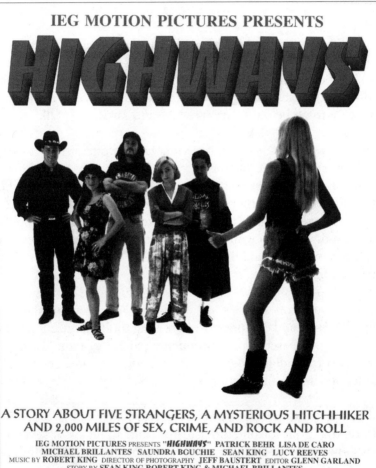

Poster art for Sean King's "Highways"
Photo courtesy of Imagery International

Because most of the film was shot outdoors -- in and around the car -- the crew was kept small. To keep it even smaller, they brought a makeup artist in at the beginning of the production to teach the actors to apply their own makeup. "That cut down having to have a makeup artist," King reasoned. "Each actor would go every morning and pick up the kit and do their own makeup and then be checked. We'd also check again after lunch, just to make sure everything was fine."

Besides handling their own makeup, several of the actors were also required to drive and act simultaneously. "We didn't tow the car, ever," King explained, "so whoever was driving in the scene was actually driving the car. Then you add on that the brakes were bad, and if you were to go below a certain RPM, the car would stall."

Adding to the pressure, Kings said, was the time it took to set up the camera rig once the car was started. "They would start the car -- and you'd have to keep it high revved, or else it would stall -- the hood would come down, and they would put the camera on it, and it would take probably ten minutes to strap it down. And then you would get rolling. And when you would eventually stop, if you didn't get it into neutral, it would stall, and they'd have to take the camera off and start all over for the next take."

Post-production was less troublesome and even proved to be profitable. King and composer Robert King took a large chunk of the budget and purchased a post-production sound system: a synchronizer, a two-track digital editor that triggers from time code, a DAT recorder and a handful of effects.

"It's been the best investment for us," King said. "Since then, we've rented it out for one other feature and about six or seven television shows and videos. Last year we did nine albums for other people. All kinds of things. It's actually made us money and it allowed us to spend three or four months on our film, then another month to re-mix it."

King recommended planning for this investment up front, and then sticking to that plan. "If you don't put that money aside at the beginning you won't have it at the end, and you'll end up skimping on the sound. A post house can get you in and out, but on low-budget films, sound is generally where you need the most work. You can really enhance with music, with sound effects. Having your own system allows you, the person who has the passion to do it, to sit by yourself and lay in sound effects at night."

Distribution for "Highways" has not been quite as smooth. The pair signed up with a small Los Angeles distribution company that never quite lived up to their promises. "They know that what you want to hear is that they're going to make money for you," King explained. "And so they do the most brilliant production number, singing and dancing, telling you how they're going to make you all kinds of money. Of course, the finale to this song and dance is that they take all your money and never give you a penny."

That deal tied up the film for nearly two years. "We finally managed to get the domestic rights out," King continued, "at least to shop it at HBO."

HBO purchased the film for an unlimited run, along with a 3-month exclusive. "We're not a typical genre film; we'll admit that we were as surprised as anyone when they accepted it," King said. "But since we didn't have any names, or sex and violence, we really needed an HBO-type of credit for the film. And that's now opened up more avenues to us."

Since the HBO deal, the pair have signed a deal for foreign television distribution and are looking at other options. "It's amazing, just being able to say 'HBO bought the film,' how many doors it will open," King continued. "The film is still the same, it's the same 90 minutes. There are so many films out there; the press and the hype are really what it's about. If you can find a hook or a niche or some phrase that will get people to actually look at it, you have a much better chance."

With "Highways" behind them, King and Brillantes said they are planning their next project using their experiences on "Highways" as a guide, particularly when it comes to the challenges of distribution. "There's no education that's worth what we learned," King said. "I would put this at the bottom of every single page in your book: When you deal with distributors, get it in writing. No matter what they say. Get it in writing."

* * *

As writer-director Jeff Butcher tells it, his black and white film "Criminals" is about "these New York characters who have the absolute worst New York sensibilities. They're Middle America's worst idea of what New Yorkers are. And, in the course of their travels, they encounter a New Yorker's worst idea of what the Midwest is like."

Stephen Blackehart as Johnny (left) and
Robert Margolis as Eddie in a scene from "Criminals"
Photo courtesy of Criminal Pictures

To tell this story, Butcher created two characters, Johnny and Eddie, who are self-described "petty criminals." Johnny, the brains of the duo (although clearly a default position) decides to take up an old girlfriend on her proposal to travel to Las Vegas and help her pull off a robbery, with ironic consequences. As Butcher explained, "Part of the joke of the movie is that it's anticlimactic. They go to Las Vegas, but they never really see the glorious lights. They actually are a success at the robbery, but 25 minutes later they've lost the money. They drive all the way across the country, but they don't get the girl. These guys are continually missing the boat -- there isn't any glory in this movie."

Although Butcher planned from the start to make "Criminals" an ultra-low-budget film, once he started pre-production he discovered a flaw in his low-buck premise. "In writing the story, I thought, let's make this simple," Butcher recalled. "Let's make it two guys in a car -- which is a really stupid statement. The only way to keep an audience interested in two guys in a car for 90 minutes is if they stop at a lot of different places and encounter a lot of different people. Of course, when you first read the script it doesn't seem like, 'Oh, man, they're stopping again, oh, they're encountering another person.' It doesn't really seem like there are that many stops or people. But when you look at it from the perspective of a producer, a locations person, a casting person -- oh boy."

Rather than literally follow Johnny and Eddie's cross-country trek, Butcher and the film's producer, his wife Nelle Stokes, devised a three-part shooting plan for their five-week shooting schedule. The first week was spent in New York shooting exteriors and the main characters' apartment; the last week was spent in and around Las Vegas; and the three weeks in between were spent in Minnesota, which stood in for all the states between New York and Las Vegas, as well as for several major Las Vegas locations.

Although the on-screen results look good, there was no question during shooting that this was a low-budget production. "This was filmmaking with no pride," Butcher explained. Stokes' point of view is more poetic: "We looked like the Joads. Instead of road warriors, we were road trash."

That impression was a result of the two vehicles that made up their cross-country convoy: A beat-up van covered with graffiti and rust, and the film's fourth main character, a dilapidated, primer-gray 64 Fairlane. Like the producers of "Highways," their biggest nemesis turned out to be vehicle repairs. "The van started dying on the way to Las Vegas," Stokes remembered. "The car did die in the middle of the Arizona desert at night. We ended up having to rent another van and tow the car into Las Vegas because the entire engine blew in Arizona."

This inopportune breakdown posed a unique problem for the team as a significant bit of action -- a car chase -- was to take place in Las Vegas. "We had to figure out how to shoot a car chase without a car that would run," Butcher explained. "We had to rethink every shot of them driving during the getaway." As with many other ultra-low-budget producers, Butcher and Stokes soon learned that problems -- if looked at from the right angle -- can become opportunities.

"If you'd told me in pre-production that we couldn't shoot it that way, I would have kicked and screamed," Butcher confessed. "But once it became obvious that this scene's not going to be in the movie, or this shot's not going to be done the way we wanted to do it, literally every time we'd go, 'Okay, let's do it this way,' and then ended up liking the new idea better."

Because so much of the action takes place in the car at night, they experimented with several different methods of lighting the car's interior. "Our lighting scheme evolved during production," Butcher recalled. "We started out by wiring tail light bulbs to the dashboard. That became problematic, because it cast shadows. So then we went to Christmas lights -- fifty of those little, white Christmas lights -- stapled to a piece of foam core that was attached to the interior roof of the car, to create an overall ambience inside the car. At the same time we used a single 60-watt light bulb on the console, which acted as the dashboard light and moonlight. That was a pretty good combination, and we did most of the movie with that. The only problem with that set up is that we really didn't have very much light on the outside of the car, so in some scenes it looks like they could be sitting in a movie theater -- it was black everywhere. So sometimes we'd hook up a 350 watt Fresnel to the hood."

Also attached to the hood was the camera, although like the lighting, the camera rigging evolved during the course of the production. "It started out complicated and got simpler," Butcher explained. "We needed to have the camera low on the hood sometimes, so you could see out the back window. We thought the only way you could get the camera low enough to see that angle was to build a rig on the front of the car, so the bottom of the camera and the head are below the hood. We eventually figured out that you could work without the head and without its base. We ended using just scraps of wood nailed together and attached the camera to that. That let us actually get the camera on the hood and be low enough. And this was a rig that we could move really quickly, and that made shooting a lot faster."

"Once we were able to actually mount the camera on the hood," Butcher continued, "we were able to mount lights with it and that was the best looking stuff, where we had a little bit of light on the hood, so you felt like there was some moonlight or some street light hitting the car. And then they were lit by the dashboard bulb and the Christmas lights were adding ambience inside."

The production definitely traveled light, shooting most of the film with a few small lights, a 1-K, and two small generators (a 650 watt Honda generator and a 1750 Coleman generator). Their biggest lighting expenditure was for a short party sequence that took place in the desert at night -- so, of course, it was shot in Minnesota. For that scene they had a 5,000 watt generator and two 2-Ks.

Before embarking on their five-week trek, they took time to rehearse for three weeks with the two main characters. "That paid off in spades," Stokes said. "It was one of the smartest things we did. It meant that they really knew who they were before we got started, and it also meant that when we said, 'We're going to do scene 18 followed by 23 followed by whatever,' with just a click of the slate in between (or sometimes not even that, we'd just do a really long take of three different scenes where they're in the car) they were able to do it. We were blessed."

Butcher agreed. "They were really good. At the drop of a hat you could say, 'Oh, the sun's come up. We didn't anticipate this, but let's do Eddie's angle from scene 72.' And they'd know it."

Butcher and Stokes opted to shoot their film in black and white, not just for artistic reasons, but also because it would allow them more latitude in shooting and in continuity. "We couldn't have made the movie in color," Butcher explained. "I don't think we could have shot a swimming pool in Minnesota and expected people to think that was in Las Vegas if we'd shot it in color. Also, it helped in the coverage between scenes, all the different variables. In one shot there's a big red light off in the distance out the back window. In the next shot it's gone. You'd notice that in color, but not in black and white. It forgave a lot."

Just as forgiving were the police, who stopped the convoy at least 19 times. "We lost count," Stokes confessed.

"Almost every time they would look at the camera and say, 'Oh,'" Butcher recounted. "Then they'd let us go. Cinematic immunity ruled. We were shooting at night, out of the back of the van, with the doors taped open, with a traffic cone hanging off the back to alert people that we were a hazard. We'd have our flashers on, but you could only do that sometimes because you're shooting this car out the back and you can't have the lights. We were safe, but I think we looked unsafe a lot of the time. But generally the police would just scratch their heads, because they really didn't know what to do, so they'd just say, 'Um, well, why don't you just be careful out there.' And we'd take off again."

With the rigors of production behind them, and a fine cut of their film nearing completion, both Butcher and Stokes have finally had a chance to begin to sort out their experience. "A huge lesson I learned from this experience," Butcher explained, "was to edit before you start shooting. Take into account that you've got a million locations. Which ones can go? There are a million characters here. Which ones can go? Because you're going to have to do it at some point. In the beginning, the script is so precious, and you're thinking, 'I can't imagine the movie without this scene.' Imagine it. If I'd gone through in advance and cut out everything that didn't make it into the movie for one reason or another, we would have had more time to shoot, and we would have been able to do a better job of it, and it would have been a better film because of it. When you're working at this level, you have to be aware of the fact that reality is going to set in, and anything you can do in advance to simplify things is worth it."

Stokes agreed, but came away from the production with a different lesson. "For anyone who wants to produce an ultra-low-budget movie, my biggest word of advice is don't ever be afraid to ask questions," Stokes advised. "I went into this thinking, 'I'm not sure how to do this.' And, because I knew I didn't know how to do some things -- pieces of equipment that I didn't know about, processes that I didn't know about -- I was able to just forget about my pride, take a deep breath and be very honest and say, 'I don't understand this. Can you explain this to me the way you would to a five-year old?' People really took the time to explain things step by step. I think that was the best thing I did, being willing to not look so smart, and to say, 'I don't get this. Can you explain it to me?'"

Now that "Criminals" is nearing completion, both Butcher and Stokes are taking a fresh look at their film and beginning to see it in a new light. "We thought we knew the niche for our movie," Stokes said. "I thought that it was going to be a little, grungy art-house movie. But it's a lot sweeter than I thought. And not half as grungy as we were after five weeks on the road."

As they prepare to take their film into the distribution process, the couple provided one final piece of advice about what they felt was the most important element necessary in making a successful ultra-low budget feature. According to Butcher, "The most important thing is actually three things: Good casting, a good cameraman, and a strong commitment."

"And a good garage," added Stokes. "If you're making a road movie, you really need a good garage."

AFTERWORD

This may be the end for us, but it's only the beginning for you. We've given you some tools — and you've probably thought up a few of your own along the way — to make your own ultra-low-budget feature, and now you're ready to take the plunge. Making that dive from the safety of the shore into the cold, deep waters of ultra-low-budget feature-film production is a scary first step, but believe us, once you hit the water it gets easier.

In reviewing these pages for publication, one thought has repeatedly struck us: We had no idea we had learned so much from producing two films. Which begs the question, would we still have made the films if we knew then what we know now?

Absolutely. We set out to make two stories that we believed in, and we're certainly proud of the results. We've had a tremendous amount of fun, met and worked with some truly exceptional people, and made two films that we and audiences seem to enjoy.

And would we do it again? In a heartbeat. With the right script, the right cast, and the right crew, we'd happily put it all on the line one more time. With what we've learned setting these words on paper — and what we've learned from the many filmmakers, actors, agents, editors, composers, and distributors who generously gave of their time and their thoughts for this book — we know we could do even better than before.

We mentioned up front that one of the goals of writing this book was to let other ultra-low-budget filmmakers know that they weren't alone. Ironically, in the process of writing the book, we also learned that we weren't alone either. The filmmakers we met and interviewed reminded us why we've spent the last few years pouring our extra time and extra dimes into small films that may never be seen by a large audience. It's that silver addiction, the lure of the film stock, that gets us every time.

So remember that you aren't alone. Keep us posted on your progress. Be persistent with your vision. And don't be a stranger.

John Gaspard
Dale Newton
c/o MICHAEL WIESE PRODUCTIONS
11288 Ventura Boulevard
Suite 821
Studio City, CA 91604

GROUP RELEASE FORM

Date _____

In exchange for screen credit under the names listed below, each of the under-signed grants the producers of the production tentatively titled [FILM NAME] the right, but not the obligation, to use her or his name, voice, likeness or any simula-tion thereof, or any film or photographs taken by the producers of us individually or with others in connection with this production.

These usage rights are given forever and thoughout the world, and include (but are not limited to) the production, distribution, advertising and exploitation of this motion picture by any means whatsoever by the producers.

Name (Print)	Signature	Address

LOCATION RELEASE FORM

Date _____

I hearby grant permission to [PRODUCTION COMPANY] to enter and use my property located at: _____ for the purpose of photographing and recording scenes (interior and exterior) to be used in the motion picture tentatively titled _____, which is anticipated to begin production on _____(date) and continue until _____ or later.

I give permission for the producer to bring personnel, equipment, props and temporary sets, and any other necessary materials and supplies onto this property for this purpose. I give [PRODUCTION COMPANY] or any person or company it licenses, the right to use, exhibit, distribute, advertise or otherwise exploit worldwide forever any scenes photographed and recorded on this property in connection with this motion picture.

[PRODUCTION COMPANY] agrees to use reasonable care to prevent damage to this property and to remove any and all materials placed on the property in connection with this production. The property will be restored as nearly as possible to its original condition, excepting ordinary wear and tear.

During the photographing and recording on this property, [PRODUCTION COMPANY] agrees to indemnify and hold the property owner harmless from any claims and demands of any members of the cast or crew of the production arising from personal injuries or death suffered while working on this property.

I hearby state that I have full right and authority to enter into this agreement concerning the property described above, and that the permission of no other person, company or corporation is necessary in order for [PRODUCTION COMPANY] to enjoy full rights to use this property. I also indemnify and hold harmless [PRODUCTION COMPANY] from all losses, costs, liability, damages, or other claims that arise out of any false statements or representations made by me in this agreement.

For the right to use this property, [PRODUCTION COMPANY] has paid me the sum of ___ [usually $1].

Approved and accepted by,

_____ (Print name)
_____ (signature) Property owner
_____ [PRODUCTION COMPANY]
authorized agent

EQUIPMENT RENTAL LIST

Camera
- Eclair NPR with 12 - 120mm zoom lens
- Tripod with fluid head
- 2 battery belts
- 2 400 ft. film magazines
- Camera slate
- Changing bag
- Series 9 Filters
  - 85N3, 85N6, 85N9
- Spectra Light Meter

Sound
- Nagra 4.2
- Headphones
- Extra batteries
- ME-80 Shotgun microphone
- Windscreen
- Shockmount
- Fish pole
- 200' mike cable (4 @ 50')

Lighting
- 4 - 1000 watt Arriflex lights w/ barndoors
- Stands
- 4 extra lamps
- 38" Flexfill (white/silver)
- 2 - 1000, 1500, 2000 watt Lowell softlights
  - With barndoors
  - Stands
  - 4 extra lamps

Expendable Supplies
- 1 roll 2" grey gaffer tape
- 1 roll 1" black camera tape
- 8' x 36" spun (105 Roscolux tough spun - 1 stop)
- 16'x 58" daylight to 3200 K correction gel (3401 RoscoSun 85)
- 4'x 36" 3200 K to daylight correction gel (3202 Rosco Full Blue CTB)

PRESS KITS

"BEYOND BOB" PRESS KIT: SAMPLE SYNOPSIS

BEYOND BOB
Granite Productions, Ltd.
(Color, 100 minutes, English)

"Beyond Bob," a winner at the WorldFest International Film and Video Festival in Houston, is a romantic comedy-ghost story about Isaac, who for years has been secretly in love with Tracy. Tracy, on the verge of becoming a big pop star, is about to marry the wrong man.

Tracy announces her wedding plans at a weekend get-together of old friends who were members of a band. Although appalled by her choice, Isaac is prepared to passively accept this marriage until he nudged into action by Bob, Tracy's old boyfriend . . . who has been dead for ten years.

Bob, a ghost visible only to Isaac, pushes Isaac to reveal his true feelings to Tracy. Bob's plan hits a snag, however, when he discovers that he still has strong feelings for Tracy.

"Beyond Bob," an award-winning comedy from the other side, is a story of love and friendship, of passion from beyond the grave, of a love that was made in heaven . . . and was just too darned important to stay there.

"BEYOND BOB" PRESS KIT: SAMPLE PRODUCTION NOTES

"BEYOND BOB" — HOLLYWOOD, MIDWEST STYLE

"Immigrants learning about our country from movies would think that Newark is next door to Anaheim," according to writer-director John Gaspard. "With independent films like "Beyond Bob," we're trying to offer that "no-coast" perspective that's missing from most American films."

Gaspard and producer Dale Newton are presenting that "no-coast" viewpoint with "Beyond Bob," the second independent feature from their Minnesota-based Granite Productions, Ltd. "Beyond Bob" is about a ten-year reunion of Bob's Band, except that Bob is only there in spirit. In the film's setting of music, romance and comedy, love isn't dead . . . just some of the lovers. The supernatural romantic comedy was shot in Minnesota and Wisconsin with local cast and crew and stars Leslie Ball, Patrick Coyle, and co-writer Michael Paul Levin.

Newton said that the production company has had no shortage of skilled technicians and talented actors to work with on the film.

"It's not well-known that Minneapolis and St. Paul have more live-theater seats than New York City, and are the fourth-largest production market for commercials and corporate videos," Newton said.

Gaspard finds another advantage in this talent pool.

"I like using actors who are new to feature-film audiences. The performers become the characters for the audience without first having to bury their last well-known role," Gaspard said.

Minnesota and Wisconsin also provided unique backdrops for such varied scenes as midnight skinny dipping with a levitating stick, a conga line and slapstick at a small-town roller rink, antagonizing bikers on a lonely country road, an impromptu rock concert in a hick bar, and driving endlessly past towns with "lake" names. Gaspard recalled one of the most exciting locations as being a hang-gliding sequence on a windy, 300-foot river bluff.

"However, the actors mainly remember the 20 straight hours we spent at a roller rink," Gaspard recalled. "They affectionately refer to it as the Bataan Death Skate."

In addition to entertaining settings, the script for "Beyond Bob" offers up witty dialogue by Gaspard and Levin.

"With lines like 'Hey, I'm a ghost. If I don't spook somebody, I can't join the union,' you know the script is full of fun," producer Newton said. "But its real strength is a serious message about what love is when the candy coating has worn off . . . about what makes friendship and romance endure."

Both Newton and Gaspard come from screenwriting backgrounds and agree that solid storytelling is the heart of any good feature film.

"If you have nothing to say, millions in production values can't buy you an audience. As long as we have good screenplays, the financial limits of an independent production don't really hamper us," Gaspard said.

"I'd even say that the inevitable money shortages in an independent production force us to solve our problems with creativity, not cash, and the result is a better film," Newton added. "Besides, working independently lets us present the story and performances we want, not the ones some executive is demanding."

Obviously, the Gaspard-Newton method works. An early work print of "Beyond Bob" — without a finished soundtrack — won in the feature film/low budget category at the WorldFest International Film and Video Festival in Houston.

Additionally, the pair have chronicled their working methods for other potential producers in a new book, <u>Persistence of Vision: An Impractical Guide To Producing A Feature Film For Under $30,000</u>, which will be published in the fall of 1995 by Michael Wiese Productions and distributed by SCB.

Count on seeing more projects from Granite Productions, according to Newton.

"It's in our veins. Where else can you spend an afternoon enticing a racing pigeon to walk down a branch on cue?" he said.

Granite Productions previously produced "Resident Alien," a science-fiction comedy feature.

"BEYOND BOB" PRESS KIT: SAMPLE CREDIT LIST

BEYOND BOB

Cast

Isaac..............................	Patrick Coyle
Bob..............................	Michael Paul Levin
Tracy..............................	Leslie Ball
Neal..............................	Peter Moore
Ginny..............................	Kathryn O'Malley
Kris..............................	Julie Briskman Hall
Augie..............................	Dan Rowles
Pops..............................	Paul R. Smith
Head Biker..............................	Steve Gronwall
Minister..............................	Richard Gibbons
Bar Waitress..............................	Eve Black
Bar Woman..............................	Jayme Lee Misfeldt
Bar Geek..............................	Jon Schumacher
Older Sister..............................	Amelia Barnes
Younger Brother..............................	Adam Goldberg

Crew

Writers..............................	John Gaspard & Michael Paul Levin
Director..............................	John Gaspard
Producer..............................	Dale Newton
Unit Production Manager..............	Kathy Erickson
Assistant Unit Production Manager	Vonne E. Jönsson
Director of Photography..............	Scott Lee Dose
Assistant Camera Operator..........	Stephen Knudsen
Film and Sound Editor................	Bruce V. Assardo
Second-Unit Director..................	Dale Newton
Sound Recordists........................	Bill McGuire

& Bruce V. Assardo
Lighting Gaffer and Boom Operator. Bill McGuire
Makeup and Hair Supervisor...... Cheryl Nick
Special Visual Effects.................. Dale Newton
Music Supervisor and Composer. Dave Reynolds
Assistant Arranger and Assistant Music Editor..John W. McKone

Camera Report

Sheet #____ of #____

Roll # _____

Date _____

Company_____ Address _____

Production Title _____

Camera Operator _____ Film Loader _____

Locations _____

Camera	Magazine #
Film Stock Type	Emulsion #
Footage (Length)	Date Loaded

Scene #	Take #	Starting Footage	Snd/ MOS	Day/ Night	Int./ Ext.	Remarks

Instructions To Laboratory

Sound Report

Sheet #____ of #____

Date ____

Sound Roll # ____

Company _____ Address _____

Production Title _____

Sound Recordist _____ Boom Operator _____

Locations _____

Tape Recorder	Mixer
Tape Stock Type	Inches Per Second
Equalization	Type of Sync

Camera Roll #	Scene #	Take #	Starting Footage	Sync/ Wild	Mike Type	Int./ Ext.	Remarks

Instructions To Transfer Laboratory

FILM COMMISSIONS

ALABAMA

Alabama Film Office
401 Adams Avenue
Montgomery, AL 36130
(205) 242-4195

ALASKA

Alaska Film Office
3601 C Street
Suite 700
Anchorage, AK 99503
(907) 562-4163

ARIZONA

Arizona Film Commission
3800 N. Central Avenue
Building D
Phoenix, AZ 85012
(800) 523-6695

Globe Miami Film Commission
1360 N. Broad Street
U.S. 60
Globe, AZ 85502
(602) 425-4495

Greater Flagstaff
Economic Development Office
1515 E. Cedar Avenue
Suite B-1
Flagstaff, AZ 86004
(602) 779-7658

Holbrook Film Commission
465 N. First Avenue
Holbrook, AZ 86025
(602) 524-6225

Lake Havasu Area Film Commission
1930 Mesquite Avenue
Suite 3

Lake Havasu, AZ 86403
(602) 453-3456

Navajo Nation
PO Box 2310
Window Rock, AZ 86515
(602) 871-6656

Page / Lake Powell Film Office
106 S. Lake Powell Boulevard
Page, AZ 86040
(602) 645-2741

Phoenix Motion Picture Office
200 West Washington
Tenth Floor
Phoenix, AZ 85003
(602) 262-4850

Prescott Film Office
PO Box 2059
Prescott, AZ 86302
(602) 445-3500

Scottsdale Film Office
3939 Civic Center Boulevard
Scottsdale, AZ 85251
(602) 994-2636

Sedona Film Commission
PO Box 2489
Sedona, AZ 86339
(602) 204-1123

Tucson Film Office
32 North Stone Avenue
Suite 100
Tucson, AZ 85701
(602) 791-4000

Wickenburg Film Commission
PO Drawer CC
216 N. Frontier
Wickenburg, AZ 85358
(602) 684-5479

Yuma Film Commission
PO Box 230
Yuma, AZ 85336
(602) 726-4027

ARKANSAS

Arkansas Motion Picture Board
One State Capitol Mall
Room 2C-200
Little Rock, Arkansas 72201
(501) 682-7676

CALIFORNIA

Big Bear Chamber of Commerce
PO Box 2860
Big Bear Lake, CA 92315
(714) 866-6190

California Film Commission
6922 Hollywood Boulevard
Hollywood, CA 90028
(213) 736-2465

Catalina Island Film Commission
PO Box 217
Avaion, CA 90704
(310) 510-7646

City of Los Angeles Motion Picture &
TV Commission
6922 Hollywood Boulevard
Suite 614
Los Angeles, CA 90028
(213) 461-8614

El Dorado / Tahoe County Film Office
542 Main Street
Placerville, CA 95667
(916) 626-4400

Greater Stockton Chamber of
Commerce
445 W. Weber Avenue
Suite 220
Stockton, CA 95203
(209) 547-2767

Kern County Board of Trade/Film
2101 Oak Street
Bakersfield, CA 93301
(805) 861-2367

Los Angeles Motion Picture Office
6922 Hollywood Boulevard
Los Angeles, CA 90028
(213) 485-5324

Madera County Film Commission
PO Box 126
Bass Lake, CA 93604
(209) 642-3676

Mammoth Location Services
1 Minaret Road
PO Box 24
Mammoth Lakes, CA 93546
(619) 934-0628

Merced Convention & Visitors Bureau
PO Box 3107
Merced, CA 95344
(209) 384-3333

Monterey County Film Commission
PO Box 111
801 Lighthouse Avenue
Monterey, CA 93942
(408) 646-0910

Oakland Film Commission
505 14th Street
Suite 715
Oakland, CA 94612
(510) 238-2193

Orange County Film Office
1 City Boulevard West
Suite 401
Orange, CA 92668
(714) 634-2900

Oxnard Department of Economic
Development
300 West Third Street
Oxnard, CA 93030
(805) 984-5611

Palm Springs Desert Resorts CVB
69-930 Highway 111
Suite 201
Rancho Mirage, CA 92270
(619) 770-9000

Ridgecrest Film Commission
100 West California Avenue
Ridgecrest, CA 93555
(619) 375-8202

Sacramento Area Film Commission
1421 K Street
Sacramento, CA 95814
(916) 264-7777

San Diego Motion Picture & Television
Office
402 W. Broadway
Suite 1000
San Diego, CA 92101
(619) 234-3456

San Francisco Film & Video Arts Office
City Hall
Room 200
San Francisco, CA 94102

San Jose Film & Video Office
333 West San Carlos Street
Suite 1000
San Jose, CA 95110
(408) 295-9600

San Luis Obispo Film Office
1041 Chorro Street
Suite E
San Luis Obispo, CA 93401

Santa Barbara County Film Office
504 State Street
Santa Barbara, CA 93190
(805) 962-6668

Santa Clarita Valley Film Liaison
23920 Valencia Boulevard
Santa Clarita, CA 91355
(805) 259-4787

Sonoma County Film Office
5000 Roberts Lake Road
Suite A
Rohnert Park, CA 94928
(707) 586-8100

Temecula Valley Film Council
27450 Ynez Road
Suite 104
Temecula, CA 92591
(909) 676-5090

CANADA

Alberta Economic Development
9940 108 Street
Starling Place
Edmonton, Alberta T5K 2P6
(403) 427-2005

British Columbia Film Commission
750 Pacific Boulevard South
Third Floor
Vancouver, British Columbia
(604) 660-2732

Burnaby Film Office
4949 Canada Way
Burnaby, British Columbia
(604) 294-7231

Calgary Film Services
P.O. Box 2100
Station M
Calgary, Alberta T2P 2M5
(403) 268-8844

Edmonton Motion Picture and
Television Bureau
9797 Jasper Avenue
Edmonton, Alberta T5J 1N9
(403) 424-7870

Film Nova Scotia
1724 Granville Street
Halifax, Nova Scotia B3J 1X5
(902) 422-3402

Location Manitoba
100.93 Lombard Avenue
Winnipeg, Manitoba R3B 3B1
(204) 947-2040

London Film Commission
c/o City Office
Room 1109, Box 5035
London, Ontario N6A 4L9
(519) 661-4524

Montreal Film Commission
425 Place Jacques Cartier
Montreal, Quebec H2Y 3B1
(514) 872-2883

New Brunswick Film/Video Commission
P.O. Box 12345
Fredericton, NB E3B 5C3
(506) 453-2553

Niagara Regional Development Office
PO Box 1042
2201 Saint David's
Thorold, Ontario L2V 4T7
(416) 685-1308

Okanagan Film Commission
P.O. Box 1177
Kelowna, BC V1Y 7P8

Ontario Film Development
81 Wellesley Street East
Toronto, Ontario M4Y 1H6
(416) 965-8393

Ottawa Film Office
55 ByWard Market Square
Ottawa, ONT K1N 9C3
(613) 564-1632

Quebec Film & TV Office
1755 East Rene-Levesque Boulevard
Montreal, Quebec H2K 4P6
(514) 873-4388

Thompson-Nicola Film Commission
2079 Falcon Road
Kamloops, British Columbia
(604) 372-9336

Toronto Film Commissioner
18th Floor East Tower
New City Hall

Toronto, ONT M5H 2N2
(416) 392-7570

Victoria / Vancouver Island Film Office
525 Fort Street
Victoria, British Columbia V8W 1E8
(604) 386-3976

Yukon Film Promotion Office
P.O. Box 2703
Whitehorse, YK Y1A 2C6
(403) 667-5400

COLORADO

Boulder County Film Commission
2440 Pearl Street
Boulder, CO 80306
(800) 444-0447

Breckenridge Film Commission
PO Box 7579
Breckenridge, CO 80424
(303) 453-0568

Colorado Film Commission
1625 Broadway
Suite 1700
Denver, CO 80202
(303) 620-4500

Colorado Springs Film Commission
30 South Nevada Avenue
Suite 405
Colorado Springs, CO 80903
(719) 578-6279

Fremont / Custer County Film Office
PO Box 8
Canon City, CO 81212
(719) 275-5149

Grand Junction Area Film Office
360 Grand Avenue
Grand Junction, CO 81501
(303) 858-9335

Greeley Convention & Visitors Bureau
1407 8th Avenue
Greeley, CO 80631
(303) 352-3566

Lakewood Film Commission
445 South Allison Parkway
Lakewood, CO 80226
(303) 987-7050

Trinidad Film Commission
136 West Main Street
Trinidad, CO 81082
(719) 846-9412

Yampa Valley Film Board
PO Box 772305
Steamboat Springs, CO 80477
(303) 879-0882

CONNECTICUT

Connecticut Film Commission
865 Brook Street
Rocky Hill, CT 06067
(203) 258-4301

DELAWARE

Delaware Film Office
99 Kings Highway
PO Box 1401
Dover, DE 19903
(800) 441-8846

DISTRICT OF COLUMBIA

District of Columbia Film Commission
717 14th Street NW
Tenth Floor
Washington, DC 20005
(202) 727-6600

United States Forest Service
201 14th Street SW
Washington, DC 20250
(202) 205-1438

FLORIDA

Broward County Film & TV Office
200 East Las Olas Boulevard
Suite 1850
Fort Lauderdale, FL 33301
(305) 524-3113

Clearwater Film Commission
PO Box 4748
Clearwater, FL 34618
(813) 462-6893

Florida Entertainment Commission
112 West Adams Street
Suite 100
Jacksonville, FL 32202
(904) 798-4300

Florida Keys and Key West Film Office
402 Wall Street
PO Box 984
Key West, FL 33040
(305) 294-5988

Gainesville / Alachua County Film Office
300 E. University
Gainesville, FL 32602
(904) 334-7100

Jacksonville Film & TV Office
128 E. Forsyth Street
Suite 505
Jacksonville, FL
(904) 630-2522

Manatee County Film Office
1111 Third Avenue West
Suite 180
Bradenton, FL 34206
(813) 746-5989

Miami / Dade Office of Film & TV
111 Northwest First Street
Miami, FL 33128
(305) 375-3288

Ocala / Marion County Film Office
110 E. Silver Springs Boulevard
Ocala, FL 32670
(904) 629-2757

Orlando Film & Television Office
200 EAst Robinson Street
Suite 600
Orlando, FL 32801
(407) 422-7159

Palm Beach County Film Liaison
15555 Palm Beach Lakes Boulevard
West Palm Beach, FL 33401
(407) 233-1000

Polk County Motion Picture &
Television Office
PO Box 1839
Bartow, FL 33830
(813) 534-4371

Space Coast Film Commission
2725 St. Johns Street
Melbourn, FL 32940
(407) 633-2110

Tampa Motion Picture & Television
Office
306 East Jackson
Tampa, FL 33602
(813) 274-8419

Volusia County Film Office
PO Box 910
Daytona Beach, FL 32115
(800) 544-0415

GEORGIA

Georgia Film & Videotape Office
285 Peachtree Center Avenue
Atlanta, GA 30303
(404) 656-7830
HAWAII

Hawaii Film Office
PO Box 2359
Honolulu, HI 96804
(808) 586-2570

Kauai Film Commission
4444 Rice Street
Lihue, HI 96766
(808) 241-6390

Maui Film & Television Promotion
180 Dickenson Street
Lahaina, Maui HI 96761
(808) 243-7710

IDAHO

Idaho Film Bureau
700 West State Street
Second Floor
Boise, ID 83720
(208) 334-2470

ILLINOIS

Chicago Film Office
One North LaSalle
Suite 2165
Chicago, IL 60602

Illinois Film Office
100 West Randolph
Chicago, IL 60601
(312) 814-3600

Quad Cities Development Group
1830 Second Avenue
Rock Island, IL 61201
(319) 326-1005

INDIANA

Indiana Tourism & Film Office
1 North Capitol
Indianapolis, IN 46204
(317) 232-8829

IOWA

Cedar Rapids Area Convention Bureau
119 First Avenue SE
Cedar Rapids, IA 52406
(800) 735-5557

Dubuque Film Bureau
770 Town Clock Plaza
Dubuque, IA 52004
(319) 557-9200

Fort Dodge Film Office
PO Box T
Fort Dodge, IA 50501
(800) 765-1438

Greater Des Moines Film Office
601 Locust
Des Moines, IA 50309
(800) 451-2625

Iowa Film Office
200 E. Grand Avenue
Des Moines, IA 50309
(800) 779-3456

KANSAS

Kansas Film Commission
700 SW Harrison Street
Topeka, KS 66803
(913) 296-4927

Manhattan Film Commission
555 Poynta
Manhattan, KS 66502
(913) 776-8829

Wichita Convention & Visitors Bureau
100 South Main
Wichita, KS 67202
(316) 265-2800

KENTUCKY

Kentucky Film Office
500 Metro Street
Frankfort, KY 40601
(800) 345-6591

LOUISIANA

Jeff Davis Parish Film Commission
PO Box 1207
Jennings, LA 70546
(318) 821-5534

Louisiana Film Commission
PO Box 44320
Baton Rouge, LA 70804
(504) 342-8150

New Orleans Film Commission
1515 Poydras Street
Twelfth Floor
New Orleans, LA 70112
(504) 527-0058

MAINE

Maine Film Office
State House, Station 59
Augusta, ME 04333
(207) 287-5707

MARYLAND

Baltimore Film Commission
303 East Fayette
Suite 300
Baltimore, MD 21202
(410) 396-4550

Maryland Film Commission
601 N. Howard Street
Baltimore, MD 21201
(410) 333-6633

Prince George's County Film Office
9475 Lottsford Road
Suite 130
Landover, MD 20785
(301) 386-3456

MASSACHUSETTS

Massachusetts Film Office
10 Park Plaza
Suite 2310
Boston, MA 02116
(617) 973-8800

MICHIGAN

Detroit Office of Film & TV
1126 City/County Building
Detroit, MI 48226
(313) 224-4034

Michigan Film Office
525 W. Ottawa
PO Box 30107
Lansing, MI 48909
(800) 477-FILM

MINNESOTA

Minnesota Film Board
401 North Third Street
Suite 460
Minneapolis, MN 55401
(612) 332-6493

Minneapolis Office of Film, Video &
Recording
323M City Hall
Minneapolis, MN 55415
(612) 673-2947

MISSISSIPPI

Mississippi Film Office
PO Box 849
Jackson, MS 39205
(601) 359-3297
Mississippi Gulf Coast Film Office
PO Box 569
Gulfport, MS 39502
(601) 863-3807

Oxford Film Commission
PO Box 965
Oxford, MS 38655
(601) 234-4651

Tupelo Film Commission
PO Box 1485
Tupelo, MS 38802
(800) 533-0611

Vicksburg / Warren County Film Office
PO Box 110
Vicksburg, MS 39180
(601) 636-9421

MISSOURI

Greater Kansas City Film Office
10 Petticoat Lane
Kansas City, MO 64106
(816) 221-0636

Missouri Film Office
PO Box 1055
Jefferson City, MO 65102
(314) 751-9050

Saint Louis Film Office
100 South Fourth Street
Suite 500
Saint Louis, MO 63102
(314) 444-1174

MONTANA

Montana Film Commission
1424 Ninth Avenue
Helena, MT 59620
(800) 553-4563

Northern Montana Film Office
815 Second Street South
Great Falls, MT 59403
(800) 735-8535

NEBRASKA

Nebraska Film Office
301 Centennial Mall South
Lincoln, NE 68509
(402) 471-3790

Omaha / Douglas County Film Office
1819 Farnam Street
Omaha, NE
(402) 444-7736

NEVADA

Nevada Motion Picture Division
3770 Howard Hughes Parkway
Las Vegas, NV 89109
(702) 486-7150

Reno / Tahoe Motion Picture Office
5151 South Carson Street
Carson City, NV 89710
(702) 687-4325

NEW HAMPSHIRE

New Hampshire Film & TV Bureau
172 Pembroke Road
Concord, NH 03302
(603) 271-2598

NEW JERSEY

New Jersey Motion Picture & TV Office
153 Halsey Street
Newark, NJ 07101
(201) 648-6279

NEW MEXICO

Albuquerque Film/TV Commission
121 Tijeras Avenue NE
First Floor
Albuquerque, NM 87125
(505) 842-9918
Las Cruces Film Office
311 N. Downtown Mall
Las Cruces, NM 88001
(800)-FIESTAS

New Mexico Film Commission
1050 Pecos Trail
Santa Fe, NM 87503
(800) 545-9871

NEW YORK

New York City Office of Film
254 West 54th Street
New York, NY 10019
(212) 489-6710

New York State Office for MP/TV
Pier 62 West 23rd Street
Suite 307
New York, NY 10011
(212) 929-0240

Rochester Film Office
126 Andrews Street
Rochester, NY 14604
(716) 546-5490

NORTH CAROLINA

Durham Convention and Visitors Bureau
101 E. Morgan Street
Durham, NC 27701
(800) 446-8604

North Carolina Film Office
430 North Salisbury Street
Raleigh, NC 27611
(919) 733-9900

Western North Carolina Film Office
PO Box 1010
Asheville, NC 28802
(704) 258-6121

Wilmington City Manager's Office
PO Box 1810
Wilmington, NC 28402
(919) 341-7810
Winston-Salem Film Commission
601 West Fourth Street
Winston-Salem, NC 27101
(910) 777-3787

NORTH DAKOTA

North Dakota Film Commission
604 E. Boulevard
Second Floor
Bismarck, ND 58505
(800) 435-5663

OHIO

Greater Cincinnati Film Commission
435 Elm Street
Cincinnati, OH 45202
(513) 784-1744

Ohio Film Commission
77 South High Street
29th Floor
Columbus, OH 43266
(800) 230-3523

OKLAHOMA

Lawton Film Commission
PO Box 1376
Lawton, OK 73502
(800) 872-4540

Logan County Film Commission
PO Box 995
Guthrie, OK 73044
(405) 282-0060

Oklahoma Film Office
440 S. Houston
Room 505
Tulsa, OK 74127
(800) 766-3458

OREGON

Oregon Film Office
One World Trade Center
Suite 300
Portland, OR 97204
(503) 229-5832

PENNSYLVANIA

Pennsylvania Film Bureau
Forum Building
Room 455
Harrisburg, PA 17120
(717) 783-3458

Philadelphia Film Office
1650 Arch Street
19th Floor
Philadelphia, PA 19103
(215) 686-2668

Pittsburgh Film Office
Benedum Trees Building
Suite 1300
Pittsburgh, PA 15222
(412) 261-2744

RHODE ISLAND

Rhode Island Film Commission
150 Benefit Street
Providence, RI 02903
(401) 277-3456

SOUTH CAROLINA

Low County Colleton County Film
Office
500 Memorial Avenue
Walterboro, SC 29488
(803) 538-5000

South Carolina Film Office
PO Box 927
Columbia, SC 29202
(803) 737-0490
El Paso Film Commission
One Civic Center Plaza
El Paso, TX 79901
(915) 534-0698

Houston Film Commission
801 Congress
Houston, TX 77002
(713) 227-3100

Irving Texas Film Commission
6309 N O'Connor Rd.
Suite 222
Irving, TX 75039
(800) 2-IRVING

San Antonio Film Commission
PO Box 2277
San Antonio, TX 78230
(800) 447-3372

Texas Film Commission
PO Box 13246
Austin, TX 78711
(512) 463-9200

UTAH

Carbon-Emery Film Commission
PO Box 764
Price, UT 84501
(801) 637-2788

Central Utah Film Commission
51 South University Avenue
Provo, UT 84601
(800) 222-8824

Kanab Film Commission
41 South 100 East
Kanab, UT 84741
(801) 644-5033

Moab Film Commission
59 South Main Street
Suite 4
Moab, UT 84532
(801) 259-6388
Park City Film Commission
PO Box 1630
Park City, UT 84060
(800) 453-1360

Utah Film Commission
324 South State Street
Suite 500
Salt Lake City, UT 84111
(800) 453-8824

VIRGINIA

Metro-Richmond CVB & Film Office
550 E. Marshall Street

Richmond, VA 23219
(804) 782-2777

Virginia Film Office
PO Box 798
Richmond, VA 23206
(804) 371-8204

VERMONT

Vermont Film Bureau
134 State Street
Montpelier, VT 05602
(802) 828-3236

WASHINGTON

Tacoma-Pierce County Film Office
PO Box 1754
Tacoma, WA 98401
(206) 627-2836

Washington State Film & Video Office
2001 Sixth Avenue
Suite 2700
Seattle, WA 98121
(206) 464-7148

WEST VIRGINIA

West Virginia Film Office
State Capitol Complex
Building 6
Charleston, WV 25305
(304) 558-2234

WISCONSIN

Milwaukee Film Liaison
809 N. Broadway
Milwaukee, WI 53202
(414) 286-5700

Wisconsin Film Office
123 W. Washington Avenue
Sixth Floor
Madison, WI 53702
(608) 267-FILM

WYOMING

Casper Film Group
1814 East Second
Casper, WY 82601
(307) 265-2266

Jackson Hole Film Commission
PO Box E
Jackson, WY 83001
(307) 733-3316

Northwest Wyoming / Park County
Film Office
109 West Yellowstone
Cody, WY 82414
(307) 587-6074

Sheridan County Film Promotion
150 South Main
Sheridan, WY 82818
(307) 672-2481

Wyoming Film Commission
I-25 and College Drive
Cheyenne, WY 82002
(800) 458-6657

DISTRIBUTOR LIST

DISTRIBUTORS

When Dorothy, in "The Wizard of Oz," commented, "My goodness, people come and go so quickly here," she could well have been referring to the distribution business in general and any number of individual distributors specifically.

While the following list is reasonably current as of this printing, by next week a few of these names may be gone and an equal number may have joined the list.

But don't let a company's supposed longevity fool you. Just because they've been doing business for a number of years doesn't mean they've been doing it honestly.

Before you sign anything with anyone, check their references. Talk to half a dozen of their clients. Get promotional materials from other films they've distributed, and track down those filmmakers. In short, don't listen to what they say but listen to what they do.

Nowadays anyone with a fax machine and a phone can call themselves a distributor, so be wary as you tread down this path. You've come a long way to make your film, and this is no time to be seduced by fancy letterheads and false promises.

501C3
c/o Voyager Company
578 Broadway Suite 406
New York, NY 10012
(212) 431-5199

ABC Distribution
825 Seventh Avenue
New York, NY 10019
(212) 456-1725

A.I.P. Distribution
10726 McCune Avenue
Los Angeles, CA 90034
(213) 559-8805

Alaiyo Films
37 Carmine Street
New York, NY 10014
(212) 465-2510

Alliance Communications Corp.
920 Yonge Street
Suite 500
Toronto, Ontario M4W 3C7
Canada
(416) 967-1174

Alternate Filmworks
259 Oakwood Avenue
State College, PA 16803-1698
(814) 867-1528

Amazing Movies
7471 Melrose Avenue
Suite 7
Los Angeles, CA 90046
(213) 852-1396

American First Run Studios
14225 Ventura Boulevard
Sherman Oaks, CA 91423
(818) 981-4950

Angelika Films International
110 Greene Street
Suite 1102
New York, NY 10012
(212) 274-1990

ARD Filmredaktion
First German Television
Am Steinernen Stock 1
Frankfurt, 60320
Germany
69 59 05 06

Aries Film Releasing
315 West 57th Street #609
New York, NY 10019
(212) 246-0528

Arista Films
16027 Ventura Boulevard
Suite 206
Encino, CA 91436
(818) 907-7660

Arrow Entertainment
1 Rockefeller Plaza
16th Floor
New York, NY 10103
(212) 332-8140

ATA Trading Corp.
50 West 34th Street
Suite 506
New York, NY 10001
(212) 594-6460

Atlas International Film GMBH
Rumfordstrasse 29-31
80469 Munich
Federal Republic of Germany
49 89 22-75-25

Aventura Pictures
300 Park Avenue
17th Floor
New York, NY 10022
(212) 572-6236

Babylone Films
162 Bis Rue de Paris
Bolougne, 92100
France
33 14 909-9539

Barenholtz/Keyes Productions
381 Park Avenue South
Suite 819
New York, NY 10016
(212) 779-2191

Beyond Films Limited
1875 Century Park East
Suite 1300
Los Angeles, CA 90067
(310) 785-2255

Big Bear Licensing Corporation, Inc.
12400 Wilshire Boulevard
Suite 360
Los Angeles, CA 90025
(310) 820-5161

Blue Ridge Entertainment
1640 S. Sepulveda Boulevard
Suite 308
Los Angeles, CA 90025
(310) 444-0097

Broadstar Entertainment Corporation
6464 Sunset Boulevard
Suite 1130
Hollywood, CA 90028
(213) 962-4950

Broadway Video Entertainment
1619 Broadway
Ninth Floor
New York, NY 10019
(212) 265-7621

Buckeye Communications
425 Park Avenue
27th Floor
New York, NY 10022
(212) 888-9115

Buena Vista Pictures Distribution, Inc.
4111 West Alameda Avenue
Burbank, CA 91505
(818) 562-3750

Canal Plus Cochise Group LTEE/Canada
467 East Boulevard St. Joseph
H2J 1J8 Montreal, Quebec, Canada
(514) 987-9866

Capella International, Inc.
9242 Sunset Boulevard
Suite 280
Beverly Hills, CA 90210
(310) 247-4700

Carolco Pictures, Inc.
880 Sunset Boulevard
Los Angeles, CA 90069
(310) 859-8800

Century Group, Ltd.
8436 West Third Street
Suite 650
Los Angeles, CA 90048
(213) 655-5001

Cinema Connection
250 West 57th Street
Suite 1017
New York, NY 10019
(212) 581-0697

Cinema Consultants Group
8033 Sunset Boulevard
Suite 93
Los Angeles, CA 90046
(213) 650-5646

Cinema Esperanca International
96 Spandina Avenue
Suite 301
Toronto, Ontario M5V 2J6
Canada
(416) 865-1225

Cinema Guild
1697 Broadway
Suite 506
New York, NY 10019
(212) 246-5522

Cinematic Soulmate Productions
19 Eresby House
Rutland Gate
London, SW7 1BG
England
44 071 589-2504

Cinetel Films, Inc.
8255 West Sunset Boulevard
Los Angeles, CA 90046
(213) 654-4000

Cinetrust Entertainment Corporation
2121 Avenue of the Stars
Sixth Floor
Los Angeles, CA 90067
(310) 551-6504

Cinevest Entertainment / Castle
Communications PLC
450 Seventh Avenue
Suite 2702
New York, NY 10123
(212) 465-0866

City Pictures
200 Second Avenue #30
New York, NY 10003
(212) 982-0063

Concorde - New Horizons
11600 San Vicente Boulevard
Los Angeles, CA 90049
(310) 820-6733

Connexion Film Vertriebs & Produktions
GMBH & COKG
Harvestuhder Weg 45
20149 Hamburg 13, Germany
(011) 49-40-41997-0

Crown International Pictures
8701 Wilshire Boulevard
Beverly Hills, CA 90211
(310) 657-6700

Crystal Sky International
1800 Century Park East
Sixth Floor
Los Angeles, CA 90067
(310) 843-0223

The Curb Organization
3907 West Alameda Avenue
Burbank, CA 91505
(818) 843-8580

Cypress Films
135 West 26th Street
New York, NY 10001
(212) 691-8565

Dean Silvers Associates
1560 Broadway
Suite 707
New York, NY 10036
(212) 302-7890

Dino De Laurentis Communications
8670 Wilshire Boulevard
Third Floor
Beverly Hills, CA 90211
(310) 289-6100

Druna Ltd.
9 Forylidou St.
Athens, 10673 Greece
(301) 360-2766

Elendil Productions
853 Broadway Suite 1118
New York, NY 10003
(212) 473-8980

Epic Productions
3330 Cahuenga Boulevard West
Los Angeles, CA 90068
(213) 969-2837

European Film Finance
17304 Preston
Suite 800
Dallas, TX 75252
(214) 380-0995

Facets Multimedia, Inc.
1517 West Fullerton Avenue
Chicago, IL 60614
(312) 281-9075

Films Fonds Hamburg
Friedensallee 14-16
Hamburg, 22765
Germany
49 40 390 58 83

Films Transit
402 East Rue Notre Dame
Montreal, Quebec H2Y 1CB
Canada
(514) 844-3358

Film World Entertainments / Miracle
Films
6311 Romaine Street
Suite 7309
Hollywood, CA 90038
(213) 466-0676

Fine Line Features
888 Seventh Avenue
Second Floor
New York, NY 10106
(212) 649-4800

First Run / Icarus Films
153 Waverly Place
New York, NY 10014
(212) 243-0600

Forefront Films, Inc.
507 17th Street
Brooklyn, NY 11215
(718) 832-3395

Fox/Lorber Associates
419 Park Avenue South
20th Floor
New York, NY 10016
(212) 686-6777

Fries Distribution Company
6922 Hollywood Boulevard
Twelfth Floor
Hollywood, CA 90028
(213) 466-2266

Full Moon Entertainment
3030 Andrita Street
Los Angeles, CA 90065
(213) 341-5959

G.E.L. Distribution
11075 Santa Monica Boulevard
Suite 250
Los Angeles, CA 90025
(310) 479-5619

Good Machine, Inc.
526 West 25th Street
New York, NY 10001
(212) 229-1046

Grainey Pictures, Inc.
44 Market Street
Cold Spring, NY 10516
(914) 265-2241

Gramercy Pictures
9247 Alden Drive

Beverly Hills, CA 90210
(310) 777-1960

Grand AM Ltd.
6649 Odessa Avenue
Van Nuys, CA 91406
(818) 780-9000

Green Communications, Inc.
3407 West Olive Avenue
Burbank, CA 91505
(818) 557-0050

Haut Et Court
1 Rue Des Gatines
Paris, 75020
France
33 14 797 3461

Headliner Productions
2238 Redondo Beach Boulevard
Torrance, CA 90504
(310) 327-0729

Hemdale Communications, Inc.
7966 Beverly Boulevard
Los Angeles, CA 90048
(213) 966-3750

Hunnia Plus LTD
H 1145 Budapest Rona U 174
Hungary
(361) 183-0746

Iltis Sikich Associates
680 North Lake Shore Drive
Suite 1328
Chicago, IL 60611
(312) 337-6012

Image Organization
9000 Sunset Boulevard
Suite 915
Los Angeles, CA 90069
(310) 278-8751

I.N.I. Entertainment Group, Inc.
11150 W. Olympic Boulevard
Suite 700
Los Angeles, CA 90064
(310) 479-6755

International Creative Exchange
3575 Cahuenga Blvd. West
Suite 475
Hollywood, CA 90068
(213) 850-8080

International Forum of New Cinema
Budapesterstrasse 50
Berlin 30, 10787
Germany
49 30 254 89246

Inter-Ocean Film Sales, Ltd.
6100 Wilshire Boulevard
Suite 1500
Los Angeles, CA 90048
(213) 932-0500

I.R.S. Media International
3939 Lankershim Boulevard
Universal City, CA 91604
(818) 505-0555

ITC Entertainment Group
12711 Ventura Boulevard
Third Floor
Studio City, CA 91604
(818) 760-2110

Kinowelt Filmverleih GMBH
Pfisterstrasse 11
Munich, 80331
Germany
49 89 296 963

L'Age D'or
Spefsipov 39
Athens, 10676
Greece
301 725 3701

Lapsus
11 Rue de Malte
75011, Paris
France
331 4355 0570

Largo Entertainment
10201 West Pico Boulevard
Los Angeles, CA 90035
(310) 203-3600

Lenfilm
10 Kisovsky Prospest
St. Petersburg, 197101
Russia
812 232 83 74

LEO Home Video
1509 1/2 N. Hoover
Los Angeles, CA 90027
(213) 913-3038

Lone Star Pictures International, Inc.
4826 Greenville Avenue
Dallas, TX 75206
(214) 696-8830

Majestic Films & Television International
PO Box 13
Glouchester Mansions, Cambridge Circus
London, WC2H 8XD
England
44 71 836-8630

Marquee Entertainment, Inc.
9044 Melrose Avenue
Third Floor
Los Angeles, CA 90069
(310) 859-8250

Mayfair Entertainment International
110 St. Martin's Lane
London, WC2N 4AD
England
44 71 304-7911

MCEG Sterling Entertainment
1888 Century Park East
Suite 17777
Los Angeles, CA 90067
(310) 282-0871

Melrose Entertainment
8383 Wilshire Boulevard
Suite 310
Beverly Hills, CA 90211
(213) 653-3191

Miramax Films
375 Greenwich Street
Third Floor
New York, NY 10013
(212) 941-3800

Monarch Home Video
P.O. Box 7006
La Vergne, TN 37086
(615) 287-4760

Moonstone Entertainment
9242 Beverly Boulevard
Suite 230
Beverly Hills, CA 90210
(310) 247-6060

Montana Productions
114 West 86th Street
New York, NY 10024
(212) 724-2042

Morgan Creek International
1875 Century Park East
Suite 200
Los Angeles, CA 90067
(310) 284-8884

Motion Picture Corporation of America
1401 Ocean Avenue
Suite 301
Santa Monica, CA 90401
(310) 319-9500

The Movie Group
1900 Avenue of the Stars
Suite 1425
Los Angeles, CA 90067
(310) 556-2830

Myriad Pictures
250 West 57th Street
Suite 1701
New York, NY 10107
(212) 581-0400

Mystic Entertainment
1312 Centinela Avenue
Suite 101
Los Angeles, CA 90025
(310) 207-9829

New Line Cinema
888 Seventh Avenue
20th Floor
New York, NY 10106
(212) 649-4900

New Video Group
250 Park Avenue South
Suite 201
New York, NY 10003
(212) 982-9000

New World Entertainment
1440 South Sepulveda Boulevard
Los Angeles, CA 90025
(310) 444-8100

Norstar Entertainment, Inc.
86 Bloor Street West
Suite 400
Toronto, Ontario M5S 1M5
Canada
(416) 961-6278

North American Releasing, Inc.
808 Nelson Street
Suite 2105
Vancouver
British Columbia V6Z 2H2
Canada
(604) 681-2165

Northern Arts Entertainment
Northern Arts Studios
Williamsburg, MA 01096
(413) 268-9301

Oak Island Films
320 West 13th Street
New York, NY 10014
(212) 807-7780

October Films
45 Rockefeller Plaza
Suite 3014
New York, NY 10111
(212) 332-2480

Odyssey Distributors, Inc.
6500 Wilshire Boulevard
Suite 400
Los Angeles, CA 90048
(213) 655-9335

Original Cinema
419 Park Avenue South
20th Floor
New York, NY 10016
(212) 545-0177

Orion Pictures
1888 Century Park East
7th Floor
Los Angeles, CA 90067
(310) 282-2473

Overseas Film Group /
First Look Pictures
8800 Sunset Boulevard
Suite 302
Los Angeles, CA 90069
(310) 855-1199

Palomar SRL
Via Silvio Pellico, 14
Rome, 00195
Italy
38 6 3251483

Pandora Cinema
955 South Carillo Drive
Suite 100
Los Angeles, CA 90048
(213) 954-3900

Panorama Entertainment
125 North Main Street
Portchester, NY 10573
(914) 937-1603

PFG Entertainment
1401 Ocean Avenue
Suite 302
Santa Monica, CA 90401
(310) 393-5788

Prism Pictures
1888 Century Park East
Suite 350
Los Angeles, CA 90067
(310) 277-3270

Promark Entertainment Group
3599 Cahuenga Boulevard West
Suite 300
Los Angeles, CA 90068
(213) 878-0404

Quigley and Company
1075 Old Country Road
Belmont, CA 94002
(415) 595-4922

Reel Movies International
8235 Douglas Avenue
Suite 770
Dallas, TX 75225
(214) 363-4400

Republic Pictures International
12636 Beatrice Street
Los Angeles, CA 90066
(310) 306-4040

The Robert Lewis Company
8755 Shoreham Drive
Suite 303
Los Angeles, CA 90069
(310) 854-3714

Saban Pictures International
4000 West Alameda Avenue
Burbank, CA 91505
(818) 972-4800

Samuel Goldwyn Company
10203 Santa Monica Boulevard
Suite 500
Los Angeles, CA 90067
(310) 552-2255

Seventh Art Releasing
7551 Sunset Boulevard
Suite 104
Los Angeles, CA 90048
(213) 845-1455

SGE Entertainment Corp.
12001 Ventura Place
Suite 404
Studio City, CA 91604
(818) 766-8500

Showcase Entertainment, Inc.
Warner Center
21800 Oxnard Street
Suite 150
Woodland Hills, CA 91367
(818) 715-7005

Sony Pictures Classics
550 Madison Avenue
8th Floor
New York, NY 10022
(212) 833-8833

Strand Releasing
225 Santa Monica Boulevard
Suite 810
Santa Monica, CA 90401
(310) 395-5002

Summit Entertainment
2308 Broadway
Santa Monica, CA 90404
(310) 315-6000

Tapestry International
920 Broadway
15th Floor
New York, NY 10010
(212) 505-2288

Taurus Entertainment
113 Middle Neck Road
Great Neck, NY 11021
(516) 829-1520

Tramstar Entertainment
257 West 19th Street
New York, NY 10011
(212) 969-0683

Trans Atlantic Entertainment
10351 Santa Monica Boulevard
Suite 200
Los Angeles, CA 90025
(310) 772-7300

Trident Releasing
8401 Melrose Place
Second Floor
Los Angeles, CA 90069
(213) 655-8818

Trimark Pictures
2644 30th Street
Second Floor
Santa Monica, CA 90405
(310) 314-2000

Troma, Inc.
733 Ninth Avenue
New York, NY 10019
(212) 757-4555

Twentieth Century Fox Film Corporation
10201 West Pico Boulevard
Building 78, Room 3
Los Angeles, CA 90035
(310) 203-2921

Unapix Entertainment
1040 First Avenue
Suite 329
New York, NY 10022
(212) 355-3857

Universal Pictures
100 UNiversal City Plaza
Building 500, 10th Floor
Universal City, CA 91608
(818) 777-5598

Vauban Productions
9 Avenue Franklin D Roosevelt
Paris, 75008
France
331 4225 6604

VPS Film Entertainment GMBH
825 Shenandoah Street
Suite 302
Los Angeles, CA 90035
(310) 289-7970

Women Make Movies
462 Broadway
Fifth Floor
New York, NY 10013
(212) 925-0606

Worldvision Home Video
1700 Broadway, 11th Floor
New York, NY 10019
(212) 261-2900

Zeitgeist Films
247 Centre Street, 2nd floor
New York, NY 10013
(212) 274-1989

TELEVISION LIST

American Playhouse
1776 Broadway, 9th floor
New York, NY 10019
(212) 757-4300

BBC Television
Kensington House
Richmond Way
London, W14 OAX
England
44 081 6136/6885

Bravo Cable Network/
The Independent Film Channel
150 Crossways Park West
Woodbury, NY 11797
(516) 364-2222

Canal Plus/Ecriture
85/83 Quai Andre Citroen
75015 Paris
France
(011) 33-1-46-10-11-54

Central Television
35-38 Portman Square
London, W1H 2JP
England
44 071 486-6688

Channel 4 Televison
60 Charlotte Street
London, W1P 2AX
England
44 071 927-8742

Edge Television / Applause Network
7805 Sunset Blvd.
Suite 203
Los Angeles, CA 90046
(213) 850-5000

Encore Media
5445 DTC Parkway
Suite 600
Englewood, CO 80111
(303) 771-7700

Fox Latin American Channel
11833 Mississippi Avenue
Second Floor
Los Angeles, CA 90025
(310) 447-7307

HBO Showcase
1100 Avenue of the Americas
New York, NY 10036
(212) 512-1901

HBO/Cinemax
1100 Avenue of the Americas
New York, NY 10036
(212) 512-1000

ICE Television
3575 Cahuenga Boulevard West
Suite 475
Hollywood, CA 90068
(213) 850-8080

Latin American Independent Network
400 South Point
Suite 1409
Miami, FL 33139
(305) 532-7339

Lifetime Television
309 West 49th Street
New York, NY 10019
(212) 424-7000

MTV Networks, Inc.
1515 Broadway
New York, NY 10036
(212) 258-8000

Norwegian Broadcasting Corporation
Bj Bjornsons Plass 1
Oslo 3, N-0340
Norway
(001) 47-22-45-93-57

Showtime
10 Universal City Plaza
Universal City, CA 91608-1097
(818) 505-7700

Showtime / The Movie Channel
1633 Broadway
New York, NY 10019
(212) 708-1600

Special Broadcasting Service
14 Herbert Street
Artarmon, NSW 2064 Australia

Turner Pictures Worldwide
1888 Century Park East
Twelfth Floor
Los Angeles, CA 90067
(310) 788-6890

21st Century Film Corporation
11080 West Olympic Boulevard
Los Angeles, CA 90064
(310) 914-0500

USA Networks
1230 Avenue of the Americas
New York, NY 10020
(212) 408-9100

VPRO-TV
PO Box 11
Hilversum, 1200 JC
Netherlands
(035) 71-29-11

WNET/13
356 West 58th Street
New York, NY 10019
(212) 560-2000

WNYC-TV
1 Centre Street
Room 1450
New York, NY 10007
(212) 669-7736

World African Network
11 Piedmont Center
Suite 620
3495 Piedmont Road NE
Atlanta, GA 30305
(404) 365-8850

ZDF/Arte
Postfach 4040
Mainz 1, 55100
Germany
06 131 702 349

Zweites Deutsches Fernsehen
ZDF-Strabe 1
Mainz, 55127
Germany
49 61 31 70 2452

FESTIVAL LIST

AFI Film Festival
American Film Institute
2021 N. Western Avenue
Los Angeles, CA 90027

Amiens International Film Festival
36 Rue De Noyon
Amiens, 80000
France

Ann Arbor Film Festival
P.O. Box 8232
Ann Arbor, MI 48107

Asian-American International Film
Showcase
NAATA
346 9th Street
Second floor
San Francisco, CA 94103

Asian-American International Film
Festival
Asian Cinevision
32 East Broadway
Fourth Floor
New York NY 10002

Aspen Film Festival
P.O. Box 8910
Aspen, CO 81612

Athens International Film & Video
Festival
P.O. Box 388
Athens, OH 45701

Atlantic Film Festival
1541 Barrington St.
Suite 326
Halifax, N.S. B3j 1Z5

Australian International Film Festival
Drummoyne Avenue
Drummoyne, NSW 2047
Australia

Baltimore International Film Festival
Baltimore Museum of Art
Baltimore, MD 21218

Banco Nacional Film Showing
Rua Paulo Barreto 107
22280 Rio de Janeiro
Brazil

Banff Television Festival
Banff Center
P.O. Box 1020
Banff, Alberta
Canada

Big Muddy Film Festival
Department of Cinema
Mailcode 6610
Southern Illinois University at
Carbondale
Carbondale, IL 62901

Black Film Festival
The Newark Museum
49 Washington Street
P.O. Box 543
Newark, NJ 07101

Brescia Funny Film Festival
Paizza Einaudi 2
Boario Terme 26041 Brescia
Italy

Brussels International Festival of Fantasy
Avenue de la Reine 144, B-1210
Brussels, Belgium

Brussels International Film Festival
Chaussee de Louvain 30
1030 Brussels
Belgium

Cabourg International Festival of
Romantic Films
106 bis Ave. du Villiers
75017 Paris
France

Cairo International Film Festival
17 Kasr El Nil St.
Cairo, Egypt

Cambridge International Film Festival
8 Market Passage
Cambridge CB2 3PF
United Kingdom

Carolina Film & Video Festival
Broadcasting/Cinema Division
100 Carmichael Building
2 UNCG
Greensboro, NC 27512

Charlotte Film Festival
Mint Museum of Art
2730 Randolph Road
Charlotte, NC 28207

Chicago International Film Festival
415 N. Dearborn
Chicago, IL 60610

Chicago Latino Film Festival
600 South Michigan Avenue
Chicago, IL 60605

Cinequest/The San Jose Film Festival
P.O. Box 720040
San Jose, CA 95172

Cleveland Film Festival
6200 Som Center Road #C20
Solon, OH 44139

Copenhagen Gay & Lesbian Film
Festival
Bulowsvej 50A
1870 Frederiksberg
Copenhagen, Denmark

Denver International Film Festival
999 18th Street
Suite 1820
Denver, CO 80202

Dublin Film Festival
1 Suffolk Street
Dublin 2, Ireland

Durban International Film Festival
University of Natal
King George V Avenue
Durban 4001
South Africa

The Edinburgh International Film
Festival
800 Lothian Road
Edinburgh EH3 9BZ
Scotland

Exground On Screen
Erbacher Str. 9
65197 Wiesbaden, Germany

Festival Internatzionale Cinema Giovani
Via Monte di Pieta
1 - 10121 Torino, Italy

Festival Internazionale
Del Film Locarno
Casella Postale
Via Della Posta 6
Locarno, CH 6600
Switzerland

Florence International Film Festival
Via S, Zonobi 54R
Firenze 50129
Italy

Florida Film Festival
1300 South Orlando Avenue
Maitland, FL 32751

Frankfurt International Children's Film
Festival
Kinder und Jugendfilmzentrum in der
Bundesrepublik Deutschland
Schaumaninkai 41
60596 Frankfurt am Main
Germany

Funny Film Festival
Piazza Ainaudi, 2
25041 Boario Terme
Italy

Gay & Lesbian Film Festival
The National Association of Gays and
Lesbians
Knarbrostrade 3
P.O. Box 1023
DK-1007 Copenhagen
Denmark
Geneva Film Festival

2, Rue Bovy-Lysberg
Case Postal 5615
1211 Geneva 11
Switzerland

Giffoni Children's Festival
84095 Giffoni Valle Piana
Salerno
Italy

Gijon International Film Festival for
Young People
Calle Matermidad2, Z
33207 Gijon
Asturias
Spain

Gothenburg Film Festival
P.O. Box 7079
S-402 32 Gothenburg
Sweden

Hawaii International Film Festival
700 Bishop Street
Suite 400
Honolulu, Hawaii 96813

Heartland Film Festival
613 N. East Street
Indianapolis, IN 46202

Helsinki International Film Festival
Cinema Mondo
Unioninkatu 10A27
SF-00130
Helsinki, Finland

Human Rights Watch Film Festival
Human Rights Watch
485 Fifth Avenue
New York, NY 10017

Independent Feature Film Market
104 West 29th Street
12th Floor
New York, NY 10001

International Film Festival Berlin
Budapesterstrasse 50
Berlin 30, 10787
Germany

International Festival of Comedy Films
House of Humor & Satire
P.O. Box 104
5300 Gabrovo
Bulgaria

International Film Festival in Abitibi-
Temiscamingue
215 Mercier Avenue
Rouyn-Noranda
Quebec J9X 5WB
Canada

International Forum of New Cinema
Budapesterstrasse 50
Berlin 30, 10787
Germany

International Thessaloniki Film Festival
36 Sina Street
Athens, 10672
Greece

International Women Directors' Film
Festival
Maison des Arts
Place Salvador Allende
94000 Creteil
France

Jerusalem International Film Festival
Hebron Rd. P.O. Box 8561
Jerusalem, 91083
Israel

Lesbian And Gay Film Festival
National Film Theater
South Bank, London
SE1 8XT
United Kingdom

Locarno International Film Festival
Via Della Posta 6 Case Postale 465
CH-6600 Locarno
Switzerland

London Film Festival
National Film Theatre
South Bank
London, SE1 8XT
England

The Long Island Film Festival
Suffolk County Motion PIcture/TV
Commission
Department of Economic Development
220 Rabro Drive
P.O. Box 6100
Hauppauge, NY 11788-0099

Los Angeles Asian Pacific American
International Film and Video Festival
Visual Communications
263 South Los Angeles Street
Suite 307
Los Angeles, CA 90012

Mannheim Festival
Collini-Center, Gallerie
D-68161 Mannheim 1
Germany

Margaret Mead Film Festival
American Museum of National History
Central Park West at 79th Street
New York, NY 10024

Maverick Film / Black International
Cinema
94 Nassua Avenue
Suite 296
Brooklyn, NY 11222

Melbourne International Film Festival
207 Johnston Street
P.O. Box 2206
Fitzroy 3065
Melbourne, Australia

Midnight Sun Film Festival
Jaamerentie 9
SF-99600 Sodankyla
Finland

Montreal International Film & Video
Festival
3726 Boulevard Saint-Laurent
Montreal, Quebec H2X 2V8
Canada

Montreal World Film Festival
1455 De Maisonneuve West
Montreal, Quebec H3G 1M8
Canada

Moscow International Film Festival
10 Khokhlovsky Pereulok
Moscow, 109028
Russia

Munich International Film Festival
Kaiserstrasse 39
80801 Munich,
Germany

New Directors / New Films
Film Society of Lincoln Center
140 West 65th Street
New York, NY 10023

Newark Black Film Festival
Newark Museum
49 Washington Street
Box 540
Newark, NJ 07101

New England Film and Video Festival
Arts Extension Service Division of
Continuing Education
604 Goodell Building
University of Massachusetts
Amherst, MA 01003

New Orleans Film & Video Festival
821 Gravier Street
Suite 600
New Orleans, LA 70112

New York International Film Festival
70 Lincoln Center
New York, NY 10023

Palm Springs International Film Festival
431 S. Palm Canyon Drive
Suite 219
Palm Springs, CA 92262

Pesaro Film Festival
Mostra Internazionale del Nuovo
Cinema
Via Yser 8
00198 Rome
Italy

Philadelphia Festival of World Cinema
International House
3701 Chestnut Street

Philadelphia, PA 19104

Philadelphia International Film Festival
2623 Sorrento Drive
Suite A
Philadelphia, PA 19131

Raindance Film Festival
6 Chelsea Wharf
15 Lots Road
London SW10 OQJ
England

Rivertown International Film Festival
University Film Society
Minnesota Film Center
425 Ontario Street SE
Minneapolis, MN 55414

Rome-Florence Film Festival
Palazzo Delle Esposizioni
Via Nazionale 194
Rome, 00184
Italy

Rosebud Entertainment / Festival
Hans-Sachs- Str 22
D Munich 80469
Germany

Rotterdam Film Festival
P.O. Box 21696
Rotterdam, 3001 AR
Netherlands

San Francisco International Film Festival
1521 Eddy Street
San Francisco, CA 94115

San Francisco International Lesbian &
Gay Film Festival
Frameline
346 Ninth Street
San Francisco, CA 94103

San Remo Auteur Festival
La Mostra Internazionale del Film
d'Autore
Rotanda dei Mille
1, 24100
Bergamo, Italy

San Sebastian International Film Festival
Apartado de Correos 397
San Sebastian 20080
Spain

Santa Barbara International Film Festival
1216 State Street
Suite 201
Santa Barbara, CA 93101

Sao Paulo International Film Festival
Renata de Almeida
Alameda Lorena 937
303-01424 Sao Paulo
Brazil

Seattle International Film Festival
801 East Pine Street
Egyptian Theater
Seattle, WA 98122

Silver Images Film Festival
9848 S. Winchester Avenue
Chicago, IL 60643

Southampton Film Festival
Marketing and Special Events (DLTA)
Union Castle House
Canute Road
Southhampton S01 1AG
England

South By Southwest Film Festival
P.O. Box 4999
Austin, TX 78765

Stockholm Film Festival
P.O. Box 7673
S-103 95 Stockholm
Sweden

Sundance Film Festival
PO Box 16450
Salt Lake City, UT 84116

Sydney International Film Festival
P.O. Box 25
Glebe NSW 2037
Australia

Taormina Film Festival
Palazzo Firenze
Via Pirandello 31

Taormina
Sicily

Taos Talking Picture Festival
216M North Pueblo Road
#216
Taos, NM 87571

Telluride Film Festival
53 South Main Street
Suite 212
P.O. Box B1156
Hanover, NH 03755

Texas Film Festival
MSC Film Society of Texas A&M
PO Box J-1
College Station, TX 77844

Torino International Film Festival
Piazza S. Carlo 161
10123 Turin
Italy

Toronto Festival of Festivals
70 Carlton Street
Toronto, Ontario M5B 1L7
Canada

Troia International Film Festival
2902 Setubal Codex
Troia
Portugal

U S International Film & Video Festival
841 North Addison Avenue
Elmhurst, IL 60126
Valladoid International Film Festival
P.O. Box 646
Valladoid 47003
Spain

Vevey International Comedy Film
Festival
CP 325
CH-1800
Vevey
Switzerland

Virginia Festival of American Film
PO Box 3697
104 Midmont Lane
Charlottesville, VA 22903

Washington, D.C. International Film
Festival
P.O. Box 21396
Washington, D.C. 20009

Wine Country Film Festival
P.O. Box 303
12000 Henno Road
Glen Ellen, CA 95442

Women in Film Festival
6464 Sunset Boulevard
Los Angeles, CA 90028

Worldfest Houston
The Houston International Film Festival
P.O. Box 56566
Houston, TX 77256

FILM LABS LIST

Allied Film Laboratory
1322 W. Belmont
Chicago, IL 60657

Astral Tech, Inc.
2101, rue Ste-Catherine Quest
Montreal, Quebec H3H 1M6

Astro Color Laboratory
61 West Erie
Chicago, IL 60610

Colorlab
5708 Arundel Avenue
Rockville, MD 20857

Continental Film Laboratory
1998 NE 150th Street
North Miami, FL 33181

Delden Film Laboratory
9530 James Avenue S.
Minneapolis, MN 55431

Deluxe Toronto
380 Adelaide Street W.
Toronto, Ontario M5V 1R7

DuArt Film Laboratories
245 West 55th Street
New York, NY 10019

Filmack Studios
1327 S. Wabash
Chicago, IL 60605

Medallion P.F.A. Film and Video
111 Peter Street, 9th Floor
Toronto, Ontario M5V 2H1

National Fast-Time
3809 North Clark
Chicago, IL 60613

RGB Color Lab
816 North Highland Avenue
Hollywood, CA 90038

Spectrum Laboratory
399 Gunderson Drive
Carol Stream, IL 60613

Western Cine
312 South Pearl Street
Denver, CO 80209

WRS Motion Picture and Video
Laboratory
1000 Napor Boulevard
Pittsburgh, PA 15205

Yale Laboratory, Inc.
1509 North Gordon Street
Hollywood, CA 90028

OTHER RESOURCES

The following lists are not comprehensive; they are only a starting point in your search for the services and supplies that you need. These listings do not imply any endorsement by the authors. Buyer beware.

INDEPENDENT FEATURE FILM OFFICES

Independent Feature Project - East
104 West 29th Street
12th Floor
New York, NY 10001
(212) 465-8200

Independent Feature Project - Midwest
3600 North Lakeshore Drive, Suite 1205
Chicago, IL 60613
(312) 868-4140

Independent Feature Project - North
401 North Third Street, Suite 450
Minneapolis, MN 55401
(612) 338-0871

Independent Feature Project - Northern California
PO Box 460278
San Francisco, CA 94146
(415) 431-5890

Independent Feature Project - Seattle
1011 Western Avenue
Suite 520
Seattle, WA 98104
(206) 682-3025

Independent Feature Project - South
Greenwich Studios
12100 NE 16th Avenue
Suite 201
North Miami, FL 33161
(305) 899-0280

Independent Feature Project - West
1625 Olympic Boulevard
Santa Monica, CA 90404
(310) 392-8832

EDUCATIONAL RESOURCES

The American Film Institute
2121 North Western Avenue
Los Angeles, CA 90027
(213) 856-7600

Association of Independent Video and Filmmakers
625 Broadway
Ninth Floor
New York, NY 10012
(212) 473-3400

Film Arts Foundation
346 Ninth Street
Second Floor
San Francisco, CA 94103
(415) 552-8760

Dov S-S Simens
Hollywood Film Institute
5225 Wilshire Boulevard
Suite 410
Los Angeles, CA 90036
(800) 366-3456

Sundance Institute
10202 W. Washington Boulevard
Culver City, CA 90232
(310) 204-2091

FILM SUPPLIERS

NEW FILM

F.R. Film Supply
25 West 45th Street
New York, NY 10036
(212) 221-4399

Steadi Systems
321 W. 44th Street, Suite 412A
New York, NY 10036
(212) 974-7666
Steadi Systems
1014 N. Highland Avenue
Los Angeles, CA 90038
(213) 461-6868

FILM STOCK EXCHANGES

New York Raw Stock Exchange
1133 Broadway, Room 1606
New York, NY 10010
(212) 255-0445

Studio Film and Tape / NY
630 Ninth Avenue
New York, NY 10036
(212) 977-9330

Studio Film and Tape / LA
6674 Santa Monica Boulevard
Los Angeles, CA 90048
(213) 466-8101

AUDIO AND VIDEO TAPE SUPPLIERS

NEW TAPES
The Tape Company
700 Creel Drive
Wood Dale, IL 60191
(708) 595-3113

The Tape Company
9852 Crescent Park Drive
West Chester, OH 45069
(513) 755-0200

The Tape Company
1140 Cambridge Circle Drive
Kansas City, KS 66103
(913) 342-7900

Tape Distributors
7630 Washington Avenue
Eden Prairie, MN 55344
(612) 947-4007

Tape Distributors
1525 Capital Drive, Suite 110
Carrollton, TX 75006
(214) 394-8273

Tape Distributors
Folcroft West Business Park
Darby Commons, Fairfax #5
Folcroft, PA 19032
(610) 237-0711

RECYCLED VIDEOTAPE

Coarc Video
P.O. Box 2]
Route 217
Mellenville, NY 12544
(800) 888-4451

EVALUATED VIDEOTAPE

Carpel Video
429 E. Patrick Street
Frederick, MD 21701
(800) 238-4300

TAPE-TO-FILM TRANSFERS

Ringer Video Services, Inc.
2408 W. Olive Avenue
Burbank, CA 91506
(818) 954-8621

VIDEO AND SOUND SERVICES

We have not included a listing of film-to-video-transfer services or sound-engineering services because most larger metropolitan areas have several competent companies doing this work. Break out those yellow pages.

WHERE TO BUY MOVIE SCRIPTS

Script City
8033 Sunset Boulevard Suite 1500
Hollywood, CA 90046
1-800-676-2522

Book City
308 North San Fernando
Burbank, CA 91502
(818) 848-4417

PUBLICATIONS

Hollywood Reporter
5055 Wilshire Boulevard
Los Angeles, CA 90036
(213) 525-2000

Variety
475 Park Avenue South
New York, NY 10016
(212) 779-1100

Variety
5700 Wilshire Boulevard, Suite 120
Los Angeles, CA 90036
(213) 857-6600

EDGE NUMBERING

Code 16
262 West 91st Street
New York, NY 10024
(212) 496-1118

COPYRIGHT AND SCRIPT REGISTRATION

Register of Copyrights
Library of Congress
Washington, D.C. 20559
Registration Office
Writers Guild of America, West
8955 Beverly Boulevard
Los Angeles, CA 90048

PHOTO PROCESSING

Skrudland Photo
5311 Fleming Court
Austin, TX 78744-1197
(512) 444-0958

INCORPORATING IN DELAWARE

State of Delaware
Division of Corporations
P.O. Box 898
Dover, DE 19903
(302) 739-3073

BIBLIOGRAPHY

While we don't recommend blowing your budget on a new library, we also recognize that this one book is by no means the final word. Most of the following books can be found at the library or can be read while standing in the stacks at your favorite book store.

Abbott, L. B. Special Effects: Wire, Tape and Rubber Band Style. Hollywood: The ASC Press, 1984.

Bayer, William. Breaking Through, Selling Out, Dropping Dead And Other Notes On Filmmaking. New York: Limelight Editions, 1971, 1989.

Blake, Larry. Film Sound Today: An Anthology of Articles From Recording Engineers and Producers. Reveille Press, 1984.

Bobker, Lee R. Elements of Film. New York: Harcourt Brace Jovanovich, Inc., 1974.

Brady, John. The Craft of the Screenwriter. New York: Simon and Schuster, 1981.

Buchanan, Mark A., and Thomas, David John. Simplified Business Incorporation: A Self-Help Manual — Minnesota Procedure. St. Cloud, Minn.: Small Business Development Center, St. Cloud State University.

Chamness, Danford. The Hollywood Guide to Film Budgeting and Script Breakdown for Low Budget Features. Los Angeles: The Stanley J. Brooks Company, 1988.

Clark, Frank P. Special Effects in Motion Pictures. Hollywood: Society of Motion Picture and Television Engineers.

Corman, Roger, with Jerome, Jim. How I Made A Hundred Movies In Hollywood And Never Lost A Dime. New York: Random House, 1990.

Detmers, Fred H., ed. American Cinematographers Manual. Hollywood: The ASC Press, 1986.

Eisen, Peter J. Accounting. New York: Barron's Educational Series, Inc., 1985.

Engel, Joel. Screenwriters on Screenwriting. Hyperion, 1995.

Field, Syd. Screenplay: The Foundations of Screenwriting. New York: Dell Publishing Co., Inc., 1979, 1982.

Field, Syd. The Screenwriter's Workbook. New York: Dell Publishing Co., Inc., 1984.

Froug, William. The New Screenwriter Looks At The New Screenwriter. Los Angeles: Silman-James Press, 1992.

Gelmis, Joseph. The Film Director As Superstar. New York: Doubleday, 1970.

Glimcher, Sumner, and Johnson, Warren. Movie Making: A Guide to Film Production. New York: Simon & Schuster, Inc., Pocket Books, 1975.

Goldner, Orville, and Turner, George E. The Making of King Kong. New York: Ballantine Books, 1976.

Goldman, William. Adventures In The Screen Trade New York: Warner Books, 1983.

Goldman, William. William Goldman: Five Screenplays. Applause Books, 1994).

Goodell, Gregory. Independent Feature Film Production. New York: St. Martin's Press, 1982.

Grodin, Charles. It Would Be So Nice If You Weren't Here. Vintage Books, A Division of Random House, Inc., 1989.

Hamilton, Peter, and Rosen, David. Off-Hollywood: The Making and Marketing of Independent Films. New York: Grove Weidenfeld, 1990.

Hunter, Lew. Lew Hunter's Screenwriting 434. New York: Perigee Books - Putnam Publishing Group, 1993.

Hurst, Walter E., and Hale, Wm. Storm. Motion Picture Distribution (Business and/or Racket?). Hollywood: Seven Arts Press, 1975, 1977.

Karlin, Fred. Listening To Movies - The Film Lover's Guide To Film Music. Schirmer Books, 1994.

Karlin, Fred, and Wright, Rayburn. On The Track - A Guide To Contemporary Film Scoring. Schirmer Books, 1990.

Katz, Steven D. Film Directing Shot By Shot. Los Angeles: Michael Wiese Productions, 1991.

Litwak, Mark. Deal Making In The Film And Television Industry. Los Angeles: Silman James Press, 1994.

Litwak, Mark. Contracts In The Film And Television Industry. Los Angeles: Silman James Press, 1995.

Lumet, Sidney. Making Movies. Alfred A. Knopf, 1995.

Lyons, Donald. Independent Visions. New York: Ballantine Books, 1994.

Rosenblum, Ralph, and Karen, Robert. When The Shooting Stops ... The Cutting Begins. New York: Penguin Books, 1979).

Sautter, Carl. How To Sell Your Screenplay: The Real Rules Of Film And Television. New York: New Chapter Press, 1988.

Schanzer, Karl, and Wright, Thomas Lee. American Screenwriters: The Insiders' Look At The Art, The Craft, And The Business of Writing Movies. New York: Avon Books, 1993.

Schmidt, Rick. Feature Filmmaking At Used Car Prices. New York: Penguin Books, 1988.

Sherman, Eric. Directing The Film: Film Directors On Their Art. Boston: Little, Brown and Company, 1976.

Seger, Linda. Making A Good Script Great. New York: Dodd, Mead & Company, 1987.

Vogler, Christopher. The Writer's Journey. Los Angeles: Michael Wiese Productions, 1993.

Warshawski, Morrie. Shaking The Money Tree. Los Angeles: Michael Wiese Productions, 1992.

Wiese, Michael. Film & Video Financing. Studio City, CA: Michael Wiese Productions, 1989.

Wiese, Michael. Film & Video Marketing. Studio City, CA: Michael Wiese Productions, 1988.

Wiese, Michael. The Independent Film & Videomakers Guide. Studio City, CA: Michael Wiese Productions, Revided 1990.

Wiese, Michael. Producer To Producer. Studio City, CA: Michael Wiese Productions, 1993.

Wiese, Michael, and Simon, Deke. Film & Video Budgets-2nd Edition. Studio City, CA: Michael Wiese Productions, 1995.

Wolff, Jurgen, and Cox, Kerry. Top Secrets: Screenwriting. Los Angeles: Lone Eagle Publishing Company, 1993.

THE FILMS IN THIS BOOK

You can learn a lot by reading about an ultra-low-budget film. You can learn even more by seeing it. Here's how to find the films profiled in this book.

All The Love In The World
c/o Facet Multimedia, Inc.
1517 West Fullerton Avenue
Chicago, IL 60614

Beyond Bob
c/o Granite Productions, Ltd.
P.O. Box 852
Stillwater, MN 55082

Criminals
c/o Criminal Pictures
21 Webster Place
Brooklyn, NY 11215

Grief
c/o Strand Releasing
225 Santa Monica Boulevard
Suite 810
Santa Monica, CA 90401

Highways
c/o Imagery International
22647 Ventura Boulevard
Suite 521
Woodland Hills, CA 91364

Plan 10 From Outer Space
c/o Plan 10 Productions
262 East 100 South #215
Salt Lake City, UT 84111

Internet Homepage: http://mcchurch.org/plan10
Resident Alien
c/o Granite Productions, Ltd.
P.O. Box 852
Stillwater, MN 55082

Slack Trek: The X Generation
c/o Fish Productions
298 Mulberry Street
Suite 3K
New York, NY 10012
Fish21@aol.com

Someone Special
c/o Caspian Films
1832 Albans
Houston, TX 77005-1706

The Usual
c/o Periferia Films
1760 Hennepin Avenue South
Suite 33
Minneapolis, MN 55403

World And Time Enough
c/o Strand Releasing
225 Santa Monica Boulevard
Suite 810
Santa Monica, CA 90401

ABOUT THE AUTHORS

When it comes to producing successful films on a shoestring, John Gaspard and Dale Newton know of what they speak.

Together they created "Resident Alien" and "Beyond Bob," two critically acclaimed ultra-low-budget features, each produced for under $30,000 using the tactics and strategies outlined in this book.

Dale Newton wrote and produced "Resident Alien," along with producing "Beyond Bob." He's an award-winning writer of numerous screenplays and scripts. He's also received awards for his work producing and directing films, videos, and audiovisual projects, which he has done for more than 20 years. An early goal in life was to avoid working as an accountant or business manager. Sadly, producing two feature films has dashed both those dreams.

Besides "Resident Alien" and "Beyond Bob," John Gaspard has also directed, written, or produced four other features, one with a budget of only $900 — get three shots of tequila in him, and he'll tell you all about it. John got into filmmaking when he heard it was the fastest route to fame, riches, and meeting intriguing women. It was only after doing it for 20 years that he realized he'd been misinformed. His writing credits include American Public Radio's "Good Evening" and "First House On The Right" programs, along with episodes of the popular European comic-western television series "Lucky Luke," starring Terence Hill.

You've Read The Book.

Now See The Movies.

The two ultra-low-budget feature films profiled in <u>Persistence Of Vision</u> are now available by mail order. Each was produced for less than $30,000 and dramatically demonstrates the techniques outlined in the book.

"Beyond Bob" is an award-winning comedy from the other side. It's a story of love and friendship, of passion from beyond the grave, and of a love that was made in heaven . . . and was just too darned important to stay there.

"Resident Alien" mixes comedy, science fiction and romance to create a memorable story about the dangers and complications that occur when you wish on a star — and your dreams come true.

"Beyond Bob"	(VHS, Color, 100 Minutes) (List price $49.95)	$29.95
"Resident Alien"	(VHS, Color, 105 Minutes) (List price $49.95)	$29.95
Special Offer —	Buy both films for only	$58.00

(Minnesota residents, add 6.5% sales tax.)

Send check or money order to:
GRANITE PRODUCTIONS, LTD.
P.O. Box 852
Stillwater, MN 55082

FILM & VIDEO BOOKS

FROM MICHAEL WIESE PRODUCTIONS

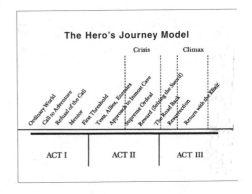

THE DIGITAL VIDEOMAKER'S GUIDE
by Kathryn Shaw Whitver

Digital video is a hot topic. The jargon is new and it's difficult to sort out what's real, what's likely to be achieved, and what's just hype.

Digital video (including Video CD) is expected to revolutionize the film and video industry in the same ways that audio CDs changed the face of the recording industry. Understanding digital video technology and taking advantage of its uniqueness is the foundation on which success in this industry will be defined.

The Digital Videomaker's Guide explores the creation of digital videos from concept to finished product.

Contents include:

- An overview of the digital video market including movies, music videos, educa tional products, and training videos.
- Explanations of the various platforms for digital video including CD-i, Video CD, CD-ROM, CD-based game machines, and interactive TV.
- The digital video studio.
- How to build a production team.
- The design, production, and manufacturing process.
- Information about marketing a finished title.
- How to copyright, duplicate, and distribute your title
- .• Complete Bibliography and Resource Guide and more.

Kathryn Shaw Whitver is an award-winning technical writer specializing in digital technologies. She currently works for OptImage, a leading multimedia and software design company.

$24.95, ISBN 0-941188-21-3, Approx 300 pages, 5 1/2 x 8 1/4

From Our Best – Seller List! Get the Money For Your Next Production!

SHAKING THE MONEY TREE
How To Get Grants and Donations for Film & Video
by Morrie Warshawski

Dazed and confused by the frustrating world of grants and donations? This book demystifies the entire maze of grant world hustling and provides easy-to-follow guidelines.

Warshawski is a leading fundraising consultant for media artists. His clients include The National Endowment for the Arts, The MacArthur Foundation, and the Center for New Television.

"Most how-to books are instantly disposable. Not this one. Put it on your shelf, under your pillow, give it to your trustees, and always have your copy handy. You'll be using it a lot."

    - Brian O'Doherty, Director, Media Arts Program
    National Endowment for the Arts

$24.95, ISBN 0-941188-18-3, 188 pages, 6 x 8 1/4

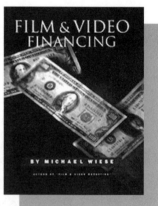

Mo' Money, Mo' Money!!!
FILM & VIDEO FINANCING
by Michael Wiese

Praised as **the** book that prepares producers to **get the money!** A complete "palette" of creative strategies for the independent producer looking to finance their feature films and video projects.

Contents include information on current attitudes and approaches to finding investment through limited partnerships, equity investments, banking issues, split-rights deals, debt equity deals, blocked funds, foreign pre-sales, and much more. Plus insider's tips from independent producers and money-raisers for such films as *"sex, lies & videotape," "A Trip to Bountiful,"* and *"Terminator 2."*

If you are looking for financing for your film or video project, this book will give you the ideas and strategies you need to get the job done!

$22.95, ISBN 0-941188-11-6, 300 pages, 6 x 8 1/4

A fabulous follow up to Katz's best selling book, "Shot by Shot"

FILM DIRECTING: CINEMATIC MOTION
by Steven Katz

"...a valuable and relevant guide...(features) interesting interviews with film professionals."   3D Artist

This is a practical guide to common production problems encountered when staging and blocking film scenes. It includes discussions of scheduling, staging without dialogue, staging in confined spaces, actor and camera choreography in both large and small spaces, sequence shots, and much more. Interviews with well-known professionals–a cinematographer, a director, a production manager, a continuity person, and an actor–enhance this comprehensive study of stylistic approaches to camera space as they address the requirements of the production manager.

Katz is an award-winning filmmaker with over 20 years of experience in the fields of writing, directing, and editing.

$24.95, ISBN 0-941188-14-0, 200 pages, 7 x 10, illus.

PRODUCER TO PRODUCER
by Michael Wiese

"This book is like having a private consultation with Wiese. Invaluable information presented in a clear, concise manner."

Straight one-on-one talk from one of America's leading independent media producers. In 26 knockout chapters, you'll hear Wiese's latest thoughts on everything from program development, financing and production, to marketing, distribution and new media. Articles include: "Self-Distribution," "Infomercials: Where's the Info?," "Where Do You Get the Money?" and much more.

$19.95, ISBN 0-941188-15-9, 175 pages, 6 x 8, illus.

TO ORDER CALL 1-800-379-8808

INDEPENDENT FILM & VIDEOMAKER'S GUIDE
by Michael Wiese

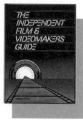

The classic best-seller and independent filmmaker's best friend. Advice on limited partnerships, writing a prospectus, market research, negotiation, film markets, pay TV, and home video buyers.

"Basic survival information that any working filmmaker hoping to make a first, much less a second film, needs to know."

— *Film Quarterly*

$18.95, ISBN 0-941188-03-5, 386 pages, 6 x 8 1/4

FILM & VIDEO MARKETING
by Michael Wiese

Secrets of marketing you can use today! This insider's book shares industry marketing techniques you can use with investors, audiences, distributors, home video companies, wholesalers and retailers. From the inception of the project to the final sale to an audience, the author presents clear, step-by-step strategies that should address the needs of any independent film or video producer. Topics include: developing hit ideas, market research, marketing and promotion, packaging and key art, publicity and advertising, and more. You can't afford *not* to read this book.

$22.95, ISBN 0-941188-05-1, 512 pages, 6 x 8 1/4

SPECIAL REPORTS

DISTRIBUTOR'S LIST 6 pages, $14.95 Up-to-date addresses and phone numbers of the top home video distributors and wholesalers.

DOES YOUR VIDEO HAVE WHAT IT TAKES? (Self-quiz) 6 pages, $14.95 Find out whether your video idea has commercial potential.

SAMPLE VIDEO DISTRIBUTION CONTRACTS - 8 pages, $14.95 Negotiate the best deal for yourself by understanding this distribution contract with comments on what is in **the producer's** (not distributor's) best interest. Worth it's weight in gold.

TO ORDER CALL 1-800-379-8808

SOFTWARE

MovieMagic: Budgeting
Regular Price: ~~$595~~
MWP Price: $495

MovieMagic represents a major leap forward in budgeting software. Fast and flexible, MOVIE MAGIC: BUDGETING has become the industry standard for producers, production managers, and estimators and other film professionals. Features include: "What-if" Functions, Database of rates, Globals for speedy entry, instant recalculation, chart of accounts, etc.

Requires:
Macintosh
•MacPlus or better including Classic, Classic II, SE, SE30, II, IIILC, IIX, IICX, IISI, IIci, IIfx, Quadras, Performas, Notebooks, etc.
•Minimum 512K RAM memory, 4 Megabytes (or more) recommended for use with System 7.
•Minimum system 6.0.5 or higher. System 7-friendly.
•Two disk drives; one may be a hard disk. •Any Macintosh compatible printer & most serial printers.
IBM
•Any IBM compatible with 384K RAM memory •DOS 3.1 or higher; DOS 5.0 recommended.
•Two disk drives; one may be a hard disk.
•A printer; it can be a dot matrix, daisy-wheel or laser printer. The printer must be able to print condensed fonts (15 to 17 characters per inch) or elite fonts (12 characters per inch).

FilmProfit
MWP PRICE: $99

Created by the former CFO of Lucasfilm, FILMPROFIT is a dynamic new spreadsheet program for the MAC or PC which enables you to track cash flow through all phases of distribution and generate reports for business plans and investor presentations. Features include: Income Revenue Projections for film, TV, home video, and foreign markets, "What If" Scenarios, Calculation of Distribution Fees, Producer's Financial Reports, etc. Great for business plans and projections!

Special Bonus! Includes a <u>free</u> 100 page book titled, *The User's Guide to Film Distribution.*

Requires:
Macintosh •Hard disk • Microsoft Excel 3.0 or higher
PC   •500K hard disk •DOS version 2.1 or higher

FREE CATALOG for all our books.
CALL 1-800-379-8808

ORDER FORM

To order these products please call 1-800-379-8808 or fax (818) 986-3408 or mail this order form to:

MICHAEL WIESE PRODUCTIONS
11288 Ventura Blvd., Suite 821
Studio City, CA 91604
1-800-379-8808

BOOKS:

_____

_____

_____

_____

Subtotal $_____

Shipping $_____

8.25% Sales Tax (Ca Only) $_____

TOTAL ENCLOSED_____

Please make check or money order payable to
Michael Wiese Productions

(Check one) ____ Master Card ___Visa _____Amex

Company PO#_____

Credit Card Number_____

Expiration Date_____

Cardholder's Name_____

Cardholder's Signature_____

SHIP TO:

Name_____

Address_____

City_____State_____Zip_____

Country_____Telephone_____

CREDIT CARD ORDERS

**CALL
1-800-379-8808**

OR **FAX
818 986-3408**

OR E-MAIL
WIESE@EARTHLINK.NET

SHIPPING

1ST CLASS MAIL
One Book - $5.00
Two Books - $7.00
For each additional book, add $1.00.

AIRBORNE EXPRESS
2nd Day Delivery
Add an additional $11.00 per order.

OVERSEAS (PREPAID)
Surface - $7.00 ea. book
Airmail - $15.00 ea. book

COMING IN 1996

FILM & VIDEO ON THE INTERNET
The Top 500 Sites

by Bert Deivert and Dan Harries
400 pages, 150 illustrations
Price to be announced.

Love film but overwhelmed by the Internet's maze of terrific (and not so terrific) information? Want to get to the good stuff fast and not spend needless hours searching for the treasures? Then this book is for you.

FILM & VIDEO ON THE INTERNET separates the wheat from chaff by identifying (and then rating) the top 500 home page sites on the World Wide Web.

This is an excellent book for film and videomakers, students, academics and film buffs who are looking for the latest resources on film, video, or new media.

Each site is identified with its name and address and categorized by subject, (e.g. Cinema, expand here). A brief review and a rating follow each section as to its usefulness to the different interests of its readers (directors, writers).

A index cross references the categories. There are also excellent sections on e-mail, usenets, and The Web.

A must for everyone interested in filmmaking.

CALL FOR INFORMATION or ask us to notify you when it's available.